INVENTING POLEMIC

Inventing Polemic examines the ways in which the new technology of print and Reformation polemic together dramatically transformed the literary culture of early modern England. Bringing together recent important work in two distinct areas, the history of the book and the history of religion, it gives an innovative account of the formation of literary culture in Tudor–Stuart England. Each of the central chapters of the book focuses on specific publishing events: Foxe's *Actes and Monuments*, the Marprelate pamphlets, the first two quartos of *Hamlet*, Donne's *Pseudo-Martyr* and *The Anatomy of the World*, and Milton's *Areopagitica*. In a discussion of the Restoration publisher Jacob Tonson and the eighteenth-century literary entrepreneur Samuel Johnson, Lander also considers the way in which subsequent understandings of literature and the literary were shaped by a conscious and conspicuous rejection of polemic. This study is an important reconsideration of some of the most influential texts of early modern England, focusing on their relation to the charged religious environment as it is reflected in and shaped by the products of the emergent print trade.

JESSE M. LANDER is Assistant Professor of English at the University of Notre Dame. His research interests include Renaissance drama, the Reformation, and Shakespeare studies.

INVENTING POLEMIC

Religion, Print, and Literary Culture in Early Modern England

JESSE M. LANDER

CAMBRIDGE
UNIVERSITY PRESS

CAMBRIDGE UNIVERSITY PRESS
Cambridge, New York, Melbourne, Madrid, Cape Town, Singapore, São Paulo

CAMBRIDGE UNIVERSITY PRESS
The Edinburgh Building, Cambridge CB2 2RU, UK

Published in the United States of America by Cambridge University Press, New York

www.cambridge.org
Information on this title: www.cambridge.org/9780521838542

© Jesse M. Lander 2006

First published 2006

Printed in the United Kingdom at the University Press, Cambridge

A catalogue record for this book is available from the British Library

ISBN-13 978-0-521-83854-2 hardback
ISBN-10 0-521-83854-1 hardback

For Kim, Max, Gordon, and Alice

Contents

List of illustrations   *page* viii
Acknowledgments   x

Introduction: the disorder of books   1

1   "Foxe's" Books of Martyrs: printing and popularizing
    the *Actes and Monuments*   56

2   Martin Marprelate and the fugitive text   80

3   "Whole Hamlets": Q1, Q2, and the work of distinction   110

4   Printing Donne: poetry and polemic in the early
    seventeenth century   145

5   *Areopagitica* and "the true warfaring Christian"   180

6   Institutionalizing polemic: the rise and fall
    of Chelsea College   201

    Epilogue: polite learning   222

Notes   232
Works cited   291
Index   319

Illustrations

1 Author, Thomas Williamson, *The Sword of the Spirit* (1613).
By permission of the Huntington Library, San Marino,
California.   *page* 22
2 Print shop, Thomas Williamson, *The Sword of the Spirit* (1613).
By permission of the Huntington Library, San Marino,
California.   23
3 Martyr, Thomas Williamson, *The Sword of the Spirit* (1613).
By permission of the Huntington Library, San Marino,
California.   24
4 Traitor, Thomas Williamson, *The Sword of the Spirit* (1613).
By permission of the Huntington Library, San Marino,
California.   26
5 Whitgift, *The Defense of the Aunswere* (1574).
By permission of the Folger Shakespeare Library.   28
6 John Colleton, *A Supplication* (1604). By permission
of the Folger Shakespeare Library.   32
7 Matthew Sutcliffe, *The Supplication* (1604). By permission
of the Folger Shakespeare Library.   33
8 Special Note, Timothy Bright, *An Abridgement* (1589).
By permission of the Pierpont Morgan Library.   73
9 Henry VIII, Timothy Bright, *An Abridgement* (1589).
By permission of the Pierpont Morgan Library.   76
10 Title page, Timothy Bright, *An Abridgement* (1589).
By permission of the Pierpont Morgan Library.   77
11 Title page, John Foxe, *Actes and Monuments* (1563).
By permission of the Folger Shakespeare Library.   78
12 Bishops' Bible (1572). By Permission of the University
of Illinois at Urbana–Champagne.   86
13 Thomas Blundeville, *The Art of Logike* (1599). By
permission of the Folger Shakespeare Library.   98

14 John Foxe, *Actes and Monuments* (1570).
    By permission of the Folger Shakespeare Library.   99
15 Martin Marprelate, *The Epitome* (1588).
    By permission of the Folger Shakespeare Library.   99
16 William Shakespeare, *Hamlet* Q2 (1604).
    By permission of the Huntington Library,
    San Marino, California.   111
17 William Shakespeare, *Hamlet* Q1 (1603).
    By permission of the Huntington Library,
    San Marino, California.   112
18 A Table, John Donne, *Pseudo-Martyr* (1610).
    By permission of the Huntington Library,
    San Marino, California.   154
19 A Table, John Donne, *Pseudo-Martyr* (1610).
    By permission of the Huntington Library,
    San Marino, California.   155
20 Frontispiece, John Darley, *The Glory of Chelsey
    Colledge Revived* (1662). By permission of the Huntington
    Library, San Marino, California.   214

Acknowledgments

Long in gestation, this book has accrued debts to both individuals and institutions. The research began at the Folger Shakespeare Library and continued at the Huntington Library, and I am deeply grateful to have had the opportunity to work at two such congenial centers of early modern scholarship. I am also grateful to have been granted permission to reproduce images of works in the collections of the Folger, Huntington, and Pierpont Morgan libraries. I would also like to thank the Institute for Scholarship in the Liberal Arts at the University of Notre Dame for covering the cost of photographic reproductions. Ashgate Publishing has graciously allowed me to republish (in slightly revised form) an essay that first appeared in *Reformation* 7 (2002). The germ of this project was planted long ago by Nigel Smith, who introduced me to Marprelate. Thomas Tanselle supplied another crucial component by teaching me the importance of bibliography. At Columbia, my exploration of print and religious controversy flourished under the guidance of an extraordinary Renaissance faculty. David Armitage, Jean Howard, Anne Prescott, and Jim Shapiro have all provided critical insight and crucial support. Beyond the privileged precincts of Morningside Heights, various pieces of this book have benefited from the comments and responses offered by Sharon Achinstein, Cyndia Clegg, Steve Fallon, Lori Ferrell, Tom Freeman, Graham Hammill, Jennifer Lander, Rich McCoy, David Norbrook, Bill Sherman, and Steve Zwicker. I am also grateful for the measured and helpful criticisms supplied by the anonymous readers for the press and am confident that the book is better as a consequence. My final acknowledgment goes out to David Kastan. A superb supervisor, admirable scholar, engaging interlocutor, and generous friend, he remains my ideal reader.

Introduction: the disorder of books

This book is about the consequential intersection of religious controversy and print technology in early modern England. Together the printing press and the Reformation produced polemic, a new form of writing, that animated the literary culture of mid sixteenth- to late seventeenth-century England. This was a period of robust disagreement and, at times, outright stridency, but it was also a time of intense ferment and innovation, and polemic, I argue, was central to the literary culture of the time. With the Restoration of 1660, polemic did not disappear, but it no longer commanded the respect that it had claimed before the Civil Wars. An important new feature of this changed cultural landscape was a restricted notion of the literary. No longer conceived of expansively as that which is written, literature began to assume a recognizably modern form. Politeness and irony, which may work at cross-purposes, become the hallmark of the literary, which is now widely perceived as an antidote to polemic with its fierce enthusiasm and unsophisticated earnestness. The demise of polemic as a legitimate form of writing is inextricably bound up with the birth of the literary.

Beginning at the end, I would like to suggest that this development is perfectly captured in *The Battle of the Books*, published as an addendum to the anonymous *Tale of the Tub* in 1704. Jonathan Swift's title furnished the English language with a durable phrase used to describe, and occasionally ridicule, an academic or literary controversy. Yet Swift did more than popularize a convenient and memorable formulation. His mock-heroic account of the epic struggle between the ancient and modern books in the King's Library has often been seen as documenting a cultural watershed, the emergence of a new antipathy between literary and scientific cultures or between rhetoric and philology.[1] The work also provides an eloquent, if idiosyncratic, document for the historian of books. Swift's attention to the physical details of books as they engage in spirited combat within the confines of the library reveals a sensibility engaged by the possibilities and problems attending the proliferation of print. Of course, the literary conceit of animated books in battle formation serves to heighten the reader's sense of the fantastic and ridiculous and produces a satiric effect by exposing the enormous gulf separating the verbal strife of the pedants from actual warfare. But there is something more to it: Swift's vivid fable, with its focus on the organization of the library and its volumes, testifies to a profound dislocation in the order of books.

Describing the arrangement of libraries, Swift makes a curious claim: "*Books* of Controversy, being of all others, haunted by the most disorderly Spirits, have always been confined in a separate Lodge from the rest; and for fear of mutual violence against each other, it was thought Prudent by our Ancestors, to bind them to the Peace with strong Iron Chains."[2] Combining the language of pneumatology and corporeal bondage, Swift suggests that these books are infused with an enthusiasm that requires the rigor of penal discipline. But what is perhaps more remarkable is the assertion that "*Books* of Controversy" have always been recognized as a coherent category and that, moreover, their forced and physical segregation from other books has been necessary in order to keep peace in the library. At the risk of self-contradiction, Swift then goes on to explain how this state of affairs originated:

> When the Works of *Scotus* first came out, they were carried to a certain great Library, and had Lodgings appointed them; but this Author was no sooner settled, then he went to visit his master *Aristotle*, and there both concerted together to seize *Plato* by main Force, and turn him out from his antient Station among the *Divines*, where he had peaceably dwelt near Eight Hundred Years. The Attempt succeeded, and the two Usurpers have reigned ever since in his stead: But to maintain Quiet for the future, it was decreed, that all *Polemicks* of the larger Size, should be held fast with a Chain. (223)

Intellectual history is here conceived of as a violent succession, marked by faction, intrigue, and ambition. Though the coup that led to the dominance of an Aristotelian scholasticism is regrettable, Swift's chief concern is to suggest that a workable arrangement, the chaining up of controversial books and implicitly their limited circulation, has been disrupted by "a new Species of controversial Books . . . instinct with a most malignant Spirit" (223).[3]

These books, unlike the ponderous "*Polemicks* of the larger Size," are fugitive and ephemeral pieces, the products of a lively commercial press. "For a very few Days they are fixed up in all Publick places," and from there the "chiefest and largest are removed to certain Magazines, they call, *Libraries*, there to remain in a Quarter purposely assign'd them, and from thenceforth, begin to be called, *Books of Controversie*" (222). The books of this sort that find a place in the library assume a common denomination, "*Books of Controversie*," but those that circulate at large "are known to the World," writes Swift, "under several Names: As, *Disputes, Arguments, Rejoynders, Brief Considerations, Answers, Replies, Remarks, Reflexions, Objections, Confutations*" (222).

The etiological myth explaining the practice of chaining books alongside the taxonomic identification of "a new Species of controversial Books" suggests an affinity between classification and confinement; both are attempts, imaginative and not entirely serious, to impose order on disorderly books. Yet, *The Battle of the Books* appears deeply ambivalent on this score – it is itself a disorderly book with a text marred by ostentatious gaps (accompanied by Latin notes acknowledging deficiencies in the manuscript) and lacking a conclusion. The notion that the entire Western tradition of philosophy and literature is riven by contention and dispute justifies Swift's own participation in controversy: if intellectual antagonism is a constant, then engagement involves belligerence. But the claim that "a new Species of controversial Books" has emerged is historical, and these books, "moved by a most malignant Spirit," constitute a cultural innovation that must be resisted in order to restore the peaceful decorum of a less turbulent past. The tension between Swift's own animated polemic and his wish to discipline disorderly books may be reduced, but not resolved, by pointing to the qualities of Swift's literary satire that distinguish it from the ardent and ingenuous controversial works that freighted the bookshops. Parodic wit and subtle irony do not, however, entirely overcome this difficulty: *The Battle of the Books* remains an entrant in the very combat that it deplores and ridicules.

Despite its ambivalence, Swift's fable represents a widespread reaction to the burgeoning print world of the late seventeenth century. To most of his readers the claim that a new sort of disorderly book was abroad in the world would have appeared a self-evident truth. Indeed, the phenomenon was soon to attract the attention of Myles Davies, whose *Eikon Mikro-Biblike Sive Icon Libellorum, or, a Critical History of Pamphlets* was published in 1715. Davies's account of the "Republick of Pamphlets" acknowledges that little treatises are to be found in antiquity, as the Greek and Latin titles suggest, but focuses on the rise and growth of pamphlet writing since the beginning of the Reformation. "The Figure Pamphlets make in the World at present is so very considerable," writes Davies, "that there is a necessity laid now-adays on most People to make their Court to them, or at least, to have an Eye upon them."[4]

The disorder of books, diagnosed by both Swift and Davies, was largely the consequence of print technology and religious controversy. The claim here is not that earlier periods did not witness polemical exchanges; they most certainly did. The point is rather that the category of polemic only emerges in response to the spread of hostile disputation in print.[5] The long tradition of academic controversy, a central practice in the medieval university, was fundamentally transformed by the hostilities of the Reformation and the effects of the press. Acrimonious public dispute does not readily produce a stable world picture, or indeed an articulate consensus; it does, however, promote recognition of polemic as a category of writing that has become common. Swift is not the first to observe the prevalence of controversial books in post-Reformation England; what distinguishes his remarks is their acute awareness that these books constitute a "new Species." Swift's insight, in fact, comes at the end of two centuries of development and definition during which English speakers came to acknowledge the existence, if not necessarily the desirability, of polemic. Intimately related to the invention of polemic is the simultaneous restriction of the literary to the imaginary. The authentically literary comes to be perceived as the antithesis of the polemical: it is aesthetic, not political; disinterested, not tendentious; exploratory, not restrictive; imaginative, not dogmatic. These oppositions, with their obvious evaluative content and their central place in the modern articulation of the literary, are produced by a long history, and it is the contention of this book that the invention of polemic was a crucial development in that history.

In the chapters that follow, I analyze a series of books: *Actes and Monuments*, the Marprelate tracts, the early quartos of *Hamlet*, Donne's *Pseudo-Martyr* and his *Anatomy of the World*, and Milton's *Areopagitica*. This sequence is followed by a chapter treating King James's College at Chelsea, an important, albeit unsuccessful, attempt to institutionalize the writing of religious polemic in England. Finally, I conclude with a short account of the way in which the literary came to be understoood in the post-Restoration world as the antithesis of polemic. The books chosen for consideration provide the basis for case studies that have, I argue, wide-ranging, though by no means uniform, implications. None of these books is straightforwardly representative of early modern English culture. Indeed, the sort of synecdoche that allows a specific text, event, or individual to represent an entire culture is invariably homogenizing and simplifying in its effect. However, taken as an ensemble or constellation, these books (and many more could be added) illuminate the polemical world of early modern England.

In each case, the principal object is to examine the way in which an important discursive form – ecclesiastical history, theological controversy, tragedy, elegy, and political tract – is manifested in a particular publishing event. Though such publishing events appear discrete, a book is after all produced at a given place and time, they are in fact protracted: the book is the culmination of a collective project that involves the intentions, ambitions, and animosities of authors, editors, publishers and printers, and it goes forth into a world of readers hostile, friendly, and indifferent. If all the agents engaged in the circuit of communication have a part to play, it does not follow that in every case the roles played by the various figures will be of equal interest. Consequently, an attention to publishing events does not entail a rigid uniformity of focus. In the second, third, and fourth chapters, publishers and printers are prominent; in the fifth and sixth, authorial intentions, exemplified by Donne and Milton, become an important part of my account. This shift in emphasis reflects the increasing prominence of the author as a figure in the seventeenth century – both Donne and Milton are exceptionally self-conscious about what it means to assume the title of author in a world of print, and this awareness is registered in their texts and their books – but it also reflects my attempt to be responsive to the documents themselves. The printed matter of early modern England is an enormously rich archive, and each document in that archive is the concrete residue of the multiple intentions of a plurality of agents.

The constellation that I have assembled here is, of course, selective. It could not be otherwise. I have attempted to bring together both books not usually considered under the aegis of literary history and books considered central to the aesthetic achievement of Tudor–Stuart England in order to reveal just how thoroughly polemic, produced by religious controversy and print technology, shaped the literary culture of early modern England. My selection is partial, both incomplete and motivated, but adequate to the task of showing how polemic emerged as powerful concept and ubiquitous practice. In juxtaposing books that are usually thought of as highly literary – Shakespeare's *Hamlet* and Donne's *Anatomy of the World* – with books usually thought of as non-literary – *Actes and Monuments*, the Marprelate pamphlets, and *Pseudo-Martyr* – I am making two related arguments. In the first instance, I seek to demonstrate the way in which polemical concerns mark even those texts from the period that we have found most emphatically literary. In the second instance, I hope to show how the modern notion of "the literary" is in part constituted through a repudiation of polemic that imposes a historical amnesia, a wilful forgetting of the polemical engagements of the past.

In the remaining part of this introduction, I elaborate on the concept of polemic in order to elucidate the theoretical implications of my argument and place it in relationship to recent work in literary and intellectual history as well as political and cultural theory. Of central importance are the connections between polemic and questions of the public and publicity as well as the connections between polemic and questions of dialogue and the dialogic. Whereas print is frequently imagined as regulative and regulariz-ing, an attention to polemic suggests that print is also fractious and divisive. In the first instance, print contributes to a disordering of books. Related to the regulative conception of print is the notion that print, by encouraging impersonality and abstraction, fosters a rational exchange of views and, ultimately, promotes deliberative democracy. However, such accounts depend on the repudiation of polemic: either it is relegated to the pre-history of the public sphere as that which must be overcome in order to usher in the free exchange of ideas or it is marginalized as a form of irrationality. My focus on early modern polemic finds it at the very center of the movement toward a world of public debate, but rather than seeing this as an unequivocally positive development, the glimmer of a democratic dawn, I find evidence of the durability of fundamental antagonisms. One of the major consequences of such an argument is that the privileged terms in literary analysis come into a new focus. The cultivation of ambivalence, the celebration of ambiguity, the appeal to dialogue and the dialogic, all look quite different when seen as a response to the troubling presence of polemic.

That print aided and abetted Protestantism is a textbook truism. Indeed, the notion that the press was God's gift to the Reformation was first promulgated by the reformers themselves. Luther himself held print to be "God's highest and extremest act of grace, whereby the business of the Gospel is driven forward; it is the last flame before the extinction of the world."[6] Invested with the unremarkable obviousness of common sense, this relationship has received little sustained attention.[7] Macaulay writes of the Reformation, "The fulness of time was now come. The clergy were no longer the sole or the chief depositories of knowledge. The invention of printing had furnished the assailants of the Church with a mighty weapon which had been wanting to their predecessors." Macaulay's echo of Galatians 4:4 – "But when the fulness of time was come, God sent forth his Son" – associates the invention of print with the dispensation of the gospel itself. Behind this formulation lies a serene confidence in the fundamental affinity between the technological innovation of print, per-haps all technological innovation, and Protestantism; both are seen to be part of the "long progress from poverty and barbarism to the highest degree of opulence and civilisation."[8] In making this claim, Macaulay is articulating what has been called a "mini-fable" from "the collective memory of Western culture."[9]

The alliance between Reformation and press perceived by the reformers depends on a strictly instrumental conception of print that regards print technology as a transparent means to an end – in this case, the spread of the gospel. Print is not held to be capable of acting as itself a source of cultural or social change – it only succeeds in extending innovations that arise elsewhere and for other reasons. This vision of the relationship between print and Protestantism has been vigorously contested by Elizabeth Eisenstein, whose work remains, despite recent and premature claims about its obsolescence, central to the field of print history. Eisenstein recognizes not only that print was an "important precondition for the Protestant Reformation," but that "the new medium also acted as a precipitant."[10] In making this claim, Eisenstein significantly reverses the usual order of causality implied by accounts that see the Reformation as *using* print. Pointing to the chronological priority of print, emerging in Germany at least half a century before Luther's break with Rome, Eisenstein rejects the tradition that would seek solely religious and political causes for the Reformation. She objects that historians of the Reformation have underestimated the new technology, seeing it as a neutral platform for the ideas it carries and limiting its function to the process of dissemination: print "is given no part in shaping new views but only seen to diffuse them after they have been formed" (I, 368).

Eisenstein is surely right to see traditional accounts of print as a neutral medium of communication as thin and inadequate; rather than being merely a technology for distribution, print enables new social practices and encourages new habits of mind. To be fair, Eisenstein claims only that print is *a* precipitant of the Reformation not *the* precipitant. Nonetheless, Eisenstein's work – marked by what Perry Anderson has referred to as "a monomania familiar in historians of technology" – has often been interpreted as making the singular claim, as elevating print to the level of historical agent and attributing to this agent a primary role in not only the Reformation, but also the Renaissance, the scientific revolution, and the Enlightenment.[11] As a corrective to intellectual histories that have concentrated on the development of disembodied ideas, her focus on the material practice of print is salutary. However, the great strength of her book – its enormous chronological, geographical, and disciplinary range – is also a weakness. When so much is covered, detail is invariably lost, but, more importantly, the constant presence of print in so many different contexts creates the impression of a single epic narrative with the printing press in the role of protagonist.

The impression of a mono-causal technological determinism can be avoided by a dialectical account of the relationship between print and various cultural and social movements.[12] Technologies do not descend from the heavens; they emerge from a particular social and cultural matrix. Technologies are put forward as solutions to perceived problems and are adopted to the degree that they are recognized as efficacious. While the use and meaning of a technology are largely determined by this social and cultural matrix, it would be a mistake to dismiss the shaping force of technology itself, the way in which it can have a recursive effect on the very social world that has produced it. As Febvre and Martin write, "All such inventions were the result of great social transformations, but in turn gave further impetus to their development."[13] Their account, while recognizing in general this recursive relation, pays little attention to the specifically cultural transformations that accompanied the emergence of the printed book, relegating their consideration of humanism and the Reformation to a final chapter on "The Book as a Force for Change" and creating the impression that such cultural changes are epiphenomenal. Yet cultural developments themselves are, in fact, crucial to the emergence and deployment of new technologies.

A forceful argument for the social construction of print has recently been made by Adrian Johns, who insists that any attempt to invest the press with "inherent" characteristics that then shape the social and cultural world is to mistake effect for cause. The terms that we have come to associate with print – most importantly for Johns, authority, fixity, and permanence – are the result of a long social and cultural history during which print practitioners had to work hard to legitimate their craft; as Johns puts it: "Printers and booksellers were manufacturers of credit."[14] While this is certainly true, Johns is so determined to avoid the perceived oversimplifications of technological determinism and the attendant notion of a unitary "print culture," which he consistently associates with Eisenstein, that he dissolves print technology almost entirely into social relations. Admittedly, without the multitudinous hopes and fears, ambitions and resistances, of a variety of individual agents and specific institutions, the printing press would not have had the effect that it did, but for all that, the machine itself required a reorganization of textual reproduction that had dramatic consequences. Rather than asking whether history is conditioned by print or print by history, one might more fruitfully pursue the reciprocal relationship between print technology and particular cultural and social developments, as Johns himself does in his excellent account of the complicated relationship between the practices of print and the history of science in early modern England.[15]

Despite the far-reaching implications of *The Nature of the Book*, the work has a fairly restricted focus both in terms of its geography and its subject. Indeed, Johns justifies his concentration on the development of scientific discourse with the assertion that this is the form of knowledge with the greatest authority in the present: "the widely accepted status of modern science as the most objective, valuable, and robust kind of knowledge currently available makes it a peculiarly appealing subject for the historian of printing" (6). Despite the repeated claim that his is only one possible history of print, Johns gives the impression that the science–print nexus is *primus inter pares*: "Conclusions demonstrated about science should be acknowledged as credible a fortiori for less authoritative fields" (623). But the decision to make science central in the treatment of a period in which it is not yet acknowledged to be the "most objective, valuable, and robust kind of knowledge" has two immediate consequences: epistemology assumes priority over ontology or metaphysics, and religion, arguably the source of the most objective, valuable, and robust kind of knowledge known to the period, is marginalized.

Not only does theology, the queen of the sciences, get dethroned, the entire complex known as humanism with its intense and insistent focus on the question of a specifically literary authority and its concomitant attention to matters of both rhetoric and philology is sidelined. Indeed, the way in which Renaissance humanism and Reformation theology together pursue a deep engagement with the very question of language itself, a problem that has recently been luminously explored by Brian Cummings, is not part of the picture.[16] The point is not that Johns should have written a different book but that he should have given it a different title. *The Nature of the Book: Print and Knowledge in the Making* asserts, despite demurrals, a punning claim to comprehensiveness, and yet the thesis Johns develops about the very gradual emergence of "print culture" focuses attention on the mid and late seventeenth century and so underestimates the importance of earlier cultural developments. The Reformation and humanism, two legs in the tripod that supports Eisenstein's concept of "print culture," affect not only chronology but substance. The notion that two cultural movements deeply committed to language and the written would have a different relationship to technologies of communication than would an embryonic science is hardly surprising. Indeed, the great achievement of

Johns's book has been to show how a technology of communication like print played a fundamental role in the development of science, a discourse that has until rather recently emphatically denied the role of language in the constitution of knowledge. However, it would be a mistake to read this as a definitive debunking of the "print culture" concept. Johns has exposed a set of almost metaphysical ideas that lurk in complacent invocations of print culture and has forced those who would use the term to think hard about the historical process that produces "print culture." However, to acknowledge the uneven development of "print culture" is not to advocate for a plurality of print cultures; the very point of retaining the concept of "print culture" is that it addresses important continuities across a variety of discourses and geographical regions.

What follows contributes to our understanding of the emergence of print culture by charting the complex cultural consequences of the reciprocal relationship between print technology and religious controversy. If print enabled the Reformation, it is equally true that Reformation and Counter-Reformation attempts to secure consent and conformity gave momentum to the proliferation of print. Of course, it is not easy to assess the degree to which such strategic deployments of print by publicists penetrated beyond the rarefied world of the intellectual elite, but it is crucial to recognize that there were concerted attempts to reach a broader segment of the population through print. If, however, print was thought to allow for the imposition of regular forms of worship and the dissemination of theological orthodoxy, it succeeded less in securing uniformity than in constructing polarities, producing not a common language but polemic.[17] The relationship between print and the Reformation is, therefore, not only reciprocal and mutually reinforcing, but dynamic and volatile.

This complex dynamic is exemplified by the printing of the Bible in English under Henry VIII. As David Kastan has written, "The English Bible did not produce a nation unified in and by a common faith, but neither did it, as its opponents feared and often claimed, leave England ravaged by division and sedition."[18] It did, according to Kastan, "encourage literacy . . . and provoke debate." Concentrating on the marginal notes that Bible producers hoped would make manifest the unitary meaning of the scripture, Evelyn Tribble similarly argues that: "The only way the institution can establish its own authority is by producing more translations and marginal glosses"; and yet these only succeed in providing "a model for contention and proliferation."[19]

Though the relationship between print and the Reformation cannot be reduced to a one-way causality, together they created a culture that formed not homogeneously but continually in debate, a culture that can itself be seen as polemical. In the wake of the Reformation, polemic becomes ubiquitous, leading William Barlow, himself an accomplished polemicist, to remark in 1609, "*There is no* End *of making of many books* (saith the *Preacher* in the end of his Booke) *especially if they be Bookes of Encounter.*"[20] Barlow's citation of Ecclesiastes 12:12 might appear to indicate that polemic is an ancient practice, but his extra-scriptural qualification – "*especially if they be Bookes of Encounter*" – reveals the form and pressure of recent history. A modern ear may miss the adversarial aspect of *encounter*, which in early modern English invariably carries connotations of conflict and battle; Barlow's "*Bookes of Encounter*" are what Swift later calls "a new Species of controversial Books." They are, I will argue, a recognizably new phenomenon distinct from an early tradition of apologetic and controversial writing. Though strenuous argument and violent invective are ubiquitous in the sixteenth century, such arguments and invectives were not christened as *polemic* until the 1630s.

Though it clearly bears a resemblance to the entire constellation of words dealing with verbal strife, *polemic* is not strictly synonymous with any of them. Argument, animadversion, apologetic, controversy, defense, invective, libel, logomachia, pasquinade, and propaganda all have slightly different referents. *Controversy* is nearly synonymous with *polemic*, and it is frequently used in the early modern period to refer to what I define as *polemic*. However, controversy, as a familiar part of the medieval university system of training, lacks the emphasis on enmity that makes *polemic* distinctive.[21] An account of polemic might usefully begin with the etymology of the word: stemming from the Greek *polemos* meaning war or battle, the word designates a particular kind of engagement.[22] A military metaphor when it first appears in English, *polemic* never escapes from its metaphoric origins; such writing is consistently conceived as a weapon, wielded by one camp against another in an effort to defend and solidify a collective identity. Accordingly, polemic is seen as the opposite of dialogue and negotiation: uncommunicative language deployed to destroy an opponent rather than convince an interlocutor. Such thinking lies behind the negative assessment of polemic as aimed not at communication and resolution, but at conquest and differentiation. Polemic understood in these terms is about retrenchment, the hardening of partisan identities and ideas, a sort of discursive calcification. However, a more interesting understanding of polemic emerges if one dispenses with the bipolar model of addresser and addressee and recognizes instead that the audience for polemic is variegated and split. The polemicist's aim is not to convert the object of attack but to convince a wider audience that the case is so. Though polemic has genuine argumentative content, there is no denying that it functions to divide and polarize, the product of a line of thinking that eschews a premature peace and pursues instead what Milton calls the "wars of truth."

The earliest example of the English noun that I have been able to locate is from Simon Birckbek's *The Protestants Evidence* (1634) where an interesting taxonomy of patristic writing is offered: "The Fathers writings bee either Dogmaticall, Polemicall, or Popular. In their Dogmaticall, and Doctrinall, wherein they set downe positive Divinity, they are usually very circumspect: in their Polemickes, and Agonistickes, earnest and resolute: in their Homilies, and popular discourse, free and plaine." In appraising their polemics, Birckbek notes that occasionally "whiles they oppose one errour, they slip into the opposite" and offers the example of Jerome, who "while he affronts such as impugn'd virginity, himselfe quarrels at lawfull Matrimony." However, "the Fathers in their Polemiques, whiles they keepe themselves close to the question in hand, their tenets are ever most sound, and direct."[23] Another early example appears in the preface to Joseph Mede's *The Name Altar* (1637), which explains that "*by occasion of the late* polemicks" his treatise was "*copied out, to communicate to some friends.*"[24] Though Mede's use of *polemicks* to refer to disputes over the proper placement of the altar is neutral, the adjectival form of the word appears in a number of clearly positive contexts. In 1642, Sir Edward Dering, pleading for a better endowed clergy, suggests that present graduates are far short of "perfect Polemy in letters."[25] "This holy warfare" requires that efforts be made so "that wee may be alway sure in all Polemicke learning, to have some men of valour." Similarly, Lord Brooke, arguing that bishops are ill-suited by their scholastic preparations to assume civil rule, anticipates the objection "that one of these Studies may fit for another. All truthes, *Polemicke, positive*, whether Politique, Philosophicall, or Theologicall, are of neere consanguinity."[26] He responds by asserting that "they spend their time in Criticall, Cabalisticall, Scepticall, Scholasticall Learning: which fills the head with empty, aeriall, notions; but gives no sound food to the Reasonable part of man." They fail, in part, because they lack "*Cotem Scientiæ & ingenii* [the whetstone of knowledge and talents], a Reall Adversary, that by contradiction might raise their Parts, and much inlarge their judgements." Brooke here derides the artificial oppositions of an academic curriculum built on regulated disputation and champions instead public and polemical engagement. A "Reall Adversary," a genuine enemy as opposed to an academic sparring partner, is needed in order to increase knowledge and judgment.

Though the *OED* gives 1640 as the date of the earliest instance of the adjective *polemical,* it can be found as early as 1615, indicating that the word does not arise as an immediate response to the crisis precipitated by the attempt to impose an English Prayerbook on Scotland. Joseph Hall, in a dedication to King James, promises to display several different sorts of divinity: "Speculation interchanged with experience; Positiue Theologie with Polemicall; Textuall with Discursorie; Popular with Scholasticall."[27] John Lewis alludes, in 1624, to the "*knotty study of* Polemicall Theologie."[28] Similarly, Daniel Featley, in his dedication of *Cygnea Cantio* to Charles I, observes: "I thought it my duty to offer unto your Majestie the ensuing Relation of the last polemicall discourses of his Majesty your Father, in matter of controversie in Divinity."[29] Another pre-1640 example appears in the seventh edition of *Actes and Monuments* printed in 1632, which included in its prefatory material a new "Table of Tables; shewing to a whole Alphabet of sundry sorts of Readers, to each kinde a particular catalogue of instances: giuing him an account wherein the reading of this great Booke of *Martyrs* may abundantly giue contentment to his vein of study."[30] The catalogue for Divines is broken into a number of sub-topics, including "Schoole Diuinitie," "Polemicall Diuinitie," "Positiue Orthodox Diuinitie," and "Textuarie Diuinitie" (()2^v–()3^r).[31] This last example of *polemical* is significant not only for its association with the Book of Martyrs, but also because it, like the three earlier instances, is associated with divinity.

Such a connection was not, however, without exception; in several early examples *polemical* is used, in accordance with its original Greek sense, to mean pertaining to war. For example, two different news pamphlets both published in 1637 by Nicholas Bourne (an important publisher to whom I will return) announce on their title pages that they treat matters both political and polemical.[32] An earlier example, marked as a Latinism, appears in the title of a sermon by Abraham Gibson published in 1619: *Christiana-Polemica, or a Preparative to Varre.*[33] The continued use of the word *polemical* in its Greek sense only insured that discursive polemic would be understood in a similar way as the verbal equivalent of war. Polemical divinity, then, is argument and exposition aimed at identifiable opponents and intended to refute theological errors. The terms of salvation are at stake, and the contest, as in war, is a matter of life and death. This line of thought is aptly expressed in Thomas Fuller's character of "The Controversiall Divine": "*He engageth both his judgement, and affections in opposing of falsehood.* Not like countrey Fencers, who play only to make sport, but like Duellers indeed, at it for life and limbe."[34]

What distinguishes polemic from earlier forms of contentious writing is its connection to print. Both print and polemic share an orientation toward what can be described as a public, a public that is neither a mass nor a monolith. A geographically dispersed and socially indeterminate aggregate of individuals, this public is, without modern theories of popular sovereignty, not invested by contemporaries with a unitary will but is rather conceived in largely negative terms as that which is not private. When Josias Nichols regrets that he and other seekers after reform employed "diuers publicke wrightinges, partlie apologeticall, partlie supplicatorie," he is using "publicke" as a synonym for printed and confessing misgivings over a strategy that was designed to jump the traditional channels of political complaint by taking an argument directly to "the people."[35] Such a print campaign obscures, though it does not necessarily displace, precisely the personal face-to-face contact between clients and patrons, subjects and sovereign, that was held to be central to the process of governance. Indeed, Nichols now admits that it was a fault "That wee did not present our cause to the Queenes most excellent Maiestie"(D4ᵛ). This same set of concerns is vividly displayed by Matthew Sutcliffe in his response to *A Petition Directed to Her Most Excellent Maiestie* (1592). The anonymous *Petition* begins with a direct address to the queen: "Crauing vppon my knees pardon for my boldness, I beseeche your most excellent Maiestie, to heare me a litle."[36] This conceit provokes Sutcliffe to ask, "Seeing this petition is directed to her Maiestie, to what ende is the same put in print?"[37] The answer is, according to Sutcliffe, obvious: the writer cares nothing for the queen's "wisedome" but seeks rather to rouse the people: "for the same was neuer presented to her Maiestie, but onely to the people [i.e. printed]." And, of course, it is for this very reason that Sutcliffe must take up the task of answering *A Petition* in print.

A very similar dynamic is visible in George Hakewill's response to Benjamin Carier's *Letter to His Majestie*, a printed pamphlet in epistolary form that purports to explain to King James I Carier's reasons for converting to Roman Catholicism. In his dedication to the king, Hakewill explains why he has answered the now dead Carier:

Had this Letter of D. Carier beene imparted, or the drift of it onely reached to your Maiestie, it would haue deserued none other answere then your Maiesties priuate censure; and might well haue been buried in silence with the Author of it: But now that it not only aymes in particular at all the members of the bodie Politike, First the Nobles, then the Commons, and lastly the Clergie; but withall is published to the view of the World, and spread through all the quarters of your Land, for the better effecting of that it aymes vnto; and is not a little magnified by the Romish faction: It must needs argue in vs, either want of wisedome in preuenting a mischiefe, or of power in prouiding for our own safetie, or zeale and sinceritie in our loue to the Trueth, if it should passe without some discouery, as well of the malicious scope to which it tends, as to the weaknesse of the argument by which it endeuours to persuade.[38]

Unlike Sutcliffe, Hakewill does not accuse the author of hypocrisy in pretending that a printed appeal to the public is a private missive to the monarch, but he does fasten on the public purposes of the document. Had the letter remained the private communication of an apostate subject to his king, it would have deserved no other answer than the king's "priuate censure"; but since it has been "published to the view of the World," a printed response is now necessary.

It is this public quality of "Bookes of Encounter" that guarantees their endlessness, for it becomes common to assume not simply that polemics can be answered but that they *must* be answered.[39] In such a world to have had the final word was considered a victory. Martin Marprelate is not merely engaged in special pleading when he asserts that Cartwright bettered Whitgift in the Admonition Controversy simply because Whitgift failed to answer Cartwright's last book.[40] A printed book, far more than a circulated manuscript, was perceived to require a printed response, a response required because such a document was immediately seen to be attempting to reach a diverse audience, but also because from its beginnings print conferred a certain authority.

This may seem paradoxical given the resistance with which print was greeted in many circles, a resistance that was frequently articulated by associating the press with rude artisans and diabolical spirits. But even scorn and derision constitute a recognition of the way in which print makes concrete a complex network of production that might range from quasi-literate workers to learned press correctors, from entrepreneurial printer–publishers to writers of varying sorts; put another way, a printed book requires far more capital investment than scribal reproduction does – this is one of the factors that allowed scribal publication to remain viable long after the establishment of the press. Thus print reveals that a given text has the backing of capital. To use Pierre Bourdieu's terms: print converts economic capital into cultural capital.[41] The threatening nature of the printed book lay not only in its ability to reach a wide audience but also in the way that it concretized a set of social relations. A printed book cannot be dismissed as the solitary ravings of a singular heretic, disgruntled reader, or political dissident. Obviously print does not compel belief, but the deployment of print technology by a network of artisans, entrepreneurs, and writers, often working within complex institutions of licensing and censorship, does confer authority upon the text. As the shepherdess Mopsa says, in *The Winter's Tale*: "I love a ballad in print alife, for then we are sure that they are true" (4.4.259–60). Similarly, William Winstanley ridicules those who believe "idle Romances . . . and for this only reason, *Because they are Printed*."[42]

While the vast majority of print productions strive to forge a unified body of readers (students of English law, lovers of lyric poetry, or readers of a Book of Common Prayer), polemic seeks to divide its readers into friends and enemies. On the one hand, there is the object of polemical attack, the direct addressee. On the other, there is a wider audience of potential friends, those whose consent is sought in the condemnation of the enemy's opinion. This sorting operation reveals an affinity between polemic and the radically dichotomized concept of the political as defined by Carl Schmitt – "The specific political distinction to which political actions and motives can be reduced is that between friend and enemy."[43] Polemic is a perfect instance of political action as understood by Schmitt. Nonetheless, the notion of polemic as the verbal equivalent of war must not be stressed to the exclusion of the practice's other aspect – the attempt to consolidate a particular community of conviction. It is in this aspect that one may see the essentially public nature of polemic – a private polemic would be oxymoronic, and it is in this publicity – an orientation toward an indeterminate body of readers – that one finds polemic's peculiar relationship to print, for print from its beginnings creates the imagined possibility, if not the reality, of a vast and potentially distant readership.

Polemicists and publishers alike struggle to win over an audience of diverse individuals with a multitude of interests and abilities. What separates a scribal readership from a print public is precisely the new need to impose the book on a set of readers. The resilience of scribal publication is in large part due to the fact that the bespoke production of manuscripts could perfectly match demand. In contrast, print runs of even limited size require an attempt to anticipate the market, a requirement that leads directly to attempts to incite consumer interest, and as a consequence print production puts new emphasis on the idea of an anonymous public, a group of potential consumers only limited by literacy and income. A telling and familiar example is provided by the address "To the great Variety of Readers" that appears at the front of the First Folio edition of Shakespeare's plays: "From the most able, to him that can but spell. There you are number'd. We had rather you were weighd. Especially, when the fate of all Bookes depends vpon your capacities: and not of your heads alone, but of your purses" (A3^r). Though the gesture is seemingly genial and inclusive, the aggression subtending this address becomes obvious when its allusion to the biblical Daniel is recalled: asked by Belshazzar to interpret the writing on the wall, Daniel explains, "God hath numbered thy kingdom, and finished it . . . Thou art weighed in the balances, and found wanting" (Daniel 5:26–27). The Folio address uses the same conceptual distinction between the enumerative and the evaluative. Expressing their desire that the audience's capacities of head and purse might be determined, the writers move on with a shrug: "Well! It is now publique . . ." This imagined diversity, then, is, however much a commercial desideratum, frequently a source of anxiety, but the important point is that writers, publishers, and printers have become increasingly aware of the diverse collectivity that is at once a nascent market and an emerging public.[44]

The idea that something like a public sphere existed in Tudor–Stuart England has recently attracted significant scholarly attention.[45] Leaving aside for the moment the question of the accuracy of Habermas's account of the eighteenth century, it would be a mistake to simply back-date the emergence of the public sphere to the sixteenth or seventeenth centuries. A simple adjustment in chronology is inadequate because Habermas's account, as David Zaret argues, "glosses over the relevance of religion for the emergence of a public sphere in politics at a time when religious discourse was a, if not the, predominant means by which individuals defined and debated issues in this sphere."[46] While Zaret sees the neglect of religion as the result of Habermas's economic determinism (a common and, I think, not entirely fair criticism of *The Structural Transformation of the Public Sphere*), I would argue that a greater difficulty is posed by Habermas's assumptions about the rational–critical debate that typifies the public sphere.

Religious conviction cannot be admitted into the rational–critical debate of the public sphere precisely because, for Habermas, it is irrational. In his ideal and idealized vision of Augustan reason engaged in unconstrained debate, one can clearly see the set of concerns and concepts that led Habermas to develop his theories of communicative action and discourse ethics. Whatever purchase these theories may claim in contemporary debates, they are of little help in illuminating the conflictual world of early modern England. This point needs stressing because in a post-cold-war world, Habermas's account of the public sphere as a place of rational debate existing between the state and the private realm has assumed a new attractiveness.[47] Annabel Patterson, for instance, has identified the sixteenth-century chronicle writer Raphael Holinshed with Habermas and John Rawls, seeing all three as expressing the liberal principle of "rational conflict resolution."[48] Patterson's desire to see Holinshed and his successors as proto-liberals is, if historically improbable, politically intelligible, confirming Chantal Mouffe's assertion that, "With the demise of Marxism, the illusion that we can finally dispense with the notion of antagonism has become widespread."[49]

By emphasizing the practice of polemic I am insisting on the importance of intention, conviction, and argument. And yet it must be added that my concern is with a broadly conceived polemical culture, one in which antagonisms proliferate, refusing to remain within the traditionally defined realm of politics. Accordingly, I find that a narrow focus on constitutional arguments, though an important corrective to histories that insist on consensus and deference, fails to capture either the extent or terms of conflict. Moreover, my attention to print introduces a material aspect to my analysis of early modern culture, while my focus on religion, rather than stressing the continuity between civic humanism and modern liberal democracy, insists on a degree of discontinuity. In fact, if anything, my account of the relationship between print and polemic should serve to defamiliarize the present, calling into question common accounts of modernity that stress the twinned processes of secularization and rationalization. I do not intend, however, to supplant one continuity with another, replacing self-determination, toleration, and rationality with violence, conflict, and transcendental longings.

By making a claim for the affinity between polemic and print, I may appear simply to be reiterating Macaulay's view that print was a "mighty weapon." However, I diverge from Macaulay's position in two important respects. First, I do not agree that print has an inevitable Protestant valence; more particularly, I reject the narrowly instrumental vision of print implied by the weapon metaphor. Let me be clear: this metaphor is symptomatic and therefore significant, it reveals a deep association between print technology and violence, but it is also misleading to the degree that it suggests a strictly instrumental understanding of print and ignores the way in which print transforms its users. Print did not lead directly to "opulence and civilisation." Indeed, the new medium seems initially to have encouraged new levels of venomous invective, and the harshest language of all invariably appears in religious polemic. In the midst of an argument for the pacification of culture brought about by print, Walter J. Ong observes:

No one has yet provided us with a hostility index to assess with exactitude the relative vigor of the polemic spirit in various ages, and yet it seems not imprudent to say that probably no culture has been more riotously polemic in its verbal production than that of Europe in the two centuries after Gutenberg.[50]

Ong, however, claims that this outburst of vitriol was a transitory phenomenon, the final efflorescence of an earlier oral, polemical culture. Ong's argument is here vitiated by his essentializing assumptions about print as an objectified and objectivizing medium: "the letter killeth, but the spirit giveth life" (II Corinthians 3:6).[51] His robust account of the classical and medieval predilection for verbal violence and contest does, however, raise a pertinent question.

Verbal violence has many sources, and obviously religious controversy is only one. Indeed, one could argue that the tendency toward vituperation in the period is a clear consequence of an educational system oriented toward a rhetorical tradition that is essentially agonistic and an honor culture that sanctioned aggressive self-assertion in the name of kin and lineage.[52] However, these practices were capable of sustained reproduction; by institutionalizing conflict, they often reinforced social and cultural hierarchies. The attitudes and capacities produced within the competitive hierarchies of the rhetorical tradition and honor culture undoubtedly contributed to the creation of print polemic; however, the printing of religious polemic significantly altered the terms of conflict. The pursuit of honor or academic distinction presupposes a consensus, however fragile, over the attributes of successful performance that gives such endeavors a game-like aspect. But religious polemic emerges out of the failure of consensus and the institutions of adjudication – it acts as a powerful social solvent at the very same time that it constitutes new communities.

"As a result of the split in ecclesiastical unity," writes Reinhart Koselleck, "the entire social order became unhinged."[53] While this apocalyptic claim may exaggerate the consequences of conceptual innovation for lived experience, it is, nonetheless, instructive. For Koselleck, the crucial point is that the Reformation, having split the universal community of Christianity, creates a plurality of collectives all putting forward absolutist claims to the legacy of universalism. The immediate consequences are wars of religion – wars that are more often than not perceived to be civil wars.[54] If England avoided its own religious civil war, and this remains a point of contention,[55] the polemical battles that raged over the course of its slow and uneven Reformation provided a discursive equivalent. Together print and religious controversy worked to erode the local solidarities of parish and county, encouraging allegiances that were imagined as transcendent.

Though such generalizations are both necessary and useful, the relationship between print and polemic is best approached through example. This is above all because polemic, though it exhibits broad regularities, to be understood fully must be localized. The specific meanings of polemic only emerge when it is placed within the context of a particular engagement.[56] A piece of writing by John Foxe provides an apt illustration of this point. One hundred and thirty-four years after it first appeared, an excerpt from *Actes and Monuments* was printed in 1704; the title page proclaimed:

THE | Benefit and Invention | OF | PRINTING | By John Fox, | That Famous Martyrologist. | Extracted out of his Acts and Monuments, | Vol. I. pag. 803, 804. Edit. 9. *Anno* 1684 | Where he Shews, | I. When and by Whom *Printing* was Invented. | II. The Excellency and Usefulness of the Art. | III. The Disadvantage that Accru'd to *Popery*. | IV. The great Advantage that the *Protestant Religion* hath reaped thereby. | *Faithfully Transcribed, and Humbly Recommended to the* | *Reading and Consideration of all* True Protestants. | *London*, Printed and Sold by *T. Sowle*, in *White-Hart-* | *Court*, in *Gracious-Street*, 1704.

Printed on a single sheet of paper, this quarto pamphlet does, as advertised, provide an excerpt from Foxe describing how "the Lord began to Work for his Church, not with Sword and Target, to subdue his exalted Adversary, but with Printing, Writing, and Reading, to Convince Darkness by Light, Error by Truth, Ignorance by Learning" (5).[57] Foxe goes on to suppose that "either the Pope must abolish *Printing*, or he must seek a new world to reign over: For else as this World standeth, *Printing* doubtless will abolish him." This certainty is next expressed in terms of historical inevitability: "If he will not, let him well understand that *Printing* is not set up for nought. To strive against the Stream it availeth not."

The implications of this assertion are enormous: Protestantism and print are both part of the historical unfolding of truth. This is not Foxe the historian of the persecuted church, the saving remnant, but Foxe the student of Apocalypse. The printing press is a mark of God's endorsement of the Reformation, the spiritual equivalent of "Sword and Target." The fact of technological innovation allows for a narrative of divinely sanctioned historical progress that supplements the Reformation's claim to have recovered the historical truth of the primitive church.

This identity of truth and Protestantism insists on a unity of identity and practice among all those who have rejected the corruptions of Rome, and yet Protestantism hardly achieved unity and conformity of belief or believers. Indeed, as Mark Edwards has put it, "Printing, propaganda, and Martin Luther together ushered in an age that saw the repeated splintering of Western Christianity."[58] This point has more than incidental value, for the 1704 pamphlet excerpting Foxe was published not by an Anglican divine but by a Quaker woman, Tace Sowle. Such a redeployment of Foxe must be set against the High Church attempt to legislate against occasional conformity, the attendance at Anglican services by dissenters in order to qualify for public office. Between January 1703 and December 1704, three Occasional Conformity Bills went down to narrow defeat. At the very same time the High Church party in an alliance with the Stationers' Company was urging the restoration of the lapsed Licensing Act, provoking Defoe's *Essay on the Regulation of the Press*, also printed in 1704.[59] Under these circumstances, the pamphlet is revealed to be a Quaker polemic against High Church Anglicans; those who would regulate printing and repress nonconformists are identified with the obstinate papists. Such an identification, which serves to equate the polemicist's particular target with a widely acknowledged enemy, is a standard polemical strategy; nonetheless, what is truly fascinating is the way in which a passage from *Actes and Monuments* is appropriated, a process facilitated by Foxe's own vocabulary, that inevitably identifies Protestantism in abstract and universal terms such as light, truth, and knowledge. The claimed alliance between print and Protestantism was, long before it became a staple of Whig history writing, an element in anti-Catholic polemic, and yet the ease with which it is appropriated for the Quaker cause indicates that the notion of a divinely sanctioned technological revelation could be used against Protestants as well as Catholics.

Another example of the early modern polemical conception of print appears in Thomas Williamson's *The Sword of the Spirit*, an octavo treatise printed in 1613 in response to John Wilson's *The English Martyrologe* (1608), an account of all the true Catholics who had suffered in England since the time of Henry VIII.[60] In many ways, a standard piece of anti-Catholic polemic, *The Sword of the Spirit* is focused on fixing the relationship between sign and thing, most particularly by establishing the difference between a martyr and a traitor. One of the most striking features of this book is its use of a series of woodcuts (most of them drawing on the iconography of *Actes and Monuments*) to illustrate the argument being made.

The first two cuts, however, do not resemble any of the images that appear in *Actes and Monuments*. Facing the title page is a small woodcut of an author writing at a table; on the wall above his head is a single shelf of books, on the table there is a skull and an hour glass (fig. 1). This scene of solitary writing, the author surrounded by books and reminders of mortality, exists in an interesting tension with the next image. Across from the

Fig. 1 Author, Thomas Williamson, *The Sword of the Spirit* (1613)

table of contents there appears a woodcut of the interior of a print shop in
which three men (an inker, pressman, and compositor) work (fig. 2). The
solitary thoughts of the author give way to the society of the shop where
people work together. Initially, this movement seems to simply recapitu-
late the genesis of the book itself – a manuscript composed in Williamson's
study was given over to the printers who made the book that the reader
scans. However, the claim being made is not so narrow, as a short poem
under the second woodcut explains:

> Loe here the forme and figure of the presse
> Most liuelily obiected to thine eye.
> The worth whereof no tongue can well expresse
> So much it doth, and workes so readily:
> For which let's giue vnto the Lord all praise,
> That thus hath bless'd vs in these latter daies.

(A2^{r})

Fig. 2 Print shop, Thomas Williamson, *The Sword of the Spirit* (1613)

Indeed, the treatise first establishes the benefit of printing and the ground-ing of true religion in the word of God before arguing that the religion of Rome is idolatrous. Williamson has, in effect, promoted the press itself to a position of priority – it is the first piece of evidence in the argument. The poem that accompanies the woodcut concentrates on revealing as well as praising the press. The liveliness of the "forme and figure of the presse" inheres both in the woodcut's faithful rendering of the print shop and in the press's almost infinite productivity. In this assertion of efficacy lies a network of allusions to controverted issues of doctrine.

That the press "workes so readily" sets it apart from what the Protestants held to be the dead works of Catholicism. That such a claim should be made using images seems to run counter to the increasing tendency toward what Patrick Collinson has termed iconophobia.[61] Indeed, the poem seems to insist on the visual image that has been "obiected to thine eye." One might discount this by arguing that the woodcuts are a matter of

Fig. 3 Martyr, Thomas Williamson, *The Sword of the Spirit* (1613)

expediency, included in order to make the book's message accessible to a
variety of readers. Williamson suggests something along these lines in the
preface: "it is profitable that there be many bookes of many persons made
of like matters in a diuers stile & method, so that they be not contrarie in a
diuers faith, that from the same truth may more clearly appeare to some in
one manner, to some in an other" (¶5ᵛ–¶6ʳ). It is precisely this insistence on
making things appear clearly that motivates the woodcuts. They are not
concessions to expediency but a fundamental part of the book. As a group,
the woodcuts juxtapose images of idolatrous Catholic religion with images
depicting the literary practices of Protestant religion – in effect, constructing a pictorial argument for literacy.

This is true even of the emblematic images such as the depiction of scales
weighing the Bible against "Popish drosse" (B3ʳ). Here the Bible, a large and
very physical book, is counterpoised against the rosaries, crucifixes, bells,
candles, and books of Catholicism. Their books of decrees and decretals
are, of course, smaller and, more importantly, plural. The unity of the
single book, "The Bible conteyning the word of god," is captured in this
image. By focusing on the material book, the emblem avoids the obvious
problems of interpretation that confront all readers of any text. Indeed, *The*

Sword of the Spirit perfectly exemplifies the dynamic of polemic by relent-lessly distinguishing friend from enemy; critical to this process is the insistence that the distinctions being made are manifest, visible, available to all with eyes to see. The images are thus not merely expedient aids for the unlearned; they delineate a polemical vision in which the distinction between true and false religion is obvious, requiring no careful discrimina-tions or abstruse definitions.

From the image of the scales follows a series of woodcuts displaying the contending forces of Protestantism and papistry. The seemingly inert book gives rise first to preaching and then to martyrdom. The woodcut of the godly preacher, showing women, men, and even a child in the audience with books in their laps, closes what Robert Darnton has called the communication circuit (E7^r).[62] In contrast, the Catholic priest cele-brating mass has his back to the viewer, while four priests kneel in adora-tion of the raised Eucharist (CI^r), an image that insists on the division between clergy and laity. The concluding pair of images is perhaps the most interesting, for it is here that the attempt to fix polemical categories reaches its height. A woodcut of a single, male, Protestant martyr chained to a stake and in flames (fig. 3) is contrasted with the picture of a long-haired, bearded head fixed on a pole and raised from the battlements of a castle (fig. 4). The poem that interprets this image asserts that interpreta-tion is necessary only to forestall the perverse reading of the pope and his followers:

> The Beast of Rome, when he this picture see
> Will not forthwith a Traitors head it deeme:
> But him as Martyr canonize to be,
> Yea with the saints to place him hee will seeme:
> If Martyrs they, that seeke a kingdomes ruth,
> Then what are they that suffer for the truth?

That this is indeed a traitor's head is as plain as day; explication is only needed in order to draw attention to the enemy's misprision. Insisting on the legibility and the legitimacy of the means of execution, this is de factoism with a vengeance: the patient suffering of plain Protestant martyrs is counterpoised against the subversive plotting of Machiavellian traitors.

The Sword of the Spirit draws a stark picture of the polemical conscious-ness that I see operating unevenly but extensively throughout early modern English culture. Though extraordinary in the way in which it condenses a number of complex issues into a series of woodcuts, the book is at the same time unremarkable in its conventional anti-popery.[63] What is most

Fig. 4 Traitor, Thomas Williamson, *The Sword of the Spirit* (1613)

striking, however, is the way in which it represents the relationship between
print and Protestantism. On one level, it is nothing more than a reiteration
of the story told by Foxe. On another level, while it continues to conflate
truth, gospel, and Protestant polemic, it also provides a succinct map of the
circulation of print, displaying writer, printers, and readers, and insisting
on the material practices that occupy the various agents in the communication circuit. One could make of this a story about the institution of the
author in the age of print; however, it seems more plausible to see the series
of images as culminating in the volatile notion of the Protestant nation.
This is the import of the book's final woodcut, which attempts to secure
the political meaning of execution by drawing a sharp line between true
martyr and false traitor. The author at the beginning is not an originary
figure; his prominent books indicate that he too is a reader, his work a labor
of transmission rather than creation.

Both *The Benefit and Invention of Printing* and *The Sword of the Spirit* are printed polemics that attempt to claim the technology of print as a weapon in the arsenal of a particular camp, a camp claiming universality. Though Foxe, in praising print, resists explicitly identifying the technology as a weapon and asserts that God began to work for his church not with "Sword and Target . . . but with Printing, Writing, and Reading," it is clear that he envisions the press as another kind of sword, one that may not inflict mortal wounds but is nonetheless able to "abolish" its opponents out of this world. Indeed, the thrust of Foxe's account is nicely captured by the title of Williamson's book: *The Sword of the Spirit,* which is itself a quotation of Ephesians 6:17: "And take the helmet of salvation, and the sword of the spirit, which is the word of God." Foxe's sanctification of the press marks it not as a neutral tool to be wielded by all comers but as the weapon of reform. However, experience on the ground made clear that the press was not the proprietary technology of the Reformers; rather than the baldly triumphalist claims of an ascendant Protestantism articulated later by the likes of Macaulay, such statements are the rhetoric of an embattled minority responding to the all too visible fact that Catholics, and Anglicans too, were able to use the press advantageously.[64]

Foxe himself, in the introduction to his edition of *The Whole Workes of W. Tyndale, Iohn Frith, and Doct. Barnes,* wishes that those who occupy the trade of printer might "vse the same to the glory of hym which gaue it, and to the ende wherefore it was ordayned, and not to abuse vnworthely that worthy facultie, eyther in thrusting into the worlde euery vnworthy trifle that commeth to hand, or hauing respecte more to their owne priuate gayne, then regarde to the publike edifying of Christes Church."[65] Foxe's worry here is most obviously the threat of a commercial market driven by a profit motive rather than evangelical commitment. Not only is the press abused by those who would peddle profane trifles, it is also corrupted by the open opponents of the gospel. This difficulty is admirably described by the printer of Thomas Cartwright's *A Replye to an Answere* in his address to the reader:

It is to be lamented / that the noble Science of Printing / giuen of the Lorde for the maintenance of the truth / should be readyer to wayte vpon the defence of corruptions / then upon the sincerity of the trueth: whilest those whych are cunning in it / and are enryched by it (I knowe not vpon what sinister respecte) refuse to bestowe their knowledge / and employ their wealth / wherwyth God hath blessed the[m] thys wayes. Where vpon it falleth out (gentle Reader) that I neyther hauing wealth to furnish the Print with sufficient varetie of letters / haue bene compelled (as a poore man doth / one instrument to diuers purposes) so to use one letter for three or four tongues.[66]

¶ Of the authoritie of the Church in things indifferent. Tract.2.

Some things may be tollerated in the Church touching order, ceremonies, discipline, and kinde of governments, not expressed in the word of God. Chap.1. the first Division.

Admonition.

S Eing that nothing in this mortall life is more diligently to be sought for, and carefully to be looked vnto (a) than the restitution of true religion and reformation of Gods Church: and seeing that your parts (dearly beloued) in this present Parliament is, aswell in freeing your selues from all kinde of Popery, and to employ your whole labour and studie not onely in abandoning all popishe remnantes both in ceremonies and regiment, but also in bringing in and placing in Gods Church those things onely, whiche the Lorde him selfe (b) in his worde commaundeth. Because it is not inough to take paynes in taking away euill, but also to be occupied in placing good in the stead thereof. Nowe because many men mine not the right way...

margin references:
a 1.Reg.23.
2.Chro.17.
2.Chro.29.
30.31.
Psal.132.1,4.
b Mat.21.12,13.
Ioh.2.15.
c Deut.4.+.2.
Deut.12.32.
d Psal.17.17.27.
Rom.12.2.
1.Cor.12.14
e Psal.1.6.
Psal.119.21.
John.15.11.10.
g 1.Tim.3.8.
h Math.7.64.
i Mat.10.31

☞ Answere to the Admonition.

Pag.20.Sect.1.6.2.

I VVill not answere two bookes, but matter, not bare affirmations or negations, but reasons: and therfore in as fewe woordes as I can, I will comprehende many lines. But before I enter into their reasons, I thinke it not amisse to examine that assertion which is the chiefe and principall grounde (so farre as I can gather) of their bookes, that is, that those things onely are to be placed in the church, which the Lord himselfe in this worde commaundeth. As though they shoulde saye, nothing is to be tolerated in the Churche of Christ, touching either doctrine, order, ceremonies, discipline, or gouernment, except it be expressed in the word of God. And therfore the most of their argumentes in this booke be taken ab authoritate negatiue, whiche by the rules of Logike proue nothing at all.

T.C. Pag. 9. Sect. 1.

Y Ou in the end of this confutation, that your enemies will be faint good, whiche haue made to taile a beginning. For before you doe the gathering out of the Admonition, that nothing shuld be placed in the Churche, but that which the Lord hath commaunded, as though the wordes were not playne inough, you doe interpret them further by your exposition. And what is that, you answere touching order, doctrine, order, ceremonies, discipline, or gouernment in the Churche of Christ, word of God. Is this to interprete it as alowed to say, Nothing is to be tolerated in the word of God. Is this to interprete or is adde vnto it? behalfe but small matters of the Churche, that can not tell, that certayne things may be tolerated in the Churche for a time, whiche by the word of God...

Tract.2:

Io. Whitgifte.

This my interpretation of their bookes is grounded vpon the whole discourse and diuise of their booke, as it may euidently appeare to be true to any that hathe eyes to see, and eares to heare: and therfore yf you can any one place in their booke, whiche bathe ouerthrowe this my interpretation of their woordes. I knowe it is one thing to saye, that nothing muste be placed in the Churche, and an other thing to saye, that nothing muste be tolerate, but I (as that they make no difference betweene them neither in their writing, nor yet in their practise. And I thinke also that there is some difference betweene these two manner of speaches, except it be commaunde in the woorde of God, and except it be expressed in the worde of God. For, I knowe sundrie thinges to be expressed in the woorde of God, whiche are not commaunded: as Christ his fasting fortie dayes, and his other miracles, and therfore by that interpretation I haue giuen vnto them a larger scope than they them selues require, whiche yf it be an iniurie, it is to my selfe, and not to them.

But I thinke you were not well aduised, when you saye, that many things are both commaunded and forbidden, of whiche there is no expresse mention in the worde of God, for this is meante that many things are commaunded or forbidden in the worde, which are not expressly set downe in the worde, in my opinion you speake contraries: For, howe can it be commaunded or forbidden in the worde, except it be also expressed in the same? If you meane, that many things are commaunded or forbidden to bee done, necessarie vnto saluation, whiche notwithstanding are not expressed in the worde of God, then I see not howe you differ from that opinion, whiche is the grounde of all papistrie, that is, that althings necessary vnto saluation are not expressed in the scriptures. For whatsoeuer you meane it, it cannot be true: for there is nothing necessarie to eternall life, whiche is not bothe commaunded and expressed in the Scripture. I counte it expedite, when it is either in manifest woordes contayned in Scripture, or thereof gathered by necessarie collection. If I had to doe with a papist, I coulde proue this to be true by the many manifest testimonies of the Scripture it selfe, and also by sundrie other, bothe auncient and late writers, but bicause I thinke it bathe but ouerslipped you, and that vpon better aduise you will reforme it, therfore I will cease to deale further in it, vntill I vnderstande more of your meaning.

By conclusion touching Argumentes negatiue ab authoritate, (as I vnderstande it, and haue expounded it, in the wordes following) is very true, and muste of necessitie be so. You saye, that some drops out of the authoritie of a man, whiche neither affirma...

margin references:
Luem.7.
vers.31.33.
Edy.30.v.2

Though the phrase, "one instrument to diuers purposes," reveals a definite anxiety over the many uses to which print can be put, the specific polemical target here is the lavish printing by Henry Bynneman of Whitgift's *An Answere to a Certen Libel,* the book that Cartwright is attempting to refute. *An Answere,* an excellent example of the protocols that develop around the printing of polemic, uses a wide variety of fonts to distinguish the different voices that it is representing: quotations from the *Admonition* (the target text) are given in a large black letter; Whitgift's commentary appears in a smaller black letter font, roman is used for names and other quotations, and italic for Latin. The result is a page that carefully discriminates between a number of voices, some confirming, others contradicting (fig. 5).

Before the development of quotation marks, direct quotations were often indicated by changing the font, a procedure modeled on the sixteenth-century manuscript convention of using italic for emphasis and quotation.[67] As C. J. Mitchell points out "the early editors of Shakespeare felt free to indicate quotations as they chose, sometimes leaving them to the context, sometimes using italic, sometimes, especially for short quotations, using brackets, sometimes using a colon at the start of reported speech; and when they did use inverted commas being quite content, as though these were a different kind of colon, merely to open a quotation and to leave its termination to the reader's common sense."[68] Printed polemic displays a similar variety of conventions, but it typically reveals a much more exacting use of the chosen convention. Polemic is, after all, a citational form that depends on precise quotation and often focuses on the parsing of particular sentences. The care with which this is done often surprises modern readers who expect all polemic to be fiercely opportunistic. Indeed, Whitgift's book is a luxurious establishment production that presents large block quotations of the opponent's book, a procedure that becomes vastly easier with the invention of print, followed by a text block devoted to Whitgift's attempt to demolish the argument presented in the preceding section. The comprehensive nature of the rebuttal – no claim goes unchallenged – makes the book appear to be a model of conscientious disputation. But the complaint of the printer of Cartwright's *Reply* should be recalled, deprived by poverty of "sufficient varietie of letters" he is compelled to "use one letter for three or four tongues." If the "varietie of letters" used by Bynneman suggests a punctilious observation of the decorum of academic controversy, it is also the case that such variety conspicuously bespeaks wealth.[69]

Fig. 5 Whitgift, *The Defense of the Aunswere* (1574)

Whitgift and Bynneman deploy the full resources of typography in order to guide the reader's interpretation. Taking a scholastic form of argument into print, they faced a variety of readers, many of whom might not have any extensive training in dialectic and might, therefore, fail to hear the commanding voice of reason. The typographical polyphony created by the use of different fonts is one way of addressing this situation by distinguishing authorial and authoritative from suspect voices. Quotations from the adversary's text could be further debilitated by the addition of sarcastic marginal glosses, such as Whitgift's succinctly dismissive, "Surely the man is in a dream."[70] Such practices were in part an attempt to reconstitute in print the sort of legible hierarchy visible in the academic institutions where the protocols of debate were inculcated.[71]

Given that polemic frequently involves the recreation of the voice it would counter, these techniques were developed in an attempt to overcome the risk that a reader might be taken by the wrong set of arguments. Bishop Parkhurst of Norwich expressed precisely this concern in his response to Archbishop Parker's suggestion that the churches of Norwich be furnished with copies of Jewel's *A Defence of the Apologie of the Churche of England* (London, 1567), a painstaking response to Thomas Harding's *A Confutation of a Book intituled An Apologie of the Church of England* (Antwerp, 1565):

Touching the bishop of Sarum's work, as I have singular cause to allow as well of the author as of his works, so do I conjecture that the placing of the such controversies in open churches may be a great occasion to confirm the adversaries in their opinions, that have not wherewith to buy Harding's books, shall find the same already provided for them; where like unto the spider sucking only that may serve their purposes, and contemning that is most wholesome, will not once vouchsafe to look upon the same.[72]

Despite its tinge of paranoia, Parker's image of spider-like readers is astute. It is tempting to claim that he recognizes quite clearly that on some fundamental level all readers are opportunists, that they take away that which will "serve their purposes"; however, to do so would be to neglect the distinction between adversaries and friends. Adversaries are by definition incompetent and perverse readers. Indeed, the figure of the spider is conventional, used also by Williamson: "as the Bee from the wholesome herbe and fragrant flower gathereth hony, but the spider poison," so "the faithful Preachers and teachers of the word … gather most excellent knowledge … But contrariwise, false teachers and diabolical seducers … pervert the same good word of God to their own destruction" (¶4ᵛ). Unlike Parker who worries that including argument and refutation will give aid and comfort to the enemy, Williamson is concerned with the interpretive abuse of the Bible, a putatively single text. "It is that which the learned call *Glossa viperina*," explains William Barlow, "when an interpretation like a Viper, eates out the bowels of the text."[73] While the threat of malevolent interpretation haunts all writing, polemic is particularly vunerable. In polemic, the opponent's argument must be rehearsed, if not directly quoted, in order to be effectively refuted. But in order to forestall the possibility that a reader will be convinced by the opponent's argument, elaborate protocols of quotation and citation, of both authorities and opponents, are developed in the maelstrom of polemic. Here, the "fixity" of the printed book matters, as polemicists accompany their copious quotations with exact page citations, which allow the reader to check for accuracy. Though admittedly speculative, it seems likely that the paper trail of printed polemic initially contributed to the hardening of opinion and argument, promoting an intellectual sclerosis. Though heavily annotated and glossed medieval manuscript books also present a multiplicity of voices arranged on a single page, early modern printed polemic materializes cultural conflict as opposed to the largely consensual, if not entirely pacific, literary culture of the Latin Middle Ages.[74]

This dynamic is taken to ridiculous extremes (or extremes of ridicule) in Matthew Sutcliffe's *The Supplication of Certaine Masse-Priests Falsely Called Catholikes* (1604). A response to John Colleton's *A Supplication to the Kings Most Excellent Maiestie* (1604) (fig. 6), Sutcliffe's book reproduced his target text adding sarcastic and critical annotations. Sutcliffe even includes a simulacrum of Colleton's title page, which glosses *supplication* as "And partly commination, terrifying vs with their forces, numbers & friends, abroad and at home" (fig. 7). The mimetic potential of print is brilliantly exploited, but the fact remains that Sutcliffe effectively insured that Colleton's tract would have an even wider circulation than it would on its own.

It is, perhaps, counterintuitive to insist on the dialogic aspect of polemic, for it is precisely the collapse of real dialogue that seems to define polemic. Conversation and genuine argument appear to give way to bald assertion and the force of rhetoric. Polemic is often described as the epitome of the monological; single-minded in its pursuit of victory, it is considered to be a polarizing discourse that recognizes no moderation or middle way. Foucault, for instance, in an interview with Paul Rabinow, explained that he did not take part in polemics and insisted on the difference between those who do and those who do not, "as something essential: a whole morality is at stake, the morality that concerns the search for the truth and the relation to the other."[75] Asserting that "the rights of each person are in

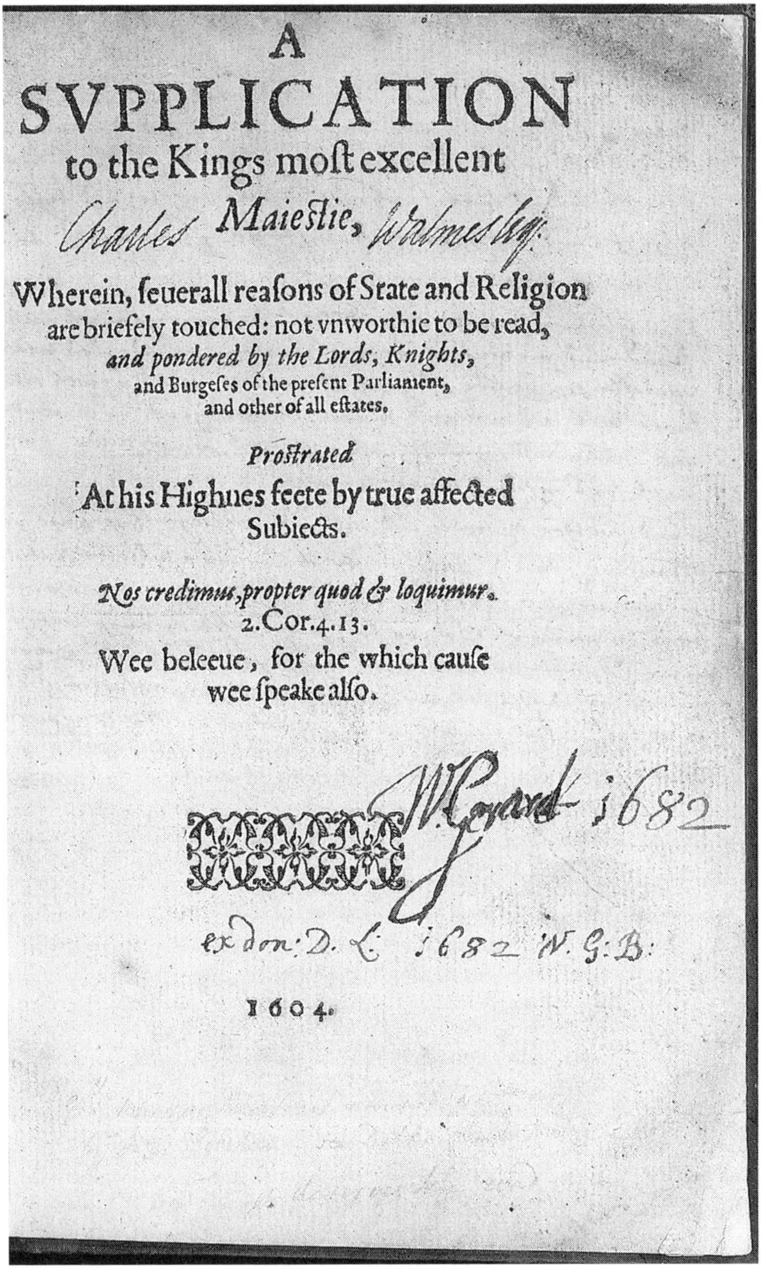

A
SVPPLICATION
to the Kings moſt excellent
Charles Maieſtie, *Walmesley*

Wherein, ſeuerall reaſons of State and Religion
are briefely touched: not vnworthie to be read,
and pondered by the Lords, Knights,
and Burgeſes of the preſent Parliament,
and other of all eſtates.

Proſtrated
At his Highnes feete by true affected
Subiects.

Nos credimus, propter quod & loquimur.
2.Cor.4.13.
Wee beleeue, for the which cauſe
wee ſpeake alſo.

W. Conard 1682

ex don: D. L 1682 W. G. B:

1604.

Fig. 6 John Colleton, *A Supplication* (1604)

A
ᵃSVPPLICATION
to the Kings ᵇ moſt excellent
Maieſtie.

Wherein,ſeuerall reaſons of State and Religion
are briefely touched: *not vnworthy to be read,*
and pondered by the c Lords, Knights, and
Burgeſſes of the Parliament,and other.
of all *d* eſtates.

Proſtrated

At his Highneſſe feete by   true affeĉted
Subieĉts.

Nos credimus,propter quod & loquimur.
f *2.Cor.4.13.*
Wee beleeue, for the which cauſe
we ſpeake alſo.

ℰ **1604.**   A 4

---

a *And partly a*
commination,
terrifying vs
vvith their
forces, numbers
and friends,
abroad and at
home.

b *To Papiſts*
the Pope is
more excellent.

c *The Lords*
ſpir it uall ſup-
preſſed.

d *They ende-*
uor to ſtirre all
eſtates.

e *Truely affec-*
ted to the Pope,
rather then to
the King.

f *If they be-*
leeue all they
ſpeake after-
vvard,they be-
leeue lyes.

g *VVhere and*
by vvhom vvas
this geare
Printed?

Fig. 7 Matthew Sutcliffe, *The Supplication* (1604)

some sense immanent in the discussion," Foucault sounds very much like Habermas. Here and elsewhere, the dialogue is celebrated as that which fosters debate, discovery, and freedom, while polemic is excoriated as that which attempts to foreclose debate, violently curtails exploration, and insists on boundaries and limits.[76] Obviously such a description is part of a normative vocabulary, a vocabulary that has received very little critical scrutiny. Indeed, *polemic* becomes a label reserved for bad and violent arguments. This evaluative vocabulary is, I would suggest, frequently misleading when it is used to analyze the complexities of controversy in the early modern period.

My attempt to rehabilitate the category of polemic is intended to illuminate the conditions of communication in early modern England. Such a project is not a celebration of polemic, nor does it mean that theoretical attempts to locate the genuinely dialogic are misguided; indeed, the paucity of such dialogic moments may well be strong evidence of the need for just such theorizing.[77] My own use of the term *dialogic* is minimalist and neutral: *dialogic* describes language that reveals the characteristics of a dialogue, which is defined as an exchange between at least two voices. Polemics, "books of encounter" in William Barlow's phrase, always attack a target, usually another text. The process of recapitulation or ventriloquization is often parodic, usually subversive, and always hostile. "Al his foolish dialogisme," William Fulke writes of one opponent, "is a fighting with his owne shadow."[78] Fulke recognizes that his Catholic adversary has attempted to write in a dialogic form, but he denies the reality of the imagined exchange. The opponent is only fighting with shadows of his own creation, refusing to engage with the genuine arguments of the Protestants. Such texts manage to combine, to varying degrees, playfulness and enmity, but their outstanding characteristic is that they take clear positions by negating, rather than incorporating, a competing argument. Such writing, with its unbecoming certitude, passionate conviction, and remorseless logic, is likely to strike modern readers as alien and unpleasant. Rather than consign polemic to the waste bin of history as a sterile exercise best forgotten, an unfortunate cultural *cul de sac*, I want to insist on the productivity, if not the prettiness, of polemic. Along with heat and noise, polemic produces arguments and identities: early modern polemic is not only polarizing but also pluralizing.

If polemic is dialogic, it is also dialectic, both in its use of logic and in its embodiment of social and intellectual conflict. Such an understanding requires that we see polemic as a strategic social practice given new velocity by the printing press and the Reformation. Polemic is not only a literary form; it is also a social and cultural practice, a practice devoted to the constitution of particular communities. Located within a social context, polemic is always revealed to be part of a dialogue, not the face-to-face dialogue seeming to promise true communication, but a temporally and geographically extended exchange. No matter how vicious, polemic invariably claims a pre-text (a book that came before) and provokes responses. Describing polemic as dialectic emphasizes its commitment to strenuous argument and its dynamic role within social and cultural history. Indeed, Mark Goldie has argued that enlightenment critique arises out of religious polemic: "the language of unmasking is rooted in the intellectual culture of the Protestant revolt."[79]

Polemic is simultaneously a genre, a concept, and a practice. In chapter 2, focusing on the Marprelate pamphlets, I argue that the practice of polemic in the early modern period achieves a generic regularity, becoming a discursive form with its own recognizable set of conventions. In chapter 6, I elaborate on the history of polemic by describing the attempt, under James I, to institutionalize its practice by founding a unique institution dedicated to the pursuit of controversial divinity. Such episodes indicate the prominence of polemic as a specific form of writing in early modern culture; however, my account is not limited to the genre of polemic. A useful, though by no means absolute, distinction exists between a formal entity, genre or kind, and a discursive dynamic or mode.[80] This distinction helpfully allows one to see the ways in which other genres, such as history, prose fiction, the elegy, and drama, were capable of being put to polemical use. In combination the Reformation and the printing press not only created a genre of polemic, they also rendered a number of popular discursive forms polemical.

A particularly illuminating example of such a discursive form is the dialogue. The move from dialogic polemic to polemic dialogue is not simply a fashionable chiasmic inversion. Dialogues provide a striking introduction to the polemical orientations of the period not only because they simultaneously depict and engage in a polemicized world but also because the efflorescence of the dialogue form during the Renaissance has led some to typify the entire period as dialogic. Polemical dialogues thus provide a useful starting point because they complicate received notions of the literary Renaissance and because they provide rich evidence of the ways polemic permeated discursive, aesthetic, and social practice. There is a lingering atttachment to the idea that the Renaisance saw a great burst of dialogue writing and that this form of writing reveals a new expansiveness of mind and culture; the playful arts of dialogue are associated with a new-found

interest in rhetoric and the ability to argue *in utramque partem*. The dialogue
in such narratives is understood as a special cultural achievement, the high-
water mark of Renaissance sophistication and elegance, subsequently
betrayed by the modern insistence on the univocal and the methodical.[81]

Peter Burke, for example, suggests that despite the existence of medieval
dialogue forms, it still makes sense to talk about the rise of the dialogue in the
Renaissance; moreover, he concludes, "the genre went into relative decline in
the seventeenth century and it has been more or less dead, or at least very
sick, ever since." Burke associates the Renaissance dialogue with the revival of
classical forms and the new interest in rhetoric, but also suggests that an
important factor in the efflorescence of dialogue may have been "the impact
of printing on a culture that was still in many ways oral."[82] Positioning such
dialogues as hybrid or transitional documents situated between a putatively
oral culture and one shaped by print collapses the difference between the
literary form of the dialogue and the Renaissance (the period that marks
the transit from pre-modern to modern); dialogue thus epitomizes the
Renaissance. The association between dialogue and Renaissance has been
given a more precise elaboration by Virginia Cox, who has convincingly
argued that "When any age adopts on a wide scale a form which so
explicitly 'stages' the act of communication, it is because that act has, for
some reason, come to be perceived as problematic."[83]

While the ubiquity of the dialogue form does attest to an increasing
alertness to the difficulties associated with communication, the vast majority of dialogues do not directly represent communication as significantly
problematic. The volume of didactic dialogues suggests that writers saw the
form as particularly well-suited for teaching complex subjects to a broad
audience: the dialogue could ameliorate the austere complexities of an
academic or theological discourse that remained inaccessible to the unini-
tiated. Question and answer dialogues struck many as an ideal pedagogic
form for print, enabling the oral colloquy of student and teacher to be
represented and replicated for readers, a perception that, in part, accounts
for the explosion of printed catechisms under Elizabeth.[84] Furthermore,
dialogues were well suited to take advantage of the possibilities offered by
the printing press. As in the polemics of Whitgift described above, different
fonts could be used not only to differentiate but to characterize different
voices. George Gifford's *A Dialogue betweene a Papist and Protestant* (1582),
for example, presents the words of Professor of the Gospel in black letter,
while Papist's claims are given in roman type. Black letter here signifies the
antiquity of the native Protestant tradition; roman indicates that papistry
is a foreign novelty. Such significations are always relational and were

capable of reversal. The same author's *Countrie Diuinitie* (1581) appears to invert the terms.[85] Here, the godly speaker, Zelotes, is rendered in roman, his interlocutor, Atheos, in black letter. In this case, black letter is associated with the popular and unlearned; roman with the elite and erudite. What remains constant is the use of different type faces to represent different voices. Clearly, such books were open in the sense that they were hospitable to their readers, but this does not mean that they were open-ended or indeterminate. Indeed, most such books clearly focus on the development of a specific argument or the transmission of a particular body of knowledge.

Polemic dialogues do, however, reveal what Cox sees as the fundamental aspect of dialogue: "a concern with communication; with the problem of what people do with language and what they do with knowledge" (6). These books simultaneously represent a polemicized culture and engage in polemical exchange: they depict a world in which religious identity is perceived as shifting and unstable, a world in which language is used to conceal as well as reveal, and, at the same time, they pursue polemical arguments of their own, seeking to deploy language in defense of an unambiguous truth. This dynamic is particularly evident in the spate of dialogues that appeared in 1548, attacking the mass in anticipation of the first Book of Common Prayer. With varying degrees of sophistication, dialogues like *John Bon, A Newe Dialogue Wherin is Conteyned the Examination of the Messe*, and *The Endightment agaynste Mother Messe* attempt to convince their readers that the Catholic mass is an act not of worship but idolatry, and yet they inevitably raise the question of how one legitimates such an argument.[86] Not all of these dialogues resort directly to the authority of scripture. *John Bon*, a dialogue between a simple farmer and a parson, relies entirely on the deflations that a "common sense" view offers to the doctrine of transubstantiation. John wants to know, for instance, how if the corpus is a man, it is able to fit in the pyx. The Parson responds, "Nowe I maye perceyue ye loue thys newe geare" (AI[v]). John denies that he is of that "facion," insisting that he is a simple man. But he persists in raising objections until, at the end of the dialogue, the Parson concludes: "Why art thou suche a one and kept it so closse / Wel al is not golde that hath a fayre glosse / But farewel John Bon god bring thee in better mind" (A4[v]). This moment of recognition suggests that hypocrisy assumes new prominence as soon as religious identity is perceived to be labile; the problem of deception – always a threat to the ideals of community and communication – is enormously exacerbated by confessional division and the concomitant attempt to impose orthodoxy upon a recalcitrant or

resistant population. Paradoxically, polemic, which works to make confessional distinctions obvious, also creates conditions that encourage
duplicity.

Recognizing that John is a lover of the "newe geare," the Parson proposes
to leave him in God's care. The exchange between the two does not result
in either interlocutor changing his mind; there is no attempt at synthesis.
The dialogue is designed to juxtapose the plain language and perceptions of
John with the mystifying obfuscations of the Parson. The final word goes
to John, who asks the Parson not to pray for him before addressing his
horse: "driue furth God spede vs and the plough" (A4ᵛ). John's own prayer
associates his plainness with piety and productivity, identifying him with
the tradition of pious ploughmen stretching back to Langland's Piers.[87]

The failure of the two speakers in *John Bon and Mast Person* to come to
any agreement is found in other polemic dialogues. An excellent example is
A Dialogve, Concerning the Strife of Our Churche (1584). Printed by Robert
Waldegrave, who would later become infamous as the printer of the first
four of the Marprelate tracts and later still would become printer to King
James VI of Scotland, this anonymous dialogue, set in an inn, takes place
between Orthodoxos, a divine; Philodoxos, a lawyer; Philochrematos, a
bishop's chaplain; and Philodonos, an innkeeper. The two principal
antagonists are the godly Orthodoxos and the corrupt Philochrematos.
Unlike *John Bon*, this dialogue presents a developed argument. Indeed the
address to the reader insists on the verisimilitude of the dialogue: "I haue as
faithfully as I can, set downe the greatest accusations, and most vsuall
crimes, that haue any colour, which are slaunderouslye cast foorth, and laid
to the charge of Gods faithfull messengers: with a short answer to shew the
vanitie of the same."[88] An accurate rehearsal of the standard charges against
the godly is not, however, neutrality. "On the other side," the writer claims,
"I haue lightly touched as it were, the heades or fountaines of diuers
corruptions, maintayned by the contrarye part, which are so grosse &
manifest, that he which shall saye he knoweth not of them, maye well be
suspected for vntruth: and he that shall defende them, must put on his
foreheade of brasse" (A3ᵛ). In other words, the dialogue consists of a
rebuttal of the charges laid against the godly and the prosecution of the
case against the defenders of the establishment.

Despite the fact that there is no pretense of neutrality, the dialogue is
presented as allowing the judicious reader to decide between the two
parties: "My sute vnto thee, gentle reader, is no more but this, that thou
wilt well waigh, and iudge vprightly, which part follow the steppes of the
blessed Apostles, and so be the true ministers of Iesus christ" (A3ᵛ). The

writer anticipates that some will be offended by "this kind of dealing" but claims that he is bound by conscience to speak out. Indeed, this issue is treated in the argument between Orthodoxos and Philochrematos. Philochrematos makes the familiar argument that public exposure of ministers' failings will only bring "the calling" into "contempt." Furthermore, such denunciations impugn those who have authorized the ministers, bringing men of honor into contempt and "the people into vnquietness." This psychic discomfort clearly carries the threat of genuine social unrest. The people will not know what or whom to believe and follow: "Thus do you marre al vnder a pretence of zeale in reprooving sinne" (F8^v).

Orthodoxos does not exactly deny that "vnquietness" will be one result; rather he maintains that to countenance an incompetent ministry is to "famish mens soules" (G1^r). Men of honor are not exempted; God's ministers are sent "vnto high and low, to reproove them when they do amisse" (G1^v). Therefore, "it is God that bringeth such as bee of great dignitie into contempt" (G4^r–G4^v). If the people are "vnquieted," he concludes, "It is a lamentable thing that they haue in these dayes beene kept in such blindnesse, that they can not trie the Spirits" (G4^v). This text, identified in the margin as I John 4:1, is constantly invoked in the polemics of the period. For example, John Foxe exhorts prospective readers of his edition of Tyndale, Firth, and Barnes, to set "aside all partialitie and preiudice of opinion . . . to taste what they doe teach, to vewe their reasons, and to try their spirite" (A3^v). Indeed, to try the spirit is a mainstay of Protestant hermeneutics.

The dedication of the 1560 Geneva Bible to Elizabeth celebrates her attempt to create a spiritual temple for the "great flocke" of godly Christians but asserts that the church is threatened by various adversaries. "We persuaded ourselues," the translators explain, "that there was no way so expedient and necessarie for the preseruation of the one, and destruction of the other as to present vnto your Maiestie the holy Scriptures faithfully and playnely translated according to the langages wherein thei were first written by the holy Gost. For the word of God is an euident token of Gods loue and our assurance of his defence, wheresoeuer it is obediently receyued: it is the trial of the spirits" (*2^v–*3^r). The verb in I John 4:1 – "Derely beloued, beleue not everie spirit, but trye the spirits whether they are of God: for many false Prophets are gone out into the worlde" – is here transformed into a noun that construes the efficacious working of the scripture itself. Rather than being an interpretive process whereby the spirits are brought to book, their claims compared to those of the scripture, the process here is rendered almost automatic, an action not of human agents but of the "holy Gost" and the sacred text.

Far from being the exclusive mark of a radical agenda, I John 4:1 was also used by defenders of the established church. Richard Bancroft used it as his text for a Paul's Cross sermon in the wake of the Marprelate controversy.[89] To Bancroft, it appeared obvious that Marprelate and his crew were among the false prophets warned against in the text. Inevitably this passage, along with I Thessalonians 5:21 ("Prove all things; hold fast that which is good"), worked to license polemical debate and invited readers and listeners to pass judgment. Though Orthodoxos expresses dismay at the thought that the people may be unprepared to assume such a position, the dialogue as a whole operates on the assumption that those exposed to it will be capable of seeing the truth.

However, unlike the translators of the Geneva Bible who invest the scripture with a machine-like efficiency that sorts godly Christians from their impious adversaries, the writer of the dialogue draws attention to the difficulties of textual authority and interpretation. The writer of the epistle to the reader anticipates that "Some will say these are but words, and who can not easilye make the like pretence for anye matter whatsoeuer." A problem for fictional dialogue in particular and for extra-scriptural discourse in general, the suggestion that words can be made to say anything is countered in this case by an appeal to experience. The writer asserts: "I will therefore note some particular causes, to shew the truth of my words" (A4^r). The "particular causes" are manifest corruptions, specific examples such as the ecclesiastical courts, that are known to all through experience. This line of argument, deployed by polemicists of all camps, clearly leavens the tendency toward an austere scripturalism and assumes that "ye shall know them by their fruits." Moreover, the appeal to common experience is a crucial step in the application of scripture to the contemporary social world.

A Dialogve, Concerning the Strife of Our Churche depicts a world in which communication has, indeed, become problematic. After welcoming the gentlemen, Philodonos, the innkeeper, complains that his trade has fallen: "Nowe all good fellowship is laide aside, the worlde is waxen stark nought" (B1^v). This nostalgic theme is taken up by Philochrematos who claims that "men waxe more couetous & worldlie." Though the innkeeper is uncertain "whether they be more couetous," he is convinced that "new-fangled Preachers" are responsible for the destruction of "all good house-keeping" (B2^r). This, predictably, provokes Orthodoxos who chastises Philochrematos for encouraging the innkeeper in his "euill speeches," which reveal him to be a "grosse and carnall man." The lawyer, Philodoxos, defends the innkeeper: "Yee mistake mine hoste, ye do him great wrong, to giue such seuere and sharpe sentence against him: I obserued and weied all his speeches, so farre as I can conceiue, he uttered nothing worthie rebuke" (B2^v). The lawyer puts himself forward as the enemy of acrimony, an impartial observer who weighs words and reaches right judgment. He quickly explains that the host's only intention was to defend "honest recreation": "If he had any worse meaning, I am deceived" (B3^r).

Philodoxos here occupies the position established for the reader, who has been exhorted in the prefatory epistle to "well waigh, and iudge vprightly" (A3^v). However, Philodoxos' judgment is immediately deemed faulty by Orthodoxos:

I do not thinke that his meaning was worse then yours: neither doth that colour of words which you go about to colour it with all, hide the nakednesse thereof: so farre off is it, from prooving his meaning or yours to be good, having scarce a shew of reason. (B3^r)

"The colour of words" recalls the epistle writer's attempt to forestall the objection that "these are but words" (A3^v). Orthodoxos' rejection of the colors of rhetoric serves to establish his credentials as a plain speaker, one whose arguments are grounded on the word of God. Yet Philodoxos, unwilling to concede that Orthodoxos is a legitimate interpreter of the scripture, accuses him of using rhetorical "colour": "You colour the matter with this, that we must obey onely in things which are not repugnant vnto Gods worde: who shall be iudge in these cases, or to which part shall men giue credite?" (C1^r). The specter of social chaos and the collapse of authority does not daunt Orthodoxos, who insists that invoking the threat of inter- pretive anarchy is a papist argument. He raises the possibility that a great reformer may arise in England but concludes that "in the mean time euery wise man will iudge as he findeth" (C5^r).

This is precisely the position of the reader at the end of the dialogue. Orthodoxos has failed to convince any of his auditors that his is the right position. Indeed, Philochrematos complains that it is vain to engage in a dialogue with one who is so obstinate and willful: "You will be singuler." This frequently made charge against the godly is intimately connected to the claim that precisians are against good fellowship and the unity and community of the church. Certainly Orthodoxos is singular to the degree that he is depicted as isolated; however, he vehemently denies the charge of singularity with its suggestion of an anti-social self-assertion: "For a man can not be too stedfast in the truth" (K1^v). The claim for conscience and commitment, with its intimations of martyrdom, here oscillates between extreme self-assertion and total self-negation.

Philodoxos reacts to this assertion of extremism by urging unity and concord, but Orthodoxos insists on the impossibility of agreement between God's faithful messengers and the devil's ungodly instruments. Philodoxos, ever the moderate, finds it incredible that any should "fight against God": "I dare not iudge so euill of anie man" (κ3ʳ). This refusal to judge is immediately attacked as "grose ignorance" masquerading as "excellent modestie." Orthodoxos sums up with the claim that "whosoeuer do fight against his word, or anie parte thereof, they are his enemies" (κ3ᵛ). The dialogue then concludes with a brief statement by the innkeeper: "I am sorie there is anie such talke in my house: If you will go to your chambers all things are readie, the Night is well spent" (κ4ᵛ). The argument ends without reaching any clear conclusion; nobody has capitulated or even modified their position; there is no image of victory or reconciliation. However, this does not mean that the polemic is somehow softened or rendered indeterminate. *A Dialogue* stages polemic, and precisely because the battle between God's messengers and the instruments of the devil will only end with the apocalypse, it is impossible for there to be a conclusive conclusion. Rather than being a form that is in some sense ideally suited to the development of open-ended thought, dialogue here functions to represent an endless opposition that does not give way to a higher synthesis or new consensus, offering instead a highly partisan map of a fractured social world.

Shortly after the Marprelate scandal, Waldegrave, presumably while in La Rochelle, printed *A Dialogue. Wherein is Plainly Laide Open, the Tyrannicall Dealing of the L. Bishopps against Gods Children.* Though there are a number of similarities to *A Dialogve, Concerning the Strife of Our Churche*, there are also significant departures. Most obviously, while the first book had addressed itself most directly to questions of law and obedience during the subscription crisis provoked by Whitgift's push for conformity in 1584, this polemic is clearly engaged in a series of arguments precipitated by the Marprelate pamphlets. The world it depicts seems several removes from the scene at the inn, where despite acrimony the hostile parties could spend the night under a single roof.

The characters are, for starters, themselves "plainly laide open": they are are not given even the slight cover of pseudo-classical allegorical names. Instead, the speakers are: "Puritane," "Papist," "Jacke of both sides," and "Idoll minister." The entire exchange takes place on the open road as the several speakers converge on their way to London. The knowledge granted to the reader by the speech prefixes is denied to the characters themselves who must establish the uncertain identities of their traveling companions by asking questions.

The first two to meet are Puritan and Jack; after exchanging greetings, they discover that they have both been in France. Puritan explains that he has been at La Rochelle; Jack has been at Orleans. Puritan inquires after the news, especially whether there is "Any likelyhoode of peace there?" (A2^r), an immediate reminder of the religious civil wars across the channel. Jack expresses optimism over the prospects for peace, but Puritan is suspicious: "but by the way, I pray you, if you came from *Orleans*, there they haue the masse, for they are of the league: & then I suppose you haue been partaker of their Idolatrie?" (A2^v). Jack vehemently proclaims his hatred of idolatry, but Puritan requires something more than a simple assertion: "I pray you let me heare if you can giue me some profe out of the word of God, for the confirmation of this your protestation against Idolatrie?" Jack cites with facility Deuteronomy 6:13, "Thou shalt worship the Lorde thy God, and him onely shalt thou serue," and I Corinthians 10:14, "Flye from Idolatrie." Admitting that these passages are "wel applied," Puritan nonetheless remains suspicious: "I am very glad if it be done in singlenesse of hart: For me thinks you could not possibly be in that place but you must be forced to be present at their Idolatrous Masse." Aware that the devil can cite scripture for his purpose, Puritan does not consider an ability to quote from the Bible to be proof that one is a friend of the gospel. Against the fluency of Jack's words stands the fact of his stay in the Catholic city of Orleans.

Jack thanks God that he has never been present at the mass, and though Puritan seems to harbor doubts, they are both soon distracted by the arrival of the minister. Immediately, the question of religious identity is again raised; Jack asks, "I pray you M. Vicker or parson, (for so you seeme to be) what good newes is there here at home, in England, for we haue bin both of vs in Fraunce?" (A3^r). Acknowledging that he is a poor vicar, Minister complains that there is no "great good newes here ... for our Church is so sore pestered with sectes & scismes." Puritan asks whether he is referring to the papists, only to learn that he means those who are "worse then papists ... the fantasticall *puritans* and *Brownists*" (A3^r–A3^v). When Puritan objects, Minister responds: "I perceue you are one of these fantastical *puritans* or *Brownists*: I pray you out of what place in Fraunce cam you?" The response, "La Rochelle," confirms Minister's suspicion: "I thought from *Rochel, Geneua* or *Scotland,* you seeme to be a birde of one of those nests." Like Puritan's earlier identification of Orleans with

Catholicism, this association of place names with confessional identity insists on a variegated religious geography, and yet it also suggests that fantastical puritans are not really English – they are hatched elsewhere. Puritan's rejoinder denies the importance of place: "Sir whatsoeuer I am, I doe not dout but to be able to prooue by the word what I haue saide." Puritan claims an identity founded on the scripture, an identity that does not depend on the localities of place and time. Such a notion provokes a scoff from the minister: "You are very full of scripture" (A4^r).

In the ensuing debate, Jack consistently takes the side of Puritan, who airs a number of the complaints earlier made by Martin Marprelate. When they are joined by Papist, who asks for good news, Puritan answers: "I knowe none good, for the land is sore troubled with these trecherous *Papists*, and filthy *Atheists*; and our church pestered with the Bishopps of the Diuel, nonresidents, Popish priests, and dumbe dogges, that there is no place, nor being for a faithful minister of the word" (D2^r). The rejoinder, "It was neuer merry worlde since there was so many puritans," incites Jack, who proclaims, "I smell you already, I perceue you are a Papist." Papist, like Puritan, does not deny the charge: "whatsoeuer I be, you may be sure I am noe puritane, for a Papist, is alwaies better then a puritan, and more friends shall he finde, both at home and abroad" (D2^r–D2^v). This claim to popularity will prove prophetic; it also demonstrates a fondness for the merry world of good fellowship. Unlike Puritan's claim for an identity grounded on scripture, Papist identifies himself by gesturing toward a social world.

The constellation of apparent identities shifts, however, when Jack, in an aside, explains to Papist, "I doe nothing but to see what this puritane will saye." He claims to have convinced Puritan that "I am one of his fraternity" (D4^r). Furthermore, while at Orleans he heard mass every day. Papist expresses incredulity, only to be told by Jack that had he not attended he would have been taken for a Huguenot, "and so should hardly escaped with my life" (D4^v). This confession of hypocritical conformity reveals Jack to be an opportunist with scant regard for religion, and yet this politic explanation does not disturb Papist. Together the two of them plot to have Puritan seized and taken before the Bishop when they arrive at London.

Final word is given to Puritan who reasserts his willingness to justify all he has said, "if not let me loose my life" (D4^v). This echoes Orthodoxos, who asserts: "For if I can not shew it to be true, let me loose my life" (H5^r). In both cases, the speakers are invoking the discourse of martyrdom, testifying to their willingness to suffer death as witnesses to the truth.

Here Puritan contrasts conspicuously with Jack who is without conviction. The reader may well wonder whether Puritan escapes to safety or goes to the martyrdom he so readily invokes. What is perfectly clear is that Puritan is alone in a world of betrayers. Equally clearly, though the dialogue acknowledges the existence of a plurality of voices, there is only one voice that is to be taken seriously. The pamphlet is itself a polemic that was, apparently, printed in La Rochelle, the very place that Puritan claims to have recently left. The action of the dialogue represents the scene of polemic; like Puritan, the pamphlet relies on scripture and argument to convince its readers and, again like Puritan, the pamphlet, an illicit publication, is in danger of being captured by the agents of episcopal authority or the crown.

There is no question that the two dialogues discussed above are relentless in their focused attack on the corruption of the ecclesiastical hierarchy. The pursuit of a pointed argument in dialogue form is hardly unusual; indeed, the form itself is far more likely to be exploited for its pedagogical utility than for its assumed affinity to dialogic thinking.[90] This split is recognized by Hans Robert Jauss who makes a familiar move when he divides dialogues into two discrete types, posing the magistral dialogue typical of the New Testament against the Socratic dialogue. In the first, "discussion is guided throughout by the teacher, and an authoritatively prescribed meaning is concretized in an interpretation of the current situation; in the second, a free-floating discussion moves in a roundabout fashion from the question to answer until it finally produces a meaning that is the result of mutual inquiry, and that emerges out of a knowledge of one's lack of knowledge."[91] Jauss readily admits that these are ideal types and that actual dialogues almost always partake of both types.

However, both types in Jauss's taxonomy leave out conflict: the top-down, authoritative dialogue is monolithic; the free-floating discussion that produces knowledge is based on the participants' amicable recognition of their own ignorance. The examples of dialogue considered thus far do not sit easily in either group. Certainly they promulgate specific arguments, but they also embrace a world of discursive conflict. As I have argued, they at one and the same time represent a world of polemic and engage in it. Yet, to understand the extent of the polemicization of early modern English culture one must consider books that are less obvious in their polemical orientation. The presence of religious polemic in two dialogues, Thomas Lodge's *Catharos. Diogenes in His Singularitie* and Robert Greene's *A Quip for an Vpstart Courtier*, which self-consciously proclaim their fictional status, provides evidence of the pervasiveness of polemical concerns. These works appear to assemble a variety of conventional themes and motifs that seem to have little direct connection to religious controversy. Indeed, for many, this is precisely what gives these works some claim to the title of literature: they are imaginative works of fiction not partisan tracts.

Nonetheless, *Catharos. Diogenes in His Singularitie*, described by C. S. Lewis as "arrant book-making," would, if not for its fictional frame, certainly be considered an uninspired didactic tract attacking contemporary corruption.[92] Constructed as an exchange between Diogenes and two men who come to seek his advice, Cosmophilos and Philoplutos, the book is a perfect example of what Jauss designates as a magistral dialogue. The scene described resembles the world envisioned in the Waldegrave dialogues: Diogenes is alone and marginalized. Lacking material and social prestige, his moral authority depends on the force of the arguments he advances in an effort to reform the worldly men who seek his advice. And yet the fact that he is recognized as a sage and sought for his wisdom suggests that he enjoys an intellectual prestige not shared by Orthodoxos and Puritan.

In his address to the readers, Diogenes remarks, "If any of you read and like, why then it likes me: if read and mislike, yet it likes me: for Philosophie hath taught me to set as light by enuie, as flatterie."[93] A pose of haughty indifference also marks the conclusion of the address: "Greedines hath got vp all the garden plots, and hardly haue I a roome left to turne my Tub around in: the best field flowers now fade, and better than Nettles my lands will not affoord. They that list may take, the rest leaue, and so I leaue you." Diogenes' imperious independence, his refusal to observe decorum, guarantees that his vision is uncorrupted by social concerns. Alone in his tub, Diogenes exemplifies the isolation of the classical satirist. Indeed, *singularity* is a word that comes up repeatedly in this dialogue. In one context, it marks the exemplary status of the rude philosopher who speaks truth to power. In other contexts, it indicates the stubborn waywardness of unruly subjects. And in still other contexts it seems to mean isolation and withdrawal. This appears to be the operative meaning in Diogenes' opening lament on the corruption of Athens: "What should *Diogenes* then doo but be singular, to see the better sort so sensuall?" (B1ᵛ). Later Philoplutos commends Diogenes using the very same term: "O *Diogenes*, this thy plaine methode, farre from Ironicall captions, prooueth thy singularitie" (G3ᵛ). Here the word is used to describe his rare virtue of plain speaking, a discursive singleness and sincerity that rejects duplicitous cavillation. Yet when discoursing on Spiritual Blindness, one of Lechery's daughters, Diogenes refers to those who have "dronken of this diuelish singularitie in thought, blinding their vnderstanding" (F4ᵛ). This singularity separates the heretic from the community of orthodoxy and is diabolical. Lodge's use of *singularity* reveals an extremely labile term that moves easily from the laudatory to the condemnatory, a fluidity that registers the dislocations that attended the English Reformation.

A particular example brings the term to bear on contemporary debates about religion. Diogenes begins his lesson with a series of beast fables, a point I will return to, and in one of them he describes the fate of a mother quail who, captured by a hawk and a goshawk, chooses to die alone rather than lead the predators back to her offspring. Asked how he applies this, Diogenes explains:

> After the manner of this Quaile ought our truely qualited diuines demean them selues, of two harmes they must choose the lesse: better had they suffer with a good conscience, than their whole flock should be deuoured in error, or misled through their enuie, and made insolent with their singularitie. They are bound to die rather for a Common profit, than to liue for a singular auaile. (D3^r)

The fable and its explication set up a series of associations and resonances, and yet it is hard to settle its meaning. Diogenes had begun with the assertion that concerning divines and lawyers, "I cannot admit in these sorts any mediocritie: for lukewarm professors in these things are lost professors" (C4^v). Indeed, his program for divines is uncompromising; they must apply themselves in "speaking the truth without hypocrisie, in reprehending all sinnes without flatterie, in liuing himselfe vprightly, and discoursing on the scriptures reuerently, in affecting no partialitie, but ordering all things in sinceritie" (D2^r). Cosmophilos finds this hard given the present state of the world. "Such therefore as will thrive in the worlde," he explains, "they must some times dissemble: for since of two euils the least is to be chosen, I thinke it better to forbeare than to beare the fagot, & more meete to beare the fagot, than to burne by the fagot" (D2^r). "To beare the fagot" is an allusion to a shaming ritual in which recanted heretics went in procession carrying a piece of firewood (emblematic of the averted burning) before making a formal public abjuration, and Cosmophilos here advocates dissimulation and submission to authority. Such a claim, issuing from a flexible attitude toward principle, would have met with stinging rebuke at the hands of Orthodoxos or Puritan, but Diogenes is more understanding. He explains that those who are "called to the service of the Gods" are under a special obligation, a claim that he develops with the parable of the quail.

This tale, then, at first appears to be an orthodox argument for the necessity of martyrdom on the part of those who serve God. But the language is far from straightforward. Clearly, Diogenes rejects a self-centered ethic, insisting that common profit trumps "singular auaile." Nonetheless, the application of the principle remains murky. Those who "suffer with a good conscience" are contrasted with those who allow their congregation to be "deuoured in error, or misled through their enuie, and made insolent with their singularitie." The language of error, envy, and insolence is usually used to describe the divisive attitude of the godly as a form of schism.[94] But if the bad divines are associated with the puritan faction, the identity of the "truely qualited diuines" who are prepared to suffer with a "good conscience" remains obscure. The logic of Diogenes' own opposition would appear to dictate that the quail who willingly accepts death rather than expose her children to the predations of the hawk and goshawk represents those Roman Catholic priests who continued to minister to adherents of the old religion and were subject to the rigors of the law. No great imaginative leap is required to understand the predatory birds as priest hunters and the quail as a martyred priest who refuses to expose the network of English recusants. Interpreted in this fashion, the parable of the quail presents a stark opposition between the integrity of Catholicism and the corruptions of Geneva, leaving no space for the so-called *via media* of the Elizabethan establishment. Admittedly, such a reading is an attempt to find coherence in a text that may simply exhibit contradictory impulses. The fable insists at once on the legitimacy of the single martyr and the illegitimacy of the singular schismatic, and though the proximity of martyr and schismatic may appear unsettling, few contemporary readers would have disagreed on these basic principles.

Though the text leaves open the precise application of its general principles, at least one reader seems to have read Lodge's tract as an attack on forward Protestantism. Thomas Bowes, in *The Second Part of the French Academie* (1594), concludes his epistle to the reader with a long diatribe against profane authors who promote atheism.[95] His first target appears to be Robert Greene, who is described as a machiavel and atheist. Bowes is infuriated that such a man should have "had the Presse at his commaundment to publish his lasciuious Pamphlets" (B4^r). Nor has the death of this notorious corrupter improved the situation, for "the rest of his crew" continue "without controlment to instill their venimous inuentions into the minds of our English youth by meanes of printing" (B4^v). The obvious consequence, Bowes explains, will be a flood of impiety. "Are they not already growen to this boldnes," he asks, "that they dare to gird at the greatest personages of all estates and callings vnder the fables of sauage beasts, not sparing the very dead that lie in their graues?" It has been argued that this is an allusion to *Catharos* and that Philoplutos and Cosmophilos are figures for Walsingham and Burghley.[96] Without doubt, Bowes goes on to allude to Nashe's *Pierce Penilesse*, which also contains a notorious beast fable.[97] In any case, Bowes, one suspects, would have been happy to lump Nashe and Lodge together as members Greene's "crew" and promoters of atheism and Catholicism, positions that he conspicuously fails to distinguish. "It were too long to set downe the Catalogue of those lewde and lasciuious bookes," laments Bowes, "which have mustered the[m]selues of late yeeres in Pauls Churchyard, as chosen souldiers ready to fight vnder the deuils banner" (B4^v).

Thomas Bowes insists in his dedication to Sir John Puckering that he, the Lord Keeper of the Great Seal, is a proper dedicatee because report holds that he takes great care that his retinue and household harbors none "whose hearts are possessed with a liking of that Antichrist of Rome, within the compasse of whose iurisdiction, this dangerous infection of Atheisme beganne first in this latter age of the world to breake foorth" (A3^v). The pope is responsible because it was in Florence that the "monster *Machiauel* first began to budde" (A4^r). This stance, as well as the orientation of the Huguenot de la Primaudaye's work, indicates the militancy of Bowes's Protestantism. Indeed, his dismay over bawdy books, which, he asserts, "preuaile no lesse (if not more) to the vpholding of Atheisme in this light of the Gospel, then the Legend of lies, *Huon of Burdeaux*, *King Arthur*, with the rest of that rabble, were of force to maintaine Popery in the dayes of ignorance" (B4^r), is an echo of Roger Ascham's insistence that the new "merry bookes of Italie" are more dangerous to youth than the notoriously corrupt medieval tales of chivalry with their celebration of "open manslaughter and bold bawdrye."[98] Both Bowes and Ascham imagine themselves to be fighting a cultural war against the depredations of a literature imbued with the corrupt and corrupting values of Catholicism.

Bowes's response to such books makes clear the degree to which even the fictional dialogue participates in religiously inflected polemics. Yet such fables do not admit stable readings. The claims put forward by Lodge appear entirely conventional: few deny that it is better to suffer with good conscience than to lead people into error. Diogenes expends a great deal of energy excoriating atheism (a word that in this period invariably designates irreligion rather than committed disbelief), a move that puts him on the side of religion. Indeed, his biting attacks on usury and lechery are so typical of the moralist that there appears to be little reason to distinguish his position from those of a wide range of social critics. In fact, it is hard to account for Bowes's hostility in terms of a moral stance. Diogenes inveighs against "amorous books" as an occasion for lechery, just as does Bowes. The provocation lies rather in the religio-political position embedded in *Catharos*. Diogenes concludes his account of divines on a deferential note: "Such should divines be, but I will leaue to talke of them who are best able to teach vs; they that weare the shooe can best tell where it wringeth, and no doubt they will against newfanglenes at last speake" (D3^r). Such a desire clearly places Diogenes in opposition to those who hoped to see further reform of the English church. In response to a question from Philoplutos about the problem of "ignoraunt and vnlettered Curates" (EI^r), a source of scandal in the eyes of the godly, Diogenes conspicuously refuses the question: "In faith I leaue to speake of them, till such as you bridle the impietie of Farmers, Grasiers, and such greasie Patrones, who neither are able to supply the place, nor will part with any indifferent maintenance for a sufficient man" (EI^r). Identifying greedy landlords as the true source of the problem serves to neutralize the argument for the immediate ouster of unlearned clergy, the dumb dogs so reviled in Puritan polemic. While a common and reflexive conservatism does not constitute a fully articulated political program, within the context of the early 1590s even such conventional wisdom could assume a polemical dimension.

Diogenes is a philosopher in the city but not of the city. Inhabiting his tub and advocating austerity, he is a figure of singularity in the midst of a vast, thriving, and, by his account, corrupt community. But the singularity of the sage easily shades into the frowardness of the schismatic. Diogenes was himself a doubtful exemplar. Though Greene used him as a figure of repentance and reform ("Diogenes, Gentlemen, from a counterfeit coiner of money, became a currant corrector of manners"), Nashe would hold him up as a paragon of hypocrisy ("*Diogenes* ... for all his nice dogged disposition and blunt deriding of worldly drosse and the grosse felicitie of fooles, was taken notwithstanding a little after verie fairely a coyning monie in his cell").[99] This unstable reputation reveals a deep ambivalence toward expressions of individualism. The tension within the word *singularity* between laudable excellence and culpable idiosyncrasy constantly confronts the many writers of the period who seek distinction in their defense of a traditional social order.

This difficulty is perfectly exemplified in the last dialogue that I will consider, *A Quip for an Vpstart Courtier*. Robert Greene was a notorious figure in his time; a person who, according to Richard Helgerson's influential account, became a celebrity by rehearsing and repudiating his own prodigality.[100] Though Greene and Lodge were associates who collaborated on *A Looking Glass for London* and wrote prefaces for each other's books, they finally reveal divergent orientations on questions of religion and community. Both writers present themselves as defenders of the traditional social order – what Lodge calls "*sacrum societatis vinculum*, the sacred bond of society" and Greene refers to as "*diebus illis.*"[101] Nonetheless, there is an enormous difference between *Catharos* and *A Quip for an Vpstart Courtier*. The first ends with hard words between Diogenes and his visitors; though much has been said, there is little sense that positions have changed, which makes it similar to the two Waldegrave dialogues discussed above. In contrast, Greene's fiction, after surveying many of the same social ills, attempts to reach a resolution.

Structured as a lawsuit between Velvet Breeches and Cloth Breeches, the book concludes with the jury's judgment in favor of Cloth Breeches, who represents "the old and worthie customs of the Gentilitie and yeomanrie of England" (A3ᵛ). The majority of the narrative, advertised as "a quaint dispute between Veluet breeches and Cloth breeches," is taken up with the impaneling of the jury, a process that allows for a survey of estates and trades. The whole is framed by the narrator's account of how, in a melancholy mood, he went alone into the fields where he fell asleep and had a dream. This medieval literary convention emphasizes the narrator's solitude. In contrast, the device of trial by jury draws attention to an integrated, though hierarchical, community. The jury as a locus of authority is far removed from the singular sage found in *Catharos*.

Despite this apparent pluralizing of moral authority, the final vision is of almost seamless consensus. Unlike the other dialogues discussed in this chapter, *A Quip* does not use speech headings to distinguish between various voices. Instead, the narrator, recounting his dream, identifies and quotes the various speakers. As a result, the dispute never threatens to splinter into a plurality of unaccommodating and unaccommodatable voices. The achievement of consensus is largely a matter of articulating a shared history. The argument put forward again and again by Cloth Breeches is that before the arrival of the foreign Velvet Breeches all was harmony. Rejecting the Lawyer, Cloth Breeches explains that the Lawyer was never his friend, "for when lowlinesse neighbourhood and hospitality liued in *England*, Westminister hall was a dining chamber not a den of controuersies, when the king himselfe was content to keep his S. *Georges* day in a plaine pair of Kersie hose, when the dukc, earle, lord, knight, gentleman and esquire, aimed at vertue, not at pride, and wore such breeches as was spun in his house." Law courts limited themselves to serious matters until "that proud vpstart Veluet-breeches, for his maintaynance inuented strange controuersies" (EIʳ).

The attitude toward religion displayed by Cloth Breeches is predictably conservative. Cloth Breeches is anxious to determine whether the parson who appears is "some puritan ... or some fellow that rayseth vp new scismes and heresies" and is relieved to learn that he is an inveterate enemy of all innovators (o2^v). As the parson declares:

A plague on them all ... for the world was neuer in quiet, deuotion, neighbour-hoode nor hospitality neuer flourished in this land since such vpstart boies and shittle witted fooles became of the ministrie, such I mean as *Greenwood Martin, Barrow, Wigginton,* and such rakehels, I cannot tel, they preach faith, faith, and say that doing almes is papistry, but they have taught so long *Fides solam iustificat,* that they haue preached good workes quite out of our parish. (G2^v)

The parson admits that he is no scholar but asserts that he "can read an homilie" and keeps company with his neighbors at the alehouse. If "good-fellowship" calls him away on a Sunday, he says "both morning & evening praier at once, and so let them haue a whole afternoon to play in" (G2^v). This is enough to convince Cloth Breeches that he is an "honest vickar." Yet such pastoral laxity was condemned by a wide range of Protestant opinion, and it is easy to see how a reader like Bowes might conclude that Greene was a promoter of atheism. Indeed, the language is strikingly similar to that put in the mouth of George Gifford's Atheos who describes his curate as "a verye good fellowe, hee will not stick when good Fellowes and honest men meete together too spende his groate at the Alehouse." In Gifford's work, such a mistaken attitude is typical of rustics who apply an easy, common-sense logic to the principles of religion. One result is the sort of popular pelagianism that assumes good intentions and basic decency are enough to merit salvation.[102] It is not difficult to see how this attitude fits with the notion that the charity exemplified by good fellowship is more important than the cramped austerity of scripturalism. The parson's humble assertion, "This is my life, I spend with liuing with my parishioners, I seek to do al good, & offer no man harm," has, then, a pointed polemical thrust.

This polemical thrust is even greater in the earliest printed version of *A Quip,* a book with a very complex publishing history. Six editions were published in the first year, and the first edition exists in two states.[103] The major difference between the first two states lies in the deletion of a passage satirizing the three Harvey brothers (E3^v–E4^r) and the excision of the names of Greenwood, Martin, Barrow, and Wigginton from the indictment of "shittle witted fooles." Richard and Gabriel Harvey had both attempted to strike a moderate stance during the Marprelate controversy, refusing to grant the arguments of either side. To the staunch defenders of episcopacy, this was perceived as siding with the enemy. Greenwood and Barrow were avowed separatists, who, after five years' imprisonment, were executed on April 4, 1593, and Wigginton, a deprived Yorkshire minister, had been suspected by Archbishop Whitgift of involvement in producing the Marprelate tracts. These names establish that the parson is on the side of the government; their deletion, along with the allusion to the Harveys, suppresses the personal and magnifies the principle. Rather than attacking specific individuals, the tract argues for an organic vision of a well-ordered community.

A Quip not only celebrates such a community, it suggests that it, rather than the activist minority of the godly sort, is the proper source of authority and judgment. Velvet Breeches requests that the Knight be disqualified because "he houldeth not the worth of his Gentrie to be and consist in Veluet breeches, but valeweth true fame by the report of the common sort whoe praise him for his vertue, Iustice, liberality, housekeeping and almesdeeds: *Vox populi vox dei*, his tenants and farmers would if it might be possible make him immortall with their prayers and praises" (F2^r–F2^v). This, of course, guarantees that he is seated. Indeed, the Knight serves as foreman, and it is he who delivers the final verdict against Velvet Breeches. The jury is the voice of the people, which is, in turn, the voice of God.

It is hardly surprising that Greene, an enormously popular writer, should locate legitimacy in the "true fame by the report of the common sort." There is, however, a tension between his condemnation of a market in luxury apparel and his own participation in the book market: if there were no velvet breeches, then nor were there professional pamphlet writers in *diebus illis*. Indeed, the constantly repenting Greene included an ironic gesture in the book's first edition. Having agreed to seat the Printer, Cloth Breeches cannot refrain from remarking that "some of his trade will print lewd books, and bawdy pamphlets (by M. R. G.)" (F3^v). Subsequent editions drop Greene's initials, making the self-referential aspect of the comment less obvious. Interestingly, the table of jurors pairs the priest and the printer – they follow the first three, the Knight, Esquire, and Gentleman (H1^r). The poet, however, comes dead last and does not even find a place on the list. Nonetheless, though he is the last person impaneled, he is also the one who completes the jury. This inclusion works to paper over the contradiction between Greene the author seeking distinction and Greene the repentant moralist advocating organic community.

Though *A Quip* does avoid the stark polemics visible in the dialogues directly treating religious controversy, it, nonetheless, remains engaged in debate with them, offering a dream about a scene in which "strange controversies" are overcome. Indeed, the book's own withdrawal from polemic – registered in the several deletions made to the first version printed and its retreat into the conspicuously medieval form of the dream poem – exemplify one important response to the development of a polemicized print culture: the elaboration of an ostentatiously apolitical literary world. The idea that normally literature is anti- or unpolemical is modern. In the sixteenth and seventeenth centuries English writers and readers seemed to have assumed the very opposite: books were, more often than not, understood to be engaged in battle.

The degree to which a polemical consciousness extends beyond the thinking of a literate elite remains a vexing question. Alexandra Walsham, for instance, finds that, "Conformists shade obscurely into a body of 'mere conformists', whose disinterest in Reformation logomachy – perhaps in 'religion' itself – challenges us to reassess our lingering pre-supposition that early modern society was fractured by the confessional dichotomies implied by contemporary polemic."[104] The same difficulty is acknowledged by Patrick Collinson when he remarks: "It is easier to trace the polemical polarities of early seventeenth-century English religious culture in principle than to follow them through on the ground."[105] It would certainly be naive to accept as accurate the account of the Catholic author of *A Petition Apologeticall* (1604), who writes in the hope that "The Godly and zealous *Artisans* and *Prentises* of *London,* and other places, may learn hereby to moderate themselves a little in their outragious alarmes of *Stoppe the Traytor,* when they see an Innocent Priest passe their streets" (A2ᵛ). One need not take this as evidence that London artisans and apprentices were regularly executing mob justice against Catholic priests in order to see it as significant. The passage reveals that a particular writer thought that such a description, associating anti-Catholicism with the unruly and often illegal behaviour of urban workers, would support an argument for greater toleration, that it would make hostility to Catholicism appear to be the irrational fear of the lower orders. Nevertheless, for such a rhetorical strategy to succeed, it would need to be at least plausible to attribute such a hostility to the artisans and apprentices of London.

That polemic reflects a commonly perceived reality seems plausible, but the focus of my argument concerns the development of a specifically literate culture. I have no doubt that many who were unable to participate directly in this literate culture nonetheless shared many of its organizing polarities, but establishing such a claim would be a vast undertaking far exceeding the scope of this book.[106] In fact, one could argue that elite polemic is merely one manifestation of a widely shared, but historically limited, tendency toward oppositional thinking common throughout early modern European culture.[107] While an underlying psychological propensity for dualism may well have contributed to polemicization, there is no question but that the printing press and religious hostilities gave the process its greatest impetus.

Arguably writers are especially susceptible to a polemical vision of the world, an observation made, and simultaneously confirmed, by Pierre Saint-Amand who pronounces: "Communication between intellectuals is necessarily polemical." A more balanced and nuanced, though perhaps less striking, formulation is provided by Pierre Bourdieu: "Literate, scholarly culture is defined by reference; it consists of the permanent game of references referring mutually to each other; it is nothing other than this universe of references which are at one and the same time differences and reverences, contradictions and congratulations."[108] Such a world is by definition elite, yet polemic is not limited to such an ambit. The commercial imperative of print, which aggressively sought to expand its market, combined with the evangelical zeal of Protestantism in an energetic attempt to draw new players into the universe of references. As a consequence, the literary culture of early modern England was fractious, robust, and deeply polemical, a fact not registered by received literary histories, which, impatient with theological squabbling and polemical exchange, have approached the period through modern editions that regularize and sanitize the hurly-burly of early modern print.

CHAPTER I

"Foxe's" Books of Martyrs: printing and popularizing the Actes and Monuments

Origins and superlatives have long been the stuff of history writing. At least since Thucydides claimed that his subject matter, the Peloponnesian War, "was the greatest disturbance in the history of the Hellenes, affecting also a large part of the non-Hellenic world, and indeed, I might almost say, the whole of mankind," historians have claimed to describe unprecedented events.[1] Unsurprisingly, Foxe's *Actes and Monuments* provokes reactions that demonstrate this tendency. Foxe was, according to one historian, "the first British author to write a Protestant apocalyptic history that attempted to explain changes in terms of an unfolding pattern of events."[2] In direct contrast to this vision of *Actes and Monuments* as an inaugural moment, another scholar finds the appropriate superlative term, declaring *Actes and Monuments* to be "the longest pamphlet ever composed by the hand of man."[3] Yet other than a certain historiographical tendency to identify events either with origins or superlatives, it is not immediately clear what these seemingly opposed assessments share.

There is clearly a wide gap between a characterization of *Actes and Monuments* that places it within a long, scholarly tradition of apocalyptic history and one that deploys a sharp and ironic oxymoron in order to insist that the work is perhaps the quintessence of polemic. Despite their contradictoriness, these two evaluations are not, however, unrelated. Indeed, both recognize Foxe's priority in the polemicization of British historiography. What Katherine Firth coolly describes as "apocalyptic history" depends, quite obviously, on identifying the agents and forces of Christ and Antichrist as they maneuver in preparation for the final, decisive battle that will end human history. In other words, apocalyptic history depends on the same sort of polarization that is central to polemic. It is not difficult to see what motivates Charles Whibley – in his entry on "Chroniclers as Antiquaries" in *The Cambridge History of English Literature* – to conclude: "No more can be said than that rage and fury are in his heart and on his tongue, that he possessed a genius of indignation which he had neither wish nor power to check and that he bequeathed to us a larger mass of invective than any writer in any age has been able to achieve" (334).

The invective mass of *Actes and Monuments* may not have been surpassed but there are competitors. Indeed, by popularizing a revised vision of the history of the true church, *Actes and Monuments* gave impetus to a religiously motivated competition between historical narratives that was not limited to martyrology and ecclesiastical history.[4] Indeed, large parts of Foxe's account were soon incorporated in the massive work known as Holinshed's *Chronicles.*[5] Prior English history writing, both medieval and early humanist, was not without controversy. However, medieval chronicle writers were only sporadically engaged in the defense or denigration of royal lineage and corporate prerogatives, and while humanist histories were more consistently focused on political matters, they might better be described as interested – interested in claims of dynasty and sovereignty – rather than polemical.[6] Foxe's history was, in contrast, radically revisionary and impressively consistent in rewriting past Christian history, and especially English history, as a constant struggle between the parties of Christ and Antichrist. Given its sweeping claims and apocalyptic militancy, it is unsurprising that the book remains controversial, and yet one of the most remarkable aspects of *Actes and Monuments* is the speed with which its adversarial polemic, which speaks for the persecuted minority, became institutionalized.[7] To examine this process it is necessary to turn our attention to the complicated publishing history of the work that came to be known as Foxe's *Book of Martyrs.*

In the Induction to *The Unfortunate Traveller* (1594), Thomas Nashe, always aware of the materiality of the book, jokingly asserts that his new work will become a fixture of sorts: "it shall be lawfull for anie whatsoeuer to play with false dice in a corner on the couer of this foresayd Actes and Monuments."[8] The *Actes and Monuments* is here a piece of furniture, the butt of a joke, an established presence that provides the foundation for discursive play. Another invocation of *Actes and Monuments* appears in Martin Marprelate's *Epistle* (1588). Attacking John Aylmer, then Bishop of London, Marprelate claims, "his grace threatened to send Mistris Lawson to Bridewell because she shewed the good father D. Perne a way to get his name out of the booke of Martyrs where the turnecoat is canonized for burning Bucers bones" (B2ᵛ). In this case, the content of the book is imagined to be – at least potentially – shifting, but more importantly for Marprelate, the book itself is a registry of iniquity that can be used as a weapon against the established church as represented by Aylmer's henchman, Andrew Perne.[9]

Perhaps the most interesting point, however, is that Nashe and Marprelate, with their radically different views of the legitimacy of the established English church, could both assume the cultural authority of the *Actes and Monuments*. A similar dynamic is visible in the Admonition Controversy in which John Whitgift and Thomas Cartwright, on opposite sides of the debate over ecclesiastical discipline and structure, both try to lay claim to Foxe.[10] Allusions such as these suggest that by the end of the sixteenth century *Actes and Monuments* was an established presence, differently marked but accepted as authoritative by a broad range of Protestant opinion.

Indeed, the *Actes and Monuments* had become canonical in the technical sense of the word in 1571, when Convocation ordered that "Euery Archbishop and bishop shall haue in hys house *The holy Bible* in the largest volume, as it was lately printed at London, and also that full and perfect history, which is intituled *Monumentes of Martyres*." It was further stipulated that the "same bookes" be purchased by every dean and "bestowed in his Cathedrall Church, in such conuenient place, that the vicares . . . and other ministers of the Church, as also straungers and forieners may easelie come vnto them, and read thereon."[11] Though the order could never effectually be enforced, the work was publicly acknowledged as the official history of the true English church, and for some time to come claimants to that historical legacy would regularly invoke the authority of Foxe's monumental book.[12]

As a result, the vast compendium known as Foxe's *Book of Martyrs* is routinely, and no doubt appropriately, invoked by modern scholars as one of the central documents of Elizabethan Protestant culture. *Actes and Monuments* was, in John R. Knott's phrase, "an inescapable text."[13] The claim that "Next to the Bible it was the most influential book in Elizabethan England" has become proverbial by sheer repetition.[14] Though historians and critics have long recognized that the work became a touchstone in debates among Protestants from the mid-70s onward, the usual tendency has been to see Foxe as providing a unifying narrative for Protestant England. According to Christopher Hill, "The English historical myth, created by Foxe, was elaborated by Hakluyt, Ralegh, Bacon, and Coke till it became the force we have all had to struggle against."[15] More recently, Richard Helgerson gives pride of place to *Actes and Monuments*, along with the English Bible, the Book of Common Prayer, and Hooker's *Laws of Ecclesiastical Polity*, in "shaping England's religious self-understanding."[16]

While Foxe's contribution to the process of nation-building has generally been acknowledged, the claim made by William Haller, in his influential work, *Foxe's Book of Martyrs and the Elect Nation*, that there is a direct link between Foxe's work and the emergence of a language of national election, has been contentious. According to Haller, Foxe's narrative promoted a view of the English nation as "a mystical communion of chosen spirits, a peculiar people set apart from the rest of mankind."[17] The intensity of the debate surrounding Haller's thesis springs from the perceived stakes of the argument; for many, the argument is, finally, about nothing less than the origins of modern national imperialism. Reduced to a narrow claim about the elect nation, Haller's book appears to make Foxe responsible for the religiously inflected exceptionalism that was to play itself out in a long history of missionary imperialism.[18] Posed in this manner the argument can only be tendentious. Rather than searching for the essence of English national consciousness or the origin of British imperialism, we might more productively explore the variety of ways in which the *Actes and Monuments* contributed to the shaping of a complex and always contested national identity.[19]

Recent scholarship has rightly raised doubts about Haller's argument that Foxe's history demonstrates the fulfillment of God's will in the triumph of a "godly" England.[20] Scholars have noted that if England is elect, it is only as an elect nation within the context of the international Protestant church, rather than the singular case that Haller defines. Richard Bauckham asserts with confidence, and no small degree of relief, "It is clear enough from all Foxe's writings that his feeling for the English nation and church could never override his dominating belief in the church as an international body, the company of Christ's elect members in all ages and places."[21]

The argument that Foxe was not himself a believer in national election is quite convincing; however, while this may require some modification of Haller's thesis, it by no means destroys it.[22] Though Foxe cannot be enlisted to the cause of such exceptionalism, meanings unintended by Foxe could be and were made available to a wide range of readers, including, at particular moments, an assertion about England's peculiar, divinely appointed role in world history. To recover these meanings we need to focus not on Foxe the singular author, but on the various material forms through which his work was circulated; by attending to these forms, we become aware of the multiple agents involved in the making of the book, agents who guarantee that the book will be both something more and something less than what Foxe intended.[23]

Both Haller and his critics have assumed that the book has a singular identity (whether this is established with the 1570 edition, which Haller believes "fixed the Book of Martyrs in the form which was to remain," or with the last "authorial" text of 1583), and, even when recognizing the various editions, have focused on these as appropriations and transformations of an apparently single text.[24] Such accounts assume the existence of two stable entities – Foxe's text and the language of the elect nation – and then attempt to articulate the relationship (or lack thereof) between them. However, these projects fail to acknowledge the implications of the multiple material forms through which "Foxe's" text was mediated. Rather than being fixed and stable, both text (a linguistic construct) and material form (a physical artifact) undergo significant alterations between editions, alterations that indicate that the work was engaged with contemporary debates and responding to immediate political pressures. Significantly, these changes in material form and text reveal the degree to which book production was a collective endeavor, influenced by numerous hands. In other words, we cannot continue to speak of this work, instantiated in a variety of different books, as though it were the creation of a single individual, John Foxe.

By attending to the various editions of the *Actes and Monuments*, I hope to establish two related points. First, as I have suggested, no account of the work's influence can rest content with a single-text model of the work. There was, in fact, a whole family of books, each member of which was produced by multiple – indeed, at times competing and conflicted – intentionalities, and we must consider the specificity of these various intentions and engagements when writing a cultural history of *Actes and Monuments*. Second, when – or rather *only* when – we recognize this polyform textual identity, can Haller's argument claiming a pivotal role for the *Actes and Monuments* in the propagation of a language of national election be seen to have a historical purchase.

Actes and Monuments was, in its origins, a polemical work written in Latin and printed on the Continent, yet at the close of Elizabeth's reign, after the publication of six English editions (1563, 1570, 1576, 1583, 1589, 1596), it had achieved the status of magisterial and unimpeachable orthodoxy, a status that would go largely uncontested, with the exception of Catholic attacks, until the work of Maitland in the nineteenth century.[25] If *Actes and Monuments* is simply identified with the language of national election, this would suggest the gradual, unimpeded rise to prominence of such a language. However, the story is actually far more complicated, involving from the start struggles over the meaning of the work, played out in the shape of individual editions. These contentions and competing claims make it clear that the association between the work and the language of national election was always problematic, and that neither the work nor the language of national election is subject to a simple "rise."

The process by which the work arrived at a position of cultural authority can be illuminated by an examination of two specific moments in its complex publishing history: the anomalous, and widely denigrated, edition of 1576 and the *Abridgement* prepared and published by Timothy Bright in 1589. Most obviously, both editions attempted to increase the circulation of the work by making it available in a format cheaper than the preceding editions. However, they also reveal divergent motivations. The edition of 1576 is clearly situated in relationship to contemporary debates between Protestants. Supplied with a new index and additional prefatory material as well as revisions of the main text, it is positioned as an intervention in the Admonition Controversy, a debate between English Protestants over the proper form of church hierarchy.[26] The *Abridgement*, on the other hand, reveals a process of deracination and popularization. Rather than engaging with disputes between Protestants within England, it focuses attention on the Catholic menace and, not surprisingly in the wake of the Armada, draws attention to England's special status in the drama of salvation.

The edition of 1576 departs significantly from the edition of 1570 in several ways. The most obvious change is in the size of the paper and the type used: both are smaller than those used in the '70 edition. The book remains a folio of two volumes, but unlike the 1,190 leaves of the second edition, its 1,033 leaves are often bound together between two boards. These changes may indicate an attempt to provide a cheaper edition.[27] Shortly after the publication of the first English edition, William Turner, Dean of Wells, had urged Foxe to reduce the size of the book "for the greater profit of the true church." In the same letter, Turner observes, "Printers like their books big because of the big gains, and regard not the profit of the poor flock of Christ." While Turner's accusation is disputable, he plausibly asserts that "not a few poor men complained of the price."[28] The '76 edition, then, can be seen as an attempt to reach a wider market by bringing the volume within reach of "the poor flock of Christ."

The '76 edition is largely a reprint of the edition of '70; there are minor changes in the body of the text, and additional matter is included at the end of the book. But significant changes occur in the preliminary matter and in the index. These elements have generally been overlooked because they have been considered extrinsic to the text, not part of the author's work.[29] In this case, an excessive focus on Foxe, the author, functions, in Foucault's words, as "the principle of thrift in the proliferation of meaning."[30] Yet in terms of the book's cultural negotiations, the preliminary matter and the concluding index are both important, because they serve as points of access, ways into the book.

The preliminary material functions – through title pages, prefaces, dedications, tables of contents, commendatory poems, addresses to the reader – as both advertisement and introduction; it reveals the way in which a particular book is positioned for an audience. For this reason, seemingly trivial changes in the preliminary matter may provide important evidence of changes in the way a book is perceived by its producers and readers. Often prefatory material answers or anticipates hostile responses.[31] Thus Foxe in the dedication of the second English edition (1570) remarks on the "fumyng & freatyng" that greeted the first edition in some quarters, claiming that "no English Papist almost in all the Realme thought him selfe a perfect Catholicke, unlesse he had cast out some word or other, to geue that booke a blow" (*1^r).

Indexes also serve to situate a book for an audience, providing an epitome of the book as well as access to particular topics. Again, indexes, like prefaces, have usually been viewed as paratextual, merely supplementary to the author's text – which is not surprising, since indexes are often prepared by someone other than the author. Indeed, in the sixteenth century, printers, aware that such aids helped to sell books, often prepared new indexes for established classics. The earliest surviving printed bookseller's catalogue draws attention to an edition of Augustine's *On Christian Instruction* by pointing out that it has "a noteworthy table, very useful for preachers."[32] Elizabeth Eisenstein has asserted that, "The act of indexing and cross-referencing which had been animated by the religious purposes of the teaching and preaching orders became more neutral and even amoral when applied to all manner of texts by printers who thought in terms of sales appeal."[33]

While indexes were certainly used to sell books, it is difficult to see how they could be thought "neutral" or "amoral"; then, as now, publishers hired indexers who brought a particular vision to their task. In fact, indexes, along with other critical apparatuses such as marginal notes, became vehicles and objects of contention. Recognizing this fact, Henry VIII, on November 16, 1538, prohibited the printing or importation of scripture "with any annotations in the margyn, or any prologe or additions in the calender or table, except the same be first viewed, examinyed, and allowed by the kynges highnes, or suche of his maiesties counsayle, or other, as it shall please his grace to assigne thereto."[34] This edict provoked Bale to complain, in *The Image of Both Churches*, "Already have they taken in England from the bibles the annotations, tables and prefaces, straightly forbidden the reading thereof . . . to take scripture clean away, they have sought out great faults in the translation of it, and therupon taken them away from the common people's understanding."[35] For Bale, the injunction against critical apparatuses, designed to make scripture available to the common reader, is part of a program of mystification which aims to deny the unlearned access to the Bible.

Though it may be the result of non-authorial labor, an index is, nonetheless, an integral part of a book; the decision to include an index and the decisions about what to include in the index announce, as do the preliminary materials, the way in which the producers wished to position the book and how they imagined it would be used. The book, as D. F. McKenzie has insisted, has a complex signifying surface, revealing the plurality of intentions that produced it, and if one starts from this assumption, then all the elements that make up the book provide invaluable evidence of the book's place in a particular historical moment.[36]

An account of the '76 edition requires a brief, and admittedly incomplete, discussion of both prior and subsequent editions. The first English edition (1563) included two Latin prefaces, both of which are dropped in the next edition (1570). However, several new elements are added; the first of these is an address "To the true and faithfull congregation of Christes universall church"; the second is a list of four questions "To all the professed frendes and folowers of the Popes procedynges"; the third is a series of commendatory poems in Latin. Despite the poems, which testify even unread (or unreadable) to the scholarly community out of which the book emerged, the clear thrust is toward the vernacular; prefaces in Latin are hardly an invitation to those who can only read English. The new prefatory material in the '76 edition could be said to continue this trend toward increasing the accessibility of the book.

The most obvious example is the addition of a page listing "Certaine places of the scripture expounded" and "Common places handled at large in their place figured" ($1 +^r$). These lists direct the reader to particular pages and serve to highlight specific lines of inquiry. The list of commonplaces includes such polemical entries as "Of the doctrine of election," "Of othes," "Of antichrist," "That there is no purgatory," and "That examples particular do not derogate from a doctrine." Clearly, this list of controversial topics provides a fund for argument according to the rhetorical tradition of commonplaces.[37] However, there is a peculiar split in the list of commonplaces between formulations beginning with "of" at the top of the list, which indicate general headings, and those beginning with "that" at the bottom, which introduce specific arguments. The first group treats commonplaces as organizing categories for a variety of arguments; the second part of the list gives determinate precepts; these may have appeared commonplace – i.e. part of a shared intellectual stock – to some readers but to others they would have appeared eminently controversial. Neither of the lists seems to have been arranged according to any system; nonetheless, their brevity makes it possible to scan them with ease. Such lists obviously position the book as a resource to be consulted for both scriptural exegesis and edifying commonplaces. Moreover, they open the book for and to polemic.[38]

An awareness of this polemical context motivates Samuel Fleming's preface, which attempts to establish the authority of the book. Fleming was a Fellow of King's College, Cambridge, along with Richard Day, the son of the printer John Day.[39] Richard Day, who resigned his fellowship of King's College in 1576 in order to take up a position in his father's printing house, is thought to have seen the edition through the press, and he is probably responsible for the presence of Fleming's preface. This preface addresses itself directly to a polemical culture, one in which reader response is conceived of as either concurrence or dissent: "In reading of philosophy and mans learning al sentences are pondered by reason, and lightly the readers wit doth run with the authors meaning, eyther to agree or disagree from those things which be vttered" (¶3^r).

Yet the Preface also goes on to make an argument (arguably a polemical one) for putting *Actes* beyond the polemical fray: "But in matters wherein naturall devises are not set out, but Gods power and wisedome, we must bring more minde to credit, then wil to examine, especially where the iudgement of the author is not to be suspected" (¶3^r). Both the divinity of the subject and the gravity of the author are adduced as reasons for suspending criticism in favor of predisposition to belief. Fleming then sketches a hierarchy of textual authority that begins, predictably enough, with scripture. Next come the apocryphal writings, while "the third place of credite is geuen to the whole church." But since the church does not speak as a whole – a point painfully obvious in the wake of the Reformation – writers are required who, like Foxe, "speak as the whole church."

Of course, others have written claiming to speak for the whole church, and Foxe's work must be distinguished from theirs. Eusebius, the chronicler of the early church, is criticized because in his "discourses mean personages are for the most part ouerpassed." Flacius Illyricus, whose account of the tribulations of the continental Protestants served as a model for Foxe, is given credit for having "more largely set out" the afflictions of the godly, "But for playne vnderstandyng, manifeste proofe, and sufficient discourses, this work of maister Iohn Foxe is to be preferred before other that haue been written in time past."

Having asserted the preeminence of the book, Fleming goes on to extoll its edifying power: as a "pattern of diligent preaching and constant suffering," it will make Christian readers "wonder at the power of that word which remaineth in broken vessels and will not be consumed by fire." Fleming then makes a point that recalls his criticism of Eusebius: "Moreouer it shal appeare in this story that they haue ben most enemies to gods Church, which haue receaued most honor in the common wealth and most nobility in kindred." But lest this anti-elitism be construed as straightforwardly populist, Fleming adds, "As for the common people they shall here finde howe variable their mindes haue bene in old time, how in one yeare they preferred the Gospell, in another oppressed it." The fickleness of the people, or mob, is a given, but what is remarkable is that the "common people" are clearly imagined as readers of the book.

According to Fleming, the book is excellent precisely because the "learned shall find reasons deep inough" and the "vnlearned shall see plainnes inough without any disceat." The idea that the book addresses a socially diverse audience is developed at length:

The common welth man, and the church man, high and low shall vnderstand a merueilous compasse of matter, to rule and be ruled, when they perceaue Gods wisedome & mans pollicy as it were in a theater building vp and pulling down: in such sort that the affaires of al mankind shal seme gouerned by an inward providence excelling nature: much agaynst those men that counte religion and scripture, but deuises to keepe the people in obedience.

The edifying and unifying power of the book is spelled out through antithesis, a figure which is used to typify both the anticipated readership and the subject matter of the book. The theater simile transforms history, with its wonderful vicissitudes, into a space for the staging of an "inward providence excelling nature." And this compelling spectacle, where "naturall deuises are not set out, but Gods power and wisdom," is not subject to the same criteria as "philosophy and mans learning." The seemingly bizarre final aside, which attempts to dispense with a Machiavellian interpretation of religion, is not a symptom of anxiety but a tactical argument. For despite Fleming's easy assertion that the testimony of the "whole Church" demands credit, there were a number of competing groups that claimed to be speaking for the "whole Church," each asserting that their opponents were operating according to an instrumental notion of religion. Fleming's aside thus is not directed at self-proclaimed Machiavellians; rather it is available to be applied by the reader to any number of groups: the presbyterians, papists, or even the bishops. "Those men," however they are identified, are the enemies of true religion. While asserting that *Actes* is somehow above and beyond polemic, the Preface nevertheless advertises the book as an authoritative resource for those who would speak for the whole church against its godless detractors.

The new index that appears at the end of the '76 edition is preceded by a short address, "To the Christian Reader." This address, signed by R. Day, begins with a careful, and defensive, explanation of the use and value of the index and then moves on to consider a topic of particular controversy: the primitive church. This is not a sudden shift of focus, for these two issues are connected. The index is designed to guide readers to a proper under-standing of the history and, perhaps more importantly, the historical significance of the primitive church. Since a particular index lays a grid over the main text and isolates a specific set of elements as potentially important or useful, the index in effect offers a reading of the main text it claims only to reference. An index thus works at cross purposes: it opens the book, providing convenient access to certain topics, but because it only identifies certain topics, directs the reader, offering a selective epitome of the book.

Richard Day unabashedly declares,

I haue in a short summe comprised the whole, and brought the large course of this famous worke to a small compasse, at the first sight shewying in a Table, as well to hym that hath perused the same as not, for the memory of the one, for the speedy and certaine knowledge of the other, what doctrine it doth containe to instruction, what examples of history to immitation.

The index then has two functions: it can refresh the memory of a reader who has finished the book, and it can allow the impatient direct access to helpful doctrine and examples. The same distinction is offered in meta-phorical terms when Day describes how a "tyred travailer" enjoys "restyng and lookyng backe," while others "had rather vewe the game by prospect then by chace." The "travailer," having completed the arduous task of working or traveling through the book, is given an opportunity for satisfied retrospection. The emphasis here is on the index as epitome or summary, a notion congruent with the language of abridgement: "in a short summe comprised the whole." In contrast, the metaphor of the hunt stresses the problem of access and suggests an object-oriented reading process, a means to "speedy and certain knowledge." Such reading techni-ques were common; Bacon's famous assertion that "Some books are to be tasted, others to be swallowed, and some few to be chewed and digested" acknowledges that different books require different reading strategies.[40] However, one might as easily argue that different reading strategies require different books: the controversialist in pursuit of supporting authorities needs a well-indexed book.

Nonetheless, the address registers a troubled awareness that the index will allow lazy readers to poach in the realm of learning. Indeed, the hunting metaphor actually seems to be saying that certain predatory readers would rather, gaining the advantage of "opportunitie and heigth of standyng," view the object of knowledge than pursue it in "chace": a glimpse or view supplants pursuit. The index is designed to instruct even such heady spirits, insuring that they do not misconstrue the book in their hunt for polemical arguments. Yet the suspicion remains that an index may actually enable a modern Nimrod to make opportunistic use of the book.

This suspicion of the index and the index user increases as a broad, popular print culture emerges in the seventeenth century. Thus Glanville opines, "Methinks 'tis a pitiful piece of knowledge that can be learnt from an index, and a poor ambition to be rich in another man's treasure." Later Swift would assert: "The most accomplisht way of using books at present is twofold: either serve them as some men do lords, learn their titles exactly, and then brag of their acquaintance. Or secondly, which is indeed the profounder and politer method, to get a thorough insight into the index, by which the whole book is governed and turned, like fishes by the tail." In remarkably similar terms, Pope laments: "How index-learning turns no student pale, / Yet holds the Eel of science by the Tail."[41] The image of the fish suggests a process that is indelicate if not obscene; those who grope for learning in this fashion are preposterous – both ludicrous and disorderly in their pursuit of knowledge. However, the mocking attitude toward the impropriety of coming at a book from the wrong end reveals a fear of another sort of reversal: that indexes will allow the unlearned to pose as learned, erasing the distinction conferred by education and culture. Like print itself, the index threatens to make learning common.

Despite a marked ambivalence, Day's Address signals to the reader that the index is new and valuable, but even more importantly it goes on to explain why a new index is particularly necessary at this moment. His labor was required so that the book might be "strengthened agaynst two sorte of aduersaries the Popish Pagane, or Paganish Papist, who glory in anti-quitie." The reference is to the presbyterians on one hand and the Roman Catholics on the other; the chiasmic formulation accusing both of a misguided "glory in antiquitie" threatens to collapse the distinction between the two.

Such polemical conflations were typical in the controversial writings of the period. Although initially Day pursues the common strategy of locating one's own "moderate" position between two erroneous extremes (the "Popish Pagane" and the "Paganish Papist"), as when defenders of the established church in England placed themselves between Geneva and Rome, he simultaneously exemplifies another tendency, driven by the polarizing dynamic of polemic, to lump opponents together. In some cases this second operation leads to startling assertions of identity between widely divergent positions. So for the presbyterians of the 1570s and beyond the English church hierarchy was identified with Roman Catholicism: the bishops are, in Martin Marprelate's formulation, "petty popes." The same strategy leads apologists for the English church to identify Roman Catholicism with paganism, and thus a pamphlet of 1605 is entitled: *Pagano-Papismus: wherein is prooued by irrefragable demonstrations that Papisme is flat Paganism.*[42] James I employs the same sort of logic when he writes "Jesuits are nothing but Puritan–Papists," and John Harington jokingly declares, "I am a protesting Catholike Puritan."[43] This tendency, then, to amalgamate one's opponents by stressing their common errors is widespread in English controversial writing of the sixteenth and seventeenth centuries; however, Day's index is addressed not to a generalized enemy but to a specific group of detractors and a specific conflict, the Admonition Controversy. To resolve this controversy, Day has "collected the doctrine, rites, and discipline of the Primitive Churche placed under the letter P."

In the debate following the publication of *An Admonition to the Parliament* (1572), Thomas Cartwright, an advocate of presbyterianism, asserted the normative status of the primitive church as outlined in the Pauline epistles. John Whitgift, Cartwright's principal opponent, was willing to grant that the structure of the church had changed, but he refused to allow that the model of the primitive church had binding force. For Whitgift, church discipline was *adiaphoron* – a thing indifferent; nonetheless, he maintained that episcopacy was a feature of the apostolic church.[44] Interestingly, both Cartwright and Whitgift invoked the authority of Foxe and the *Actes* to support their positions. After examining these references to Foxe, V. Norskov Olsen concludes that "Whitgift and not Cartwright was correct in his evaluation of Foxe," yet Olsen's primary interest is the recovery of Foxe's attitude toward the church and its ministry.[45] But perhaps more interesting is the fact that *Actes* could be read as favoring two very disparate positions. The issue then is not who was right about Foxe, but how and why such a disagreement was even possible.

Cartwright responds to Whitgift's quoting of Foxe with a demand to know why a proper citation was not provided; he acknowledges that Foxe is indeed a formidable scholar, but he denies that Whitgift has actually read Foxe's work: "I think I have read more of him than you. For I have read over his Book of Martyrs, and so I think did never you." In response Whitgift claims: "I can bring forth good testimonies of my reading in these books, though I make no brag thereof or vain comparisons."[46] It is against this contention over the meaning of the work that Richard Day's new index for the 1576 *Actes and Monuments* must be set.

Day addresses himself to those who "earnestly frame themselves to ye foresayd platforme of the first, old, and auncient, primit. Church," offering a warning: "lawes generall are not to be grounded upon commaundementes extraordinary, and particular examples as they do not impayre, so also do they not grounde a doctrine generall." Whitgift had similarly rejected the "whole mode of argument, which sought to draw general rules from particular examples and directly apply apostolic practice to contemporary conditions."[47] Day here signals his agreement with the future Archbishop of Canterbury. However, his caveat is immediately followed by a disclaimer: "But it is not my purpose to geve preceptes of doctrine or example." What Day has done is to provide a means of access to the doctrines and examples in the book. Yet his index cannot be construed as transparent or impartial.

"Primitive Church" is given its own heading in roman type that is about twice the size of the black letter that comprises the index entries. The page of citations that follows this heading is neatly divided into subcategories, also in roman type but smaller than the main head, such as "Sacramentes," "Common Prayer," "Conversation therof," "Bishop," and "Archbyshop" (4YY1ʳ–4YY1ᵛ). These last two are of particular significance because they, in effect, decide the Admonition Controversy in favor of the defenders of the episcopal hierarchy merely by asserting that it makes sense to speak of bishops and archbishops in reference to the primitive church. Despite its orthodoxy, the index also opens the book up to debate; in a sense, the index encourages readers to engage in the polemical dispute concerning the status of the primitive church merely by highlighting it as a contentious category.

The next edition of the *Actes and Monuments* (1583), also published by John Day, reverses this trend. The Latin prefaces from the first edition reappear, as does the Kalender, but the novel elements in the preliminary matter of the '76 edition – the finding aids and Fleming's preface – are gone, as are Richard Day's address to the reader and his index. The '83 index, prepared at a time when the primitive church was still a controversial issue and presbyterianism by no means a spent force, contains no entry for "primitive church."[48] The material cited in the '76 edition is still in the book; nonetheless, the indexer chose to ignore the subject. Indeed, the '83 edition, which has been described as "visually the most impressive of all the editions," seems to have been designed to realize the monumental pretensions that had always been part of the project: to lift the book above the polemical fray.[49] Of particular interest in this regard is the inclusion of a new item in the preliminary matter. Designed to balance the set of four questions for the followers of the pope's proceedings, there now appears, "Foure considerations geuen out to Christian Protestantes professours of the Gospell with a brief exhortation inducing to reformation of life," an address admonishing those who promote "contentions and vnbrotherly diuision amongst vs." The symmetrical rebukes to the Papists and the Protestants suggest that the producers of the book were determined to position it as ecumenical. By offering a highly visible rebuke to militant Protestants who advocated further reform, the '83 edition placed itself squarely on the side of the established English church. Unlike the '76 edition, which had implicitly sanctioned further argument, the '83 edition seeks to foreclose debate and urge discontented Protestants to count themselves lucky for the present dispensation. The '83 edition does allude to disputes among Protestants, but it urges quietism and discourages further contention.

A similar logic is displayed by the *Abridgement* of 1589, which further occludes the problem of division within England, whether between Protestants and Catholics or between various groupings of Protestants. While the '76 edition displayed an unseemly willingness to engage in internal debates between English Protestants, the *Abridgement* of 1589, appearing soon after the Armada victory, presents England as united against the threat of continental Catholicism. At the same time, the language of national election, always available in *Actes*, assumes greater importance, unsurprisingly perhaps in light of the astounding events of 1588.[50] The index of the '76 edition had encouraged its readers to enter into a polemical debate within the English church. Both the format and the content of the *Abridgement* work to forestall any such intramural polemic. Its readers are, instead, encouraged to identify an external enemy: European Catholics. Thus the language of national election here serves to palliate internal divisions within England, constructing an image of a unified nation.

In his address to the Christian reader, Timothy Bright – a physician who eventually took holy orders and, incidentally, invented modern shorthand – praises Foxe but then asserts that, "By reason of the largenes of the volume, and great price . . . the most were bereaved of the benefite of so necessarie an Historie" (¶2ʳ). This lack makes the work of abridgement necessary, so that "both those that are busie in affaires, or not able to reach to the price of so great a booke, might also have the vse of the historie with them that neither want leisure, nor hability sufficient." The *Abridgement*, then, will offer what is necessary and useful in the "great" book to a readership of the busy and the impecunious, joining them in community with the leisured and wealthy classes. The ambition articulated by Fleming, a wide social range of readers for the work, is here realized, or claimed to be realized, by a change in the material format of the book.

However, the status of the *Abridgement* remains problematic – an abridgement depends on the reputation of its antecedent for its legitimacy, but at the same time it claims to be an adequate substitute for its original. Economic exigencies are often acknowledged, but are also ultimately denied as insignificant: the same thing *can* be had for less. Grafton's preface to *A Manuell of the Chronicles of Englande* (1565) is an excellent example. Grafton explains, "I haue in this small volume abridged my former Abridgemente of Chronicles, to thintent the same should be more portatiue & also to be sold at a meane & small price" (A2ʳ). Nonetheless, he assures his reader that he has not "omitted any speciall note." Everything "special" – this is an important term, and I will return to it – about the earlier edition is now available in a portable volume at less expense.[51]

Uncertainty over the status of his abridgement creates contradictory impulses in Bright. Having asserted the efficacy of the *Abridgement* both to deliver what is essential in *Actes* and deliver it to the people who most need it, Bright admits that the documentary material has been left out and urges his readers to consult the "large Booke: which I doe exhort thee (gentle Reader) the rather for my Abridgements sake, to buy, and use" (¶2ʳ–¶2ᵛ). There is an ambivalence in the phrase, "my Abridgements sake"; it expresses the hope that the *Abridgement* will motivate readers to buy the larger book, but it also hints that the *Abridgement*'s survival depends on a continued market for the larger book. In fact, the *Abridgement* did provoke the Stationers' Company to sue on the grounds that it was an infringement of Richard Day's privilege. The suit was unsuccessful, and although the details of what the Stationers' Court records refer to as the "late Controversie or striffe touchinge the abridgement of the Booke of Martyrs" remain obscure, it is tempting to speculate that Bright was helped by his influential dedicatee, Sir Francis Walsingham.[52] There is no question that Bright and his *Abridgement* had the support of Archbishop Whitgift.[53]

Documentary material is not all that is left out of the *Abridgement*. Bright acknowledges that the "Treatises, Disputations, [and] Epistles" have also been omitted. This is the very material that made the large version such an effective source-book for controversialists. Indeed, the compiler of a later abridgement, Thomas Mason, was to identify the *Actes* as "a Club able to beate downe the Popish Tower of Babell," and to complain that an unnamed prior abridgement – presumably Clement Cotton's *The Mirror of Martyrs* – "was done but superficially, for all the points of Religion that the Martyrs defended, or Papists obiected were omitted; (which disputations I chiefly labour to set forth)."[54] This rich vein of polemical material is not, in Bright's view, an essential part of the work. After asserting the logical equivalence between the two books – the *Abridgement* contains all that is useful and necessary – Bright presents assurances that the *Abridgement* will not displace the larger book. The *Abridgement* is now modestly described as an advertisement: "So this my labour may geue thee an assay, and appetite, to know further, whereof thou maist here take (as it were) the taste" (¶2ᵛ). Presumably, having acquired a taste for Foxe, the busy will find time and the poor will find money.

The *Abridgement* deracinates and reduces the material of the large book, concentrating on presenting events in an almost schematic form. Where Foxe offers trial records, epistles, tracts, and disputations, Bright provides only the events themselves. Grafton, the prolific abridger, explains that those who "write short notes in the maner of Annales, commonly called Abridgements, rather touch the tymes when things were done, then declare the manner of the doyngs."[55] One might argue that, finally, the historical veracity of this chronological sequence of events, organized into a coherent narrative, is the outstanding achievement of the *Actes*.[56] However, the copious and polyphonic quality of the "large book" cannot be ignored or dispensed with as accidental (in either sense). Bright's reduction of the *Actes* produces a less complex narrative, a narrative that exploits precisely the possibilities of a discourse of national election in order to propagate a Protestant, English triumphalism.

This is achieved, on one level, through a process of compression. Presenting the entirety of *Actes* in 288 quarto pages accelerates the narrative, giving greater momentum to the unfolding of history.[57] It is made even more explicit by a further act of compression: facing the opening page of the history, is a single-page précis of the entire history, entitled, "A speciall

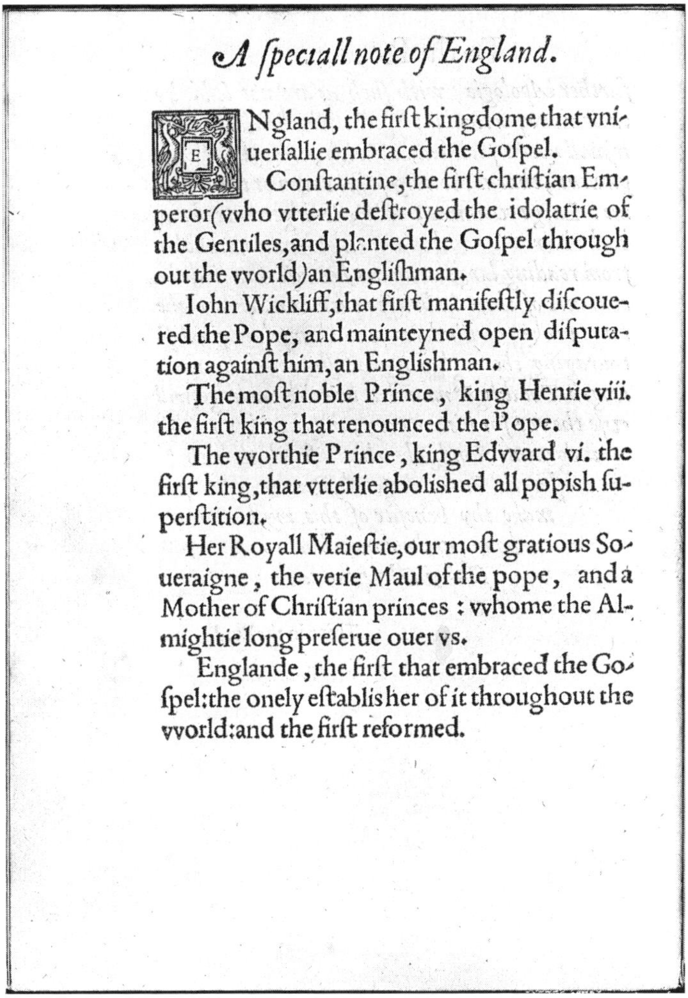

A speciall note of England.

Ngland, the firft kingdome that vni-
uerfallie embraced the Gofpel.

Conftantine,the firft chriftian Em-
peror(vvho vtterlie deftroyed the idolatrie of
the Gentiles,and planted the Gofpel through
out the vvorld)an Englifhman.

Iohn Wickliff,that firft manifeftly difcoue-
red the Pope, and mainteyned open difputa-
tion againft him, an Englishman.

The moft noble Prince, king Henrie viii.
the firft king that renounced the Pope.

The vvorthie Prince, king Edvvard vi. the
firft king,that vtterlie abolished all popish fu-
perftition.

Her Royall Maieftie,our moft gratious So-
ueraigne, the verie Maul of the pope, and a
Mother of Chriftian princes : vvhome the Al-
mightie long preferue ouer vs.

Englande, the firft that embraced the Go-
fpel:the onely eftablisher of it throughout the
vvorld:and the firft reformed.

Fig. 8 Special Note, Timothy Bright, *An Abridgement* (1589)

note of England" (fig. 8). The phrase "special note" echoes Grafton's language and may merely denote a formal device, the epitome that follows. Nonetheless, it also carries with it intimations of what Hamlet will refer to as "special providence": the note distinguishes England from other nations, it is marked out by God's providence to play a special role in world history. The list that follows, the quintessence of the *Abridgement*, presents a now familiar litany of English Protestant achievement. "England, the first kingdome that vniuersallie embraced the Gospel" heads the list, referring to the early conversion to Christianity. The keyword, "uniuersallie," asserts that the kingdom was united in faith in antiquity, and, by a certain vagueness in the language – embracing the gospel can as easily refer to the adoption of Protestantism as to the conversion to Christianity – it implies that the kingdom is united in faith now. Constantine, Wyclif, Henry VIII, Edward VI, and Elizabeth appear in order before the list concludes with a recapitulation: "Englande, the first that embraced the Gospel: the onely establisher of it throughout the world: and the first reformed." This triumphant assertion of the originality and uniqueness of the nation is in tension with the expansive and ecumenical vision offered by the "large book"; nonetheless, each of the elements found on the list that justifies this claim can be found in any of the large editions of *Actes*. Abstracted from context and presented in schematic form by Bright or John Windet, the printer, these events make a compelling claim for the special status of England in the drama of salvation.[58]

Of course, this list of successes leaves out the equally long history of failure and back-sliding, a history that reveals a nation divided by faith. For those who maintained their allegiance to the Roman church as well as those who ardently hoped for further reform, such successes were little cause for celebration. As Patrick Collinson has pointed out, under such pressure, the language of the elect nation was available as a unifying force only for a very short historical period; this is a strong argument against constructing a narrative which runs easily from Foxe to Milton to modern imperial nationalism.[59] Nonetheless, it would be overly scrupulous to deny any connection between the language of national election, however chrono-logically limited, and subsequent articulations of a national destiny.[60]

Bright's *Abridgement* certainly appears to be strong evidence that a discourse of the elect nation was indeed taking shape as the sixteenth century drew to a close. Moreover, it reveals that Protestant international-ism is not incompatible with a sense of England's unique role and status: "the onely establisher of it throughout the world." The viability of such a position is visible in the way the work treats the St. Bartholomew's Day Massacre, an event which solidifies an English Protestant identity against a continental Catholic threat and also raises the problem of vulnerable Protestant minorities on the Continent.

Indeed, the recollection of the Massacre is the most prominent feature in the dedication to Sir Francis Walsingham. Bright asserts that the dedica-tion is an act of gratitude for many favors received, particularly, "that especiall protection from the bloody massacre of Paris, nowe sixteene yeeres passed: yet (as ever it will be) fresh with me in memory" (¶3ᵛ). That Bright was able to find refuge in Walsingham's house makes the dedication appropriate: "Had not your Honour beene, my selfe, with a number mo, sholde at that bucherie of Paris novve long agoe beene martyred" (2¶1ʳ). It seems that his own narrow escape from inclusion *in* the book as a martyr gives Bright the authority to abridge the work. His experience as a persecuted minority, taking refuge in the household of an English diplomat, establishes his own identity as a loyal, English Protestant. This personal account at the beginning of the book connects to and contrasts with the summary account of the Massacre which appears in its final pages. Nonetheless, the Massacre serves as a frame; by directing attention to the continental scene, it suggests that the battle within England has been won and that future struggles will be between a besieged, but united, England and the forces of Catholic reaction on the Continent.

This point is made clearly by the two woodcuts that appear in the front of the book. The first leaf folds out to reveal the familiar image of Henry VIII enthroned, receiving the Bible from Cranmer and Cromwell and trampling on Pope Clement (fig. 9).[61] On the facing page, the title page, there is a small block depicting the pope and a friar cutting the throat of a lamb, while in the background two martyrs burn at the stake (fig. 10). This juxtaposition emphasizes England's triumph over Rome yet acknowledges the persistent threat of Catholicism. A comparison with the iconography of the large book's famous title page is instructive. That image is organized around the split between the true and false church – the antithesis between the two strikes a visual balance that suggests unresolved conflict (fig. 11). The two images at the front of the *Abridgement* are also antithetical, but the antithesis is not the universal struggle between the true and false church. On the left is a large image of the exemplar of English militarism; on the right, a small and distant depiction of Catholic bloodthirst, captioned by a citation of Apocalypse 6:10 that has profound implications for Elizabethan foreign policy: "How long Lord, holy and true?" The struggle between the true and false church is here given a national specificity that is absent on the title page of the large book: English Erastianism is here pitted against papal tyranny.

Actes and Monuments cannot in any simple sense be claimed as the source of a religious nationalism, yet its publishing history reveals a constant and nuanced engagement with the problematic of national religious identity. In a necessarily schematic way, I have attempted to show how the '76 edition and the *Abridgement* contributed to the process of diffusion that transformed the work into a part of the nation's stock of cultural capital. The '76

Fig. 9 Henry VIII, Timothy Bright, *An Abridgement* (1589)

edition is in some ways a negative example; by pointing to internal divisions within the nation, it jeopardized its own status as a work above
polemic and belied the fiction of Protestant unity. The *Abridgement*, in
contrast, denies internal division and amplifies the language of national
election. Both books, by making changes in format and content, dramatically alter the significance of the work.

Such a dispersal of meaning makes it much harder to claim a singular
identity for *Actes and Monuments*. Print led to a proliferation of versions:
not only were there successive and widely varying editions, Bright's
Abridgement was merely the first of several attempts to capture the essence
of the larger book.[62] It was followed by Clement Cotton's *Mirror of
Martyrs* (1613), Thomas Mason's *Christs Victorie over Sathans Tyrannie*
(1615), and John Taylor's *The Booke of Martyrs* (1616). These very different
publications all appeal to slightly different readers: the *Mirror of Martyrs*
clearly marked as a devotional work intended to promote meditation on

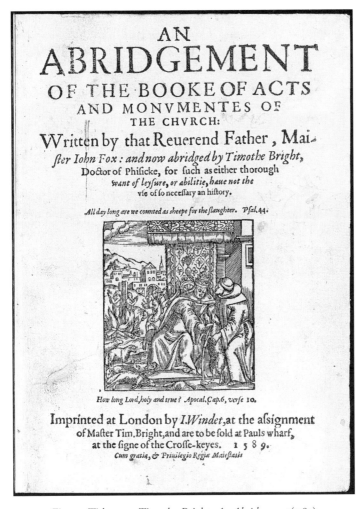

AN
ABRIDGEMENT
OF THE BOOKE OF ACTS
AND MONVMENTES OF
THE CHVRCH:

Written by that Reuerend Father , Mai-
fter Iohn Fox : and now abridged by Timothe Bright,
Do&or of Phificke, for fuch as either thorough
want of leyfure, or abilitie, haue not the
vfe of fo neceffary an hiftory.

*All day long are we counted as sheepe for the flaughter. Pfal.*44.

How long Lord, holy and true? Apocal. Cap.6, verfe 10.

Imprinted at London by *I.Windet,*at the afsignment
of Mafter Tim.Bright,and are to be fold at Pauls wharf,
at the figne of the Croffe-keyes. 1 5 8 9.
Cum gratia, & Priuilegio Regiæ Maieftatis

Fig. 10 Title page, Timothy Bright, *An Abridgement* (1589)

the exemplary lives of the English martyrs; *Christs Victorie*, mentioned
earlier, stresses the polemical and apocalyptic aspect of Foxe's work and
insistently presses the identification of the pope as Antichrist; *The Booke of
Martyrs*, first published as a tiny 64mo, reduces *Actes and Monuments* to
476 lines of rhyming verse that celebrate Britain's glory, excoriate the
popish Antichrist, and promote an uncomplicated Protestantism.[63]
While each one of these books offers its own version of *Actes and
Monuments*, together they attest to the cultural centrality of Foxe's

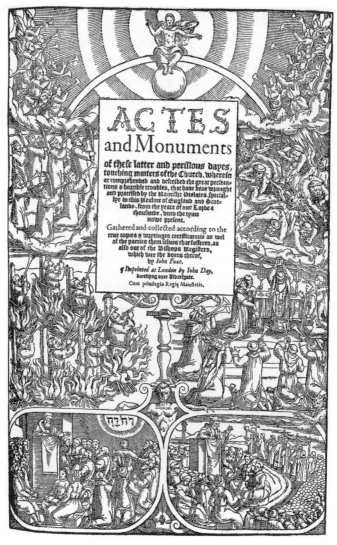

Fig. 11 Title page, John Foxe, *Actes and Monuments* (1563)

book.[64] That this centrality was manifested in a rivalrous competition to claim the legacy of the great book only confirms its power. Protestant writers could disagree about what precisely Foxe meant and could even concede that he erred on certain points of detail – according to Thomas Fuller, "it were a miracle if in so voluminous a work there were nothing to be justly reproved; so great a Pomgranate not having any rotten kernell must only grow in paradise" – but there was widespread acceptance of two key points: Foxe taught that the true church in England had suffered and survived horrible persecutions at the hands of the Antichrist and that the Elizabethan settlement was a decisive turning point in the historical struggle for truth.[65]

At the level of narrative, *Actes and Monuments* insisted on the inevitability of struggle and conflict, a strife played out variously at the level of the individual, the nation, and the church; at the same time, the physical book – in all its myriad forms – served as a reminder of the importance of discursive warfare. It was, to repeat Thomas Mason's violently physical metaphor, "a Club able to beate downe the Popish Tower of Babell" (A3[r]). For some, the book was an affirmation of the efficacy of print; for others, an example of the baneful consequences of innovation; for all it was palpable evidence that books mattered.

CHAPTER 2

Martin Marprelate and the fugitive text

Martin Marprelate was the pseudonym adopted by the writer or group of writers who penned a series of anti-episcopal tracts advocating a presbyterian form of ecclesiology between October 1588 and September 1589. The name quickly became a virtual synonym for religiously motivated polemic. As provocative as their unorthodox views on ecclesiastical polity, was their very publication, for the pamphlets were not printed abroad, as was the great majority of anti-establishment polemic both Catholic and puritan, but on a hidden press within England. Indeed, this press was moved repeatedly in an attempt to avoid the authorities. Both this clear contravention of the laws regarding the proper licensing of printed matter and the anti-episcopal argument created scandal enough, and the irreverent and calumnious manner of Marprelate's writing itself added enormously to the obloquy.

Martin was and remains anonymous, and this insolent and enduring anonymity has also contributed to the notoriety of his name.[1] A proper name lacking a person is a signifier available to be attached to a variety of individuals and concepts – a possibility that precipitated an immediate struggle both to identify Martin and to define "Martinism." Some of those responsible for the pamphlets were, in fact, captured and punished. John Hodgskin, Valentine Simmes, and Arthur Thomlin, occupying a rented house near Manchester, were caught in the act of printing *More Worke for Cooper* by agents of the Earl of Derby. Soon after, the bookbinder, Henry Sharpe, was arrested. The combined testimony of these individuals allowed the authorities to reconstruct the printing history of the pamphlets, and it was soon revealed that the Martinist press had been sheltered by several members of the puritan gentry. However, no conclusive proof regarding the actual authorship of the pamphlets emerged. Of those implicated, Roger Wigston and his wife, Sir Richard Knightley, John Hales, and Elizabeth Crane, members of the gentry who had harbored the press, were fined and imprisoned, while John Udall, condemned to death and then reprieved, died in prison and John Penry, after a sojourn in Scotland where he continued to produce books arguing for a presbyterian form of church discipline, was finally captured, tried and executed in 1593. Robert Waldegrave, the printer of the first four tracts, escaped to Scotland where he became the future king of England's printer.[2]

As a result of this failure to identify the writer or writers responsible, the Marprelate episode, when it has received sustained attention, has most often been treated as a literary whodunit. It is tempting to argue that such investigations simply pose the wrong question, that time would be better spent examining the production, circulation, and reception of the tracts; nonetheless, there is something to be gained by paying attention to these arguments for they are not without consequence.[3] These are, however, largely unintended consequences. The most recent book on Marprelate, Leland Carlson's *Martin Marprelate, Gentleman: Master Job Throckmorton Laid Open in His Colors*, provides impressive evidence for two of Foucault's arguments about the author function. On the one hand, Carlson's use of stylistic evidence to convict Throkmorton of being Martin only continues the case first made by Matthew Sutcliffe and confirms Foucault's argument that "Texts, books, and discourses began to have authors . . . to the extent that discourses could be transgressive." The purpose is to locate the originating agent, to assign responsibility, and, in the case of the government, to convict and to punish. On the other hand, the insistence on a singular author with a distinctive style is, as Foucault also pointed out, a way of limiting the proliferation of meaning.[4]

When a particular historical individual is assigned the role of authorship, particular readings of the tracts become more or less plausible. For instance, Donald McGinn, believing Marprelate to have been John Penry, who was executed, sees the pamphlets as earnest and courageous. If, however, one accepts Carlson's argument that Job Throckmorton, a *quondam* Member of Parliament and gentleman from Warwickshire, who escaped serious punishment, was the author, then it becomes much easier to see the entire affair as a bout of irresponsible radicalism.

Furthermore, to argue for *any* single author is to stress the singular and exceptional nature of the tracts.[5] Celebrated genius and isolated crackpot are two sides of the same coin. The idiosyncrasies of a single consciousness and conscience are the logical ground of an argument that would see Marprelate as a loose cannon or lone gunman. And yet, what we do know of the production of the pamphlets suggests that the network of agents responsible was remarkably extensive. As John Benger puts it, "A microcosm of Elizabethan society can be discerned amongst the

Martinists."[6] Rather than insisting on a single author, we might better assume that the pamphlets were a collaboration.[7] Indeed, as print productions they were by necessity the result of a collective effort.

The busy scene of printing is well described in the testimony of Valentine Simmes: "When Martin Senior was in printinge Symmes pervsinge the copye found fault wth some thinge in it towardes the ende as beinge written wth owt sense. Whereupon Hoskins caryinge the copye to Penrye, he strok owt certayne lines, and interlined that wch shold be supplyed."[8] Such testimony was used by the government in attempting to make the case for Penry's authorship – but as was well known then many printers employed correctors who were not themselves authors. The point here is not to exculpate Penry, but rather to see that all those involved in the printing of the Marprelate tracts helped to shape the meanings that they made available.

Apart from the efforts to identify their author, the Marprelate tracts have failed to attract, with few exceptions, the sustained attention of either literary or intellectual historians.[9] Undoubtedly, there are myriad explanations for this neglect. One might argue that when a certain narrative about the emergence of English liberty fell into disrepute, Marprelate's fortunes underwent a similar decline.[10] I think, however, that there is another explanation that deserves consideration: the Marprelate pamphlets resist easy classification and therefore end up as lost property outside the particular domains of the various disciplines. On the one hand, Marprelate fails to merit the attention of intellectual historians because he is too frivolous and literary. On the other hand, literary historians are perhaps put off by his underlying religious seriousness and his startling polemic intent. Both aspects of Marprelate's writing – the playful rhetoric and the strenuous controversy – should be considered together: Marprelate is neither an incoherent religious controversialist nor a frustrated poet, but a polemical writer exploiting a wide repertoire of techniques in an attempt to reach a broad audience.

Crucial to my argument is the assertion that texts are always in a sense "fugitive" for they do not exist apart from a particular material form and that these material forms are themselves meaningful. If this is the case, then the vexing collaborations of the Martinists should not be seen as a problem to be overcome, but rather as a felicitous condition, one that opens up an analysis of the tracts. As a result, my argument falls into two sections. The first part takes up the issue of the material book, arguing that the tracts display a sophisticated awareness of the many ways in which a book may signify. This section will first consider the significance of Marprelate's attacks on the material form of the books produced in defense of episcopacy, before examining the way in which the tracts exploit print conventions in an attempt to construct a godly community of true believers. The second part of the chapter explores the way in which this project is pursued on the level of explicit argument. In particular, I claim that the tracts attempt to forge a collective identity through polemical engagement with both the bishops and the puritans.

The first Marprelate tract, comprised of 54 pages and commonly referred to as the *Epistle*, appeared in October of 1588 under the title, *Oh read over D. Iohn Bridges / for it is a worthy worke: Or an epitome of the fyrste Booke / of that right worshipfull volume / written against the Puritaines / in the defence of the noble cleargie / by as worshipfull a prieste / Iohn Bridges / Presbyter / Priest or elder / doctor of Diuillitie / and Dean of Sarum.* In contrast, John Bridges's book is a ponderous tome of 1,401 pages entitled, *A Defence of the Government Established in the Church of England for Ecclesiastical Matters,* and designed as a refutation of arguments for a presbyterian form of church government. Marprelate exclaims against the incongruity in size between these two volumes. In the *Epistle,* he asserts, "I cannot very often at one breath come to a full point" (A2^v), and in the *Epitome* he worries, "I was never so affraid in my life that I shoulde not come to an end till I had bene windlesse"(C3^v–C4^r).[11] Perhaps more significant than his indictment of Bridges's verbosity is Marprelate's attack on the physical size of the book. After a brief epistle, the *Epitome* begins:

The whole volume of M. Deanes containeth in it 16 bookes besides a large preface and an Epistle to the reader. The Epistle & the preface are not above 8 sheets of paper and very little under 7. You may see when men have a gift in writing howe easie it is for them to daube paper. The compleat worke (very briefely comprehended in a portable booke if your horse be not too weake of an hundred threescore and twelve sheets of good Demie paper) is a confutation of *The learned discourse of Ecclesiastical gouernement.* (B1^r)

There are two elements in this opening that deserve careful attention: Marprelate's joke about portability and his focus on the material construction of the book. To take the second of these issues first, Marprelate's precise tabulation of the number of sheets of demy paper consumed in the production of *A Defence* advertises the material resources underwriting Bridges's polemic. In contrast, the *Epitome* and the *Epistle* are each printed on a mere seven sheets, the amount of paper Bridges consumes with his prefatory matter. As a subsidized writer, Bridges is able to command resources beyond the reach of all but the wealthy, and yet the ability to publish a monumental text does not guarantee an audience. As Marprelate jibes: "I think you had more need to gather a benevolence among the Cleargie to pay Charde toward the printing of your booke or els labour to his grace to get him another protection for men will give no mony for your book unles it be to stop mustard pots" (*Epistle* A2^v).

Even with a strong horse, Bridges's *A Defence* is not comfortably portable. An imposing book, it was clearly designed to take its place alongside other learned volumes in a library. The Marprelate tracts, in contrast, are designed to travel. Though all texts are in a sense fugitive, the Marprelate tracts present an especially clear case of this general textual condition. Produced on a pirate press and intended for speedy circulation, these little books were always moving. In this respect the Marprelate tracts bear a family resemblance to a range of ephemeral forms that had the imprimatur of the authorities such as sermons and scaffold speeches. Assessing the importance of such material is complicated because so much of the evidence has disappeared, leaving behind libraries full of books designed to endure. Nonetheless, a concerted effort must be made to recover an awareness of the wide variety of material forms in which print circulated.[12] An examination of the Marprelate tracts, which range from a 50-page pamphlet to a single-sheet broadside, suggests that ephemeral print was an important part of an emerging print culture that had far-reaching consequences.

The notion that books are static objects is often complemented by the idea that print performs a regulative function. According to this view, print promotes uniformity by producing duplicate copies lacking the human touch of scribal error and emendation. Such a view, however, assumes passivity on the part of readers, an assumption that is perhaps more in accord with modern habits of consumption than with the active reading, often accompanied by the writing of marginal annotations, engaged in during the early modern period.[13] Furthermore, while print may indeed be employed to enforce or extend uniformity, it can also, quite obviously, be used to contest precisely such impositions. The Marprelate tracts are an excellent example of the political inertness of print;[14] print is not itself a historical agent, though it is instrumental in constituting historical actors. Marprelate delights in exploiting the subversive possibilities of print when attacking the orthodoxy of the episcopal order; at the same time, he is attempting, through print, to promulgate a uniform vision of the true presbyterian form of church government. Whether using print to criticize the incoherence of the bishops or to constitute a new interpretive community, Marprelate is always aware that the format, the type face, the disposition of the text on the page, all contribute to the meanings of the book.

Marprelate's attack on the Book of Common Prayer strikes at the very heart of a print-enforced community. John N. Wall has argued that by printing the Book of Common Prayer "the English reformers took advantage of the press's ability to achieve simultaneous use of the same document over a wide area to bring about a Reformation that was more liturgical and behavioral than it was theological and intellectual."[15] Moreover, Elizabeth herself was unyielding in her advocacy of a single use, declaring: "Nay, I have heard there be six preachers in one diocese the which do preach in six sundry ways. I wish such men to be brought to conformity and unity: that they minister the sacraments according to the order of this Realm and preach all one truth."[16] One might point out, however, that the inadequate theological reformation registered in the Prayer Book was in conflict with the Thirty-nine Articles, especially regarding the crucial doctrine of predestination. Indeed, as Wall acknowledges, the exploitation of print to impose a single use may instead have "exacerbated fragmentation" (219).

Martin's awareness of the potential of print leads him to focus withering criticism on the Prayer Book. Yet, interestingly enough, Marprelate's critique fixes not on theological corruptions, though these are mentioned, but on an error in the print itself. Marprelate, arguing that the bishops are "verie notorious for their learning and preaching" (F3^v), gives as his first example the fact that Travers was able to set Whitgift and Cooper at "a non plus" with an argument against the Prayer Book's translation of Psalm 105. The "corruption of the translation of the 28. verse" is contrary to "the translations allowed by the Bb. themselves" (F3^v). The disputed passage does represent a "contrarietie": "For in the book of Common prayer you shal read thus: And they were not obedient unto his word (which is a plain corruption of the text) in other priviledged English translations it is / And they were not disobedient unto his word / which is according to the veritie of the originall" (F3^v–F4^r). While Marprelate's reading of this crucial obedience / disobedience crux is not beyond dispute, he is quite accurate in claiming the support of other "privileged English translations."

The "not disobedient" reading is given by the Geneva Bible (1560); however, the Prayer Book incorporates the version given in the Great Bible (1540): "they were nat obedyent unto his worde" (2C4^v). But when the Bishops' Bible appeared in 1569, it followed the Geneva translation: "they went not from his words" (D8^v). Perhaps most interesting is a version of the Bishops' Bible (1572) produced by the queen's printer, Richard Jugge, which sets the Great Bible and the Bishops' Bible versions of the Psalms in parallel columns identified as "The translation used in common prayer" and "the translation after the Hebrewes" (3A2^r). Predictably, the Common

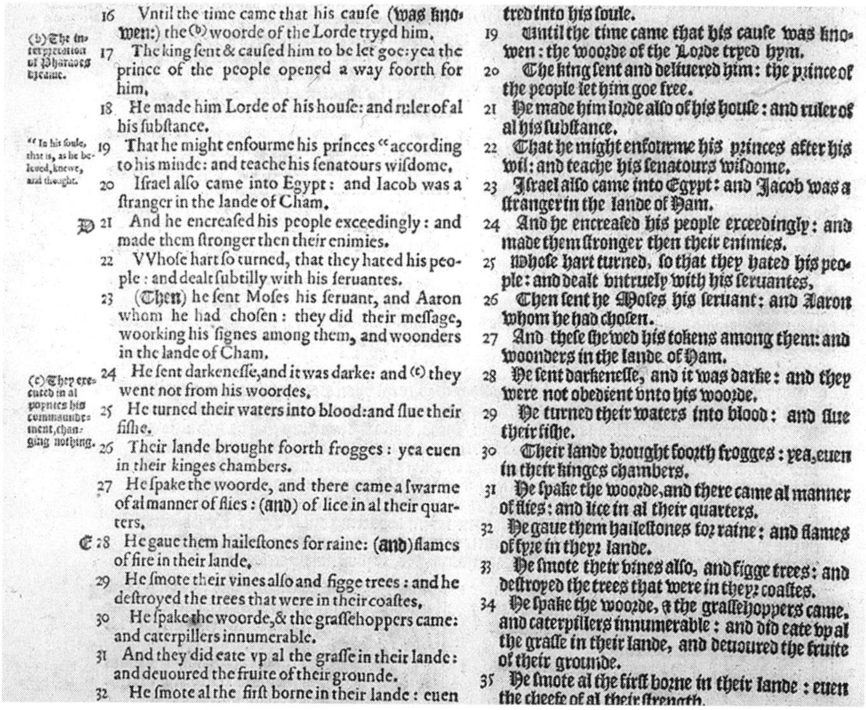

16 Vntil the time came that his cauſe (was kno-
wen:) the (b) woorde of the Lorde tryed him.
17 The king ſent & cauſed him to be let goe: yea the
prince of the people opened a way foorth for
him.
18 He made him Lorde of his houſe: and ruler of al
his ſubſtance.
19 That he might enfourme his princes "according
to his minde: and teache his ſenatours wiſdome.
20 Iſrael alſo came into Egypt: and Iacob was a
ſtranger in the lande of Cham.
21 And he encreaſed his people exceedingly: and
made them ſtronger then their enimies.
22 VVhoſe hart ſo turned, that they hated his people: and dealt ſubtilly with his ſeruantes.
23 (Then) he ſent Moſes his ſeruant, and Aaron
whom he had choſen: they did their meſſage,
woorking his ſignes among them, and woonders
in the lande of Cham.
24 He ſent darkeneſſe, and it was darke: and (c) they
went not from his woordes.
25 He turned their waters into blood: and flue their
fiſhe.
26 Their lande brought foorth frogges: yea euen
in their kinges chambers.
27 He ſpake the woorde, and there came a ſwarme
of al manner of flies: (and) of lice in al their quarters.
28 He gaue them haileſtones for raine: (and) flames
of fire in their lande.
29 He ſmote their vines alſo and figge trees: and he
deſtroyed the trees that were in their coaſtes.
30 He ſpake the woorde, & the graſſehoppers came:
and caterpillers innumerable.
31 And they did eate vp al the graſſe in their lande:
and deuoured the fruite of their grounde.
32 He ſmote al the firſt borne in their lande: euen

(b) The interpretation of Pharaoes dreame.

" In his ſoule, that is, as he beleued, knewe, and thought.

(c) They executed in al poyntes his commaundement, changing nothing.

tred into his ſoule.
19 Until the time came that his cauſe was kno-
wen: the woorde of the Lorde tryed hym.
20 The king ſent and deliuered him: the prince of
the people let him goe free.
21 He made him lorde alſo of his houſe: and ruler of
al his ſubſtance.
22 That he might enfourme his princes after his
wil: and teache his ſenatours wiſdome.
23 Iſrael alſo came into Egypt: and Iacob was a
ſtranger in the lande of Ham.
24 And he encreaſed his people exceedingly: and
made them ſtronger then their enimies.
25 Whoſe hart turned, ſo that they hated his people: and dealt vntruely with his ſeruantes,
26 Then ſent he Moſes his ſeruant: and Aaron
whom he had choſen.
27 And theſe ſhewed his tokens among them: and
woonders in the lande of Ham.
28 He ſent darkeneſſe, and it was darke: and they
were not obedient vnto his woorde.
29 He turned their waters into blood: and ſlue
their fiſhe.
30 Their lande brought foorth frogges: yea, euen
in their kinges chambers.
31 He ſpake the woorde, and there came al manner
of flies: and lice in al their quarters.
32 He gaue them haileſtones for raine: and flames
of fyre in theyr lande.
33 He ſmote their vines alſo, and figge trees: and
deſtroyed the trees that were in theyr coaſtes.
34 He ſpake the woorde, & the graſſehoppers came,
and caterpillers innumerable: and did eate vp al
the graſſe in their lande, and deuoured the fruite
of their grounde.
35 He ſmote al the firſt borne in their lande: euen
the cheefe of al their ſtrength.

Fig. 12 Bishops' Bible (1572)

Prayer version is set in black letter, while the relatively novel Bishops' version is in roman type.[17] The disputed passages are simply set side by side, and the only gloss repeats the comment made in earlier versions of the Bishops' Bible: "They executed in al poyntes his commaundement, changing nothing" (fig. 12). This version makes no attempt to smooth over the contradiction in the official position that so infuriates Marprelate. The fact that a variant of the readings given by both the Geneva and Bishops' Bibles was later taken up in the King James version – "they rebelled not against his word" – suggests that the reading fossilized in the Book of Common Prayer was losing support among biblical translators.

This shift in scholarly opinion begins to explain why Marprelate is able to go on to typify the Prayer Book version as a misprint: "And can he have no time in 3 or 4 yeares to correct most grose and ungodly faultes in the print / whereof the putting out of one syllable / even three letters (dis) would have amended this place" (F4^{r}). Rejecting the possibility of a substantive reading, Marprelate identifies the fault as a slip that might easily have been corrected. His rhetoric insists on the enormous disproportion between the physical slip (a misplaced syllable of three letters) and its consequences (the corruption of scripture). This description thus serves to emphasize the arbitrariness of the archbishop who would rather promulgate manifest error than admit to having made a mistake. By depicting Whitgift as willing to defend the status quo at any cost, Marprelate is able to make this textual crux serve as a fitting emblem of the archbishop's refusal to admit the argument for further reform.

In a rather typical paean to the stabilizing virtue of print, Myron Gilmore writes, "The mere fact that a single emendation by a great scholar could now circulate, without the danger of a copyist's error, signified a complete revolution in the conditions of activity of the learned world."[18] While there is, of course, an element of truth in this view, it overlooks the degree to which printing itself introduced errors; furthermore, it ignores the fact that unlike a scribal error which may be corrected by the next copyist, "faultes in the print" may be produced in thousands of copies, introducing an entirely new magnitude of error. Indeed, this is the very point made by Marprelate: "For if the unitie of the Church had bene his end / why hath not he amended this fault in all the books that have bene printed since that time / which now is not so little as 3 yeares / in which time many thousand of books of Common praier have bin printed" (F4^r).

The implications of this critique are extensive. At the heart of what has been called the Admonition Controversy was a debate over the correct reading of certain passages from the New Testament.[19] But along with this debate came a series of attendant questions regarding the status of scripture, the Book of Prayer, the Homilies, and preaching. Marprelate, in this instance, avoids the difficulties of exegetical dispute by claiming that the bishops have disqualified themselves by allowing a misprint to corrupt the scripture, a slip that exposes a lack of proper reverence for the Word. In the *Epistle*, Marprelate recalls Cooper's declaration, in a sermon, that, "men might finde fault / if they were disposed to quarrel / as well with the Scripture / as with the booke of Common praier" (E2^r). His immediate response is to wonder, "Who could heare this comparison without trembling?" While Cooper's point is clear enough, Marprelate gives it a strong reading, suggesting that the Prayer Book has been equated with scripture. The trembling that this provokes is a horror at the mixing of the profane and the sacred. This same attitude is visible in Marprelate's response to "a commaundement from his grace into Paules Churchyard that no Byble should be bound without the Apocripha": "Monstrous and ungodly wretches that to maintaine their owne outragious proceedings thus mingle heaven and earth together and woulde make the spirite of God to be the author of prophane bookes" (E4^r). The same rigid binary is visible in Marprelate's insistence that ministers cannot be lords (H4^v). This dichotomy, between the spiritual and the temporal, runs throughout the Marprelate tracts; however, while it offers a certain conceptual clarity, the exact relationship between the two orders is never firmly established.

In attacking the Prayer Book version of Psalm 105, Marprelate accuses the bishops of allowing "most grose and ungodly faultes in the print," faults, moreover, that are in direct contradiction to other privileged texts. Far from being a stable monolith, the Elizabethan church settlement is revealed to contain contradictions. If Marprelate is able to exploit the failure to correct a "misprint" in order to demonstrate that the bishops are incorrigible, he is also quite happy to ridicule attempts to repair an unsatisfactory text. In both cases, print seems to inevitably entail misprint.

Rather than seeing this as a universal condition of print, a necessary falling off as the pristine authorial word is subjected to the indecencies of print, Marprelate insists that corruptions in the print accurately reveal the corruptions of the bishops. In *Hay Any Worke for Cooper*, Marprelate quotes Cooper as writing, "Touching the Praemunire let the libeler and his doe what he dare," before drawing the attention of his readers to a cancel slip appearing in the first edition of Cooper's *Admonition*: "mark how I have made the bishops to pull in their hornes. For whereas in this place they had printed the word *dare*, they bethought themselves / that they had to deale with my worship / which am favored at court / and being afraide of me / they pasted the word *can* upon the word *dare*" (F4^v). In itself this is hardly a devastating critique, though it does suggest a degree of vacillation that might be interpreted as pusillanimity, but Marprelate quickly moves onto a second cancel slip of greater consequence.

Responding to Marprelate's argument that the Apostles and the primitive church operated according to presbyterian principles, the first state of Cooper's book concedes the point – "I will not deny it" – but goes on to argue that this does not constitute a binding precedent. However, sometime between its printing and release this concession was covered over with a slip claiming, "That is not yet proved."[20] This correction leads Marprelate to conclude that "although their consciences do tell them / that the discipline was then / yet they will beare the world in hand / that that is not yet proved. Here you see that if this patch T.C. had not used two patches to cover his patcherie / the bishops woulde have accounted him to be as very a patch as Deane John" (F4^v). While this does not address Cooper's claim that the primitive discipline is no binding precedent, it does allow Marprelate to accuse the bishops of bad faith: the "patch" is the material manifestation of a fundamental duplicity; its removal, an act of unmasking. According to Marprelate, the first state is a conscientious expression of truth and the cancel slip is a conscious attempt to deceive. Both attempts at correction are taken as evidence of uncertainty and incoherence, allowing Marprelate to characterize Cooper as a "patch" (fool) and his book as a "patcherie."

Despite his severe criticism of what he considers to be corrupt and incompetent printing, which he takes to be symptomatic of an underlying intellectual incoherence, Marprelate clearly believes that print will serve to further reform. A searcher for finely articulated doctrine will be disappointed; nonetheless, the tracts do work to establish a group of followers united by their hostility to the abuses encouraged by the episcopal system. Yet, despite the vigor of this appeal, recent work on Elizabethan puritanism has paid little attention to Marprelate's attempt to gain a wider audience.[21] In part, the scholarship has been unduly influenced by an awareness of the eventual capture of the Martinist press and simultaneous collapse of the presbyterian movement. However, we must heed Marprelate's injunction and "Resone not frome the successe of thinges untoe the goodnesse of the causse" (*Protestatyon*, A3^v). The fact that the demands articulated in the tracts went unmet does not detract from the significance of Martin's appeal to a wider audience.[22]

Though the rude and boisterous Marprelate tracts were immediately recognized as a significant departure from earlier polemic, they were not entirely without precedent. Indeed, there is an extensive literature of religious controversy, some of it unlicensed and anonymous, some of it printed abroad, that precedes the Marprelate tracts.[23] It is also true that such polemic was often harsh. Patrick Collinson remarks that the official response to the *Briefe Discourse against the Outwarde Apparell* (1566) "accepted the new bitterness of invective and replied in the same coin."[24] This, in turn, provoked a reply from Anthony Gilby which is described as "an early puritan exercise in the art of 'pleasant' badinage which would one day give birth to Martin Marprelate." On the one hand, rather than being a novel rupture in an otherwise stable discourse of scholastic debate, the Marprelate tracts are merely one episode in a long line of Protestant polemic.[25] On the other hand, in their attempt to win over a popular audience, the tracts register an important departure. Despite some premonitions of things to come in the pamphlets surrounding the vestments controversy, which occurred in 1550–51 and concerned the question of appropriate clerical garb in the reformed English church, the vast majority of the puritan tracts adopted a tone of gravity and constructed their arguments by using syllogistic reasoning and scriptural citations.[26] These texts appealed to readers who already had an awareness of the importance of the issues involved. Marprelate, however, does not confine his address to the godly sort; indeed, one could argue that he deliberately risks their disapprobation, attempting instead to gain a new audience by employing a style and method that incorporates elements of a common culture.

Marprelate's sophisticated treatment of print conventions, already seen in the attacks on the various infelicities in the print of his opponents, is also visible in the attempt to use print in order to repoduce the festive, oral world of popular pastimes. Though it is true that Marprelate's writing is marked by an oral and extemporaneous style, this should not lead to a neglect of the constitutive role played by print.[27] For it is precisely in the complex combination of oral elements and print conventions that one finds one of the most innovative aspects of the Marprelate tracts.

The embodiment of particular voices in type is achieved by two distinct techniques that both depend on the manipulation of print conventions. First, the space of the page is used to establish an imagined interpretive community. Second, the conventional conflation of text and writer allows Marprelate to figure the entire series of pamphlets as a lineage, consisting of Martin and his two sons. In this way, the appearance of *Theses Martinianae* (Martin Junior) and *The Iust Censure and Reproofe of Martin Iunior* (Martin Senior) confirms Marprelate's prediction that his movement would grow. In both cases the actual printed material reinforces the arguments being made within the text, the bibliographic and linguistic codes work together.

The *Epistle* sets up a dynamic relationship between main text and margin that constitutes the page as a space for antagonistic dialogue. Rather than using the edge of the page to provide edifying glosses, the *Epistle* allows various voices to speak from the margin. The illusion created by this use of textual space is that of a fluid argument taking place in public and drawing in bystanders. The first interruption from the audience appears within parentheses: "Therefore no Lord B. (nowe I pray thee good Martin speake out / if euer thou diddest speake out / that hir Maiestie and the counsell may heare thee) is to be tollerated in any christian commonwelth" (A3ᵛ). This intrusive endorsement fails to please Marprelate, who comments in the margin: "What malapert knaues are these that cannot be content to stand by and here / but they must teach a gentleman how to speake."

The typographic conventions of margin and parentheses are here used to imagine a dynamic and fluid situation in which Marprelate, the gentleman, holds forth to an enthusiastic and unruly plebeian audience. Though the admonition to maintain order, especially its invocation of the disorderly lower classes, is ironic coming from such a transgressive persona, it serves to establish a scene of debate, governed by certain protocols. On the next page, it is the bystanders who now appear in the margin. Marprelate has constructed a syllogism to establish that bishops are "petty popes," but in the conclusion he adds that they are "proud prelates / intollerable with-standers of reformation / enemies of the gospell / and most couetous wretched priests." The marginal note complains, "M. Marprelate you put more then the question in the conclusion of your syllogisme." This provokes another outburst from Marprelate:

This is a pretie matter / that standers by / must be so busie in other mens games: why sawceboxes must you be pratling? you are as mannerly as bishops / in medling with that you have nothing to doe / as they do in taking upon them ciuill offices. I thinke for any maners either they or you have / that you were brought up in Bridewell. But it is well that since you last interrupted me (for now this is the second time) you seeme to have lernt your *Cato de Moribus* in that you keepe your selves on the margent. (A4^r)

The bystanders have been successfully disciplined, and they now make their points from the margin. However, it is important to distinguish between these bystanders and the bishops themselves. Marprelate frequently addresses the bishops directly and ventriloquizes their responses, and a similar effect is created when block quotations are inserted in the text, but the function of these standard polemical techniques is distinct from that of the play between main text and margin which serves to create an imagined space inhabited by a popular audience to be won over.[28] This space, occupied by the as yet uncommitted bystanders, is also an invitation to the reader. Crucially, Marprelate's page is not reduced to a field of battle occupied only by the godly and the forces of the Antichrist; there is space for curious listeners.

This point bears emphasis because it has recently been suggested that Marprelate's parody of the humanist page provides a radical critique of the "inflated discourse of the church apologists," but fails to provide purchase for an interpretive community: "The humanist use of the page as a locus for consensus or community is thus turned on its head in a context which points up the importance of the printed page as a territory for ideological occupation."[29] On one level, this is clearly right: Marprelate does not use the conventions of the page consistently to reinforce a sense of coherence and consensus; however, the format of the page invites the reader to join the fray by creating the illusion of an immediate, verbal exchange.

The next and last marginal note in the voice of a bystander asks, "Why Martin / what meanest thou? Certainely an thou takest that course but a while / thou wilt set thy good brethren at their wits end" (BI^v). While displaying a residual concern for the sanity of the bishops, the bystander is clearly now in sympathy with Marprelate. The marginal notes in the opening of the *Epistle* are an invitation to debate, but they do not promote an open-ended contest; indeed, the sequence of notes encourages the reader to take Marprelate's side by invoking a tumultuous scene of public disputation in which Marprelate both chastises and seduces a popular audience. A similar attempt to create the illusion of an embodied audience appears in *Hay Any Worke* when Marprelate exclaims: "and holde my cloake there somebody / that I may go roundly to work" (B4^v). The subsequent appearance of Martin Junior and Martin Senior serves as material evidence of Marprelate's evangelical powers.

At the conclusion of the *Epistle*, Marprelate claims, "I will watch you at every halfe turne / & whatsoever you do amisse / I will presently publish it: you shall not call one honest man before you / but I will get his examination ... & publish it" (FI^v). In order to accomplish this threatened program of surveillance, he will "place a young Martin in everie diocesse." The idea of a proliferation of Martins, returned to in *Hay Any Worke for Cooper* where Marprelate asserts that "the day that you hange Martin / assure your selves / there wil 20. Martins spring in my place" (D3^v), undoubtedly caused the intended anxiety in episcopal circles. But it is in the next two pamphlets that the idea takes on substance.

Theses Martinianae appeared in July, 1589, with a title page that declared that it was "published and set foorth as an after-birth of the noble Gentleman himselfe, by a prety stripling of his, MARTIN IVNIOR." This conceit is maintained in the body of the text which opens with a prefatory statement from Martin Junior: "Thou shalt receive (good Reader) before I set downe unto thee anie thing of myne owne, certeyne of those thinges of my fathers dooings which I found among his unperfect papers: I have not changed anything in them, nor added to them ought of mine owne, but as I found them, so I have delivered them unto thee" (AI^v). Thus Martin Junior positions himself as literary executor of his father's legacy. The assertion that nothing has been changed is repeated, and the reader is informed that Martin Junior has appended his own epilogue. Despite its "unfinished" state, the main text is a model of clarity and gravity, while the epilogue is in the familiar jesting style of Marprelate. In this epilogue, Martin Junior explains that his father's manuscript was "taken up (together with certaine other papers) besides a bush, where it had dropped from some body passing by that way" (C3^v), a detail that insists on the fugitive status of the text.

This "discovered" text consists of a short preface which breaks off in mid-sentence and a list of 110 theses which is also incomplete. In both cases the imperfect state of the copy is signaled in the print. The last sentence of the preface ends, "wee truelie charge them to have erred, otherwise their 812. their 1401" (A3^r). In his epilogue, Martin Junior states: "The Arithmeticall nombers in the end of his preamble shew, that when he had written so farre, he had something more in his head then all men doe conceive, which made him leave in the middest of a period" (C4^r).[30] Paradoxically, this assertion of incompleteness suggests the authenticity and integrity of Marprelate's fragment.

The last item in the list of theses displays a similar dynamic: "That our prelates. Heere the father lefte his writings unperfite, and thus perfitely beginnes the sonne" (C2^r). The printed imperfection of the text manifests the perfect fidelity of the son who has not dared to mend his father's text. This filial piety does not keep Martin Junior from expressing some reservations about the reaction of his father and his brothers to his "presuming this of mine owne head" (D4^r). In a gesture of self-exculpation, he claims, "I did all of a good meaning, to save my fathers papers: and it would have pitied your heart to see, how the poore papers were rain and weather-beaten, even truely in such a sort, as they coulde scant bee read to bee printed" (D4^r). Drawing on the common notion that print has a peculiar preservative virtue, Martin Junior figures a potentially radical act as essentially conservative: publication keeps the fragile manuscript from disintegration and saves the fugitive text. The same desire to mitigate the presumption of his action appears in Martin Junior's conclusion: "one thing me thinkes my father should like in me, and that is, my modestie, for I have not presumed, to publish mine in as large a print or volume as my father does his." This modesty *topos* ingeniously incorporates the exigencies of print production (necessities dictated by the availability of type and paper) into the very narrative of the tracts. The switch from black letter to roman type and from quarto to octavo does not, however, forestall the coming reaction.

The next tract, entitled *The iust censure and reproofe of Martin Iunior*, states on the title page: "Wherein the rash and undiscreete headines of the foolish youth, is sharply mette with, and the boy hath his lesson taught him, I warrant you, by his reverend and elder brother, Martin Senior, sonne and heire unto the renowmed Martin Mar-prelate the Great." In particular, Martin Senior charges Junior with violating his "right of inheritance," and he reminds him that their father "did not once vouchsafe to speake a worde of such a dilling as thou art" (B2^r). On the other hand, he recalls, "the honourable mention that my father ... made of me in his

writings," a reference to the invocation of Martin Senior in the *Epistle* (F4^v).
While some time is spent admonishing the younger brother for exposing
the "scrabled and weather-beaten papers," the main focus of the tract is
once again the abuses of the bishops. Nonetheless, the act of fraternal
censure is significant. Not only does it display the gentle correction that the
presbyterians claimed to be fundamental to the discipline, but it also
reveals that the Marprelate family, far from desiring an Anabaptistical
community of property, is involved in a typical squabble over an estate,
which itself presupposes the validity of a "right of inheritance." Most
importantly, the very existence of the pamphlets that come to be known
as *Martin Iunior* and *Martin Senior* is evidence of the growth of Martinism.

I have argued that the Marprelate tracts make use of recognizable print
conventions both to criticize the government's productions and to construct a community of readers by establishing a textual space of debate and
by figuring the series of pamphlets as a lineage that represents the prophe-
sied expansion of Martinism. As important as these elements are, they need
to be linked to the explicit arguments made within the pamphlets. Far too
often, the coherent argument made in the tracts gets obscured or neglected.
Raymond Anselment, for instance, suggests that "the satires remain primarily vehicles to popularize reform rather than means to dispute their
opponents' essential beliefs."[31] This view is partly true: one never gets the
sense that Marprelate expects the bishops to be satisfied with or converted
by his arguments. Marprelate's polemic does not attempt to persuade the
object of attack to change, rather it seeks to convince the uncommitted
to avoid such errors by joining with the Martinists. Nonetheless, the
"essential beliefs" of the bishops are disputed in the very process of
popularizing reform. To neglect or minimize this element of dispute is to
suggest that, in the case of the Marprelate tracts, popularizing is equivalent
to demagoguery.

An analysis of the methods used by Marprelate to prosecute his argument cannot, nonetheless, be easily separated from the issue of style.
Marprelate's innovative style has attracted enormous attention and has
recently been examined by Leland Carlson in his attempt to ascribe the
tracts to Job Throkmorton on the basis of stylistic parallels. Among other
stylistic peculiarities, Carlson notes an "extensive use of alliteration . . .
colorful writing and coined words" (180). To this I would add the use of
colloquialism and regional dialect; both help to foster the illusion that
Marprelate is a plain-speaking Englishman.[32] This boisterous and extemporaneous style, with antecedents in the drama and the jest book, is
designed to appeal to the appetite for print pastimes.[33] Though elements

of abuse, anecdote, and critique are interspersed throughout the tracts and seem to preclude the possibility of sustained argument, for all their unruliness the tracts are not without method. On the contrary, the variety of strategies used is the result not of authorial incoherence, but of a deliberate attempt to gain a non-academic readership.[34] Along with his sophisticated manipulation of print conventions, Marprelate uses two principal methods to mount his argument: the scripture-based syllogism and the *ad hominem* anecdote.

In the pamphlets, logical demonstration and invective interpenetrate to such a degree that one must wonder whether attempting to separate argument from abuse is not imposing an anachronistic standard; the tendency to conflate the two is, I believe, typical of early modern polemic. An attack on an opponent's logic always carries the imputation that one's adversary suffers from a deficit of reason. If an attack on an argument is always also an attack on the person making the argument, it is not immediately obvious that the converse is true. Is an attack on the person also an attack on the argument? Put another way, is a ridiculous or morally suspect person capable of making a good argument? The affirmative that comes readily to us would have been much more elusive for someone in the sixteenth century. For Marprelate it is not even a question: the pamphlets consistently associate logical slips, "dealing so loosely" (*Epistle* G3^v), and incontinent living, "the pattern of loosenesse" (G4^r). In Marprelate's reiterated call for an open disputation with the bishops and in his constant use of syllogistic arguments, we see a commitment to the claims of reason as defined by a scholastic tradition; alternatively, the language of *ad hominem* attack and the use of fantastic syllogistic forms provoke laughter, suggesting that the opposition and their arguments deserve only ridicule.

When Marprelate refers to a "lustie syllogisme of mine owne making" (*Epistle* B1^v), he manages to invest the scholastic mode with physical life. A similar effect is achieved when he writes, "I wil presently proue both maior and minor of this sillogisme. And hold my cloake there somebody / that I may go roundly to worke" (*Hay* B4^v). Syllogistic disputation is elsewhere figured as a duel or wrestling match: "but first you & I must go out alone into the plaine fields / and there we wil try it out / even by plaine syllogismes" (*Hay* B2^r). Despite these joking invocations, Marprelate never denies the efficacy of the syllogism; not only does he expose the "paralogisms" of the bishops, but he also makes use of the syllogism to mount his own argument.

The first tract, attacking Bridges's *Defence of the Government Established,* provides an excellent example of Martin's attention to logic. He claims to have found in Bridges's book a "syllogism concluded in no mood" (*Epistle* GI^v). *Mood* is here a technical term of logic, referring to a syllogistic form, defined by Thomas Wilson in *The Rule of Reason*, as "a lawful placyng of proposicions, in their due qualitie or quantitie."[35] Marprelate reproduces Bridges's argument: "Some kind of ministrie ordained by the Lord was temporarie (saith he) as for example / the Mosaicall priesthood / and the ministrie of Apostles / prophets / &c. But the ministrie of pastors / doctors / elders & deacons / was ordayned by the Lord: Therefore it was temporarie" (*Epistle* GI^v). Martin then proceeds to produce a series of arguments exploiting the same fallacy: "Some man in the land (say they) weareth a wooden dagger & a coxcombe / as for example / his grace of Canterburies fool ... you presbyter John Catercap are some man in the land: Therefore by this reason / you weare a wooden dagger and a coxcomb." The fourteen arguments that follow display Marprelate's usual penchant for scurrilous anecdote: "Some presbyter priest or elder in the land / is accused (& even now the matter is in trial before his grace and his brethren) to have two wives / & to marrie his brother vnto a woman upon her death bedd / she being past recouerie. As for example / the B. of Sir Davies in wales / is this priest as they saye. But you presbyter John / are some priest: Therefore you have committed all these vnnatural parts" (G2^v). Of course, Marprelate's joking use of this logical fallacy provides not demonstrative proof but an opportunity to suggest that the particular failings of certain members of the English prelacy are actually universal to the class of bishops. Marprelate admits that his syllogisms have "offended in form," yet he maintains that "many of their propositions are tried truths, having many eye and ear witnesses living" (G3^v).

Not all of Marprelate's polemic revolves around the play of logic; there is a liberal dose of straightforward invective and libelous anecdote designed to reveal the turpitude of the bishops. But as defenders of the episcopate were quick to point out, these tales of malfeasance, even if true, do not demonstrate the illegitimacy of the office of bishop. Marprelate's exuberant use of *ad hominem* attacks seems worlds away from the "Scholastical manner" of syllogistic argument, for clearly the corruption of the incumbent does not logically entail the corruption of the office.

Instead, the attack on particular individuals reveals the influence of the common practice of "libeling" or "ballading." Sometimes sung, sometimes circulated in manuscript, and only rarely printed, these "libels took many forms and were circulated across a broad social and geographic range."[36] Though the practice could, as Richard Cust has suggested, be used to disseminate news on a national level, frequently it was a local phenomenon, a process of social shaming, resorted to in an effort to correct perceived deviancy. Martin Ingram, for instance, places mocking rhymes within the panoply of techniques available to enforce social discipline.[37] Such techniques, nonetheless, could also be deployed not to insist on conformity but to attack figures of authority.

Indeed, Marprelate's use of the damning anecdote rather than representing a new polemical low only continues a procedure used by Foxe. As Collinson writes, "Martin's distinctive polemical method, the raking up of past episodes and discreditable anecdotes, grew out of the martyrological technique of 'gathering' and 'registering' the troubles of the godly, learned by Field from John Foxe and employed to good effect in the amassing of the puritans' own documentary files." This puritan archive would later supply material for *A Parte of a Register* (1593), and Collinson suggests that Marprelate drew on it for some of his material.[38] Rather than being the singular fulminations of a hot-headed puritan, Marprelate's anecdotes are part of an established Protestant tradition, and may in fact have been drawn from a collectively amassed archive. Furthermore, Marprelate's attacks have an analogue in the puritan practice of "personal preaching," the naming from the pulpit of particular offenders in the congregation. This practice was divisive and clearly an unwelcome development to many, as numerous local brawls and lawsuits attest, yet it became a standard weapon in the godly preacher's attempt to move the people to reform.[39]

Though practices such as personal preaching, "registering," and ballading provide antecedents, it must be pointed out that even in his use of defamatory anecdotes Marprelate remains within the realm of accepted dialectic technique, using inductive rather than strictly syllogistic logic. There is an incipient empiricism, what Marprelate refers to as "old mother experience" (*Epistle* A2^v), visible in Marprelate's attention to the behavior of particular prelates. However, the novelty of this development must not be overemphasized. Induction was, after all, an accepted technique of argumentation according to Aristotle. Nonetheless, a split existed in the period between humanist dialectic, which focused on a pragmatic logic to be used in court and council, and scholastic logic, which maintained an unswerving allegiance to the formal syllogism.[40] Under the influence of humanism, most contemporary English logic handbooks admitted the efficacy of *inductio* and other forms of non-demonstrative argument. As Thomas Wilson puts it in *The Rule of Reason*: "An Induction, is a kinde of argumente, when we gather sufficiently a numbre of propre names, and there vpon make the conclusion vniuersall" (18^v). Accordingly,

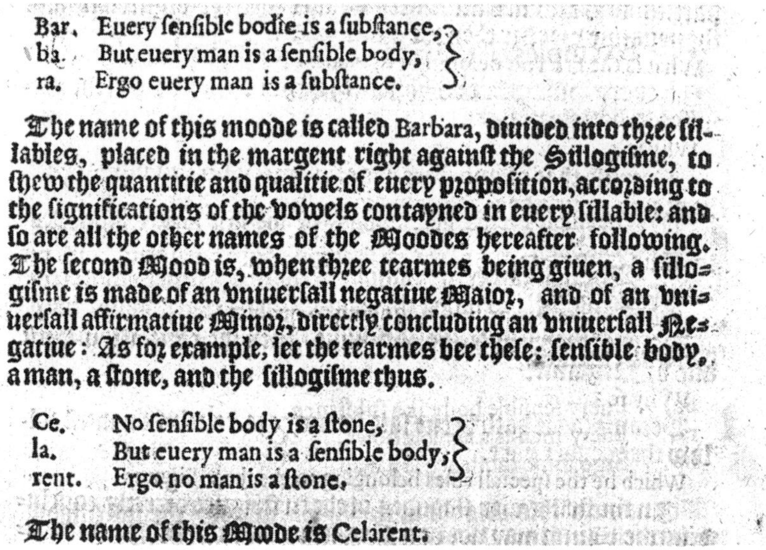

Inventing Polemic

Bar, Euery fenfible bodie is a fubftance,⎤
ba. But euery man is a fenfible body, ⎬
ra, Ergo euery man is a fubftance. ⎦

The name of this moode is called Barbara, diuided into three fil--
lables, placed in the margent right againſt the Sillogiſme, to
ſhew the quantitie and qualitie of euery propoſition, according to
the ſignifications of the vowels contayned in euery ſillable: and
ſo are all the other names of the Moodes hereafter following.
The ſecond Mood is, when three tearmes being giuen, a ſillo=
giſme is made of an vniuerſall negatiue Maior, and of an vni=
uerſall affirmatiue Minor, directly concluding an vniuerſall Ne=
gatiue: As for example, let the tearmes bee theſe: ſenſible body,
a man, a ſtone, and the ſillogiſme thus.

Ce, No fenfible body is a ſtone, ⎤
la, But euery man is a fenfible body,⎬
rent. Ergo no man is a ſtone, ⎦

The name of this Moode is Celarent,

Fig. 13 Thomas Blundeville, *The Art of Logike* (1599)

all Marprelate's examples of episcopal misbehavior, duly noted with proper names, are adduced to prove that bishops as a class are bad.[41]

One final example shall serve to demonstrate Marprelate's typical blend of playful syllogism and *ad hominem* abuse. In *The Epitome*, Marprelate offers a new argument: "It shall be concluded I warrant you in mood and figure. But indeed I have invented a new mood of mine own (for I have been a great schooleman in my daies) which containeth in it a great misterie . . . This is the syllogism / the mood answereth unto *Celarent*, elder daughter to *Barbara*, and I will have it called *Perncanterburikenolde*" (E4ᵛ). *Celarent* and *Barbara* are mnemonic words indicating moods in the first figure. Blundeville, in *The Art of Logike* (1599), explains these two words and demonstrates their marginal use (fig. 13). The use of "three sillables, placed in the margent right against the Sillogism" became a typographic convention indicating, in Wilson's phrase, "a lawful placing of proposicions." A passage from Foxe illustrates the use of such a typographic convention in setting out an argument against the doctrine of transubstantiation (fig. 14).

Here the three syllables in the margin no longer function as a mnemonic or even heuristic device. Each of the vowels *a, e, i, o*, used in the mnemonic words, indicates a different type of proposition, either what the logicians called universal affirmative, universal negative, particular affirmative, or

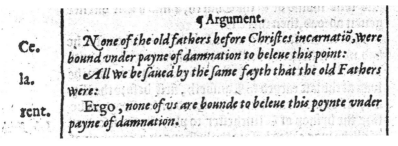

Fig. 14 John Foxe, *Actes and Monuments* (1570)

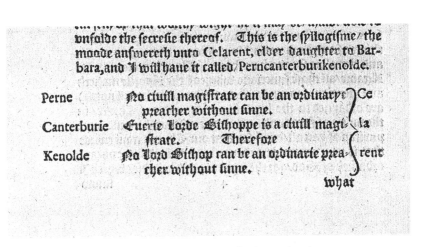

Fig. 15 Martin Marprelate, *The Epitome* (1588)

particular negative. Thus, as Blundeville asserts, *Celarent* indicates a syllogism with a universal negative major premise, a universal affirmative minor, and a universal negative conclusion. The syllogism given conforms to this pattern: no civil magistrate can be an ordinary preacher without sin; every lord bishop is a civil magistrate; therefore, no lord bishop can be an ordinary preacher without sin (fig. 15). Deftly deploying an established typographic convention, Marprelate claims a standard mood as new and christens it with a mnemonic word that combines the names of three of his opponents: Andrew Perne, Dean of Ely; John Whitgift, Archbishop of Canterbury; and Dr. Kenolde. At this moment argument and abuse are deeply, perhaps inseparably, imbricated.

Marprelate's attachment to the syllogism is complex. In the opening of the *Epistle*, after using a syllogism to prove that the bishops are petty popes,

Marprelate claims, "the syllogismes are mine owne / I may do what I will with them / and thus holde you content" (A4ʳ). Despite such constant playfulness regarding the form of the syllogism, Marprelate never gives up on its efficacy. The use of the syllogism guarantees the ultimate rationality of Marprelate's discourse, which might otherwise be open to the charge of antinomian enthusiasm, and places Marprelate not on the fringe but within the mainstream of Protestant polemic. That said, Marprelate's selective and opportunistic deployment of syllogistic logic departs from the standard form of theological controversy, which placed a premium on the systematic development of arguments.

The claim that the pamphlets represent a serious attempt to gain popular support for the presbyterian program must, however, be complicated by their condemnation by both conformists and presbyterians alike. If the pamphlets are an attempt to create a coalition of support for presbyterian discipline, who is the target audience? The beginnings of an answer can be found through an analysis that pays special attention to Marprelate's responses to criticism from both the conformists and the puritans.[42]

Though both conformists and puritans agreed in condemning Marprelate for some of the same reasons, there was a split in the focus of their respective criticisms.[43] According to the conformists, the greatest danger was posed by the leveling tendency of Marprelate's argument. For them, the transgressive style and method of the tracts reveal a desire to confound all social hierarchy. For the puritans, the profane style and method threatened to discredit a serious argument and to contaminate the scriptures: an apparently undisciplined argument for the discipline was a contradiction in terms. In response, the tracts try to limit the possibility of social leveling at the same time as they justify the use of jesting in an appeal to a wider audience. The positioning of the "puritans" in this response raises the possibility that Marprelate is seeking the support of those who did not identify themselves as "puritans," even those who did not perceive themselves to be part of the godly elite.

The presbyterian argument had, from its outset, been vulnerable to the accusation of "popularity," a vague term which invoked a number of related fears.[44] The presbyterian platform insisted that the church be ruled not by bishops but by elders each elected by the male, householding members of the church. This attack on episcopal hierarchy was claimed to be the first step in an attack on all hierarchy, just as the attack on episcopal wealth would lead to an attack on all property.[45]

These accusations of "popularity" are all haunted by the figure of the Anabaptist who was held to be a scriptural literalist, a believer in direct divine inspiration, and an opponent of personal property.[46] The Peasants' War of 1524–26 had provided dramatic evidence of the consequences of a fanatical and enthusiastic adherence to an idiosyncratic reading of the scriptures. Indeed, in his exchange with Cartwright, Whitgift had argued that presbyterianism was the highroad to Anabaptism. At the same time, he had claimed that the platform also revealed a papist tendency because the presbyterians similarly deprived the Christian prince of a clear role in ecclesiastical matters. This counterintuitive claim that presbyterianism is in fact an amalgam of Anabaptism and papistry exploits a fear of the two great evils that, according to Whitgift and other defenders of the Elizabethan settlement, threatened the true church. As Peter Lake argues, the "two opposed negative images of popery and Anabaptism" were used to delimit "a middle ground of protestant respectability between the madcap populist scripturalism of the Anabaptists and the sterile formalism and reliance on merely human authority of the papists."[47] If popery – what a later age would term "priestcraft" – is most often associated with a mystification of hierarchy, Anabaptism consistently figures mob rule.

The charge of popularity does not simply characterize the form of church government being proposed, it also suggests that the advocates of the discipline are directly seeking the support of the people.[48] This is an issue that comes up repeatedly in the first response to Marprelate, Thomas Cooper's *Admonition to the People of England*, where it is often coupled with the charge of Anabaptism. However, the title of Cooper's own tract is worth noting. It is, of course, an echo of the title of the tract written by Field and Wilcox, *An Admonition to the Parliament*, but where the presbyterian tract had addressed the political nation, the Parliament, Cooper, aware that the Marprelate tracts are seeking support from a wider range of readers, addresses himself to the "people" in general. Of course, this does not make him any less hostile to the populist tendency displayed by Marprelate.

Cooper is horrified that "at this present time, we shoulde see in mens handes and bosomes, commonly slanderous pamphlets fresh from the press against the best of the Church of Englande," and he summarizes the dire consequences of such behavior elegantly: "But if this outragious spirit of boldenesse be not stopped speedily, I feare he wil prove himselfe to bee, not onely *Marprelate*, but *Mar-prince, Mar-state, Mar-lawe, Mar-magistrate*, and all together, until he bring it to an Anabaptisticall equalitie and communitie" (29, 35). In an argument designed to refute the assertion that the clergy ought to live in a state of apostolic poverty, Cooper suggests that the same argument could be made to apply to all Christians, becoming "the very ground of Anabaptisticall communitie . . . that none can be saved, but such as renounce all their goods and possessions" (145). Attacks on the wealth of the bishops will encourage attacks on secular wealth, which will bring not only "a *Platonicall* community of all things: but also denying superioritie, and Lordship and dominion, and bringing in a general equalitie, most dangerous to the societie of man" (148).

Cooper insists on the linkage between the church and state: "their whole drift, as it may seeme, is to bring the Government of the Church to a *Democracie* or *Aristocracie*. The principles and reasons whereof, if they bee made once by experience familiar in the minds of the common people, and that they have the sense and feeling of them: It is greatly to bee feared, that they will very easily transferre the same to the Government of the common weale" (70). Later Cooper repeats the warning: "If this their doctrine spread in libelles, shall become familiar to the common people of this Realm: it may happily breed such a scab and daungerous sore, as all the cunning in this land wil scant bee able to heale it" (160). In a sermon at Paul's Cross which was subsequently published, Bancroft produced the same argument: "Now deerly beloved unto you of all sorts, but especially to you of the richest, I praie you tell me how you like this doctrine . . . The whole maner thereof is wholy Anabaptisticall, and tendeth to the destruction and overthrow of all good rule and government" (26). Clearly such arguments are designed to produce solidarity among the propertied in the face of what is described as a potentially revolutionary threat.

Marprelate responds to these criticisms in two different ways. On the one hand, while maintaining that neither he nor the puritans are seeking separation, he attempts to dissociate the bishops from the crown. On the other hand, he constantly invokes English law in an attempt to portray the bishops' proceedings as unconstitutional while maintaining that presbyterianism is consonant with the English constitution. This use of legal argument not only counters the charge of antinomian Anabaptism but also appeals to a gentry steeped in the language of the common law.[49]

Marprelate's patriotic invocation of English common law serves not to criticize the monarchy but to emphasize the tyranny and foreignness of the "petty popes." Throughout the tracts the claim is made that the queen, if she were only made aware of their abuses, would deprive the bishops. Marprelate uses this variant of the ancient charge of evil counselors in order to assert his loyalty to the queen while attacking the government of her church in the strongest possible terms. Furthermore, Marprelate manages to use the royal supremacy as evidence of the unlawfulness of the episcopacy by arguing that since the magistrate cannot lawfully maim the true church, and the magistrate can lawfully remove the bishops, therefore, the office of bishop cannot be lawful (*Hay* B4^v).

In making this argument, Marprelate invites the bishops to make the counterclaim that their offices are not dependent on the royal will. Indeed, Bridges himself had made a confused and tentative claim for *jure divino* episcopacy (s4^v). Though J. P. Sommerville has suggested that the *jure divino* case was not interpreted as a "clericalist assault on the Royal Supremacy," Marprelate encourages just such an interpretation.[50] Bridges had attacked Beza's classification of bishops as of God, of Man, and of the devil, using the logic of dichotomy to deny the existence of the middle class. Marprelate happily takes up Bridges's dichotomy between bishops of God and bishops of the devil and concludes that since the bishops are appointed by the queen, they cannot be "of God" and therefore must be of the devil (*Certaine Minerall and Metaphisicall Schoolpoints, Hay* E3^v). To claim a direct divine mandate for episcopacy would be a derogation of the queen's royal supremacy. Marprelate thus positions himself as a loyal subject intent on revealing the treasonous practices of the bishops.

The emphasis placed on English law produces the same effect. The tracts repeatedly allude to the violation of *praemunire* and the illegality of the *oath ex officio*. In both cases, the tracts contest the jurisdiction of the Court of High Commission, claiming that its procedures are contrary to the laws of the land: "May you put men to their othe against the law? Is there any law to force men to accuse themselves: No. Therefore looke what this dealing wil procure at the length. Even a plaine premunire upon your backs / for urging an oth contrary to statute: which is a piece of the forraine power banished by statute" (*Epitome* A2^v). In making these claims, Marprelate adopts the strategy of the puritan lawyers who attempted to defeat the prosecution of puritan ministers by employing a similar set of constitutional arguments. Though a debate was forestalled, a number of these arguments were formulated in a list of nineteen "motions" to be put forward in the Parliament of 1588. In Patrick Collinson's view, the list of complaints is "a portent of the future growth of legal and constitutional puritanism" (399). The Marprelate tracts would appear to portend the same.

Despite the championing of English law against the "Popes Canon laws" (*Hay* E2^r), Marprelate is aware that a positive statement describing the constitution of church and state is necessary to counter the charge of popularity. In *Hay Any Worke for Cooper*, he writes:

> The government of the church of Christ / is no popular governement / but it is Monarchicall in regarde of our head Christ / Aristocraticall in the Eldership / and Democraticall in the people. Such is the civill governement of our kingdome: Monarchicall in her Maiesties person: Aristocraticall in the higher house of Parliament / or rather at the Councell table: Democraticall in the bodie of the commons of the lower house of the parliament. (E2^v)

This claim for a mixed polity in both church and state follows the lead established by Cartwright.[51] Rather than intending the alteration of the "civill estate," as Cooper had alleged, the advocates of presbyterian discipline simply desire to bring the government of the church into line with the government of the realm. The connection, however, between these parallel structures is never established; furthermore, Christ, unlike her Majesty, is not present in person, and therefore the presbyterian system is actually a combination of the aristocratic and democratic forms. Despite these potential difficulties, Marprelate's description of the English constitution attempts to defuse the charge of popularity by assimilating the potentially outlandish discipline, what Bancroft, in *Davngerovs Positions*, calls "Geneuian Doctrine" (C3^v), to a set of specifically English institutions.

Such a strategy was not in itself sufficient, for the establishment claim that the Marprelate tracts advocated the violent overthrow of church and state was based more on Martin's insistently physical vocabulary than on any overt support of violent insurrection. Carlson draws attention to his use of "strong, aggressive and threatening verbs such as 'bangest, bepistle, bessop, buckle, bumfeg, choaked, clapperclawed, cogge, girding, leveling, lewre, mangle, stashed, thumped, thwacked'" (198). And, indeed, Bancroft would, in *Davngerovs Positions*, complain that "they vse very violent wordes" (T3^v). Perhaps the best example is Marprelate's warning to Bridges: "mark what martin tels you / you will shortly I hope have twenty fistes about your eares more then your own" (*Epistle* A2^v). In his edition of the tracts, Pierce notes that "The Bishops insisted upon interpreting this phrase perversly" (18) and cites Cooper: "So the Anabaptists, within our memory after slaunderous and opprobrious calumniations against the godly preachers and magistrates then liuing, fell to blowes and open violence. The libeller in this booke hath performed the one and threatned the other" (*Admonition* 51).

Marprelate, of course, denied making a physical threat, explaining that "I meant in deede / that many would write against him / by reason of his bomination learning / which otherwise neuer meant to take pen in hand" (*Hay* A3^r). Later in the same tract he calls Cooper, "a senseles wretch / not able to vnderstand an English phrase [who] hath giuen out upon that which he calleth the threatning of fistes" (D3^v–D4^r).[52] Though this explanation may have failed to convince his opponents, the writer of the presbyterian *A Petition Directed to her Most Excellent Maiestie*, agreed that Martin "meaneth nothing else, but that many would excercise their handes in writing against D. Bridges, which hath proued true" (F2^v).[53] Richard Harvey betrayed some sympathy for this argument when he addressed *Plaine Percivall the Peace-Maker of England* not only to Martin and "The Misbegotten Heires of His body" but also to "All Whip Iohns, and Whip Iackes: not forgetting the Caualiero Pasquill, or the Cooke Ruffian, that drest a dishe for Martins diet, Marforius and all Cutting Huffnufs, Roisters, and the residew of light fingered younkers, which make euery word a blow, and euery booke a bobbe" (A2^r). This phrase accuses the anti-Martinist writers of simultaneously misconstruing Martin's words as blows and attempting to use their own words as physical weapons; according to Harvey, they are making a category mistake and, as a result, they "fight with a mist in steed of a man" (A3^v).

A similar position is articulated by Francis Bacon in *An Advertisement Touching the Controversies of the Church of England*. Bacon's attitude is measured and moderate; though he objects to having matters of religion "handled in the style of the stage," he concedes that "bitter and earnest writing may not hastily be condemned."[54] Furthermore, he accuses the Anti-Martinists, and implicitly their patron Bancroft, of having turned the controversy into a brawl, invoking the proverb, "'the second blow maketh the fray'" (4). The ruthlessness of the government response provokes Bacon to observe: "forbidden writing is thought to be certain sparks of a truth that fly up in the faces of those that seek to choke it and tread it out" (5).

It is, nonetheless, hardly surprising to find that expressive violence is met with interpretive violence; "reciprocall inuictiues" (¶3^v), to use Dr. Bridges's phrase, are not conducive to charitable interpretation. After citing Marpelate, the judicious Hooker makes the operative principle clear: "That *things doubtful are to be construed in the better part*, is a principle not safe to be followed in matters concerning the public state of a commonweal" (48). Establishing the evil intentions of the presbyterians, Hooker writes, "ye affirm that your Pastors, Doctors, Elders, and Deacons, ought to be in this Church of England, ^{r}*whether her Majesty and our state will or no.*" The superscript *r* is keyed to a citation: "Mart. in his 3. libel. p. 28." The passage quoted in italics is actually on page 26 of *Hay Any Worke for Cooper.* In full, the sentence, addressed to the bishops, reads: "For will you say / that you ought lawfully to be here in our commonwelth whether her Maiesty and the Counsell wil or no" (E2ᵛ). In other words, Hooker attributes to Martin the very claim that Martin was attempting to attach to the bishops.

That the attempt made by the tracts to gain popular support for presbyterianism should have met with such accusations from the bishops and their supporters is not surprising; ironically, the tracts also met with rejection at the hands of the very group they were trying to defend, the puritan supporters of a presbyterian discipline.[55] In a letter of October, 1590, to Burghley, Thomas Cartwright writes: "From the first beginning unto this daie, I have continually upon any occasion testified both my mislike and sorrow for such kinde of disordered proceding."[56] Josias Nichols, in *The Plea of the Innocent* (1602), considers the appearance of Marprelate as one of "three most greeuous accidents [that] did greatlie astonish vs, & verie much darken the righteousnesse of our cause."[57] On one level, it is to be expected that known supporters of presbyterianism, faced with a massive government effort to locate the source of the pamphlets, would publicly repudiate the tracts. For this reason it is difficult to know how heartfelt such disavowals were.[58] Yet, from Marprelate's own comments we get the distinct sense that many of the puritans were sincere in their disapprobation.

The first sign of an awareness of puritan disapproval appears in the opening of the *Epitome*: "The Puritans are angry with me / I meane the puritane preachers. And why? Because I am to open. Because I jest / I jested because I dele against a worshipful jester" (A1ʳ). The initial qualification of puritans is important for although Marprelate is willing to concede that his course has been rejected by the preachers, he seems to want to leave open the possibility that he has support among lay puritans. The argument that Marprelate is only using a proper decorum is repeated on several occasions. Furthermore, Marprelate has the scriptural sanction of Proverbs 26:5: "Answer a fool according to his folly, lest he be wise in his conceit."[59] Marprelate's attitude toward those he refers to as "our precise brethren" alternates unsteadily between conciliation and condescension (*Epitome* B1ʳ).

The problem is returned to in *Hay Any Worke* where Marprelate acknowledges that "there be many that greatly dislike of my doinges" (E4ᵛ). In response he offers the following defense of his method:

I sawe the cause of Christs gouernment / and of the Bishops Antichristian dealing to be hidden. The most part of men could not be gotten to read any thing / written in the defence of the on and against the other. I bethought me therefore / of a way whereby men might be drawne to do both / perceiving the humors of men in these times (especialy of those that are in any place) to be given to mirth. I tooke that course. I might lawfully do it. I / for jesting is lawful by circumstances / even in the greatest matters. (c4^v)

Marprelate is administering, to use Sidney's expression, a "medicine of cherries." And, indeed, years later Thomas Brightman would simultaneously acknowledge the success of this strategy and voice his disapproval in a series of rhetorical questions: "How acceptable to the people were those merry conceites in wordes? How plausible almost to all men? How gladly and greedily, and with howe great pleasure were they received everywhere?"[60] Yet, Marprelate insists that he has "never profaned the word in any jest." The Lord is the "author both of mirth and gravity," and both have their appropriate uses. That this defense failed to convince the puritans of the righteousness of his method becomes clear in the subsequent tracts.[61]

At the opening of *Theses Martinianae*, Marprelate asserts: "Those whom foolishly men call Puritanes, like of the matter I have handled, but the forme they cannot brooke" (A2^r). In the epilogue written by Martin Junior, these same puritan ministers are chastised for their lack of "faithfulnes, courage and zeale" (c4^v). This criticism is recalled by Martin Senior who claims that "with more equitie thou mightest have blamed both the gentlemen and people together, with the Ministers, then the Ministers alone" (*Iust censure* c3^r). While the earlier emphasis on the ministers had left open the possibility of support among the puritan laity, Marprelate now acknowledges that "the gentlemen and the people together" have also been recalcitrant. This criticism is preliminary to Martin Senior's request: "I would have al the Puritans in the land, both lordes, knights, gentlemen, ministers, and people, to become joint suitors in one supplication to her Majestie, and the Lords of her honorable privie counsell" (c3^r).

Marprelate's relationship to "Those whom foolishly men call Puritanes," marked by both criticism and a desire to create solidarity, is further complicated by the shifting status of the label *puritan*.[62] Like *precisian*, *puritan* was initially a term of abuse. Yet, by the close of the sixteenth century, some of those to whom the label was applied, such as William Bradshaw, appropriated the term, using it to signify the godly minority within the reprobate mass.[63] Marprelate himself reveals a fundamental ambivalence toward the term; at times it is used as though it is an appropriate description, while at other times, as in the reference to "those whom foolishly men call Puritans," its use is qualified. Denigrating the godly as austere, precise, and, perhaps most of all, hypocritical is, according to Marprelate, foolish; and yet to appropriate the label in the manner of Bradshaw would be to accept that puritans are defined by their exclusivity. Rather than being the result of a headstrong unwillingness to heed the warnings of the godly sort, the tracts, by refusing to identify themselves directly with the puritans, attempt to construct a wider coalition that includes those who do not share all the views of the "precise brethren."

The attempt to appeal to a broad coalition is visible in the definition of Martinism given in the *Protestatyon*: "That to be a right Martiniste indeede, is to bee neither Browniste, Cooperist, Lambethist, Schismatike, Papist, atheist, traytor, nor yet L. byshop; but one that is at defyaunce with all men; whether he bee French, Dutch, Spanish, Catercap, pope or popeling, so far forth as he is an enimy to God and her Maiestie" (Di^r). In a culture whose public discourse was hostile to "faction," this is a bold attempt to define the Martinist as one who rejects all other factions. Martin's taxonomy mixes eponymous factions (both real and imagined), religious labels, political categories, and national identities, creating a dizzying array of conflicting loyalties and convictions. This attempt to steal the high ground insists on the foreignness of popery and concludes with Marprelate's pious assertion: "I still heartely reioyce to think that all the honestest, and best affected subiects her Maiestie hath, will one day become Martinists."

That this wish went unfulfilled ought not to detract from the seriousness of the Martinist enterprise. The tracts represent a sustained effort to mount a popular campaign in opposition to government policy, and while the specific goal of establishing a presbyterian form of worship may not have been realized, the episode reveals that the volatile combination of print technology and religious controversy had broad cultural ramifications. The Marprelate pamphlets with their complex intertwining of linguistic and bibliographic codes, the fugitive text and the physical book, adeptly exploit the resources of print in order to mount a polemical assault on the established church. And yet this polemic, leavened with abusive anecdotes and joking asides, remains committed to the syllogism and the dialectical legitimacy that it confers. Though the pamphlets may have failed to win new converts to presbyterianism, they did succeed in popularizing polemic.

In 1592, Gabriel Harvey complained of "this Martinish and Countermartinish age: wherein the Spirit of Contradiction reigneth, and everie one superaboundeth in his owne humor, even to the annihilating of any other, without rime, or reason."[64] Despite the trace of theological odium discernible in the word *annihilating*, this description of a culture of controversy driven by personal idiosyncrasy and individual competitiveness conspicuously neglects the importance of both politics and religion. While presbyterianism as a political movement after 1590 was dormant, if not defunct, anti-Catholic polemic continued to provide an officially acceptable form around which a puritan identity could coalesce. Most importantly, while the Marprelate press was silenced, the audience that Marprelate had courted did not disappear. In 1591 a tract entitled *Martine Mar-Sixtus* exploited Marprelate's fame for a standard attack on the pope. In the epistle, the writer explains his choice of title, etymologizing thus: "You shall pick his nature out of his name, the first sillable whereof implying of it selfe to *Mar*, and being headded with a *Tine*, the murdering end of a forke, it must needes be that *Mar-tine* being truely spelled and put together, signifieth such a one as galleth and pricketh men to death." However, there is a difference between the writer and "the great Martine": Martin "laid siege against his natiue soyle"; the present writer has picked "a forreine aduersary, a common enemy to play upon."[65] This suggests that the polemical energies made manifest in the Marprelate tracts did not simply dissipate when the enterprise collapsed: the threat of foreign popery became a convenient and consistent target for polemical attacks that sought a broad audience of English readers. But when internal conflict finally reemerged in the 1640s, Martin's fugitive text returned: the reprinting of *Hay Any Worke* – under the title *Reformation No Enemie* in 1641 and again, using the original title, in 1642 – indicates that at least one printer believed an audience for Marprelate still existed.[66]

CHAPTER 3

"Whole Hamlets": Q1, Q2, and the work of distinction

A reader in 1604 pausing at a bookshop might have noticed a quarto volume with a title page proclaiming: "The Tragicall Historie of Hamlet, Prince of Denmarke. By Willliam Shakespeare. Newly imprinted and enlarged to almost as much againe as it was, according to the true and perfect Coppie. At London, Printed by I.R. for N.L. and are to be sold at his shoppe vnder Saint Dunstons Church in Fleetstreet. 1604" (fig. 16). This same reader might have encountered a very similar book in the past months or even at an adjacent stall. The title page of this other book offers a slightly different account of the play: "The Tragicall Historie of Hamlet Prince of Denmarke By William Shake-speare. As it hath beene diuerse times acted by his Highnesse seruants in the Cittie of London: as also in the two Vniuersities of Cambridge and Oxford, and else-where At London printed for N.L. and Iohn Trundell. 1603" (fig. 17). Both are clearly identified as the work of Shakespeare/Shake-speare, a name that could, evidently, by the early seventeenth century be counted on to help sell a play. But despite the congruence of author and title, the title pages make clear that these are different books. The rhetoric of differentiation is part of the general cultural process of distinction that shapes and organizes the book market of early modern England.[1]

Most attempts to explain the differences between Q1 and Q2 have constructed narratives of their authorial or theatrical origin.[2] I would like to suggest, however, that the two quartos can more usefully be differentiated not in terms of their (uncertain) efficient causes but in terms of their more predictable social effects. Accordingly, each of the two quartos can be seen as a coherent text that produces a distinct readership. Q1 offers its readers a fast-paced revenge play, while Q2 offers a longer, more abstruse drama, one that dwells insistently on the problem of right action in an uncertain world. Q2 is designed to produce a readership that considers itself distinct from the readers of Q1 – they, after all, are reading a play "enlarged to almost as much againe as it was." This formulation both invokes and

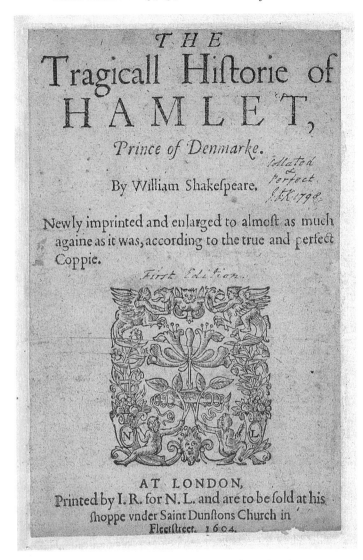

Fig. 16 William Shakespeare, *Hamlet* Q2 (1604)

repudiates the earlier quarto. Though Q1 comfortably inhabits the popular tradition of the revenge play, Q2 is pervaded by a sense of uncertainty that coalesces around the problem of the popular itself, revealing an awareness that playwrights, preachers, printers, and even monarchs themselves must now consider what it means to be "most tyrannically clapped for."[3]

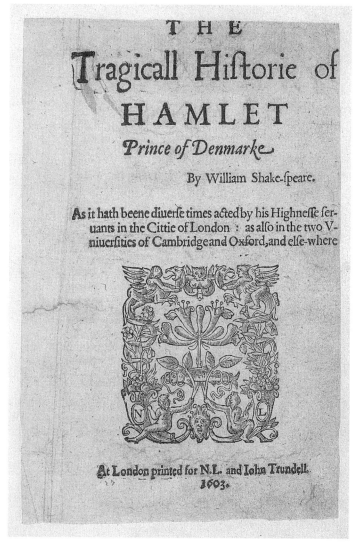

Fig. 17 William Shakespeare, *Hamlet* Q1 (1603)

The anxiety in Q2 about the tyranny of the popular is, as I shall show, not merely a reflexive elitism but a specific response to the problem of religious controversy. The fact of religious debate is, of course, incontrovertible; indeed, "An Homelie agaynst Contencion and Braulynge" acknowledges its ubiquity, condemning: "these woordes of contencion, which be now almoste in every man's mouth: he is a Pharisei, he is a gospeler, he is of the new sorte, he is of the olde faythe, he is a new broched brother, he is a good catholique father, he is a papist, he is an heretique."[4] But this and other official admonitions did not silence the pulpits or the press, both of which rang constantly with discordant controversy. Though both versions of *Hamlet* are animated by issues of religious debates, only Q2 is absorbed with the issue of controversy itself and in doing so it reveals a consistent hostility toward both dogmatism and polemic. Q1, in contrast, still operates within polemical categories. These differences are not only registered in the two competing texts of *Hamlet* but are also evident in the appearance (both lineaments and advent) of the two playbooks.

Unlike the title page of Q2 – which effaces the play's theatrical origin and sells the book on the basis of authorship, accuracy, and length – the title page of Q1 makes a clear reference to the play's origin on the stage, offering a document of a popular entertainment "As it hath beene diuerse times acted." Though the site of the stage was not itself an unproblematic source of prestige, the claim that this play was performed by "his Highnesse seruants" does confer cultural authority on the text, as does the naming of the metropolis, London, and the two universities, Cambridge and Oxford. The invocation of the new monarch, James I, also marks the play as fresh and contemporary since the Lord Chamberlain's Men did not become "his Highnesse seruants" until May 19 of 1603.

Both the reference to the stage and the invocation of the newly renamed acting company serve to advertise the currency of the play being offered to the reader. But there is further information available on the title page. The title pages of both Q1 and Q2 are dominated by the device of Nicholas Ling, a publisher. Ling was one of a new breed of entrepreneurial publishers; unlike earlier members of the Stationers' Company who had combined the role of publisher and printer, such as John Day, Ling seems to have focused on procuring copy for publication, while relegating the work of printing to others.[5] However, the Q1 title page asserts that the book has two publishers: "N.L. and Iohn Trundell." Harold Jenkins, the editor of the formidable and exemplary Arden edition, asserts that Trundle was "very much a junior partner" in the collaboration with Ling and then goes on to remark that this has led many to the speculation that it was Trundle who "secured the unauthorized copy."[6] This account conveniently (though in the absence of any facts) identifies Trundle as the source of the "bad quarto" and tends to exculpate Ling who was later involved in the production of Q2, a text that Jenkins designates "a good quarto, apparently based on Shakespeare's autograph and believed to be for the most part printed from it" (18).

Ling does not, however, entirely escape the imputation of nefarious practices – his very role in Q2 is attributed to his having gained *de facto* rights to
the play by virtue of having published it first. But Ling emerges at worst as a
naive, if opportunistic, purveyor of stolen and damaged goods. In contrast,
James Roberts, the printer of Q2, appears as a white knight nobly championing the authentic, Shakespearean *Hamlet*. According to this scenario,
Roberts, who registered the play and supposedly possessed an authoritative
manuscript, recognizes Ling's technical right to the title and is thus
compelled to collaborate with him in order to see the genuine *Hamlet*
published. Consequently, Roberts was given the job of printing Q2 by Ling
who retained both the copy and the role of publisher.[7]

    Dutiful and law-abiding, James Roberts is clearly the hero of this
particular narrative – his goodness produces the "good" quarto for the
world – and yet his status as beneficent protagonist is far from obvious.
Roberts's place in this story is in large part the result of priority, yet this
priority is entirely an effect of the extant archive. Harold Jenkins tellingly
writes, "The history of the play's publication begins with its entry on the
Stationers' Register on 26 July 1602" (13). This seemingly straightforward
claim introduces two different difficulties. First, the status of "history" is
not immediately clear; apparently it does not refer to history as such
because if it did, it would at least need to infer or explain Roberts's prior
procurement of a manuscript of the play before the claim to ownership
made in the register.[8] If, however, "history" refers to a written narrative
about the past, then perhaps this document, as the earliest extant record
concerning the publication of the play and the first known moment in that
story, deserves its place of primacy. Second, "publication," as the work of
Harold Love has convincingly demonstrated, is itself a slippery concept
that has been handled reductively by those who would limit its meaning to
print production for the market. As Love observes, the word invariably
designates "a movement from a private realm of creativity to a public realm
of consumption."[9] In the case of *Hamlet* that transit was unusually complicated, and we know at once too much and too little about it. I raise these
points not to denigrate Jenkins, whose *Hamlet* is a superb work of scholarship, but to emphasize the way in which editorial practice is frequently
supported by a recourse to conjectural histories about textual origins. Of
course, editors need to choose between texts, and an informed choice will
always consider the history of the relevant documentary witnesses. Such
procedures, however, can lead to an unfortunate emphasis on what we do
not know: the gaps in the historical record that must be filled by a plausible
narrative.

The entry in the Stationers' Register certainly indicates that the *Hamlet* associated with Shakespeare and his company was being staged prior to the accession of James: "Entred for his Copie . . . A booke called the Revenge of Hamlett Prince [of] Denmarke as yt was latelie Acted by the Lord Chamberleyne his servantes."[10] The seductiveness of the Register, in all its documentary solidity, has undoubtedly contributed to the various narratives that unfailingly cast Roberts as hero. Though the precise significance of this entry is impossible to ascertain, it, nonetheless, provides useful information. Perhaps most interesting is the title of the play: "the Revenge of Hamlett Prince [of] Denmarke." This apparently minor distinction suggests that in its earliest instantiation the work was identified as a revenge play, yet both Q1 and Q2 announce "The Tragicall Historie of Hamlet, Prince of Denmarke." However, this generic indeterminacy is further compounded by the contradictory running title: "The Tragedy of Hamlet Prince of Denmarke." It is this title, with its generic clarity and literary pedigree, that is recorded for posterity in the First Folio.[11] These shifting titles suggest a gradual transformation from revenge play – a popular form that enjoyed enormous success in the playhouse – to classical tragedy, a metamorphosis that obscures the play's origin in a theatrical economy and avoids the ethically problematic term, revenge.

The putative villain responsible for Q1, John Trundle, deserves greater consideration than he has been given in the standard narratives of the text, which are inevitably informed by the moral language of the "bad" quarto.[12] What is known of him hardly suggests he is dishonest or unscrupulous. In fact, Gerald D. Johnson concludes undramatically that Trundle was "a relatively law-abiding member" of the Stationers' Company.[13] However, Johnson also points out that Trundle achieved a certain notoriety in the period as a publisher of topical and ephemeral material that addressed itself to the low end of the print market. His name provoked puns from contemporaries such as John Taylor, who prided himself on his ability to discover value in even the lowest material: "If it were but the treatise of *Tom Thumb* / Or *Scoggins Jests*, or any simple play, / Or monstrous news came Trundling in my way."[14] Taylor's inventory of popular forms suggests that at least the "simple play" was seen as comparable to romance, jest book, and broadsheet. The tone of condescension audible in these invocations infects even Johnson's account: "Trundle devoted most of his twenty-three years in the trade to the publication of pamphlet literature meant to catch the eye of the lower-class reading public."[15] For Johnson, Trundle's willingness "to exploit the public's taste for news of the current sensation" betrays a weakness for vulgar spectacle. In light of Trundle's main stock-in-trade, the handful of plays he published appear to present us with a problem of categorization. Yet this problem disappears if one is willing to concede that the quartos of plays such *Hamlet* or Dekker's *The Whore of Babylon* – a work jointly registered by Trundle and Nathaniel Butter, though printed for Butter – were themselves "news of the current sensation" and not overtly "literary" artifacts.

Trundle also traded in controversial pamphlets. He published two well-known interventions in the debate provoked by Swetnam's *Arraignment of Lewd, Idle, Froward and Unconstant Women: Hic Mulier: Or, The Man-Woman* and *Haec-Vir: Or, The Womanish-Man* (1615). The speed with which these latter two pamphlets appeared suggests, as Johnson points out, the possibility of an organized publication strategy designed to create and profit from public interest. This does indicate that Trundle was quick to respond to perceived demand; however, it is too simple to conclude that he merely exploited an existing and stable taste. Trundle's publications undoubtedly helped to shape the very taste they catered to. "A cultural product," as Pierre Bourdieu insists, "is a constituted taste":

a taste which has been raised from the vague semi-existence of half-formulated or unformulated experience, implicit or even unconscious desire, to the full reality of the finished product, by a process of objectification which, in present circumstances, is almost always the work of professionals.[16]

Admittedly, Bourdieu is, in this case, analyzing the contemporary field of cultural production; however, the claim made for contemporary cultural goods can be extended to the early modern book trade: "the relation between supply and demand takes a particular form: the supply always exerts an effect of symbolic imposition." Certainly print production in the sixteenth century was "almost always the work of professionals." This process, however, of "symbolic imposition" must not be interpreted as a claim for the passivity of consumption. To claim that cultural producers alone are taste-makers would be as mistaken as the assertion that cultural producers slavishly cater to a preexisting taste. It is the dynamic relationship between cultural producers and consumers that constitutes demand; furthermore, demand is not unitary but is itself split and shaped by a process of distinction that sorts both publishers and readers. Moreover, such distinctions were fine and multiple; the familiar binary split between popular and elite culture is not an adequate model for late sixteenth-century England.[17]

Close attention to the actual producers of the printed book, the publishers and printers, makes it possible to begin to analyze the processes of affiliation and differentiation that shaped the burgeoning print market, and in the process the texts of *Hamlet*. Gerald Johnson, whose work has been exemplary in this regard, agrees with Jenkins concerning the division of labor in Q1, but his conclusion is based on a study of the actual publishing practices of both Trundle and Ling, rather than upon inferences deriving from the putative "badness" of the first quarto, a "badness" that quickly attaches to Trundle himself. Trundle is notable for the regularity with which he collaborated with other stationers; this tendency leads Johnson to conclude that Trundle specialized in the acquisition of copy, and that his partners often supplied the capital to cover the cost of printing. Nicholas Ling, in contrast, appears to have frequently underwritten the printing of copy initially procured by others. Often Ling is recorded as entering a copy jointly which later becomes his sole property; he also appears to have acquired a number of copyrights that had earlier been claimed by other stationers.[18] The list of sixteen copyrights belonging to Ling and assigned to John Smethwick on November 19, 1607, includes a number of popular works: *Love's Labour's Lost*, *Hamlet*, and *Romeo and Juliet* are joined by Drayton's poems, three works by Robert Greene, Lodge's *Euphues' Golden Legacy*, Nashe's *Pierce Penilesse*, and Anthony Munday's *English Roman Life*. Such works suggest a commitment to the developing category of English "literature," a commitment that puts some cultural distance between Ling and Trundle.

The initial collaboration between Ling and Trundle indicates, however, that this distance is variable. Looking at the set of copies held or handled by each publisher, it is clear that they specialized in different sorts of material. Yet there are points of contact, and the printed drama is one of them. It has long been a critical commonplace that "plays were not regarded as 'literature.'"[19] According to this view, it was Ben Jonson who first claimed literary status for his plays by including them in his collected works of 1616. The ridicule that greeted this act of self-promotion is then cited to confirm the view that Jonson's contemporaries did not share his exalted vision of drama. However, the status of drama was far more complex; Jonson's decision to include his plays would not have even been thinkable if there had not been an available tradition that identified drama not with the ephemeral world of ballads and broadsheets, but with the enduring realm of the classical genres. Any attempt to understand the status of printed drama must consider the whole range of dramatic genres – this means including academic and "closet" drama as well as moral interludes "offered for acting."[20] Indeed one might even make an argument for attending here to the ubiquity of printed dialogues and even catechisms – two forms that bear a striking typographic resemblance to plays. What scholars and editors usually mean by drama, however, is the play performed by professional actors and now embodied in print. If the focus is shifted from recovering the admittedly extraordinary cultural achievement of the Tudor–Stuart stage to the emerging print culture of early modern England, printed drama no longer appears derivative and secondary but instead is revealed to have been a protean form, aimed at a wide range of readers and put to a variety of uses, that helped to shape the terms and categories designating difference and distinction in the literary world of early modern England.

Peter Blayney has recently examined the printing of drama in an article that challenges the received wisdom that considers play texts to have been highly coveted commodities that were worth a publisher's strenuous efforts to gain access to a script. He argues that, in reality, play quartos did not sell particularly well and that, therefore, "publishing plays would not usually have been seen as a short cut to wealth."[21] Any argument for the commercial popularity of the genre, as Blayney points out, must take account not only of the number of new plays printed but also of the (in)frequency of reprints. According to his figures, of the plays first published between 1583 and 1602 the majority were never reprinted, appearing only in a single edition. *Hamlet*, which was published seven times between 1603 and 1637 if one includes the two Folio printings, fared better than all but a handful of the plays printed in the seventeenth century. Blayney's argument about the marginality of drama in the print shop suggests that a narrow focus on the printing of professional drama is less fruitful than an investigation that would locate books such as *Hamlet* within the broader set of categories that organized the market for printed books.[22]

The elusive and fluid position of drama within the field of print is inextricably bound up with the problematic notion of popularity – a notion that for some tainted the very medium of print itself.[23] The printed play was articulated on a continuum from the austerely classical to the broadly demotic. This is most evident in the stance taken, in the case of drama that was performed, toward the book's theatrical origin. This could be a point of pride, as in Q1 *Hamlet*, suggesting an attempt to make audience and readership continuous. Alternatively, the theatre could be a potent source of embarrassment to be ignored, as in Q2 *Hamlet*, or indeed repudiated, as in Q1 *Knight of the Burning Pestle*. The latter example is an extraordinary attempt to convert a dramatic failure into a print success. Walter Burre, the publisher, alludes, in his dedication, to the play's dramatic failure: "exposed to the wide world, who for want of judgement, or not understanding the privy mark of irony about it (which showed it was no offspring of any vulgar brain) utterly rejected it."[24] This very failure to excite an audience becomes a mark of distinction that guarantees the play's status as an elite book and constructs its ideal reader as a solitary and judicious gentleman, just as Hamlet takes the disdain of the "million" to be a ratification of his own singularly uncommon aesthetic judgment.[25]

The question of popular taste resonates throughout *Hamlet*, condensing especially in the scenes with the players.[26] The players are traveling because, as Gilderstone says in QI, "noueltie carries it away, / For the principall publike audience that / Came to them, are turned to priuate playes, / And to the humour of children" (E3[r]). The same concern with, even contempt for, popular taste is evident when Hamlet requests a speech:

> I heard thee speake a speech once,
> But it was neuer acted: or if it were,
> Neuer aboue twice, for as I remember,
> It pleased not the vulgar, it was cauiary
> To the million:
>
> (E3[v])

Though the thrust of this statement is clear enough, there remains something puzzling about its logic. Hamlet's uncertainty whether the play was ever "acted" presents a problem because only if it were acted could it have been subject to the scorn of the vulgar. The general scorn is what validates and distinguishes the taste of Hamlet and those few "that receiued it in like kinde." Staging such elitism runs the risk of alienating an audience, but for the solitary reader (or small group of reader and listeners) it presents not a threat but a possible enticement.

This same elitism is also evident in Hamlet's famous advice to the players in Q2 where he rejects what he considers to be a hyperbolic style of acting:

o it offends mee to the soule, to heare a robustious perwig-pated fellowe tere a passion to totters, to very rags, to spleet the eares of the groundlings, who for the most part are capable of nothing but inexplicable dumbe showes, and noyse (G3[v]–G4[r])

This advice to the players is more than simple condescension (though it is that too). Hamlet makes a plea for the sovereignty of the aesthetic judgment of the judicious individual against all forms of popularity: "Now this ouer-done, or come tardie off, though it make the vnskilfull laugh, cannot but make the iudicious greeue, the censure of which one, must in your allowance ore-weigh a whole Theater of others" (G4[r]). Though QI includes the advice to the players, there are several differences.

Instead of "groundlings," Hamlet indicts "the ignoraut." Significantly, the term of disapprobation is changed from a physical location in social space to a mental condition. (Anyone can deny ignorance; it is harder to repudiate the ground one stands upon.) While Q1 includes the chastising of clowns who take liberties with their lines in order to "set on some / Quantitie of barren spectators" (F2^r), the invocation of the single, judicious spectator whose opinion outweighs a "whole Theater of others" is lacking. This is just one moment in which Q2 seems insistently to address itself to a fit audience, though few.

The argument that Q1 is in some sense a more "popular" or populist version of the play has been made by Janice Lull. Putting the long-standing theory that Q1 is a memorial reconstruction to good use, Lull argues that as such the first quarto provides evidence of the contemporary reception of *Hamlet*: "If Q1 *Hamlet* displays neither a divided mind nor a particularly Protestant soul, it may be because the Q1 reporters were not familiar with or interested in the concerns of a relatively bookish elite."[27] The corollary of this argument is taken up by Giorgio Melchiori, who champions Q2 as "a text for the study, not for the stage, reproducing Shakespeare's original intention of giving Tragedy the full status of a new literary genre."[28]

This claim that Q2 is a text for the study needs to be separated from Melchiori's less supportable assertion that would bind it to Shakespeare's "original intention." Though Lukas Erne has recently made a vigorous case for seeing Shakespeare as a self-consciously literary author of drama that was not exclusively targeted at a theatrical audience, the conclusive evidence that would support such a claim (should one care to make it) is lacking.[29] Melchiori does, however, tell a refreshingly iconoclastic story in which Q2 is based on Shakespeare's foul papers of the first version of the play, a version "intended more for the wiser sort of readers than for the audience of the public theaters" (200). What's more, he attractively imagines this version circulating early among a coterie, "justifying Harvey's remark in or around 1601." Although it is impossible to know when it was written, Gabriel Harvey's comment has long featured in arguments about the dating of Shakespeare's *Hamlet*, and Melchiori at least attempts to make sense of what was said as well as when it was said. This marginal note, no longer extant, was transcribed from Harvey's copy of Speght's Chaucer, printed in 1598. In an extended meditation on English poetry, Harvey remarked: "The younger sort take much delight in Shakespeares Venus, & Adonis, but his Lucrece, & his tragedy of Hamlet, Prince of Denmarke, have it in them, to please the wiser sort."[30] Unfortunately, for Melchiori's case, it is impossible to know which, if either, of the two quartos Harvey was familiar with, or even when, after 1598, he wrote in the book.

However, Harvey's note does suggest that very early on an appreciation of *Hamlet* was being recognized as a sign of distinguished taste. Melchiori urges, in support of his view of Q2, the "sheer length of the text, its rich allusiveness, and, above all, the revolutionary conception of the function of tragedy."[31] The last two of these – even if one could establish that the text's allusiveness is anomalous and that its vision of tragedy is unprecedented – are hardly convincing evidence that Q2 was never intended for the stage. As for the first point, the performance time of a given text is notoriously difficult to ascertain, as is the endurance of a sixteenth-century audience. In any case, as Stephen Orgel has argued, play texts must have been routinely cut for performance.[32] Though Q2's length cannot, therefore, be construed as evidence that it was not written for the stage, it nonetheless remains, in a very literal sense, remarkable. Indeed, the title page explicitly remarks upon it, advertising the fact that the "Tragicall Historie" has here been "enlarged to almost as much againe as it was."

The size of Q2 has long been a source of temptation for editors. Beginning with Nicholas Rowe in 1709, editors have frequently used Q2 to supplement the Folio text. Rowe was selective in taking Q2 readings, but with Theobald's edition of 1733 almost all the Q2 only readings were incorporated into a text based on F.[33] When Dover Wilson made the argument that Q2 is the more "authoritative" text, this situation was reversed: Q2 became the copy text and was supplemented by readings from F.[34] For Wilson, degrees of authority are determined by proximity to the author, and, according to his analysis, Q2 shows evidence of having been set from Shakespeare's autograph (the infamous "foul papers"), while F has clearly been shaped by playhouse practice.

Nevertheless, even if uncontaminated by the theatre, Q2 cannot, unfortunately, give us direct access to what Shakespeare actually wrote: at the very least there remains the ever-present threat of printing-house error. For this reason, according to Wilson's editorial principles, a Q2 reading is not automatically preferable to an F reading. For example, a remark made by Claudius to Gertrude is longer in Q2 than in F, but the presence in Q2 of a half-line is seen to indicate corruption:

> Come *Gertrard*, wee'le call vp our wisest friends,
> And let them know both what we meane to doe
> And whats vntimely doone,
> Whose whisper ore the worlds dyameter,

As leuell as the Cannon to his blanck,
Transports his poysned shot, may misse our Name,
And hit the woundlesse ayre, o come away,
My soule is full of discord and dismay.

(Q2, KI^v)

Come *Gertrude*, wee'l call vp our wisest friends,
To let them know both what we meane to do,
And what's vntimely done. Oh come away.
My soule is full of discord and dismay.

(F, 2P2^v)

Wilson conjectures plausibly that "the lines in question were marked for omission in the original manuscript not by transverse lines of deletion but by some kind of brackets or rectangular enclosure, an arm of which accidentally appeared to delete the first half-line of the passage, so that the Q2 compositor set up all but that half-line" (1, 30).

In this case, the very plenitude of Q2 becomes the basis on which the text is judged nonauthorial, a plenitude that for Philip Edwards becomes a principal element in his account of the text: "Shakespeare's 'foul-papers,' which were used by Roberts in setting up the 1604/5 quarto, contained a certain amount of material which Shakespeare had decided he didn't want. Whatever cancellation marks he used were not observed or not understood by Roberts' compositors."[35] Edwards assumes that early modern printers and compositors, like modern editors, aim to reproduce the author's final intention, and that any failure in this regard is either an oversight or a lack of comprehension. However, even granting the existence of hypothesized deletion marks, there is another possibility: the compositors, perhaps under instruction, may have deliberately ignored them. In other words, the length of Q2 might be strategic rather than accidental. Intentions other than the author's always come into play in the printing house. Certainly in this case, Nicholas Ling, the publisher of Q2, saw the play's length – however produced – less as a problem than as a virtue.

Q2 aims to produce a distinction not merely between itself and Q1, but between different sorts of readers by offering itself as a more "literary" book and helping to constitute the taste it would appeal to. In this regard, the title page's silence regarding the stage is significant; just as modern editors in their efforts to restore and safeguard Shakespeare's words have expressed an anxiety about F "having been deformed and contaminated by playhouse influences," Q2 presents itself as a message directly from Shakespeare to the discerning reader, unmediated by the public theatre, marking itself and its readers as different from Q1 with its popular appeal.[36] Q1, in contrast, is the book of the play, whose various venues of performance advertised on the title page are indicative of its popularity. An exploration of this process of distinction between the two quartos must, however, in addition to the circumstances of their printing, consider the content of the two books.

This is not, however, to say that the two represent discrete, integral texts. Though Q1 and Q2 each reveal an internal coherence, they are not entirely independent versions, yet neither are they merely accidental variants of some essential *Hamlet*. Recent revisionist efforts to restore the "integrity" of textual versions that have suffered conflation at the hands of eclectic editors would invest each instantiation of a text with its own inviolable identity.[37] As valuable and bracing as these arguments have been, they appear, at times, to merely celebrate difference by venerating the material book in all its splendid idiosyncrasy. Alternatively, the effort to see through these versions in order to discern the ideal text (or texts) intended by the author often leads to a neglect of the specificities of the various printings, unhinging the text from the materializations in which it is realized.[38] If, however, one's object is a cultural history rather than an edited text, then the complex affiliations between the several versions of *Hamlet* are valuable evidence of social energies (and stresses) and are best captured by an attention to the individual printings considered both as commodities within a commercial environment and as documents within a discursive field.

Focus on the multiple texts of *Hamlet* has, however, more often led to the privileging of one (usually Q2) as the best representative of Shakespeare's intentions (the others in various ways defective) or, more genially, to something like Philip Edwards's contention that "the variations in the text of *Hamlet* are . . . representations of different stages in the play's development," in which case "our task becomes to choose the moment at which we would try to arrest the movement of the play" (8). Shakespeare's genius is even here the principle that connects all three texts and provides an axiology that privileges, to use the terminology of Edwards, "second thoughts" over "false starts" (19, 30). However, if attention is shifted from the author to the broader field of cultural production, the problem is refocused so that the inevitable collaborations of composition, of theatrical performance, and of print become visible and valuable.

Recent work has done much to locate play publication within the larger field of print culture.[39] However, the appearance of such work has been slowed not only by the New Bibliography's notorious ambivalence toward drama, but also by the work of revisionist textual scholars who, in an effort to reverse the anti-theatricalist bias of their predecessors, have insisted on seeing the printed play as a script for performance or at very least a document containing, in Steven Urkowitz's phrase, a "legacy of theatrical treasure."[40] While there is much to be gained from both approaches, there is also a risk that the specific attributes of the printed play as a book will be lost. The significance of *Hamlet*'s print history may be better understood not by placing it alongside other printed *plays*, but by placing it within another category of printed books in which it fits, a category determined, however, not by genre but by subject. *Hamlet* may productively be thought of as part of the vast flow of books treating religion that poured off the press in early modern England. Indeed, A. C. Bradley, generally hostile to an overtly religious reading of Shakespeare, long ago noted that *Hamlet* is set apart from Shakespeare's other tragedies by its "freer use of popular religious ideas," and speculated that "this is probably one of the causes of the special popularity of this play."[41]

Bradley, as is so often the case, is here remarkably astute, but it is more accurate to speak of the inescapable presence in *Hamlet* of controversial rather than "popular" religious ideas, for each of the religious issues invoked by *Hamlet* – ghosts, purgatory, suicide, predestination, marriage, burial rites – was subject to continuous debate and struggle. These seemingly disparate topics all relate to the ongoing attempt, visible in the several editions and abridgements of *Actes and Monuments* as well as the Marprelate pamphlets, to define the extent of the Christian community in early modern England. Bradley's reference, while it usefully focuses attention upon "religious ideas," gives the misleading impression that "popular" religion was a stable entity and that the "people" saw in *Hamlet* a reflection of their collective beliefs. In fact, the play (like the English nation itself) contains a range of conflicting views and positions, yet there is (in both) a visible discomfort over the idea that "sweet religion" is in danger of becoming "A rapsedy of words" (Q2, 12^v). The two quartos, however, tend to handle this controversial material very differently. While Q1 is conformable to what has been described as a Calvinist consensus, Q2 places greater emphasis on the language of skepticism and is, correspondingly, careful to avoid dogmatism. Q1 is not doctrinaire and does not qualify as a programmatic statement of Calvinist theology; nonetheless, the text, unlike Q2, is susceptible to a Calvinist interpretation.[42]

The interval between the entry in the Stationers' Register of 1602 and the printing of the second quarto in 1604 saw the death of Queen Elizabeth and the peaceful succession of her chosen heir, James VI of Scotland, and numerous critics have seen the play as being preeminently preoccupied with the urgent questions of succession and rebellion.[43] However, it is important to realize that this transition simultaneously held forth the threat and promise of change to the religious establishment of the realm. Indeed, the succession is not a purely political event, and once its religious dimension is acknowledged it becomes easier to understand *Hamlet*'s amalgam of the political and the theological. The last two successions had demanded major changes in the religious establishment – the very alterations dramatized and popularized by *Actes and Monuments* – creating the expectation that the new monarch might again institute changes in the church. Indeed, James would attempt to institutionalize such changes, declaring at the Hampton Court conference that the assembly was "no nouell deuise, but according to the example of all Christian Princes, who, in the commencement of their raign, vsvally take the first course for the establishing of the church."[44] James went on to assert that this was true "particularly, in this land, King *Henry* the eight, toward the end of his raigne; after him King *Edward* the 6. who altered more, after him *Queene Marie*, who reuersed all; and the last Queene of famous memory ... who setled it as it now standeth" (B2[r]–B2[v]). Not surprisingly, the prospect of religious change motivated a flurry of controversial religious works.

The king's own proclamations, printed by Christopher Barker and appearing contemporaneously with Q1 and Q2 *Hamlet*, were part of this flood of print. A proclamation of February 22, 1603 [i.e. 1604], commands Seminary priests and Jesuits, who have entertained "a vaine confidence of some Innouation in matters of Religion to be done by Us," to quit the realm by March 19. Initially, the cause of the godly seemed to fare better; a proclamation of October 24, 1603, had announced: "we are perswaded that both the constitution and doctrine" of the English church "is agreeable to Gods word, and neere to the condition of the Primitiue Church." Nonetheless, "experience doeth shewe dayly, that the Church militant is neuer so well constituted in any forme of Policie, but that the imperfections of men who haue the excercise thereof, doe with time, though unsensibly, bring in some corruptions." Therefore, James had proposed a "serious examination of the state of this Church, to redeeme it from such scandals, as both by the one side and the other were layd upon it." Unfortunately, the King's "godly purpose" has been "misconstrued." The catalogue of disruptions is extensive: "Some vsing publique Inuectiues against the state Ecclesiastical here established, some contemning their Authoritie and the Processes of their Courts, some gathering subscriptions of multitudes of vulgar persons to Supplications to be exhibited to vs to craue that Reformation, which if there be cause to make, is more in our heart then in theirs."[45] The dismay James expresses at the proliferation of "publique Inuectiues" and the presumption of the "multitudes of vulgar persons" who would pretend to a knowledge of theology is congruent with the stance of Q2 *Hamlet*, which consistently combines elite skepticism with a hostility toward the vulgar.

Though the Hampton Court conference has come to be seen as a decisive victory for the forces of orthodoxy, in the period leading up to and immediately after the conference the outcome was by no means certain or clear.[46] A royal proclamation of July 16, 1604, attempts to clarify the outcome of the conference, asserting that "no well grounded matter appeared to Us or our sayd Councell, why the State of the Church here by Law established, should in any material point be altered." Yet, to the king's dismay, at the recent Parliament the same questions regarding the Book of Common Prayer and the government of the church were renewed. The proclamation urges all English subjects to conform them-selves to the church and ignore those ministers who "vnder pretended Zeale of Reformation, are the chiefe Authors of Diuisions and Sects among our people." Throughout, James expresses disappointment over the obstinacy of the nonconforming clergy and asserts his resolve to see a uniformity "wrought by Clemencie, and by weight of Reason, and not by Rigour of Law."[47]

The Hampton Court conference was not a scholastic exercise of interest only to divines. Its proceedings aroused such intense and sustained interest that an account of the meeting, Dr. Barlow's *The Summe and Substance of the Conference*, was printed twice in 1604, and again in 1605, 1612, 1625, and 1638. This was, however, clearly an official history designed to demonstrate that the "most learned and iudicious" James was resolutely opposed to the claims of the puritans.[48] According to Barlow, Doctor Rainolds, the "fore-man" of the reformers, organized their objections under four headings: doctrine, sufficiency of ministers, church government, and the Book of Common Prayer. The first question raised under the first head was the church's still ambiguous position on the question of predestination. Reynolds desired that the 16th Article of Religion with its assertion that "*After we have received the Holy Ghost, we may depart from grace*" might be amended with the addition of the phrase "*yet neither totally nor finally*"; furthermore, he requested that the Lambeth Articles, originally drafted in 1596 under Archbishop Whitgift in order to clarify the doctrine of pre-destination but never officially adopted, be "inserted into that book of Articles" (D4^v). Bancroft, the Bishop of London, objected that "very many in these daies, neglecting holinesse of life, presumed too much of persisting of Grace, laying all their Religion upon Predestination, *If I shall be saved, I shall be saved"* (E3ʳ). Such a "desperate doctrine" is, according to Bancroft, a perversion of the "true doctrine of predestination" (E3ʳ).

Bancroft articulated this distinction by contrasting ratiocination *ascendendo* and *descendendo*. The former is the proper reasoning to apply to the doctrine of predestination: *"I live in obedience to God, in love with my neighbour, I follow my vocation, & c., therefore I trust that God hath elected me, and predestinated me to salvation:* not thus, which is the vsuall course of argument. *God hath Predestinated and chosen mee to life, therefore, though I sin, neuer so grieuously, yet I shall not be damned, for whome he once loueth, he loueth to the ende."* The target of Bancroft's criticism is clearly the militancy of the self-proclaimed saints, who, he implies, eschew the social virtue of neighborliness and neglect to practice their vocations. The alternative danger, that a conviction of reprobation would lead to despair, was a staple of Catholic polemic, and yet Burghley voiced just such a concern in response to the Lambeth Articles. According to Dr. Humphrey Tyndall of Queens' College, Cambridge, Burleigh "seemed to dislike of the propositions concerning predestination . . . drawing by a similitude a reason from an earthly prince, inferring thereby they charged God of cruelty and might cause men to be desperate in their wickedness."⁴⁹ Both responses reveal a preoccupation with the social and political consequences of predestination as opposed to its scriptural warrant. Queen Elizabeth shared the sentiment and, holding predestination to be "a matter tender and dangerous to weak ignorant minds," forbade consideration of the doctrine. James, in contrast, was willing to have it discussed but wished that "it might bee verie tenderly handled, and with great discretion, least on the one side, Gods omnipotency might be called in question, by impeaching the doctrine of his eternall predestination, or on the other a desperate presumption might be arreared, by inferring the necessary certaintie of standing and persisting in grace" (E3ᵛ). Bancroft and James agree, in Barlow's account, in their hostility toward assurance, an attitude also visible in Q2 *Hamlet*.

Q2 *Hamlet* does not, however, seem to share the king's faith in the "weight of reason," suggesting, instead, that god-like reason is all too fallible. The notion that *Hamlet* promulgates a refined skepticism in the manner of Montaigne has relied most particularly on the profound uncertainty registered in Hamlet's "To be, or not to be" soliloquy, a passage that not only exists in two distinct versions, but also appears in two different places.⁵⁰ In Q1 this speech appears before the soliloquy in which Hamlet accuses himself of being a "dunghill idiote slaue" and formulates his plan to "catch the conscience of the King" (E4ᵛ–F1ʳ). Such a movement from

irresolution to determination presents a common psychological dynamic
in the form and allows for a straighforward development of the narrative.
However, in Q2, "O what a rogue and peasant slaue am I" precedes "To be,
or not to be," disrupting the smooth developmental logic of Q1 and
providing evidence of procrastination for later critics. The issue of delay
aside, Q2's structure centers on Hamlet's character, while Q1 is driven by
plot. Q1 is hardly *Hamlet* without the prince, but its efficient narrative
and comparative inattention to Hamlet's pyschic turbulence depict a
world less anxious about human agency.

Margreta De Grazia has drawn attention to a remark made in Q1 by
Claudius as Hamlet enters: "see where he comes poring vppon a booke."[51]
When Hamlet then exclaims, "To be, or not to be, I there's the point," he
may in fact be reading from his book. The deictic *there* may indicate that
Hamlet is pointing to a passage in the text. Obviously such a possibility
raises profound questions about the status of the soliloquy and its representation of consciousness; at the same time, the speech itself unfolds in
highly conventional terms:

> To Die, to sleepe, is that all? I all:
> No, to sleepe, to dreame, I mary there it goes,
> For in that dreame of death, when wee awake,
> And borne before an euerlasting Iudge,
> From whence no passenger euer retur'nd,
> The vndiscouered country, at whose sight
> The happy smile, and the accursed damn'd.
> But for this, the ioyfull hope of this,
> Whol'd beare the scornes and flattery of the world,
> Scorned by the right rich, the rich curssed of the poore?
>
> (D4^v)

This opening clearly operates within the conventional categories of
Christian eschatology and suggests that we endure in the expectation of
final justice. The sleep or dream of death here indicates the period between
earthly death and the resurrection that precedes judgment. The decree of
the "euerlasting Iudge" irrevocably separates the "happy" from the
"accursed." Most significantly, this doctrine is converted into a "ioyfull
hope" – hope of one's own salvation and perhaps the expectation that one's
enemies will be damned. The speech continues to follow the same logic,
asking "who would this indure, / But for a hope of something after death?"
(E1^r). It is this eschatological hope that is identified as that which "pusles
the braine, and doth confound the sence." Hamlet's conclusion, "O this
conscience makes cowardes of vs all" (E1^r), locates conscience within an

explicitly Christian frame; *this* conscience is consumed by the four final things: death, judgment, heaven, and hell.

The version that appears in Q2 has a different focus. There is no mention of a book; as a result, the process of internalization that De Grazia finds absent in Q1 becomes visible. The speech opens with an invocation of nobility and continues with a series of martial images:

> To be, or not to be, that is the question,
> Whether tis nobler in the minde to suffer
> The slings and arrowes of outragious fortune,
> Or to take Armes against a sea of troubles . . .
>
> (G2^r)

Janice Lull has argued that this speech shows Hamlet brooding on the conflict between an "ancient warrior ethic" and the "newer Protestant morality."[52] However, it is difficult to see what about the speech is explicitly Protestant; indeed, the Q2 version is remarkably reticent regarding questions of the afterlife. "The dread of something after death" does not invoke precisely the same eschatology that "a hope of something after death" does. In Q2 this "something" is entirely undefined, perhaps unthinkable; indeed, it expands to include all that is unknown, all that would puzzle the will by presenting insuperable epistemological problems. Lull's dichotomy must, then, be supplemented by another discourse, a newly revived Pyrrhonism.[53] Classical skepticism held a ready appeal for many caught up in the turbulence of religious wars; combining a radical epistemology with a conservative cultural and social politics, it sought to defuse the claims to certainty that propelled sectarian conflict.

Q2's version of this soliloquy is marked by skepticism throughout, but it finds an especially condensed expression in the word *conscience*. Jenkins provides the following gloss: "(1) as in ordinary modern usage, the inner voice of moral judgment; (2) consciousness, the fact or faculty of knowing and understanding" (280). Both Philips and Jenkins agree that Hamlet is using the word to refer to an intact, internalized moral compass. Such a reading seeks to tame a wildly variable and highly charged concept; moreover, it achieves this end by making what is arguably an anachronistic fact–value dichotomy, cordoning off morality from epistemology. Though Catherine Belsey also disagrees with the reduction of *conscience* to *consciousness*, her account of "the faculty which distinguishes between good and evil" associates it with a tradition which claims that "conscience is aligned with the understanding as opposed to the will."[54] Her consideration of the burgeoning literature of casuistry makes it clear that, in contrast to the split effected by Jenkins, no rigid distinction between knowing and moral judgment was made. *Conscience* became, during the early modern period, an increasingly problematic and troublesome concept. Hooker, for example, maintained that "*Conscience* is the proper court of God," but by the middle of the seventeenth century it was clear to Hobbes that "a mans Conscience, and his judgement are the same thing; and as the Judgement so also the Conscience may be erroneous."[55] Belsey sees that the play is about "moral doubt," and by paralleling it with William Perkins's *Discourse of Conscience* she suggests that the play similarly attempts to train the conscience – though admittedly by leaving the audience with questions. In the case of the printed quartos such an account seems most appropriate to Q1; Q2, in contrast, seems to set itself against the doctrine promulgated by Perkins and other maintainers of what has been described as "experimental predestination," the belief that experience and the searching of one's conscience could provide evidence of election. Q2 consistently raises questions that seem designed to undermine any such assurance.

Calvinist casuistry frequently finds itself on the defensive against attacks claiming that the rigidity of predestination caused despair and encouraged suicide. Robert Some, for instance, felt compelled to address the problem of suicide at the end of a short tract in the doctrine of predestination. The advice given to those who are "solicited of Satan to kill themselues" is that they pray and seek the counsel of the learned and that they "not giue themselues to solitarines, least they become peeuish and vntoward."[56] It is in this light that the play's several allusions to suicide should be considered. Michael MacDonald, a social historian, argues that *Hamlet* "exploits changing attitudes to suicide," but, having set out the "current interpretations of suicide," it does not "resolve the contradictions among them."[57] MacDonald is quite convinced that the vast majority of the population considered suicide diabolical, the result of satanic temptation, a view not incongruent with the scholastic tradition that identified despair, the deliberate turning away from God, as an ultimate sin. However, MacDonald also notes that suicide was the "subject of sectarian controversy."[58] Foxe, for instance, listed Catholic suicides, suggesting that such deaths were clear evidence of divine disfavor. Robert Parsons, the Catholic polemicist, returned the favor, implying that the Protestants were like the Donatists described by Augustine, "who, rather then they would lacke martyrs, were ready to murder themselues."[59] Sectarian controversy over suicide was not, however, limited to debates between Catholics and Protestants. According to MacDonald and Murphy, with the emergence of a split between Protestant and puritan, "the religious politics of self-murder came increasingly to focus on the pernicious effects of predestinarian doctrines" (64). Of course, the revival and propagation of classical models provided alternative views, especially for the educated classes; one such view finds expression in Horatio's claim to be "more an antike Roman, / Then a Dane" (Q1 I3^v). Responding to a cultural preoccupation, both texts display a constellation of attitudes toward suicide.

When Hamlet first encounters the Ghost, Horatio, in both quartos, eloquently warns him against following the apparition. In both cases, Horatio worries that the Ghost may change its appearance and "deprive" Hamlet of his "sovereignty of reason." However, in the Q2 version he goes on to describe the effect of standing at the cliff's edge: "The very place puts toyes of desperation / Without more motiue, into euery braine / That lookes so many fadoms to the sea / And heares it rore beneath" (D2^r). Horatio, the historian and philosopher, here offers an account of self-slaughter that both naturalizes and psychologizes the act. The point is simple: if under normal conditions the cliff creates such dangerous thoughts, then how much more dangerous is it in the presence of a super-natural, potentially diabolical, being? This slight remark adds another perspective on the question of self-slaughter, a perspective that is lacking in both Q1 and F, and it gives substance to Horatio's rationalism. This rationalism, which attempts to account for both natural and supernatural phenomena, provokes Hamlet's criticism in both Q1 and Q2: "There are more things in heauen and earth *Horatio* / Then are Dream't of, in your philosophie" (Q1, D1^v; Q2, D4^v).

While the Q2 "To be, or not to be" soliloquy avoids conventional Christian categories, the opening of the first soliloquy is firmly fixed within such categories: "O that this too too sallied flesh would melt, / Thaw and resolue it selfe into a dewe, / Or that the euerlasting had not fixt / His cannon gainst seale slaughter, o God, God" (C1^r). God ("the euerlasting"), conspicuously absent from Q2's "To be" soliloquy, appears here as the author of an injunction against suicide. Q1 supplies an alternative opening: "O that this too much grieu'd and sallied flesh / Would melt to nothing, or that the vniuersall / Globe of heauen would turn al to a Chaos!" (B4^r). Taken in combination with their respective versions of the "To be, or not to be" soliloquy, these two passages present very different views of self-slaughter. Q2 Hamlet moves from an almost automatic acceptance of the canons of the "everlasting" to a position of radical doubt; in contrast, Q1 Hamlet's initial desire for self-dissolution is expressed in cosmic terms, yet in the soliloquy he comes to inhabit, however uncomfortably, a highly conventional religious structure.

The treatment of self-slaughter is not, obviously, limited to the reflections of Hamlet and Horatio. The doubtful death of Ophelia raises the
question once again and provokes the comments of the gravediggers as well
as the contest between Laertes and the priest. The discussion between the
two "Clownes" opens in Q1 with a simple opinion: "I say no, she ought not
to be buried / In christian buriall" (H3ᵛ). Asked to justify this opinion, the
first Clown proclaims "Mary because shee's drownd." Unconvinced, his
assistant continues to question:

> 2. But she did not drowne her selfe.
> *Clowne* No, that's certain, the water drown'd her.
> 2. Yea but it was against her will.
> *Clowne* No, I deny that, for looke you sir, I stand here,
> If the water come to me, I drowne not my selfe:
> But if I goe to the water, and am drown'd,
> *Ergo* I am guiltie of my own death:
> Y'are gone, goe y'are gone sir.

(H3ᵛ–H4ʳ)

The central contention is over volition, and, in the Clown's logic, going
to the water reveals an intent to commit suicide. His logic entirely denies
the possibility of mischance; indeed, death by mischance was the common alternative to the verdict of *felo de se*, one that avoided the puni-
tive confiscation of estate entailed by a finding of suicide. The Clown's
argument is strictly voluntaristic, and this strictness is marked by the use
of a technical term of logic, *Ergo*. Behind the Clown's voluntarism lurks
the possibility of what has been termed popular pelagianism.[60] This
possibility becomes explicit in the quite different Q2 version of this
exchange.

In Q2, the Clown opens with a question rather than a statement, a
question that poses the relationship of will to salvation: "Is shee to be
buried in Christian buriall, when she wilfully seekes her owne saluation?"
(M1ᵛ). In so doing, the text explicitly invokes contemporary debates about
predestination and ridicules the obstinate pursuit of grace with a malapropism that cuts both ways: against Catholic freewillers who presume to
earn salvation and Calvinist saints who are convinced of their own election.
The other Clown replies that the "crowner ... finds it Christian buriall."
The introduction of the legal apparatus, represented by the Coroner,
provides an opportunity for extended play with the language of law:
"How can that be, vnlesse she drown'd herselfe in her owne defence."
Homicide was only excusable in cases of self-defense, and because suicide is
a species of homicide it too must allow of such a defense. The joke here

depends not on the looseness of plebeian logic but on a too rigid application of logic, an application that defies common sense and creates a ridiculous paradox. In fact, the only verdict that could excuse a suicide was a finding of *non compos mentis*, a verdict which rendered the will of the deceased inoperative. A finding of death by mischance had the same effect: the death of the individual was accidental not willful. When the second Clown responds to this paradox by saying, "Why tis found so," the first Clown expands his claim: "It must be so offended, it cannot be els, for heere lyes the poynt, if I drowne my selfe wittingly, it argues an act, & an act hath three branches, it is to act, to doe, to performe, or all; she drownd her selfe wittingly"(MI$^\text{v}$).[61] This question-begging is followed by an explicit tautology: "Giue me leaue, here lyes the water, good, here stands the man, good, if the man goe to this water & drowne himselfe, it is will he, nill he, he goes" (MI$^\text{v}$–M2$^\text{r}$). The Clown's reasoning is deliriously confused and confusing; his demonstration with its conditional language and its use of deictic words only succeeds in proving that if the man goes to the water: "he goes." Furthermore, the state of the will is ruled irrelevant ("will he, nill he") in the face of this blunt fact. However, "if the water come to him, & drowne him, he drownes not himself, argall, he is not guilty of his own death, shortens not his owne life." In contrast to the compression of Q1, Q2's Clown offers a laborious statement of the obvious that is marked as specious by the malapropism of *argall* for *ergo*. This version of the exchange works as an extended joke about the baffling scholasticism of the theology of grace; as such it not only discredits the pretensions of commoners who claim to understand but also disparages the doctors who dispute endlessly, like Milton's fallen angels: "Of providence, foreknowledge, will and fate, / Fixed fate, free will, foreknowledge absolute."

Argall marks the Clown's reasoning as irregular and works to neutralize the verbal facility that Q2 Hamlet finds so threatening: "How absolute the knaue is, we must speake by the card, or equivocation will vndoo vs" (M3$^\text{r}$). The word here used to identify the knave's verbal practice, "equivocation," carries with it a very specific religious coloring.[62] Though not yet indelibly associated with the doctrine of mental reservation elaborated by Catholic casuists, as it would be in the wake of the Gunpowder Plot, the term was common in theological polemic where it invariably designated an opponent's shifty imprecision. Q1 Hamlet experiences irritation at the Clown's answers but responds not with Latinate terms about the disorder of language but with sarcasm, "An excellent fellow by the Lord *Horatio*, / This seauen yeares haue I noted it: the toe of the pesant, / Comes so neere the heele of the courtier, / That he gawles his kibe" (H4$^\text{v}$). This same sentiment is expressed in Q2; however, here, without "An excellent fellow," it functions as a generalized worry over social mobility and the potential collapse of status differences. In Q2 this concern is explicitly linked to linguistic competence. Hamlet's sense of distinction is throughout the play confirmed by his verbal facility. Like Prince Hal, he "can drink with any tinker in his own language," moving with ease between the courtly and the colloquial, yet the Clown's joking reveals the possibility that such verbal play is no longer the monopoly of the elite: it has become common. Hamlet's response to the verbal fluidity represented by "equivocation" is to invoke the "card" that fixes and stabilizes language.

The threat of indeterminacy is not simply a general linguistic condition – it has everything to do with what is being said as well as how it is being said. The anxiety that attends the exchange with the gravedigger is in part a result of the awareness that clowns have begun to ask charged questions about the theology and the social order. The linkage between theology and the social is made explicit in both texts when the Clowns affirm that Ophelia's social status accounts for her burial in sacred ground. In Q1, Hamlet recognizes that the funeral procession "shews to be some noble parentage" (I1^v), but in Q2 Ophelia's "maimed rites" indicate to Hamlet that "The corse they follow, did with desprat hand / Fordoo it owne life, twas of some estate" (M4^r). Here the procession functions as a legible sign of both soteriological (a "desprat hand" signifies a lack of grace) and social ("of some estate") fact. Q2 Hamlet's immediate identification of "maimed rites" and his ability to read them accurately as an indicator of suicide and social standing raises the possibility that such rituals are concerned more with the circulation of social meanings than with the final rest of the deceased and raises questions about the purpose and efficacy of religious ritual and ceremony.

In both Q1 and Q2 Hamlet's observation is immediately followed by Laertes's urgent question: "What ceremony else?" This plangent demand denies the appropriateness of the ritual, insisting that more be done for Ophelia. The different responses of Q1's Priest and Q2's Doctor reveal a shift that goes beyond mere expansion. In Q1 the Priest answers:

> My Lord, we haue done all that lies in vs,
> And more than well the church can tolerate,
> She hath had a Dirge sung for her maiden soule:
> And but for the fauour of the king, and you,
> She had beene buried in the open fieldes,
> Where now she is allowed christian buriall.

(I1^v)

The Priest's address recognizes Laertes's social rank ("My Lord") but uses the first person plural to identify himself as the representative of the corporate body of the church. The dirge, the singing of a psalm, was a part of the burial rite that had been under Protestant attack from the beginning of the Reformation in England. According to a strict Protestant theology, the dirge could have no effect on "her maiden soule," and thus the practice threatened to perpetuate a grievous misunderstanding of soteriology. And yet, despite attempts to inculcate a uniform and theologically Protestant rite of burial, practices continued to vary and controversy continued to swirl around what constituted a legitimate Christian burial.[63] James Pilkington, the Bishop of Durham, addressed this confused situation by offering three clear rules: first, bodies are not to be cast out or buried in "dunghils, ditches, or such like places"; second, avoid great expenses, "which do no good to the dead"; and third, "no superstition should be committed." Predictably, this last rule, "wherein the Papists infinitilie offend," is followed by an exhausting but not exhaustive catalogue of superstitious practices: "masses, diriges, trentalls, singing, ringing, holiwater, halowed places, yeares, daies & moneth mindes, crosses, pardon-letters to be buried with them, mourners, *de profundis*, by euery lad that could saie it, dealing of money solemnlie for the dead, watching of the corps at home, bell and banner, with manie moe then I can reckon."[64] Pilkington's austerity betrays his puritan inclinations, and though his position is hardly definitive, it does represent one important line of thought on the issue. The Q1 Priest, on the other hand, who has allowed the dirge cannot be committed to a strict Protestant theology.

The exchange between Laertes and the Doctor in Q2 displays a far greater degree of acrimony and a sharper command of theological technicalities:

> Her obsequies haue been as farre inlarg'd
> As we haue warrantie, her death was doubtfull,
> And but that great commaund ore-swayes the order,
> She should in ground vnsanctified been lodg'd
> Till the last trumpet: for charitable prayers,
> Flints and peebles should be thrown on her:
> Yet heere she is allow'd her virgin Crants,
> Her mayden strewments, and the bringing home
> Of bell and buriall.
>
> (M4^r)

Q2's Doctor is expansive in his consideration of both the social and theological complexities provoked by Ophelia's "doubtful" death. In contrast to the concrete language of Q1's Priest, the Doctor deploys technical language ("warrantie," "obsequies," "vnsanctified") and a conditional construction. Unlike the personal "but for fauour of the king, and you," Q2 asserts that a delicately anonymous "great commaund," readily identifiable as the secular authority of the sovereign, abrogates "the order." The order here invoked is presumably the order of burial for confirmed suicides, but the passage cannot fail to recall the preemption and suppression of other religious orders, and yet Hamlet is able to recognize the actions on stage precisely as the "maimed rites" appropriate to a suicide. Laertes, Hamlet, and the Doctor all offer different perspectives on the burial ritual that is taking place: for the Doctor there has been too much, for Laertes too little, and for Hamlet sufficient ceremony. By offering an expansive treatment of this dispute, Q2 draws attention to the very controversial question of "maimed rites" and suppressed orders.

The Q2 scene includes an additional exchange between the Doctor and Laertes. In response to Laertes's "Must there no more be doone?" the Doctor replies:

> No more be doone.
> We should prophane the service of the dead,
> To sing a Requiem and such rest to her
> As to peace-parted soules.
>
> (M4^r)

The denied requiem stands in sharp contrast to the dirge provided in Q1 for Ophelia's "maiden soule." Though there are reasons to hesitate before accepting Dover Wilson's contention that Q2's cleric is a Protestant doctor of divinity, there is no denying that the Doctor does have a precise concern for the proper ordering of church ritual, a concern that far exceeds that manifested by the Priest in Q1. Though in both Q1 and Q2 Laertes scornfully identifies the representative of the church as a "Priest," in Q2 this creates a dissonance on the page between the speech headings and the character's line. The standard editorial practice has been to emend Q2's stage direction and speech headings so that they agree with Laertes. Yet this normalizing removes an intriguing contradiction, a contradiction that draws the reader's attention to the problematic identity and contested authority of the clergy.[65]

In both Q1 and Q2 Laertes is given the final word in his exchange with the officiating cleric: "So, I tell thee churlish Priest, a ministring Angell shall my sister be, when thou liest howling" (Q1, I^v). This stinging declaration, delivered with fierce conviction, invokes the four final things: death, judgment, heaven, and hell. Laertes operates within a clear eschatological scheme and displays none of the morbid curiosity that typifies Hamlet's thoughts in the graveyard. In both Q1 and Q2, Hamlet focuses insistently on the dissolution of the physical body: "How long will a man lie in the ground before hee rots?" (Q1, H4^v; cf. Q2, M3^v). A fascination with bodily corruption leads to speculation about the transformations undergone by Alexander, recalling the exchange between Hamlet and Claudius immediately after the death of Polonius in which Hamlet remarks that "A man may fish with the worme that hath eate of a King, & eate of the fish that hath fedde of that worme" (Q2, K2^r; cf. Q1, G4^r). Though this speculation is intended, so Hamlet threateningly claims, to show Claudius "how a King may goe a progresse through the guts of a begger" (Q2, K2^r–K2^v), it is also marked by the sort of theoretical curiosity exemplified in the comment about Alexander. Both examples toy with the identity between body and person and refer to a paradox regarding the doctrine of bodily resurrection. How will each person be resurrected in his or her physical entirety when certain individuals have come to share matter? This thought raises the specter of a collapse of integrity, a blurring of distinctions that is articulated in social terms: the king becomes food for a beggar, Alexander the Great is reduced to clay and used to stop a beer barrel. One response to such a theological conundrum would be to stress the vital importance of the immortal soul as the subject of judgment. Indeed, this is an element in the earlier exchange. When Claudius for the second time asks Hamlet where Polonius is, he replies: "In heauen send thether to see, if your messenger finde him not there, seek him i'th other place your selfe, but if indeed you find him not within this month, you shall nose him as you goe vp the stayres into the Lobby" (K2^v). "Him" refers first to a soul subjected to damnation or salvation and then to a rotting corpse.

In direct contrast to the doctrine implicit in the gravedigger's riddle, which asserts that gravemakers build houses that will last until doomsday, Hamlet's later speculation on the indignities of decomposition, without any recourse to notions of the soul, harbors a materialism that hints of mortalism.[66] The issue is treated more expansively in Q2 where Horatio responds to Hamlet's initial query about Alexander with a revealing disavowal: "Twere to consider too curiously to consider so" (M3^v). Yet Hamlet continues, concluding with two couplets that only serve to reiterate the theme:

> Imperious Caesar dead, and turned to Clay,
> Might stoppe a hole, to keepe the wind away.
> O that the earth which kept the world in awe,
> Should patch a wall t'expell the waters flaw.
>
>   (M4^r)

It is Horatio's response that indicates that this moment of reflection goes beyond the conventional *memento mori* indicting human vanity and ambition. Hamlet's curious consideration reveals an unhealthy obsession with the corruption of flesh and the circulation of matter; he takes no solace from the doctrine announced by the Doctor, echoing the gravedigger, just moments later and on the same quarto page: "She should in ground vnsanctified been lodg'd / Till the last trumpet."

Ruminations of the sort engaged in by Hamlet are directly addressed by the passage from I Corinthians in the Book of Common Prayer's Order for the Burial of the Dead: "But some man will say, How arise the dead? With what body shall they come?"[67] Later in the seventeenth century, Sir Thomas Browne would reflect on this very question: "How shall the dead arise, is no question of my faith ... I beleeve that our estranged and divided ashes shall unite againe, that our separated dust after so many pilgrimages and transformations into the parts of mineralls, Plants, Animals, Elements, shall at the voyce of God returne into their primitive shapes; and joyne againe to make up their primary and predestinate formes."[68] For Browne, this thought provides an opportunity to extoll the power of God who will restore order to what has become, with time's corruption, a confused and indistinct mass of matter. Hamlet's refusal to make a similar profession of faith leads Ernst Bloch to the provocative assertion that Hamlet's attitude reveals "no liberation by the materialism germinating in the bourgeois Ratio but on the contrary a religious horror at its own irreligion."[69] Yet Bloch's conclusion that "the sole final prospect is 'how a king may go a progress through the guts of a beggar'" ignores Hamlet's subsequent invocation of divine providence.

Hamlet does, after all, make a profession of faith shortly after the burial of Ophelia. Yet, there is a wide discrepancy between the version offered in Q1 and that in Q2. The pronouncement of Q1 Hamlet regarding providence is fleeting and matter-of-fact; indeed, occurring in the brief interval between the departure of the Gentleman and the arrival of the royal entourage, it does not retard the play's forward momentum. The Q2 version, in contrast, is expansive and dilatory: Hamlet's thoughts on providence are developed at greater length and integrated into his account of his escape from Rosencrantz and Guildenstern.[70]

Q1 Hamlet decides to ignore his sense of foreboding and refuse Horatio's suggestion that he decline the duel: "No *Horatio*, not I, if Danger be now, Why then it is not to come, theres a predestiuate providence in the fall of a sparrow" (12^v–13^r). Condensed to such a degree, the thought appears almost perfunctory. Rather than being gestural, however, this brevity assumes the unproblematic nature of predestinate providence, a phrase with decidedly Calvinistic flavor.[71] Indeed, Hamlet's remarks in Q1 have the appearance of the commonplace. A similar claim regarding the imminence of danger is made, for instance, by Hugh Latimer: "For seeing that we be certain that danger and peril shall come upon us, all they that be wise and godly will prepare themselves, lest they be taken suddenly unawares, or unready."[72] Hamlet's presentiment of death proves correct: the denouement follows speedily. But he, unlike his father, is prepared, and his final words are at once a prayer and a profession of faith: "heauen receiue my soule" (13ᵛ).[73] Once again, Q1 comfortably inhabits a conventional eschatology, one that allows, if not assumes, the validity of Calvinist predestination.[74]

Q2 spends considerably more time on the problems of providence, presenting the reader with a topic of theological debate handled in an oblique fashion, and thus achieves a specific, aesthetic distance from the world of religious controversy. This disposition must not be construed as one of disinterest or indifference; by aestheticizing curious considerations, Q2 addresses the unperturbed, literate gentleman, one who can stand above, or rather sit quietly at a remove from, the fray, taking pleasure in speculation and drawing edification from the undermining of dogmatic positions.[75]

The issue of providence is first broached when Hamlet describes his shipboard exploits to Horatio. This news, narrated second-hand by Horatio to Gertrude in Q1, is given by Hamlet himself:

> Sir in my hart there was a kind of fighting
> That would not let me sleepe, my thought I lay
> Worse than the mutines in the bilbo, rashly,
> And praysd be rashnes for it: let vs knowe,
> Our indiscretion sometime serues vs well
> When our deepe plots doe pall, & that should learne vs
> Ther's a diuinity that shapes our ends,
> Rough hew them how we will.
>
> (N1ʳ)

Hamlet's psychic disturbance is significantly described in terms of an internal battle, an image familiar from pietist pastoral literature and conversion narratives.[76] Hamlet perceives his situation to be worse than that of a mutineer bound in iron shackles; more than an index of discomfort, this image of rebellion constrained vividly expresses the sense of futility that accompanies Hamlet's perception that he has no scope for effective action. Yet out of this sense of futility comes the rashness that leads Hamlet to take action, leaving his cabin to seek the commission carried by Rosencrantz and Guildenstern. The happy result of Hamlet's indiscretion increases his conviction that a divine providence determines the final consequences of human planning and action. That he is able to seal his forged commission with his father's signet is taken as further evidence of an "ordinant" heaven arranging mundane matters.

After accepting the challenge, Hamlet suddenly finds that he feels "ill all's heere about my hart" (N3^v). Though this clearly bears a resemblance to the inward fighting that disturbed him aboard the ship, he here dismisses it as "such a kinde of gamgiuing as would perhapes trouble a woman." Horatio urges him to obey his intuition, but he refuses:

> Not a whit, we defie augury, there is speciall prouidence in the fall of a Sparrowe, if it be, tis not to come, if be not to come, it will be now, if it be not now, yet it well come, the readines is all, since no man of ought he leaues, knowes what ist to leaue betimes, let be. (N3^v)

The great range of interpretations that this passage has provoked sufficiently warns against a tendentious reading.[77] Indeed, the polysemous quality of Hamlet's affirmation seems designed precisely to frustrate and forestall any reading that might attach the prince or the play to a particular religious dogma. Robert G. Hunter asserts that *Hamlet* explores the mysteries of providence "in detachment from any commitment to a specific Christian orthodoxy." It is precisely this disinterestedness, Hunter insists, that guarantees the play's status as art: not an "imaginative presentation of theology," *Hamlet* is the realization of Shakespeare's "artistic purpose."[78]

I agree that Q2 is doctrinally indeterminate; but rather than seeing this as the alchemy of literature transforming the dross of theological polemic into aureate art, I would argue that Q2 is, as Hunter terms it, a work of *bricolage*, but one that helps to constitute the very category of literature. The only partial consolidation of this category, or rather its distance from a post-romantic understanding of literature, is visible precisely in the failure of organic unity that would wipe away the traces of *bricolage*, the striations of polemical consciousness clearly visible to the reader who looks. Alan Sinfield has looked and he concludes that the play is a document of anxiety, demonstrating that the "paradoxes of Protestant theology provoked alarm and confusion." The play's reticence and indeterminacy are taken to register "a deep unease with Christian doctrine as it was customarily preached."[79] However, Sinfield's rapid slide from Protestant theology to Christian doctrine elides the very polemical distinctions that in part structure the play. *Hamlet*, I am claiming, is animated by the polemical energies of late Elizabethan culture, its immediate success – on the stage as well as in the bookstalls – a result of its having engaged not transcended those energies. Q2's overall effect, however, is to create an objectivizing distance on the controversies of religious doctrine. On this score the two different versions of Hamlet's final words are revealing. Q1 Hamlet, as noted, dies with a conventional eschatological anticipation ("heauen receiue my soule"), but Q2 Hamlet says, "the rest is silence" (G1ᵛ). Admittedly, Horatio is there to supply the missing consolation: "And flights of Angels sing thee to thy rest." However, the next line, "Why dooes the drum come hether?" signals martial music, not angelic harmony. Hamlet's last words seem to evince a final uncertainty; after so much talk, so many curious considerations, Hamlet ends with an eerie announcement of silence.[80] These final words invoke the bleak doctrine of the *deus absconditus* – a vision of the world ruled by an omnipotent but hidden and unapproachable God – but they also echo Revelations 8:1: "And when he had opened the seuenth seal, there was a silence in heauen about halfe an houre." An allusion to this same passage is also audible in the Player's speech: "But as we often see against some storme, / A silence in the heauens" (Q2, F3ᵛ).[81] The Geneva Bible's marginal gloss explains that the seventh seal signifies the great danger brought about by corrupt doctrine and "what troubles, sectes & heresies hathe bene & shalbe broght into ye Church thereby" (GGg1ʳ). Such an allusion returns the text squarely to the problems of eschatology and provides a specifically religious register for Hamlet's assertion that the time is out of joint.

Hamlet emerges out of a polemical culture, a culture that helps account for the contemporary popularity of and fascination with *Hamlet*, yet neither the play nor its printed versions are themselves polemics. My claim is, rather, that Q2 both dramatizes and repudiates polemical culture – a world of violent certitudes in which competing camps seek to name and exclude each other from the magic circle of orthodoxy. The play transforms the popular revenge tragedy into a vehicle that interrogates the genre itself and raises enduring questions about what another play calls "supernatural soliciting." In a world in which supernatural warrants were regularly invoked to justify the most implacable violence, Q2 insists that knowledge and ethics are far from obvious and never easy. However, anti-polemic cannot easily remove itself from a polemical culture; indeed, attacks on polemic, paradoxically and inevitably, partake of the polemical dynamic itself – using the condemnation of polemic to marginalize certain arguments and arguers while establishing "moderation" as the mark of legitimacy.

Yet there is a second part of my argument: while Q1 remains within that polemical culture, Q2 objectivizes and rejects polemic. This distinction is exemplified in the alternative lines given Claudius at the end of his attempt to pray in the chapel: "My wordes fly vp, my sinnes remaine below. / No King on earth is safe, if Gods his foe" (Q1, G1^v–G2^r); "My words fly vp, my thoughts remaine belowe / Words without thoughts neuer to heauen goe" (Q2, I2^r). Both passages move from a specific description to a generalization. Q1's commonplace stresses the relationship between God and king, but rather than celebrate God's support for the monarch, it insists upon the divine chastisement of guilty kings, anticipating Claudius's death and suggesting that Hamlet is indeed God's minister. In addition, the passage reveals a stark political theology based on the polemical distinction between friend and foe according to which everyone, from kings to commoners, is either with or against God. Q2's generalization, in contrast, emphasizes the possible disjunction between word and thought, reminding the reader, once again, that untethered language threatens to turn sweet religion into a rhapsody of words. Such an anxiety was not limited to any one wing or variety of Protestant opinion: the threat of empty or insincere words was used in the Protestant attack on worship in a strange tongue, by the godly in their disparagement of a reading ministry, and finally by Anabaptists in their rejection of all set forms of prayer.

Claudius does not reject the efficacy of prayer, but his reflections do foreground the dialectic between sincerity and hypocrisy that gained prominence in the confessional strife following the Reformation. As Q2 Polonius puts it: "Tis too much prou'd, that with deuotions visage / And pious action, we doe sugar ore / The deuill himselfe" (G2^r). A more problematic collocation of language, virtue, and hypocrisy appears in Hamlet's planned approach to his mother. In Q1, Hamlet asserts: "I will speake daggers, those sharpe wordes being spent, / To doe her wrong my soule shall ne're consent" (G1^v). Yet in Q2 he claims: "I will speake dagger to her, but vse none, / My tongue and soule in this be hypocrites" (H4^v). The separation between tongue and soul – the quintessential condition of hypocrisy – is here indicated with the coordinating conjunction *and*, raising the possibility that both soul and tongue are hypocrites. However, rather than being the harbinger of a subversive politics, Q2's emphasis on the turbulence created by wild and whirling words erodes at once both the assurance of the polemicist and the rigidity of polemical identities and identifications.

At the textual level Q2 displays a hostility toward dogmatic presumption, and yet Q2 as a *book* has another significance. It creates a distinction not based on confessional identity but on a nascent literary taste; Q2 repudiates Q1 – the "popular" *Hamlet* with its clear invocation of the stage – seeking not the applause of the vulgar but the approbation of the wiser sort. The play as well as the books of *Hamlet* are complexly bound up with this problem of popularity. Gabriel Harvey's assertion – that the tragedy of *Hamlet* has what is needed "to please the wiser sort" – presents one view. An alternative is offered in the preface of *Daiphantvs, or the Passions of Loue* published in 1604.[82] This Epistle to the Reader is in fact a highly ironic and self-reflexive account of what such an epistle should achieve:

> *It should be like the* Neuer-too-well read Arcadia, *where the* Prose *and* Verce, Matter *and* Words *are like his* Mistresses *eyes, one still excelling another without Corivall: or to come home to the* vulgars Element, *like Friendly Shake-speares* Tragedies, *where the* Commedian *rides, when the* Tragedian *stands on Tiptoe: Faith it should please all, like Prince* Hamlet. *But in sadnesse, then it were to be feared he would runne mad: Insooth I will not be moone-sicke, to please: nor out of my wits though I displeased all.* (A2ʳ)

The author, identified on the title page as An. Sc. Gentleman, structures his comments around a series of antitheses. Sir Philip Sidney's *Arcadia* is compared to Shakespeare's *Hamlet*: the first demands rereadings that will, nonetheless, never exhaust its significance; the second is the "*vulgars* Element" and is indelibly marked by its theatrical origin. Both works themselves contain contrasting elements. In *Arcadia*, prose and verse exist in a rivalrous but ultimately harmonious relationship, a situation described in the imagery of love poetry itself and embodied in the integrated and aesthetically pleasing figure of the mistress. "Friendly Shake-speares Tragedies" are more discordant; the generic mingling that they display is described in terms of kinetic postures that emphasize the physical bodies and shared space of the theatre. The success of this strategy of generic hybridity – lamented by Sidney as "neither right tragedies, nor right comedies"[83] – is acknowledged with the assertion that *Hamlet* pleases all, yet this achievement is immediately revealed to be a dubious one. Though the threat of madness is most obviously a joking reference to Hamlet's "antic disposition," the joke also plays on the notion that attempting to please all creates incoherence and a collapse of integrity. The epistle writer, revealing his sophistication and sounding not unlike the elitist Hamlet himself, disavows any such desire, claiming to be above such pandering.

The opinions of Harvey and An. Sc. point to the range of responses provoked by Shakespeare's *Hamlet*. Q1 and Q2 were printed to shape and profit from these varied opinions; in both cases a process of differentiation is visible. Q1 emerges as distinct from the earlier non-Shakespearean *Hamlet*, identifying itself as the play by Shakespeare recently acted by the King's Men.[84] Q2, in turn, distinguishes itself by rejecting Q1 and the taint of the theatre, claiming the virtues of authenticity ("according to the true and perfect Coppie") and abundance ("almost as much againe as it was"). This cultural process of distinction – according to which agents, texts, and practices strive to consolidate their identities against the spectral horizon of the common and customary – here operates alongside the explicit determinations of religious polemic and confessional conflict. On the one hand is incipient consumerism and a nascent market for cultural goods, and, on the other hand, furious religious strife played out through language and bodies. Though the two are inextricably bound together throughout the culture of early modern England, Q2's anti-polemic anticipates the establishment of the category of literature – a category in large part constituted through the repudiation of polemic. Eventually, literature – the creative, the autonomous, the imaginative – will, in an ironic twist, become a, if not the, repository for the very spiritual longings that once animated the religious polemic it repudiated and replaced.

CHAPTER 4

Printing Donne: poetry and polemic in the early seventeenth century

Looking back on the early part of the seventeenth century, John Aubrey, that great repository of gossip and anecdote, remarked: "The Studies in fashion in those dayes (in England) were Poetry; and Controversie with the Church of Rome."[1] This chapter pursues the seemingly incongruent yoking of poetry with polemic in the literary culture of early seventeenth-century England by examining two apparently disparate texts by John Donne: *Pseudo-Martyr* published in 1610 and *An Anatomy of the World*. Though my principal focus remains publishing events, these two books, one a religious polemic and the other a set of three poems, share a single author, and this generic range in an individual writer indicates that poetry and polemic were not entirely discrete endeavors, given over to specialists committed to one or the other. Though Donne is not alone in writing both poetry and polemic, his work usefully points to the cultural affinity between poetry and polemic, to the ways in which both endeavors are animated by similar concerns. Attempting to make such a case with Donne will strike many as counterintuitive or quixotic, but the received notion of a private, lyrical, print-phobic, and non-polemical Donne is, I believe, in need of refinement.[2] As a consequence, this chapter departs from those that precede it by focusing more attention on the figure of the author. However, my interest in Donne's role as author remains subordinate to my main argument about the shaping influence of print technology and religious controversy on the literary culture of early modern England.

Aubrey's allusion to fashionable studies is at the same time both dismissive and revealing. Such writing is held to be a transitory phenomenon, the passing interest of the social elite, and yet Aubrey also suggests that, in the early seventeenth century, the division of labor between accredited divines writing religious polemic and amateur gentlemen writing poetry was not yet rigid. The cultural context that made for an efflorescence of poetry and religious controversy is not especially mysterious. In general, the reading and writing of poetry provided Tudor–Stuart gentlemen with rhetorical training and access to a complex social network of patronage and exchange, but more specifically, the accession of James I brought to the throne a monarch who had published both poetry and polemical writings.[3] The idea of a royal controversialist was not without precedent; Henry VIII had earned the title of *Fidei Defensor* from Pope Leo X for penning an attack on Luther, but James went further and took an unprecedented pride in his scholarly aptitude as a discerning critic and an effective debater. He is the first English monarch to fashion an image of himself as author using the medium of print. Though James I clearly relished academic arguments, he was also a loud advocate for peace who seems to have sincerely believed that reasonable debate would eventually produce accommodation and agreement, and consequently controversial writing assumed a new prominence and prestige.[4]

Unlike the king, John Donne is often described as having resisted print culture. This critical commonplace owes its present currency largely to the work of Arthur Marotti, who has made a convincing case for Donne the coterie poet.[5] However, this claim about poetry, drawing on J. W. Saunders's vision of the "stigma of print," is clearly not intended to cover all other forms of printed discourse.[6] Nonetheless, perhaps because the "stigma of print" is such a resonant phrase, scholars have not always been precise in making discriminations between various genres and their changing relationships to print. Rather than exploring the ways in which different genres were constituted in *and* against print in order to make sense of Donne's embrace of print when he came to publish his polemics (*Pseudo-Martyr* and *Ignatius His Conclave*), sermons, and devotions, scholars have usually resorted instead to literary biography.

Indeed Donne's life provides a handy and seemingly clear narrative structure based on the trope of conversion: the witty and private Jack Donne of erotic lyricism and manuscript discretion becomes the grave Dr. Donne of the pulpit and the press, a public figure intent upon edification. We owe the germ of this idea of change to Donne himself, who engaged in a degree of self-mythologization. Significantly, Donne's account of his transformation is raised in a discussion that concerns print publication. In a letter to Sir Robert Carr, Donne identifies *Biathanatos* as the work of Jack Donne, not Dr. Donne, writing, "I only forbid it the press and the fire. Publish it not, but yet burn it not, and between those do what you will."[7] This is not a hostility to print *per se*, but an awareness instead that the public persona speaking through print and from pulpit is incompatible with the rhetorical persona adopted in *Biathanatos*.[8] Unfortunately, Donne's own wry awareness of the distance between Jack and the Doctor has led to an excessively polarized vision of Donne's intellectual development, which, according to Annabel Patterson, tends to oversimplify "those five or six transitional years which served as his threshold between lives, which mark his passage from outsider to one of the most notable spokesmen for the establishment."[9] For Patterson, this transition is marked by division, confusion, and, most importantly, resistance. In particular, Patterson argues that Donne was a reluctant polemicist and describes *Pseudo-Martyr* as "his partly obedient defense of obedience to the crown."[10]

Where Patterson finds evidence of psychic resistance, others have found boredom (whether Donne's or their own is not always clear). Evelyn Simpson, for example, considers it a "typical product of those 'middle years' which were the most dreary part of his life, when he was overworked and underpaid, the victim of unceasing anxiety for his family and his future"; it is "the dullest of Donne's work," showing "no passion and very little wit."[11] Behind the image of a harried or resistant Donne lies the traditional account of the book's genesis in response to the royal command of James I. Isaak Walton, himself hostile to the very idea of controversial writing, first promulgated the claim that Donne wrote *Pseudo-Martyr* in response to a royal command. The king, according to Walton, was so impressed with Donne's verbal account of the controverted issues that he asked Donne to "bestow some time in drawing the Arguments into a method ... and, having done that, not to send, but be his own messenger and bring them to him."[12] Print is not, at this point, part of the equation; the king may simply be requesting the sort of manuscript book of advice that was common in the courts of the Tudor–Stuart monarchs. However, Walton next explains: "To this [Donne] presently and diligently applied himself, and, within six weeks brought them to him under his own handwriting, as they be now printed; the Book bearing the name of *Pseudo-martyr*, printed *anno* 1610." A manuscript book, then, was first presented to the king and only later printed. Furthermore, Walton affirms that "When the King had read and considered that Book, he perswaded Mr. *Donne* to enter into the Ministery." Donne, of course, resisted, but his fate was sealed by his exemplary performance. The king had divined in the book Donne's true vocation as a preacher of the word. However, corroborative evidence for Walton's account of the origins of *Pseudo-Martyr* is hard to find. Before considering alternatives, it should be noted that Walton's narrative defuses and vitiates Donne's own polemical interests and intentions by amplifying the force of the royal will, while at the same time claiming that the result is an intellectual triumph for Donne. What's more,

Donne's distasteful polemical moment is, in Walton's eyes, actually a happy fall, for it leads ineluctably to his taking orders.

Evidence for an alternative etiology of the book is not far to seek, and the first necessity of such an account is that it not explain the book away. The very desire to belittle *Pseudo-Martyr* betrays an unwillingness to really grapple with Donne and his culture. The book is a harsh and stringent polemic, yet there seems to be little justification for assuming that some-how, on some level, Donne did not really mean it.[13] The important point is that Donne thought his emergence in print should take the form of a polemic defending the oath of allegiance against proponents of the pope's authority, especially those who held that the pope had the power either to absolve subjects of their obedience to a heretical monarch or to directly depose an apostate king.[14] As a printed book, *Pseudo-Martyr* has conse-quences not only for the narratives we tell about John Donne, but also for our histories of early modern print. It reveals a close association between print and polemic: the growing prestige of printed polemic offered the possibility of professional advancement while serious polemical purpose justified a resort to the public medium of print. Rather than dismissing polemic as a marginal and slightly disreputable practice, we must recognize that what Brian Cummings refers to as "This monstrous hydra of counter-textuality" was quite central to the literary – literary in the expansive sense – culture of the time.[15]

Treated as a publishing event and located in the broader culture of England and Europe in 1610, rather than in the inherited literary bio-graphy of Donne, *Pseudo-Martyr* appears normal rather than anomalous. There is no question that Donne had a close relationship with that important and indefatigable polemicist, Thomas Morton. Admittedly, Donne complained that "the Divines of these times, are become meer Advocates, as though Religion were a temporall inheritance; they plead for it with all sophistications, and illusions, and forgeries . . . They write for religion without it."[16] But there are few polemicists who do not claim to deplore the current state of controversy. While the case for Donne's polemical apprenticeship with Morton has been called into question, I am inclined to agree with T. S. Healy, who gives the idea a cautious endorsement.[17] Whether or not Donne helped Morton write his books, there is definite evidence that Morton helped Donne with *Ignatius His Conclave*, and good reason to think that he encouraged the writing of *Pseudo-Martyr*. Donne's close relationship with Morton assumes addi-tional significance when considered along with the wider polemical context.

The close of the seventeenth century's first decade saw a marked increase in polemical writing. The Oath of Allegiance controversy, over James I's demand that his Catholic subjects take a loyalty oath that specifically repudiated the pope's deposing power, recently described as "a diabolically effective polemical cocktail," is only part of this picture.[18] The Gunpowder Plot in 1605 had provided a new motive for anti-popery and was the subject of a vast outpouring of printed books. Furthermore, the publication of an *English Martyrloge* in 1608 – listing the true Roman Catholic martyrs who had died under Henry VIII, Edward VI, and Elizabeth – had helped to reanimate sectarian disputes about the proper definition of martyrdom, and evidence of new interest in the controversy over martyrdom undoubtedly encouraged the Stationers' Company to publish a new edition of Foxe's *Actes and Monuments* in 1610. In France, arguments between Gallicans and Ultramontanes continued, only to be given renewed energy by the assassination of Henri IV in May, 1610.[19] This regicide quickly became the subject of both news pamphlets and polemics in England, further exacerbating a period of tension and anxiety. Perhaps the best indicator of the new prominence of polemic in these uncertain circumstances was the establishment on May 8, 1610, of King James's College at Chelsea, an institution intended to serve as a "spiritual garrison" for the production of polemical divinity. Thomas Morton, Donne's associate and patron, is listed among the original fellows. So is John Boys, who in that same year gave Donne's new book a plug: "I wil not meddle with the cobwebs of learning in the schoole, which have more wit then art, yet more art then use; nor with the distorted and idle glosses of the Canonists; he that list may burthen his memorie with a shipfull of their fooleries, accuratly collected by the penner of Pseudomartyr."[20]

Donne himself identifies this polemical environment as his motive for writing. His dedication to the king begins:

As Temporall armies consist of Press'd men, and voluntaries, so do they also in this warfare, in which your Majestie hath appear'd by your Bookes. And not only your strong and full Garisons, which are your Cleargie, and your Universities, but also obscure Villages can minister Souldiours. For, the equall interest, which all your subjects have in the cause (all being equally endanger'd in your dangers) gives everyone of us a Title to the Dignitie of this warfare; And so makes those, whom the Civill Lawes made opposite, all one, Paganos, Milites.[21]

This dense military opening has understandably caused some confusion. Donne's distinction between "Press'd men" and voluntaries is not long maintained. Initially it works as a pun, associating the act of being pressed or printed with official approval and obligatory service, yet Donne goes on to insist that every subject has a right to enter the polemical fray because the cause concerns all. Indeed, the situation has, he claims, effectively collapsed the distinction made in civil law between civilians (*paganos*) and soldiers (*milites*). Under such conditions, there can be no non-combatants. This is all a rather roundabout way of justifying Donne, lacking an official position in the church or in one of the universities, in his decision to venture into the field. It also makes polemic appear heroic, the work of scholar–soldiers. Donne goes on to claim fulsomely that: "The influence of those your Majesties Bookes, as the Sunne, which penetrates all corners, hath wrought upon me, and drawen up, and exhaled from my poore Meditations, these discourses" (3).[22] These prefatory remarks focused on the public world of books offer no trace of the intimate story later told by Walton.

Donne's discourses appeared neatly printed in roman type in a quarto volume with generous margins. The large type and the small text block suggest that cost was not a primary concern. Anthony Raspa, in preparing his recent edition, has carefully surveyed the extant copies and has, on the evidence of stop-press corrections, concluded that Donne himself supervised the printing of the work (lxxix–lxxxii). In addition, the book itself suggests that Donne was attentive to the protocols of print.

In the preface, Donne warns the reader, "that when he findes in the printing of this Booke oftentimes a change of the Character, hee must not thinke that all those words or sentences so distinguished, are cited from other Authors; for I have done it sometimes, onely to draw his eye, and understanding more intensely upon that place, and so make deeper impressions thereof" (10). In other words, Donne has rejected the standard convention that sets off quotations with a distinctive type, often italic, and has instead opted to use italic for emphasis. Furthermore, Donne goes on to explain that, though those places where he is quoting will be known by the marginal notes, he does not "always and precisely and superstitiously binde my selfe to the words of the Authors." These pejorative adverbs, *precisely* and *superstitiously*, are associated with puritanism and Catholicism respectively, and Donne's apparently cavalier rejection of polemical convention serves to locate his own hermeneutic technique in the moderate middle. Donne, of course, insists that his citations "collect their sense, and express their Arguments or their opinions" (10), but he has, nonetheless, departed from the standard of precise quotation that had been and would remain central to polemical writing. The general practice is somewhat dismissively described by Sydney Anglo as "the customary tedious apparatus – generally set out in a bewildering variety of type-faces, where points are cited paragraph by paragraph, sentence by sentence, and even phrase by phrase, before being laboriously refuted."[23] This may be in good part a consequence of the way in which the argument of the book is constructed. Unlike the vast majority of religious polemics, *Pseudo-Martyr* does not attack a specific target text, which might be "laboriously refuted."

In contrast, Donne's strategy is to move from one author to another in order to display the perplexing variety of Catholic opinion on issues ranging from the pope's power to depose sitting monarchs to purgatory. Donne's chief strategy is to insist that there is too much uncertainty regarding these and other matters to justify refusing the oath. As he remarks, concerning Bellarmine's support for the pope's indirect deposing power, "neither the Doctrine, nor the Doctor are constant enough to build a Martyrdom upon" (185). Donne's avoidance of the typographical manicheanism visible in many polemics, like his decision to cite Catholic sources almost exclusively, works to erode confidence in the easy confessional binary of us and them, Catholics and Protestants. Yet it would be a mistake to conclude that this makes the book into a document of moderation. Donne, of course, uses the language of moderation – the autobiographical address in which he acknowledges his own Catholic past and that of his family is designed to establish his authority as an irenic healer of division – but its purpose, as in most polemic, is to isolate those who disagree, depicting them as fanatical extremists. Along the way, Donne has a number of astringent things to say about not only Catholic theology but also religious practices.

Addressing the cult of martyrdom that sprang up in response to the execution of Catholic priests by the English government, Donne comments: "I have seen at some Executions of Traiterous *Priests*, some bystanders, leaving all old Saints, pray to him whose body lay there dead; as if he had more respect, and better accesse in heauen, because he was a stranger, then those which were familiar, had" (163). Elsewhere he concludes, "So all discourse of Purgatorie seems to me to be but the *Mythologie* of the Romane Church, and a morall application of pious and useful fables" (92). "This *Comique-Tragicall* doctrine of *purgatory*" has, he writes, given rise to a profusion of ghost stories so incredible that "the more moderate sort of *Catholiques* have declined from any great approving of them" (94, 95). Donne's attack on the doctrine of purgatory is not the standard Protestant case against clerical greed and the selling of salvation. What chiefly concerns him is the way in which the terrors of purgatory are exploited to promote false martyrdom: the promise of an escape from purgatorial torments is, according to Donne, a strong but erroneous inducement to martyrdom.

The Jesuits, predictably, are subject to a torrent of abuse: they specialize "in kindling and blowing, begetting and nourishing jealousies in Princes, and contempt in Subjects, dissention in families, wrangling in Schooles, and mutinies in armies; ruines of Noble houses, corruption of blood, confiscation of States, torturing of bodies, an anxious entangling and perplexing of consciences" (106). But Donne is also scathing in his denunciation of ecclesiastic structures that encourage blind submission, describing clerical vows of obedience as "an *Indiscreete* surrendring of themselves, which professe any of the *rules* of Religion, to the command of their Prelate and Superior; by which, like uncleane beasts, *They swallow, and never chaw the cudde*" (134). He follows up with a long catalogue listing examples of misplaced obedience, including the story of "certaine youthes whom their *Abbot* sent with Figges to an *Ermit*, loosing their way sterved in the Desart, rather then they would eate the Figges, which they were commanded to deliver" (135). Donne gladly uses ridicule to establish the contrast between the irrational and excessive obedience demanded by the Roman hierarchy and the rational and inescapable obedience owed to the secular sovereign. These, and other similar passages, do not suggest that the book is exceptionally sensitive to the claims of Catholicism.[24]

Donne's supervision of the printing makes the book's Table of Chapters all the more striking. Some version of the Table appears to have circulated in manuscript before Donne composed the full text of *Pseudo-Martyr*. This not-quite private world of manuscript circulation allowed Donne to solicit responses before making his argument public in print.[25] His Advertisement to the Reader explains "that these Heads having beene caried about, many moneths, and thereby quarrelled by some, and desired by others, I was willing to give the Booke a hasty dispatch" (9). Additionally, "Some of the Romane profession, having onely seene the Heads and Grounds handled in this Booke, have traduced me as an impious and profane under-valuer of Martyrdom" (8). However, this prior circulation in itself does not explain the curious inclusion in the list of chapters 13 and 14 despite the fact that they are not actually in the book. This mismatch between text and para-text is remarkable; in fact, Donne complains in *Pseudo-Martyr* about Bellarmine's inaccurate indices and tables, adding, "they are so severe upon the Indices, made by some of their owne Church, that pretending still to have rased nothing in the body of the fathers, they expunge in the *Indices* many sentences, though the very wordes be in the Text it selfe" (91).[26] If an index that fails to mention passages that are in the text deserves censure, what is to be made of a table that advertises elements that are not in the book? Indeed, it is Donne's primary concern in the Advertisement to the Reader to explain that the last two chapters were dropped not just to hasten publication but to avoid offending Sir Edward Coke by intruding upon his argument with Robert Parsons.[27]

Such an explanation provokes more questions than it answers. If Donne had merely wanted to avoid Coke's terrain and speed publication, he could presumably have dropped items thirteen and fourteen from the table. In all likelihood, the ghostly presence of chapters 13 and 14 is a consequence of the decision to omit the final two chapters once the book was in the press. The Table, appearing on A4 recto and verso (figs. 18 and 19), is part of the first signature, while the Advertisement that acknowledges the inaccuracy of the Table is part of a two-leaf signature that also contains a list of errata and was clearly printed after the rest of the book was complete.[28]

Though the book's structure helps us to establish the sequence of printing and supports the notion that the decision to cut the final two chapters was made while the book was in the press, it does not in itself offer any explanation for that decision. The Table that points to an absence is not merely the residue of the material process of printing; it is also evidence of an ideological interruption. This trace naturally provokes curiosity and easily becomes an object of fantasy. Anthony Raspa, whose indispensable edition of *Pseudo-Martyr* is a model of careful scholarship, speculates: "In spite of the virulence of some of his comments about Catholicism, Donne's message in the final unwritten chapters of *Pseudo-Martyr* might have come perilously close to telling Christians to love one another as Christ had loved them" (liv).[29]

The notion that, finally, Donne would have concluded his polemic with a plea for Christian charity and toleration is not without appeal, but only specific language would allow us to gauge the balance between belligerence and reconciliation. Indeed, Raspa here reveals a tendency, common in discussions of *Pseudo-Martyr*, to mitigate, but the prevalent notion that the text is unusually moderate is misleading.[30] Although, when compared to the most toxic attacks on popery, *Pseudo-Martyr* appears restrained, it remains a polemical work intent upon eviscerating arguments against taking the Oath of Allegiance. Donne's position is exacting and unequivocal: English subjects owe an indefeasible loyalty and obedience to their sovereign, James I. Though Donne does not display the brutality of some contributors to the controversy, there is much in his book that is harsh and exaggerated, a fact that will not surprise any reader of early modern polemic.

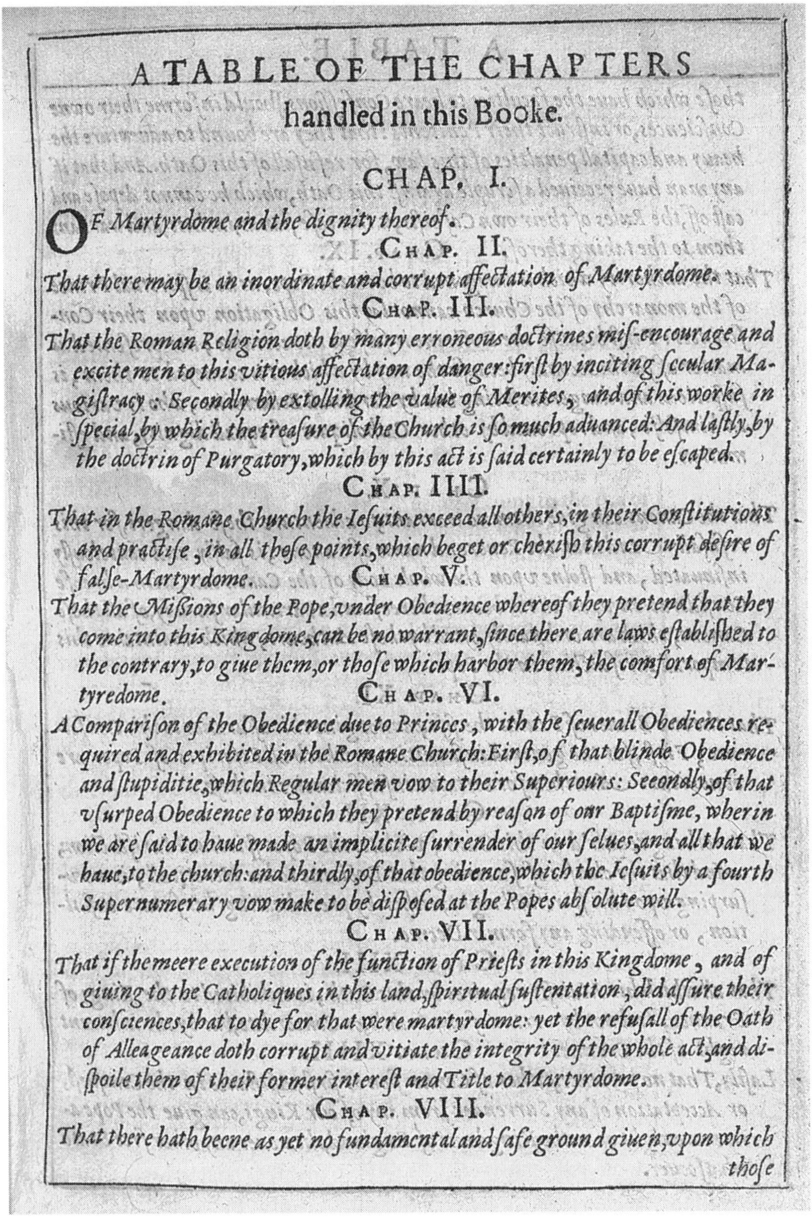

A TABLE OF THE CHAPTERS

handled in this Booke.

CHAP. I.

OF *Martyrdome and the dignity thereof.*

CHAP. II.

That there may be an inordinate and corrupt affectation of Martyrdome.

CHAP. III.

That the Roman Religion doth by many erroneous doctrines mif-encourage and excite men to this vitious affectation of danger: firft by inciting fecular Magiftracy : Secondly by extolling the value of Merites, and of this worke in fpecial, by which the treafure of the Church is fo much aduanced: And laftly, by the doctrin of Purgatory, which by this act is faid certainly to be efcaped.

CHAP. IIII.

That in the Romane Church the Iefuits exceed all others, in their Conftitutions and practife, in all thofe points, which beget or cherifh this corrupt defire of falfe-Martyrdome.

CHAP. V.

That the Miſſions of the Pope, vnder Obedience whereof they pretend that they come into this Kingdome, can be no warrant, fince there are laws eftablifhed to the contrary, to giue them, or thofe which harbor them, the comfort of Martyredome.

CHAP. VI.

A Comparifon of the Obedience due to Princes, with the feuerall Obediences required and exhibited in the Romane Church: Firft, of that blinde Obedience and ftupiditie, which Regular men vow to their Superiours: Seeondly, of that vfurped Obedience to which they pretend by reafon of onr Baptifme, wherin we are faid to haue made an implicite furrender of our felues, and all that we haue, to the church: and thirdly, of that obedience, which the Iefuits by a fourth Supernumerary vow make to be difpofed at the Popes abfolute will.

CHAP. VII.

That if the meere execution of the function of Priefts in this Kingdome, and of giuing to the Catholiques in this land, fpiritual fuftentation, did affure their confciences, that to dye for that were martyrdome: yet the refufall of the Oath of Alleageance doth corrupt and vitiate the integrity of the whole act, and difpoile them of their former intereft and Title to Martyrdome.

CHAP. VIII.

That there hath beene as yet no fundamental and fafe ground giuen, vpon which those

Fig. 18 A Table, John Donne, *Pseudo-Martyr* (1610)

A TABLE.

thofe which haue the faculties to heare Confeſſions,ſhould informe their owne Conſciences,or inſtruct their Penitents: that they are bound to aduenture the heauy and capitall penalties of this law, for refuſall of this Oath. And that if any man haue receiued a ſcruple againſt this Oath, which he cannot depoſe and caſt off, the Rules of their own Caſuiſts, as this caſe ſtands, incline, and warrant them, to the taking therof. CHAP. IX.

That the authority which is imagined to be in the Pope, as he is ſpiritual Prince of the monarchy of the Church, cannot lay this Obligation vpon their Conſciences: Firſt becauſe the Doctrine it ſelfe is not certaine, nor preſented as matter of faith: Secondly becauſe the way by which it is conueyed to them, is ſuſpitious and dangerous, being but by Cardinall Bellarmine, who is various in himſelfe, and reproued by other Catholiques of equall dignity, and eſtimation.

CHAP. X.

That the Canons can giue them no warrant, to aduenture theſe dangers, for this refuſall. And that the Reuerend name of Canons, is falſly and cautelouſly inſinuated, and ſtolne vpon the whole body of the Canon law, with a breefe Conſideration vpon all the bookes thereof: and a particular ſuruay, of all thoſe Canons, which are ordinarily cyted by thoſe Authcurs, which maintaine this temporall Iuriſdiction in the Pope.

CHAP. XI.

That the two Breues of Paulus the fift, cannot giue this aſſurance to this Conſcience. Firſt, for the generall infirmities, to which all Reſcripts of Popes are obnoxious: And then for certaine inſufficiencies in theſe.

CHAP. XII.

That nothing requir'd in this Oath, violates the Popes ſpirituall Iuriſdiction; And that the clauſes of ſwearing that Doctrine to bee Hereticall, is no vſurping vpon his ſpirituall right, either by preiudicating his future definition, or offending any former Decree.

CHAP. XIII.

That all which his Maieſty requires by this Oath, is exhibited to the Kings of Fraunce, And not by vertue of any Indult, or Concordate, but by the inhærent right of the Crowne. CHAP. XIIII.

Laſtly, That no pretence, eyther of Conuerſion at firſt, Aſſiſtance in the Conqueſt, or Acceptation of any Surrender from any of our Kings, can giue the Pope any more right ouer the Kingdome of England, then ouer any other free State whatſoeuer.

Fig. 19 A Table, John Donne, *Pseudo-Martyr* (1610)

Consequently, the received account of an unpolemical Donne has difficulty accommodating *Pseudo-Martyr*. After all, Donne was famously unwilling to confine religion to Rome, Wittenberg, or Geneva, allowing that "they are all virtuall beams of one sun."[31] A similar sentiment is visible in his declaration in the Preface to *Pseudo-Martyr*: "I used no inordinate hast, nor precipitation in binding my conscience to any locall Religion" (13). While many hear only disparagement in "locall Religion," there is a positive aspect to this designation. In fact, what from a modern perspective appears to be an easygoing ecumenical stance is, within the context of early modern debates about religion, a hard-edged argument. *Pseudo-Martyr* on more than one occasion provides a theoretical justification for what is best described as ecclesiological pluralism, a concession that there is no single legitimate form for the church.

In an often cited passage, Donne asserts that even if a company of savages should consent and concur to a civil manner of living, "Magistracie, & Superiority, would necessarily, and naturally, and Divinely grow out of this consent . . . And into what maner and forme soever they had digested and concocted this Magistracie, yet the power it-self was *Immediately* from God" (79). By denying that consent itself produces political power, Donne studiously avoids the argument for popular sovereignty common in Counter-Reformation political thought. He opts instead for a version of designation theory, which holds that though the community designates the form of rule and even nominates the particular ruler, the magistrate's power comes nonetheless immediately from God.[32] This endorsement of the divine right of kings is rarely placed within its full context. Donne's principal aim here is to make an argument concerning not political but ecclesiastical institutions. He goes on to argue that if such a community "should receive further light, and passe, through understanding the Law written in all hearts, and in the Booke of creatures, and by relation of some instructers, arrive to a saving knowledge, and Faith in our blessed Saviours Passion, they should also be a *Church*." As a result, "lawfull Ministers for Ecclesiastique function would rise up, though not derived from any mother Church, & though different from all the divers Hierarchies established in other Churches" (79). Donne pointedly breaks with the notion of apostolic succession, and thus rejects a claim maintained not only by defenders of the Roman Catholic Church but also by a range of Protestants from John Foxe, whose massive history positioned the present English church as the inheritor of a continuous Christian tradition stretching back to the early church, to Archbishop Bancroft who used the idea of *jure divino* and continuous episcopacy in his polemics against presbyterianism. Donne combines a radical ecclesiastical argument with a conservative constitutional theory in an account of the jurisdictional claims of church and state that gives priority, both theoretical and chronological, to secular authority: it comes first.

The relationship between secular and ecclesiastical authority is also treated in a chapter attacking the Jesuits, where Donne blames them for "that Distinction, Superstitious on one part, & Seditious on the other, of *Mediate* and *Immediate* institution of the two powers: for Ecclesiastique authority is not so *immediate* from God, that he hath appointed any such certaine *Hierarchy*, which may upon no occasion suffer any alteration or interruption: Nor is secular authority so *mediate*, or dependant upon men, as that it may at any time be extinguished, but must ever reside in some form or other" (78). Donne insists that ecclesiastical hierarchy is defectible, subject to the contingencies of history, and at the same time mystifies secular authority as immutable and everlasting. Such an argument invests political sovereignty with the theological trappings that had been associated with the church and strips the church of such traditional attributes as unity and perpetuity. Versions of this claim are made on several occasions. "Some States in our time seeme," Donne observes, "to have *Conditionall* and *Provisionall* Princes, between whom and subjects there are mutuall and reciprocal obligations; which if one side breake, they fall on the other, yet that *Soveraignty*, which is a power to do all things available to the maine endes, resides somewhere" (133). Even in conditions of civil war, sovereignty is only obscured not interrupted. Peaceful transitions also confirm the continuous nature of sovereignty: "in such secular states, as are provided by election, without all controversie the supreme power, in every *vacancy*, resides in some subiect, and inheres in some body, which as a Bridge, vnites the defunct, and the succeeding Prince" (78).

Donne's notion of sovereignty conforms to Bodin's account of "the most high, absolute, and perpetuall power ouer the citizens and subiects in a Commonweale."[33] Like Bodin, Donne holds that sovereignty is indivisible and has "no degrees, nor additions, nor diminutions" (133). Though Donne unsurprisingly maintains that "*Regall Authoritie*, by subordination of *Bishops*" – the present English system – is the "best and fittest way" to maintain peace and religion, he concedes that there are alternative forms of government. Yet he insists that in all cases a single sovereignty resides somewhere: "For God inanimates every State with one power, as every man with one soule" (133). An attraction to Bodin's account of sovereignty, however, need not be taken as evidence of a cringing acquiescence to the claims made by King James.

Recent work on early modern English absolutism has certainly made it clear that a range of opinion can be found marching under that flag (and indeed that the flag itself now seems to be of more recent vintage than has been commonly thought).[34] In fact, it has now become possible to speak of moderate absolutism or limited absolutism and not be accused of an oxymoronic obscurantism. In *Pseudo-Martyr* an absolutist language of sovereignty is dedicated to the establishment of the England's independence from papal jurisdiction. Donne, prudently, does not develop the consequences of his theory for government. Indeed, responding to a puzzling passage in which Bellarmine says that the power to depose resides in the pope, yet not as he is pope, Donne writes, "For other Princes, when they exercise their extraordinarie and Absolute power, and *prerogative*, and for the publique good put in practise sometimes some of those parts of their power, which are spoken of in Samuel, (which to many men seem to exceede *Regall power*) yet they do professe to doe these things as they are *Kings*" (186). This is hardly a ringing endorsement of an expansive royal prerogative. Indeed, one of the points that joins the two missing chapters is that they both would have required a more detailed examination of the prerogative rights of two particular monarchies, England and France.

The proposed thirteenth chapter would have treated the "inherent right" of the French crown to independence, while the fourteenth chapter would have shown that England's long allegiance to Rome had not impaired her claim to be a "free State," in other words a state without a superior power. The decision to omit these chapters may have been an act of prudence dictated by an unwillingness to venture into the question of the king's positive rights as opposed to a corrosively critical account of the pope's prerogatives. The omission proved fortunate; almost immediately after the printing of *Pseudo-Martyr* in mid-January 1610, a controversy arose over John Cowell's *Interpreter*, a book initially published in 1606. When Parliament met in February 1610, John Hoskyns, an acquaintance of Donne's, was to introduce the subject of Cowell's exaggerated claims for the royal prerogative, and the subsequent debate precipitated an intervention by James himself, who suppressed the book by proclamation.[35] In his address to Parliament on March 21, King James alluded to the suppression of Cowell's *Interpreter* and asserted that it is "sedition in subjects to dispute what a king may do in the height of his power . . ."[36] The royal prerogative was, according to James I, an inscrutable mystery and not to be examined. Under such circumstances, it may well have appeared advisable to drop the planned final chapters.

What the missing chapters, whether or not Donne chose to omit them, do tell us is that Donne's emergence in print was not entirely smooth, but there is little reason to think that Donne was dissatisfied with the work done by his publisher Walter Burre or the printer William Stansby. Soon after, when Donne published *Ignatius His Conclave*, the work was again given to Burre. Rather than providing evidence of a hesitant and resistant Donne, *Pseudo-Martyr*, both as book and text, demonstrates that Donne was eager to exploit the technology of print to make a public argument. In his Preface he complains that the Jesuits have "corrupted the two noble Inventions of these later ages, *Printing* and *Artillery*, by filling the world with their Libels, and Massacres" (25). This yoking of print and artillery was not, for Donne, a fleeting observation. In a sermon preached at St. Paul's on Christmas Day, 1621, he returned to the idea. Developing the claim that the "light of reason" has led to profitable and useful discoveries, he singles out two inventions: "printing, by which the learning of the whole world is communicable to one another, and our minds and our inventions, our wits and compositions may trade and have commerce together" and "artillery, by which wars come to a quicker end than heretofore, and the great expense of blood is avoided." Sanguine, if not sanguinary, this Donne is not the irenic and ironic figure familiar to us from literary biography. Donne's polemical moment provides evidence for an engagement with print and a religious animus that are rarely noticed; his first printed volume of poetry provides additional evidence of an interest in the uses of print, and yet it appears studiously unpolemical.

Sir Arthur Throckmorton, residing in Northamptonshire, acquired a copy of *An Anatomy of the World* on November 21, 1611. A steady collector of books, Sir Arthur received regular shipments from his agent in London. In this case, however, the book was delivered by Robert Pound, who brought it from London along with Marston's *Sophonisba*, Tourneur's *The Atheist's Tragedy*, and a copy of the newly completed King James Bible.[37] *An Anatomy of the World* would appear to fit somewhere between the play quartos that so clearly appealed to the rusticated gentleman, who had for a time attended court, and the new Bible, which he promptly donated to the parish church. An unprepossessing and slim octavo, the full title reads: "*AN* | ANATOMY | of the World. | WHEREIN, | BY OCCASION OF | the vntimely death of Mistris | Elizabeth Drvry | the frailty and the decay | of this whole world | is represented." Neither on the title page nor within the book is an attribution of authorship to be found. Instead of an address to the reader, a short poem, "To the Praise of the Dead, and the Anatomy," serves as an introduction to the main text, which is followed by "A Funeral Elegy." The two names that do appear on the title page are those of Elizabeth Drury, the ostensible subject of the poem, and Samuel Macham, the publisher. Either of these names might have allowed a knowledgeable reader to locate the book within a particular social context. However, of the two, the name of Macham would have been of greater significance to a regular browser of the London bookstalls. A publisher who concentrated on religious subjects and had a shop in St. Paul's Churchyard, Macham had a list that included a number of works by Joseph Hall, who was, in 1611, a rising star in the ecclesiastical hierarchy with a well-established literary reputation.[38] The association between Hall and Macham, as Geoffrey Keynes has suggested, probably owes something to the fact that both were natives of Ashby-de-la-Zouche.[39] Hall, who shared with Donne a connection to the Drurys, has usually been identified as the author of "To the Praise of the Dead, and the Anatomy" and credited with seeing the entire work through the press.[40] Whether Robert Pound knew of Donne's authorship or Hall's involvement, he clearly assumed that the new book published by Samuel Macham might well be of interest to his employer.

Though we unfortunately have no record of Sir Arthur's response to the poem, there were a number of other readers who were vocal, if not vociferous. The evidence that the poem caused a stir in some quarters is found in several reactions to the poem's reception in Donne's letters. In a letter from Paris, dated April 14, 1612, Donne explains to George Garrard:

> Of my Anniversaries, the fault that I acknowledge in myself, is to have descended to print anything in verse, which though it have excuse even in our times, by men who professe, and practise much gravitie; yet I confesse I wonder how I declined to it, and do not pardon myself: But for the other part of the imputation of having said too much, my defence is, that my purpose was to say as well as I could: for since I never saw the Gentlewoman, I cannot be understood to have bound myself to have spoken just truths, but I would not be thought to have gone about to praise her, or any other in rime; except I took such a person, as might be capable of all that I could say. If any of those Ladies think that Mistris *Drewry* was not so, let that Lady make her self fit for all those praises in the book, and they shall be hers.[41]

This often noted mea culpa regretting print is repeated in a separate letter to G.F. that employs very similar language. Though reiteration with subtle variations might be construed as evidence that Donne's repentance at having fallen into print is genuine, the self-conscious deployment of what is a rhetorical set-piece leaves room for doubt: a doubt that needs amplification in light of the many commentators who have taken Donne very much at his word.[42] In fact, the letter to Garrard exists in two versions;

the alternative version suggests that an excuse for printing is provided by "example of men, which one would thinke should as little have done it, as I."[43] Between this petulance and the generosity of "men who professe, and practise much gravitie" one detects an audible shift, a rhetorical elevation that transforms bitterness into light irony. Donne's shifting, if not exactly shifty, position on the propriety of printing verse needs to be handled with care.

Donne is conducting his own defense in these letters and, unsurprisingly given his training at the Inns of Court, he uses both legal language and tactics. The case against him – "the imputation" in the letter to Garrard and, more revealingly, "the indictment" in the letter to G.F. – is separated into two different charges. The first, the impropriety of printing verse, is not contested; the second, the impropriety of hyperbole, is. Donne scholars have naturally gravitated toward this second aspect of Donne's argument, offering as it does an apparent glimpse into Donne's own sense of his poetic method. However, to pursue this line of investigation is to accept the persuasive force of the dichotomy that splits the material from the textual, the medium from the message, the printed book from the lyric poem. Attention then shifts to the complexities of poetic form and the inheritance of genre; the fact of print is rendered accidental in both senses: it is unnecessary and it is the result of mere contingency, a lapse, a slip, a fall.

Insisting on the significance of print for an account of *An Anatomy of the World* does not deny the importance of Donne's second argument, but it does suggest that the matters of poetic technique raised by this argument need to be considered alongside issues of print. "An Anatomy" is, after all, one of the few Donne poems that does not seem to have circulated in an independent manuscript form, which suggests that it was composed for print publication. When the printing of *An Anatomy* has been considered, the focus is usually on Donne's inscrutable motives. The blankness of Donne's own professed perplexity – "I wonder how I declined to it" – serves as canvas upon which the literary scholar may portray a mercenary desire for patronage or the tentative, and revocable, ambitions of a would-be professional writer. In either case, the publishing event is understood in terms of John Donne's psychic economy, and the book is understood to be a product of his hopes and desires in all their potent ambivalence. An alternative account, one that attends to *An Anatomy* as primarily a printed book with specific physical features that was produced not simply by Donne, nor solely by the patronage complex of Sir Robert Drury and John Donne, but by these figures acting in concert with Joseph Hall, Samuel Macham, and the printer William Stansby, and intended for an extensive readership, tells us less about the travails of Donne and more about the conditions that shaped printed poetry in the early seventeenth century.

In pursuing such an approach, the evidence of reader reaction is valuable, as is Donne's own response to critical comment, because it allows us to develop a picture, admittedly fragmentary, of the book's reception. At the same time, attention to the book as a print artifact provides for a reconsideration of the project of printing itself. Far from being accidental, *An Anatomy* is a carefully conceived and printed book, a point that is rarely acknowledged and when acknowledged, never analyzed. Resort to the evidence of the printed book does not resolve the various difficulties presented by the linguistic text; however, it does promise to enrich our account of the problems presented by Donne's poem.

As Donne's letter campaign attests, the poem was quickly perceived to be a problem, and the criticism of the unnamed ladies mentioned by Donne was eventually joined by Ben Jonson's famous claim "that Dones Anniversarie was profane and full of Blasphemies / that he told Mr Donne, if it had been written of ye Virgin Marie it had been something to which he answered that he described the Idea of a Woman and not as she was."[44] This recalled, and perhaps apocryphal, exchange has had an abiding influence on the critical tradition treating the poem. Predictably Donne's "Idea of a Woman" has garnered more attention than Jonson's gibe, which is often construed as self-evidently wrong and simple-minded. Indeed, Jonson's accusation of blasphemy itself might best be understood as mimetic hyperbole, an inflated use of religious language that imitates Donne's own practice. Given Jonson's period of Roman Catholicism, which ended immediately before *An Anatomy* appeared, his suggestion that the Virgin would have been a suitable object for such praise is difficult to judge. Coming from a staunch Protestant, the comment would appear to be a not very subtle attack on Donne's residual attachment to Catholicism, a hint that what really troubles the poem is covert Mariolatry. However, the charge of blasphemy and the allusion to the Virgin work together to suggest that Donne has mistaken the earthly for the divine in his depiction of Elizabeth Drury as a mediating figure who, like the Virgin, could bring the heavenly to earth and the earthly to heaven. Her demise, as described by Donne, coincides with the loss of all mediation between the sacred and the profane, the celestial and the mundane; for Jonson, the result, an enormous amplification of the girl's virtue accompanied by a diminishment of revealed religion, is a form of theological incoherence.

Theology and religion have, unsurprisingly, continued to inform critical responses to the poem. Louis Martz, Barbara Lewalski, and Edward Tayler provide illuminating, and distinct, examples of this tendency. Each supplies a religious or theological framework that offers to makes sense of the poem's recalcitrant terms.[45] In fact, the way in which the poem continues to provoke strong claims about its religious valences (Martz's Counter-Reformation, Lewalski's Protestantism, and Tayler's Medieval Christianity) suggests that "An Anatomy of the World" is at once evasive and assertive. The poem says a great deal about the corruption of the contemporary world and about the virtue of the now dead Elizabeth Drury, but concerning the questions raised in contemporary debates about religion the poem offers only oblique comments and silence. The poem's refusal of explicit polemical engagement helps to explain the mixed reception that it received in a world shaped, in good part, by religious controversy. From the outset, the poem has incited a variety of religious interpretations. At once provocative and available for interpretation, it refuses to publicly espouse a particular creed or confession. Unlike *Pseudo-Martyr*, which gives copious detail on the author's religious loyalties and history, "An Anatomy" does not clearly locate itself within the field of religious controversy. It is left to the reader to decide where it fits, and the results have been widely, if not wildly, divergent.

Though the title page does provide a description of the contents, *An Anatomy of the World* is an austere little pamphlet. It lacks the sort of prefatory material that usually adorned volumes of poetry: there is no dedication and no address to the reader. The marginal notes that are added in the 1612 edition are a concession to reader friendliness that the 1611 volume conspicuously avoids. Instead, the printed book offers a poetic triptych: a central poem adjoined by two ancillary poems on either side. This arrangement is reinforced by the unusual decision to set the main text in italic and the two ancillary poems in roman. Like a triptych the book is best understood as an articulated whole, a claim that may seem obvious but that runs counter to much scholarly opinion, which habitually conceives of "A Funeral Elegy" as an undeveloped precursor and the prefatory poem "To the Praise of the Dead, and the Anatomy" as a derivative exercise. The critical trend has been to extract "An Anatomy" from its place within the book; if it is considered alongside another poem, it is invariably *The Progress of the Soul*, the second of the Anniversaries.[46]

The introductory poem develops two main claims. First there is a celebration of the fitness between poet and subject – the "Thrise noble maid" could not have found a better time to die "Then whiles this spirit liues; that can relate / Thy worth so well" (A3ʳ). This "mutuall grace" confirms her virtue and the poet's rare ability. Her elegy is "A taske, which thy faire goodnes made too much / For the bold pride of vulgar pens to tuch" (A3ᵛ). This assertion of ethical and aesthetic distinction, shared by the maid and her poet, is fundamental to the book itself, which invites judicious readers to join in a celebration of the private virtues exemplified by Elizabeth Drury. In fact, the second main claim modifies the exclusivity of the first: the speaker now suggests that the dead girl is herself the source of the praise that she now receives – "what we giue to thee, thou gau'st to us" – and that, furthermore, "these high songs that to thee suited bine, / Serue but to sound thy makers praise, in thine" (A3ᵛ). This conventional notion that praise of Elizabeth Drury is actually praise of God also serves to make the act of reading the poem a form of worship.[47] The first-person plural joins not only the present speaker and Donne but also those understanding readers who will join in singing the praises of Elizabeth and God. Certainly the concluding couplet invites such an interpretation: "Neuer may thy name be in our songs forgot / Till we shall sing thy ditty, and thy note" (A4ʳ). The speaker here anticipates joining Elizabeth Drury "Amid the Quire of Saints and Seraphim" – "we" again insists that this is not just the idiosyncrasy of an individual but the desire of a group, a community.

The possibility of a community of sorts is spelled out in greater detail in the opening of "An Anatomy" itself:

> When that rich soule which to her Heaven is gone,
> Whom all they celebrate, who know they haue one,
> (For who is sure he hath a soule, vnless
> It see, and Iudge, and follow worthinesse,
> And by Deedes praise it? He who doth not this
> May lodge an In-mate soule, but tis not his.)

The community of those offering praise is imagined as at once expansive, including all those who have a soul, and exclusive, rejecting any who fail to participate as unworthy. These opening lines issue a challenge and demand a judgment from the reader. To read on is, on one level, to join the community of perceptive judges, those whose discrimination allows them to recognize "worthinesse" whether found in a person, such as Elizabeth Drury, or in a book, such as *An Anatomy*.

This didactic imperative – to discern, to judge, and to act in pursuit of worthiness – is reiterated throughout the poem. Yet the precise attributes of worthiness remain obscure. As numerous critics have noted, the poem does not develop a robust account of Elizabeth Drury; instead the focus is sharpest in the satirical sections that anatomize the current state of the world. Elizabeth Drury, the embodiment of virtue, remains pallid, indeed ghostly. Hers is a spectral presence that haunts an increasingly disenchanted world: "Her Ghost doth walke; that is, a glimmering light, / A faint weake loue of virtue and of good / Reflects from her, on them which understood / Her worth" (A6ᵛ). What this might require beyond reading and understanding the poem is not evident. The poem does implore its reader to "feed (not banquet) on / The supernaturall food, Religion" (A8ᵛ), an alimentary metaphor that invests religion with solidity and associates it with sustenance, but also suggests that consumption and devotion are analogous. The antithesis between the substantial and nutritive *feed* and the insubstantial and gourmandizing *banquet* reveals a hesitancy over the voluntarism implied by the metaphor; the feeding imagined is not the frivolous selection of delicacies nor is it gluttonous carousing. And yet, despite these negations, the precise qualities of "The supernaturall food" remain deliberately obscure, a distinct impediment for those who would act upon the poem's injunctions.[48]

The poem's description of the present world is an eloquent and stark rendering of disenchantment that returns repeatedly to the fractured relationship between the heavenly and the mundane. Of celestial influences, the speaker laments: "If this commerce twixt heauen and earth were not / Embarr'd, and all this trafique quite forgot, / Shee, for whose loss we haue lamented thus, / Would work more fully' and pow'rfully on vs" (B4ᵛ). In an earlier section of the poem, the speaker considers the consequences of astronomy:

> For of Meridians, and Parallels,
> Man hath weau'd out a net, and this net throwne
> Vpon the Heauens, and now they are his owne.
> Loth to goe vp the hill, or labor thus
> To goe to heauen, we make heauen come to us.
>
> (B2ᵛ)

This description of ambitious but slothful "Man," employing technological aids in an effort to chart and ultimately control the stars, uses a spatial logic that appears in the section of the poem that treats the decay of man: "This man, whom God did wooe, and loth t'attend / Till man came vp, did downe to man descend" (A8ʳ). An impetuous Christ, eager to embrace his people, is contrasted with the current population distracted by Promethean projects and unwilling to do the "labor" necessary to go to heaven.

These dire conditions debilitate even "artists" – a term that extends to include not only makers of charms and amulets but also painters and poets: "What Artist now dares boast that he can bring / Heaven hither, or constellate anything?" (B4ᵛ). As a marginal note supplied in the second edition indicates, there is a "Weakness in the want of correspondence of heaven and earth" (1612, Sig. C6ʳ). The theme of disenchantment is, of course, given its most famous rendition in the passage on astronomical discoveries:

> And new philosophy calls all in doubt,
> The element of fire is quite put out;
> The sun is lost, and th' earth, and no man's wit
> Can well direct him, where to look for it.

(B1ʳ)

Though these familiar lines are not an epitome of the poem, they are, nonetheless, central. New philosophy – the emerging science of astronomy most obviously – is described as corroding the inherited vision of the cosmos, which imagined the universe as a series of concentric spheres. However, the speaker is quick to claim that this shift in cosmology is reflected in deteriorating social conditions:

> 'Tis all in pieces, all cohærence gone;
> All iust supply, and all Relation:
> Prince, Subiect, Father, Sonne, are things forgot,
> For euery man alone thinkes he hath got
> To be a Phœnix, and that then can be
> None of that kinde, of which he is, but hee.

(B1ʳ)

This pessimistic and fundamentally conservative diagnosis indicts antinomian individualism as a source of social anarchy and regrets the loss of assured authority and clear hierarchy that once structured the social world.[49] The phoenix, which usually figures as a type of Christ, is here the narcissistic fantasy of those who, in Grierson's revealing phrase, prefer "private judgement to authority."[50] Rather than place this social critique entirely within the context of new science, I would argue for the continuing relevance of the polemical situation addressed by *Pseudo-Martyr* a year earlier. The problem of confessional competition has not been resolved – and the poem offers to continue the argument made in *Pseudo-Martyr* by rejecting individual claims to sanctity made by would-be saints of all denominations. The singular phoenix and the convinced martyr are both examples of epistemological arrogance, a blind certitude that fails to recognize the tenuous and fallible nature of human knowledge.

Obviously the poem offers no elaborate treatments of theological complexities (though there are glancing allusions to both purgatory and transubstantiation), but rather a repeated call to a religion without content and a corresponding criticism of the social disorder that ensues when individuals claim a warrant that has no institutional standing.[51] Of course, few of Donne's contemporaries would have failed to condemn unfettered individualism and to endorse religion. The vexing question concerns the identity of the legitimate institutions that serve to curb the wayward inclinations of the individual, and on this point Donne remains silent.

The evasive nature of the poem's didacticism, its public call to pursue an indeterminate virtue, is best exemplified in the final section that treats the speaker's own role and considers the propriety of verse:

> And you her creatures, whom she works upon
> And have your last, and best concoction
> From her example, and her virtue, if you
> In reverence to her, do think it due,
> That no one should her praises thus rehearse,
> As matter fit for chronicle, not verse,
> Vouchsafe to call to mind, that God did make
> A last, and lasting'st piece, a song.
>
> (B6^r)

This direct address to the readers turns attention toward the audience as the speaker anticipates a hostile response: the followers of virtue may complain that verse is too frivolous a medium for a subject that demands the ponderous and public prose of chronicle history. Of course, the irony here is that the public language of chronicle would be entirely incapable of registering the significance of Elizabeth Drury, whose stature rests in large part on an immaculately eventless life. The juxtaposition of private verse and public chronicle, echoing lines from "The Canonization" – "And if no piece of chronicle we prove / We'll build in sonnets pretty rooms" – introduces a defense of public poetry. The decorum of public verse is supported by the example of the Song of Moses (Deuteronomy 31:19, 32:1–43), a divinely inspired piece of verse that serves to remind the Israelis of their obligation to God. This biblical allusion both attests to the divine and durable nature of verse, and associates the speaker with Moses himself. The speaker does not directly claim the status of law-giver or prophet; nonetheless, after an account that insists on the collapse of mediation between heaven and earth, the allusion to Moses points to the possibility of "commerce twixt heauen and earth." Like Moses delivering the law to the people of Israel, the speaker attempts to confine Elizabeth's "incomprehensibleness" within the strictures of "due measure." In a disenchanted and distracted world apparently cut off from heaven, he claims verse itself as a form of mediation: "Verse hath a middle nature: heauen keepes soules, / The graue keeps bodies, verse the same enroules" (B6^r). That verse has a commemorative function is expected in an elegy; however, the poem makes the more pointed claim that verse exists between the body in the grave and the soul in heaven, that it performs the very mediating function that had apparently been lost with the death of Elizabeth Drury. The printed poem is offered as a consolation and a corrective, a potential palliative in a desolate world; the "middle nature" of verse has the potential to constitute a new community of the godly.

The establishment of such a community is hampered by the difficulties of commemoration (like *Hamlet*, "An Anatomy" is obsessed with memory, mourning, and the care of the dead), a theme taken up in the last poem in the book. "A Funeral Elegy" begins with an account of the inadequacy of all physical monuments that leads on to a consideration of the form of the elegy itself: "Can these memorials, ragges of paper, giue / Life to that name, by which name they must liue?" The speaker goes on to ask whether Elizabeth can "stoope to bee / In paper wrap't; Or, when she would not lie / In such a house, dwell in an Elegie?" (B7^r). Yet these questions about the sufficiency of poetry to represent the departed girl are lightly dismissed: "But 'tis no matter; we may well allow / Verse to live so long as the world will now" (B7^r). The image of the present book composed of "ragges of paper" is soon joined by another volume: the book of destiny.

The speaker anticipates a reader of "the booke of destiny" who: "measuring future things by things before, / Should turn the leaf to read, and read no more, / Would think that either destiny mistook, / Or that some leaves were torn out of the book" (B8^r). A densely paradoxical image (mistaking destiny and its damaged book), these lines introduce the temporal process of reading a physical, and frail, book, not unlike the one held by the actual reader of the poem. The image of destiny's book appears once again in the conclusion when the speaker imagines that all those who "true good prefer" shall remain on earth as Drury's delegates: "They shall make up that book, and shall have thanks / Of fate, and her, for filling up their blanks." The book of destiny containing the unfinished story of Elizabeth Drury, a narrative that must be completed by the actions of her readers, becomes indistinguishable from *An Anatomy* itself. The printed book, rather than being an autonomous and self-enclosed aesthetic object, is an instigation to action; the virtuous deeds that it calls forth are a part of Elizabeth Drury's legacy: "And 'tis in heaven part of spiritual mirth, / To see how well the good play her, on earth" (B8ᵛ).

This notably optimistic conclusion suggests that in heaven there remains some solicitude for earthly affairs. Furthermore, the "gift of her example" is made possible by the book itself. Indeed, those who play Elizabeth on earth learn their parts from the script provided by *An Anatomy*. Like "To the Praise of the Dead and the Anatomy," "A Funeral Elegy" has been accused of failing to match the achievement of the central poem. Lewalski, for example, finds the poem conventional in its use of "Petrarchan hyperbole and of panegyric celebrations of the ideal through a particular example."[52] If one follows the accepted chronology of composition, this makes perfect sense. A first attempt that does not manage to innovate gives rise to a subsequent composition that introduces a new typological symbolism. Thus John Carey, in keeping with his psycho-biographical approach, places the "Funeral Elegy" before "An Anatomy" in his Oxford Classics edition. But the printed book gives a different order: the sequence is reversed with the most recent composition coming first and the earliest appearing last. Though the sequence of texts in the book does not guarantee a particular reading procedure, it does establish a range of possibilities, a limited number of permutations.

Though it is perfectly plausible to read the poems as documents that attest to the aesthetic and psychic development of Donne, an account of the poems as printed must consider their arrangement within the physical space of the volume. The fact that the two companion poems are often held to be conventional is not a reason to look past them. The three poems together create a complex structure in which there is both dissonance and continuity. The juxtaposition of the three separate poems invites the reader to speculate on their relationship and even place them in dialogue with each other. The death of Elizabeth Drury is a focus in each, but there is a less obvious concern running through the three poems. "To the Praise of the Dead" introduces that potent metaphor of celestial song that is developed at length in "An Anatomy"; more interestingly, its allusion to "the Quire of Saints and Seraphim" puns on choir / quire in a way that links figures of song to those of the book. "An Anatomy," in turn, asserts: "Shee's now a part both of the Quire, and Song" (A5ʳ). The obvious meaning is that she is both singer and song; one need not dwell on the fact that *An Anatomy* is composed of two quires or gatherings of paper in order to detect a resonance with images of the book. "An Anatomy" also takes up the question of verse as song as well as the problem of its material embodiment. Finally, "A Funeral Elegy" concentrates attention on the inadequacy of the materials of commemoration. Though these connections are not reducible to a single claim, they do suggest that the volume itself considers, in an oblique fashion, its status as a book of printed poetry.

As a book, *An Anatomy* is an unusual performance – a slim pamphlet in octavo it is at once austere and ostentatiously literary. Unapologetic and enigmatic, the volume manages to combine the sharply deflationary rhetoric of satire with the inflationary language of epideictic in a way that defies easy resolution. Constantly harking back to a moment, always ready to recede into a still more distant past, when things were whole, the poem insists on the impoverishment of the present. As didactic poetry this may successfully create a sense of sinful inadequacy, but the attempt to enlist readers as followers of Elizabeth Drury does not offer a specific program, save only to become appreciative readers of the book itself. As opposed to offering a clear theological orthodoxy, the book offers its readers a particular stance and a peculiar style. In short, the volume eschews the directly polemical engagement found in *Pseudo-Martyr*, offering instead a general corrective, a self-consciously witty and difficult set of poems that tests a reader's patience and ingenuity. In contrast to the hard words and uncompromisingly manifest positions of polemic, the volume offers the consolations of poetry. *An Anatomy* deplores the narcissism prevalent in contemporary society, and seeks to fashion a fellowship of discerning readers who will follow true virtue. Acknowledging the prevalence of strife and conflict, a world in which people "Argue, and agree not, till those stars go out" ($B8^r$), it nonetheless holds forth the possibility of community founded on aesthetic discernment and moral rectitude. And yet this imagined cult of Elizabeth Drury still depends for its realization on an appeal to the vagaries of the individual, and wayward, reader.

As noted earlier, the book provoked confusion and consternation when it first appeared. John Davies of Hereford supplies one extended, and under-analyzed, response in his own elegy for Elizabeth Dutton, who was daughter to Sir Thomas Egerton, himself the eldest son of Lord Ellesmere, Lord Chancellor of England. The poem appears in a section of Davies's *The Muses Sacrifice* (1612) revealingly entitled "Rights of the Living, and the Dead" that includes several elegies.[53] The title – appearing under a headline announcing "OBIT RIGHTS" – notes that Elizabeth was at age eleven married to John Dutton, who was then fifteen; John died at seventeen, "and left the said Elizabeth a Virgin-Widow" ($P6^v$). This peculiar set of circumstances provides ample scope for the elegist: "A Virgin, Wife, and Widow, three that One / Held rarely perfect in like Vnion" ($P7^r$). The paradoxical sum of female innocence and experience as defined by the conventional triad of maid, wife, and widow, Elizabeth Dutton surpasses Elizabeth Drury. Moreover, Davies asserts that "*Wit* for her *worth* can ne'er hiperbolize; / Much lesse a *Poet* in it Poetize; / Sith what or *Wit* or *Poetry* can praise / (With their best *Arte*) was found in her" (P7^v). This variation on the inexpressibility *topos* seems to glance at Donne's hyperbolic wit by suggesting that here is an individual whose worth cannot be traduced by witty hyperbole and feigning poetry.[54] Unlike the poet who lavished praise on an unknown subject, Davies claims direct and intimate knowledge of his paragon: "I best can witness how her time she spent, / Who taught her *hand* to shew her *hearts* entent" (P8^r). Furthermore, this claim insists on something more than the physical and psychic proximity of teacher and student; as a writing master, Davies taught Elizabeth to express her "*hearts* entent" in written language. As a teacher of sincere writing, he makes a strong claim for the sincerity of his own verse. Where Donne used non-acquaintance as a defense against charges of partiality ("Since I never saw the Gentlewoman, I cannot be understood to have bound myself to have spoken just truths"), Davies emphasizes intimate, personal experience as the legitimate source of evaluation and praise. Donne's insistence on "incomprehensibleness" contributes to a sense of obscurity and disenchantment; Davies's claim to clarity privileges experience and suggests that it can be captured in language.

Davies more explicitly engages Donne in a passage on the limits of proper praise:

> To say thou was the *Forme*, (that is the *soule*)
> Of all this *All*; I should thee misenroule
> In *Booke* of *Life*; which (on the Earth) they keepe
> That of *Arts fountaines* have carowsed deepe.
> Nay, so I should displease and wrong thee both:
> For, *vniust praise* thou canst not chose but lothe,
> That lothed'st it *here*; then *there*, more (past compare)
> For, hee's the *Soule* of *All* by whom they *are*.
>
> (Q2^r)

The charge that Donne is guilty of blasphemy, made familiar by Jonson's remark to Drummond, is offered here by implication. According to Donne, "Her name" gave the world (Davies's "all this *All*") "forme and frame" (A5^v), but Davies after pedantically observing that *form* means soul, objects that such an assertion is a diminishment of God's creative power. "Misenroule," furthermore, recalls and corrects the closing rhyme of "An Anatomy" ("soules"/"enroules"), which itself echoes the "enrol"/ "soul" rhyme from "A Funeral Elegy." Davies the writing master notices the language of inscription that marks Donne's poems and hints that drinking deeply from "*Arts fountaines*" may lead to a presumptuous attempt to write the "*Booke* of *Life*" or catalogue the elect. Rejecting the language of superlatives and the notion that anyone other than Christ could be the form or soul of the world, Davies also reveals a desire to reaffirm a conventional eschatology.

In an earlier invocation to his muse, he implores: "raise / Her vp my *Muse*, ere she be rais'd, at last" (P7^v), and a subsequent section of the poem takes up the question of physical resurrection in great detail. Rebuking the mortalism of an imagined "Atheist," the speaker defends the immortality of the soul and the truth of resurrection: "Each Graine that rots before the same doth spring / Is a figure of this reall thing" (Q3^r). Using language reminiscent of debates over the Eucharist, Davies asserts that the plant rising from a buried seed figures the bodily resurrection of the buried individual. Such thoughts are optimistic, not lugubrious: the God that created the world from nothing will have no difficulty restoring dissolved bodies. Davies brings these abstruse, yet not uncommon, considerations to bear on a particular possibility:

> Say *Men* eate *Men*, through some hard exigent,
> And them conuerted haue to *nutriment*,
> Yet shall their *Excrement* (how ere vnmeete)
> At last yeeld vp their Relickes *pure* as *sweet*!
>
> (Q3^v)

Hamlet's charnel meditations combine with Donne's insistent troping upon relics to produce not a melancholic and skeptical vision of death and physical degradation but an optimistic affirmation of God's "matchlesse Pow'r" (Q4^r). This consideration of divine power leads Davies to explain why he contemplates Elizabeth "Among his Praises that most praisefull be" (Q5^r). Adopting the same position articulated by Hall in "To the Praise of the Dead," Davies explains that in praising her, he praises her creator.

However, the poem is not merely an expression of the poet's piety. Davies describes the poem as "th'*Oblation* of my *Zeale*, / Which I doe offer for the *Common-weale*," and asks for Elizabeth's forbearance: "sith my scope / was but thy *glory*, and the Peoples *good*, / which in *great light*, goe right in likelihood" (Q5^v). Davies here makes an explicit claim for the poem's public function: an offering for the "*Common-weale*" that intends the "Peoples *good*" as well as Dutton's glory. As is conventional, the elegy serves a dual purpose, memorializing Elizabeth Dutton's probity and encouraging its readers to adopt her exemplary virtues as their own.

Davies shows no obstinate condolement, no sense that the death of one so young and innocent calls the order of the universe into question. Indeed, his pious optimism (signaled by *zeal,* which was to be one of the seventeenth century's most hotly contested concepts), his forthright adoption of a public role, and his invocation of a benign providence put him at some distance from Donne.

It is perhaps unsurprising, then, that the passage immediately following takes up the question of Donne himself.

> I must confesse a *Priest* of *Phebus,* late,
> Vpon like *Text* so well did meditate,
> That with a sinlesse *Enuy* I doe runne
> In his *Soules* Progresse, till it all be *DONNE.*
> But, he hath got the *start* in setting forth
> Before me, in the Trauell of that *WORTH:*
> And me out-gone in Knowledge eu'ry way
> Of the *Soules* Progresse to her finall *stay.*
> But his sweet *Saint* did *vsher* mine therein;
> (Most blest in that) so, he must needs beginne;
> And read vpon the rude Anatomy
> Of this dead World; that, now, doth putrifie.
>
> Yet greater *Will,* to this great *Enterprise*
> (Which in great *Matters* solely doth suffice)
> He cannot bring than I: nor, can (much lesse)
> Renowne more *Worth* than is in *WORTHINES!*
>
> (Q6ʳ)

This expression of deference is misleading.[55] Though Davies acknowledges himself an epigone, he nonetheless insists that what he lacks in knowledge and technique is made up for by his magnanimous will.[56] An aggressive comparison of wills may be a symptom of the anxiety of influence, a clumsy attempt by Davies to deal with his intimidating predecessor; but this language also registers a more immediately available meaning, a subtle accusation that Donne suffers from a deficiency of the will or, to use a modern idiom, bad faith.

Situated within the context of the entire volume, Davies's praise of Donne's expansive knowledge is revealed to be a backhanded compliment. The opening verse – dedicating the book to Lucy, Countess of Bedford, a patron of Donne's; Mary, Countess-Dowager of Pembroke; and Elizabeth, Lady Cary, the author of *The Tragedy of Mariam* – surveys the literary scene and professes concern for the unsophisticated multitude subject to a *"Haile of hard Conceits"* and overwhelmed by ignorance and false learning: *"What* Piles *of* Pamphlets, *and more* wordy Bookes, / *now farse the World!*" ($^{**}4^r$–$^{**}4^v$). In a passage that invokes the scholasticism of Donne, Davies asserts "Wit's *most wrong'd by priuiledge of* Schoole" ($^{**}4^v$) before developing the charge:

> *Some search the* Corpes *of all* Philosophie,
>   *and eu'ry* Nerue *and* Veyne so *scrible on,*
> *That where it should be* Truths Anatomie,
>   *they make it* Errors *rightest* Scheleton.
>
> *Some others on some other* Faculties,
>   *still (fondly) labour, but to be in* Print . . .
>
> (A1^r)

Davies's chief target is an academic discourse of commentary and epitome, but he is also criticizing the anatomizing vogue, a literary dissection that produces not truth but a skeletal and erroneous version of it.[57] He here connects the desire to "be in Print" with the derivative and parasitical discourse of the anatomy, suggesting that the pursuit of print publication produces degenerate and corrupt books. The itch to print has a deleterious effect on other departments of learning, but especially poetry:

> *But* Poesie (*dismall* Poesie) *thou art*
>   *most subiect to this sou'raigne* Sottishnesse;
> *So, there's good Cause thou shouldst be out of heart,*
>   *sith all, almost, now put thee vnder* Presse.
>
> *And* Wit *lies shrowded so in* Paper-sheetes,
>   *bound* Hand *and* Foote *with* Cords *of* Vanities:
> *That (first) with all* Obscuritie *it meetes;*
>   *so, tis impossible it ere should rise.*
>
> (A1^r)

This conventional complaint about the proliferation of bad poetry flowing from the presses, like so many similar indictments, serves as a defensive gesture differentiating the present book from all of its unworthy competitors. However, Davies gives this standard move a specific and telling valence: resisting "Obscuritie" and "hard conceits," he advocates verse that is accessibly didactic and, thus, equates poetry and rhetoric. Poets were, "in the Worlds *first* Age, / *pow'rfull'st* Perswaders; *whose sweet* Eloquence: / (*That euer, staidly, ranne from holy Rage*) / *was the first* Rethoricke *sprung from* Sapience" (A2^r).[58] The parenthetical invocation of "*holy rage*" – the Platonic furor that frequently was assimilated to Christian notions of divine inspiration – identifies it as the source of "*sweet* Eloquence" while the adverb *staidly* insists that the stream of inspired eloquence is not turbulent. Poets have, according to Davies, an obligation to use their art to teach right doctrine and to persuade readers to follow virtue. Apparently, Davies found in Donne's "Anatomy" evidence that his own approach to poetry, owing allegiance to Sidney and Spenser, was under attack.

Davies's *The Muses Sacrifice* was published by George Norton, who also published works by several of the Jacobean Spenserians.[59] He was the publisher of *The Shepheards Pipe* (1614), with a dedication signed by William Browne, containing eclogues by George Wither, Christopher Brooke, and John Davies.[60] He also published Wither's *A Satyre: Dedicated to His Most Excellent Maiestie* (1614) and *The Shepheards Hunting: Being, Certaine Eglogues Written During the Time of the Authors Imprisonment in the Marshalsey* (1615), as well as William Browne's *Britannia's Pastorals* (1613), which includes a catalogue of English poets that begins with Sidney and Spenser and ends with Wither and Davies (F2^r–F3^v). Other items on Norton's list show a marked propensity for a hard-edged, patriotic Protestantism.[61] Obviously, the writers published by Norton do not assume a uniform, corporate identity, but the evidence of collaborative work along with assorted commendatory poems suggests an awareness of shared commitments and personal relationships that justifies speaking of them as a group. In fact, the Spenserians present the intriguing and paradoxical possibility of a print coterie, a group of loosely affiliated writers who exploited print rather than manuscript. That these poets were committed to print is itself an important fact with ramifications that are both political and aesthetic.

The rejection of poetic obscurity typical of, though not limited to, the Jacobean Spenserians is connected to a commitment to print as the means by which to reach the widest reading public. Arguably the very expansion of the reading public provoked a reaction on the part of some writers, who, according to Arnold Stein, "intended to take literature away, not only from the folk, but from all but the most witty."[62] A formidable example of this trend is provided by George Chapman who, in 1595, asserts: "Obscuritie in affection of words, & indigested concets, is pedanticall and childish; but where it shroudeth it self in the hart of his subiect, vtterd with fitnes of figure, and expressive Epethites; with that darkness wil I still labour to be shaddowed."[63] Chapman's outspoken defense of a self-consciously elitist poetics presents an extreme version of the reaction against the Elizabethan sentiment captured in George Gascoigne's observation that "the haughty obscure verse doth not much delight." The Elizabethan resistance to obscurity is also visible in Thomas Campion's *Observations in the Art of*

English Poesie, which opens with the declaration: "There is no writing too breefe that, without obscuritie, comprehends the intent of the writer."[64] Brevity without obscurity is the soul of wit. The same hostility toward obscurity is audible in the seventeenth century as poets and printers react to the verse of those who would later come to be called "Metaphysical poets."[65]

A representative statement, written around 1610, is supplied by Dudley North, who professes that he "cannot approve the ridling humour lately affected by many, who think nothing good that is easie, nor any thing becoming passion that is not exprest with an hyperbole above reason."[66] "These tormentors of their owne and their Readers braines" may be "admired in their high obscure flight," but North himself aims to "procure but a familiar delight to a superficiall reading." The aristocratic pose that identifies poetry as a pleasant pastime should not be mistaken for a dismissal. North, dedicating his volume to Lady Mary Wroth, invokes, in revealing terms, the achievement of her uncle, Sir Philip Sidney, whose "extant works flourish in the applause of all, by a happy and familiar display of their beauties to the meanest" (a3^r). No one now is likely to mistake Sidney for the people's poet, but from the vantage point of the early seventeenth century, he appeared to many both profound and accessible.[67]

Jasper Mayne's allusion to *An Anatomy* is best understood within the context of this struggle over proper poetics. In his elegy for Donne, included in the *Poems of J. D. With Elegies on the Authors Death* (1633), Mayne identifies "thy Anniverse, / A Poëm of that worth, whose every teare / Deserves the title of a severall yeare. / Indeed so farre above its Reader, good, / That wee are thought wits, when 'tis understood" (Eee1^r). Mayne subtly associates technical poetic achievement with moral worth in the single word *good* and commends the reading dynamic that Davies and North deplore. A charitable interpretation of this reading process sees not empty self-congratulation but sustained edification that qualifies the successful reader for the title of wit. And yet it is also quite clearly a process of social distinction: the poem separates understanders from the ignorant, a determination apparently based on cognitive ability as opposed to status. Nevertheless, the capacity to read, enjoy, and understand Donne is not the result merely of native intelligence but the mark of a certain form of acculturation. The 1633 volume of Donne's verse promises to make this acculturation available to the purchaser. In a preface, entitled "The Printer to the Understanders," John Marriot begins: "For this time I must speake only to you: at another, *Readers* may perchance serve my turne; and I thinke this a way free from exception, in hope that few will have a minde to confesse themselves ignorant" (A1^r). What follows is a strenuous attempt to deny that the volume bears any resemblance to "ordinary publications." Marriot's strategy is similar to Mayne's; he addresses himself selectively (and proleptically) to the understanders, those who have the capacity to recognize that this is no "ordinary" book, knowing that few will have the courage to declare themselves undiscerning and insensible, but to join this club one must buy, read, and understand the book. This confluence of critical appreciation and sales pitch raises the possibility that the commercial interest of the publisher Marriot is not readily separable from the aesthetic interest of the amateur poet Mayne.

Both the reservations of Davies and the praise of Mayne locate *An Anatomy of the World* within the literary culture of early seventeenth-century England: on the one hand, an admiring but critical engagement that faults the poem for its failure to uphold an earlier poetic ideal of public persuasion and takes issue with the poem's rebarbative conceits and hyperbole; on the other hand, a laudatory account that celebrates the poem for the very same features, seeing them as a test of the reader's own skill and ingenuity. Though Davies and Mayne do not offer the only responses, they usefully point to the range of opinions provoked by Donne's first printed volume of verse.[68] While these reactions clearly respond to the specific poetic qualities of the text, contentious and varied responses were seen as an especially likely consequence of print publication because print – unlike manuscript circulation which was able to at least maintain the polite fiction of a select (and selected) readership of friends and friends of friends – exposed the text to the marketplace and made it available and vulnerable to any stranger willing to pay the asking price.

An awareness of the variety of readers and the range of their possible responses is frequently attested to in the prefaces of sixteenth- and seventeenth-century books. Indeed, the vast majority of prefatory matter is devoted to an attempt, however hopeless, to manage the reader's response by defusing criticism. Authors and printers are constantly addressing themselves to "the general reader," "the great variety of readers," "the gentle reader," and the ever popular, "Christian reader" in an effort not only to sell the book but also to defend its procedures. Such prefatory addresses and commendatory poems are often preoccupied with the figures of Momus, a minor Greek god of ridicule, and Zoilus, an infamous grammarian and critic of Homer, who together represent the endless carping of hostile readers. Unsurprisingly, readers and writers alike came to think of themselves as living in a critical (the word itself is a late

sixteenth-century coinage) age. The quarrels of poets, playwrights, historians, and editors were both highly contentious and highly visible, and
frequently they fed on and into the theological and political polemics
written by divines and statesmen. Under such circumstances print publication was perceived to be an assertive act, one that invited criticism and
required justification.

Donne was clearly taken aback by the hostile reception of his printed
poems, but we cannot take his expressions of regret at face value. The
notion of a print-phobic Donne in particular needs to be abandoned in
light of his foray into print in the years 1610–12. The poems were "at least in
part a business venture" according to Frank Manley, who suggests that at
this time Donne "thought of making his living in some fashion by writing"
(5). But Manley goes on to claim that the criticism of the Anniversaries
"cured him of any such notions" and left Donne "ashamed and humiliated." Donne appears to have overcome his shame by 1614 when he wrote
to Henry Goodyer announcing: "I am brought to a necessity of printing
my Poems."[69] Admittedly, in the same letter, he explains that the imagined
volume will be "not for much publique view, but at mine own cost, a few
Copies" (197), which suggests something short of commercial print publication. Nonetheless, the vexing terms (print–manuscript, public–private,
amateur–professional) point to the complexity of Donne's engagement
with print, as he himself remarks, "I apprehend some incongruities in the
resolution."

Critics have been less than attentive to Donne's engagement with print
because they have preferred a "manuscript" Donne: an intimate, intellectual, private, and epistolary Donne, a Donne "consciously opposing the
values of the open market and the promiscuously purchasable page created
by print."[70] In this critical discourse, Donne serves as the preeminent
example of a poet for whom manuscript circulation was "a mode of social
bonding" that produced "scribal communities." Manuscript circulation
and print dissemination of verse, in Arthur Marotti's terms, "not only
competed but also influenced each other and, to a great extent, coexisted by
performing different cultural functions." However, despite the suppleness
of Marotti's formulation, print and manuscript are frequently understood
as antithetical pursuits, and more regard is given to "different cultural
functions" than to mutual competition and influence.[71] Advocates of a
scribal seventeenth century may be forgiven to the degree that they work
to dislodge a massive misunderstanding of actual literary conditions.
Unfortunately, historical revision, as is often the case, threatens to over-
correct the deficiencies of an earlier view. Recent emphasis on the

continued vitality of scribal publication has helped to create skepticism about the once common notion of a print revolution, but the press's failure to immediately "extinguish" older methods of publication does not mean that print did not have a transforming effect on literary culture. Exaggerated claims about the influence of "print logic" or the presence of a homogeneous "print culture" are certainly vulnerable, and yet we must not forget that for the English reader in the early seventeenth century print was inescapable.

Donne's case is especially interesting because he straddles not only the divide between print and manuscript but also that between poetry and polemic. Our own sense that poetry and polemic are radically distinct activities makes their proximity in Donne appear slightly incoherent, but here we encounter the prejudices of a literary tradition that considers poetry, its composition and its reading, to be largely an affair of private individuals. John Stuart Mill's reading of Wordsworth provides a fitting, and influential, paradigm of poetry as therapeutic, a salve for the wounded psyche. For such a sensibility, poetry that pursues polemical targets forfeits its claim to be called poetry; the result is a considerable diminution of poetry's scope. Nonetheless, the divide between poetry and polemic in the seventeenth century was discernible. Though polemical verse was ubiquitous, it, along with innumerable prose polemics, gave impetus to the development of conspicuously non-polemical poetry. *An Anatomy* can be read in these terms: deliberately obscure and difficult, it does not directly engage in controversy. Indeed, the poem both describes and creates a condition in which the interpretive certitude fundamental to polemic seems both inappropriate and unavailable. And yet this characteristic, which makes *An Anatomy* resemble Q2 *Hamlet*, also makes it a confirmation of the argument offered in *Pseudo-Martyr*. In a corrupt world, fallible humans have few unimpeachable warrants for action, and thus radical skepticism becomes an argument for conformity.

CHAPTER 5

Areopagitica *and "the true warfaring Christian"*

Above all Milton *fought.*
Christopher Hill

No account of the relationship between print and religious polemic in early modern England would be complete without a consideration of Milton's *Areopagitica.* Milton is perhaps the only canonical writer of English literature who is celebrated for his polemic; indeed, Milton is frequently credited with raising polemic to the level of art.[1] Milton's tract is the first great polemic in defense of unlicensed printing and has long been identified as the beginning of a robust Anglo-American tradition of free speech and religious toleration. Alternatively, *Areopagitica* functions in my argument not as a beginning but as an end. Rather than situating Milton's tract as an inaugural celebration of freedom, I place it at the end of the wars of truth that followed the Reformation. Obviously, one could argue that in 1644 neither religious war nor its verbal equivalent, polemic, was at an end. This is quite true. However, *Areopagitica* does represent the culmination of an optimistic Protestant belief in the efficacy of printed polemic. *Areopagitica's* defense of religious polemic ("books of controversy in religion"), as opposed to its advocacy of toleration, was to find few supporters after 1660.[2]

In addition to re-establishing the monarchy and the episcopal Church of England, the Restoration enshrined the ideal of "politeness," which, as J. G. A. Pocock writes, "formed part of the latitudinarian campaign to replace prophetic by sociable religiosity."[3] Essential to the elevation of politeness was the denial of enthusiasm in all its many forms; as Christopher Hill concludes, "enthusiasm was rejected in science as in religion or politics."[4] The emergence of a new polite politics and its accompanying morality did not, of course, necessitate an end to polemic, but it did require that polemic be written in a new manner, a manner aptly described by Pocock: "The polemic against enthusiasm was to continue for another hundred years – so deep were the scars of the Puritan interregnum on the governing-class mind – and the concepts of politeness, manners, and taste were to remain integral parts of its strategy."[5] With the ascendancy of irony, wit, and innuendo, polemic became an insiders' game of deciphering and discernment, except in establishment polemics against nonconformists and Catholics where rhetorical violence was still deemed permissible.[6]

Areopagitica belongs to a different world; Milton is writing at a moment of national crisis, a moment of intense conflict when the concept of controversial writing has finally been labeled *polemic* in English.[7] As is well known, the tract addresses the threat of a renewal of the licensing system that had been abrogated by the abolishment of Star Chamber in 1641. The lapse in censorship was accompanied by an explosion of printing, especially of smaller, topical pamphlets, and to address this situation as well as the professed concerns of the Stationers' Company, which no longer had a legal warrant for the maintenance of copyright, the Long Parliament passed on June 14, 1643, a new ordinance to regulate the press.[8]

These conditions spurred Milton to articulate what had until then remained implicit in the practice of print polemic. For *Areopagitica* is far more than a polemic: it is a polemic for polemic.[9] Though Milton's argument includes claims to freedom of conscience and speech, it is most obviously an assertion of the virtues of zealous dispute, whether in the form of brotherly dissimilitudes or exchanges with the adversary. Scholars have frequently connected *Areopagitica* to Milton's personal pique at having his controversial writings on divorce threatened with censorship; what is less often noted is that *Areopagitica* provides a general defense of the mode of writing found in the early anti-prelatical tracts.[10] As Milton writes in the opening of *An Apology Against a Pamphlet,* "And because I observe that feare and dull disposition, lukewarmeness & sloth are not seldomer wont to cloak themselves under the affected name of moderation, then true and lively zeal is customably dispareg'd with the terme of indiscretion, bitternesse, and choler, I could not to my thinking honor a good cause more from the heart, then by defending it earnestly."[11] In the same tract, Milton asserts that "there may be a sanctifi'd bitternesse against the enemies of truth" and adduces the example of Luther as evidence of the benefits of "tart rhetorick in the Churches cause" (I, 901). Milton's commitment to a form of discourse animated by "true and lively zeal" has a number of consequences. First of all, it forces us to reject liberal readings that would anachronistically claim the tract as a defense of "free speech" as we understand the term.[12] This is so for a number of reasons, not least that the freedom of "unlicensed printing" that Milton advocates is not equivalent to "free speech." Even granting the limited media, Milton is, as we have so often been reminded, hardly urging a cessation of all censorship and review. Nonetheless, readers have emphasized what one critic recently described as Milton's "antinomianism," seeing the tract as, in the words of another scholar, "a rousing defence of pluralism, and ... a powerful manifesto for indeterminacy."[13] Perhaps Milton did, despite the apparent contradiction, polemicize for indeterminacy, but what such a reading neglects is that Milton is writing a religious polemic, a polemic imbued with the conviction that God has destined England, and perhaps John Milton, for greatness.

In this chapter, I argue that *Areopagitica* represents the zenith of religious polemic in English culture. In what follows I read the tract as above all a defense of, and an invitation to, strenuous and zealous argument. Fish, with characteristic astringency, asserts that "The only *positive* lesson the *Areopagitica* teaches (a lesson it also exemplifies), is the lesson that we can never stop,"[14] but I would add "never stop asserting the truth." The emphatic activism of the tract is directed toward discursive activity – arguing, writing, controverting – but this activity is not, strictly speaking, endless. Milton's particular urgency and vehemence is in part the result of an apocalypticism, a millennial enthusiasm that discerns in recent events intimations of the second coming. Such fervor was to be disappointed, and Milton later presents a very different attitude toward the world and its possibilities. But it is important to remember that at the time of *Areopagitica*'s first appearance many were preparing for Christ's return, anticipating the moment when "he shall bring together every joynt and member, and shall mould them into an immortall feature of loveliness and perfection" (II, 549). The religiously inspired enthusiasm for polemic that animates the tract dissipated in the wake of the failed experiment of the Commonwealth, and subsequent appropriations of the language and the arguments of *Areopagitica* show a conspicuous disregard for its championing of polemic itself. This chapter concludes with a close reading of two such appropriations, by Charles Blount and William Denton, in order to show what of Milton's argument still appeared viable in the late seventeenth century.

Fervent optimism and apocalyptic belief combine when, in *Areopagitica*, Milton claims that God reveals himself "first to his Englishmen" (II, 553). This element of Protestant patriotism should also warn us against assuming that the strictures against popery in the essay are mere concessions to the time.[15] Annabel Patterson has observed that *Areopagitica* does not "sort everybody into two sharply polarized camps."[16] And yet such sorting seems to be the very heart of Milton's strategy, which depends crucially on the association of the presbyterian supporters of the Licensing Act with tyr-annical bishops and inquisitorial papists. "Bishops and Presbyters are," writes Milton, "the same to us both name and thing" (II, 539). Within the next two years, Milton would give this observation a compelling and memorable formulation: "New *Presbyter* is but old *Priest* writ large,"[17] and consistently popery figures as the unassimilable adversary. The plural-ism that Milton is prepared to recognize is a pluralism within Protestantism. Furthermore, even this must be understood within the context of an optimism regarding England's future, for Milton clearly relishes the pro-spect of "a Nation of Prophets," a people "destin'd to become great and honourable in these latter ages" (II, 554, 557). As has often been noted, Milton does not here make the argument for separation of church and state, and it is clear that he still, in 1644, maintains a hope that the "many schisms and many dissections" that are evident in his England will give rise to "the goodly and the gracefull symmetry that commends the whole pile and structure" (II, 555).

This element of providentialism is not limited to the languages of edification and of the elect nation. It also permeates Milton's claim that polemic produces knowledge, a proposition that relies on a providential belief in the ultimate, as well as the occasional, victory of truth over error. At the center of Milton's argument for polemic is the claim that "that which purifies us is triall, and triall is by what is contrary" (II, 515). The implications of this claim for the productivity of conflict are multiple. As Victoria Kahn puts it, for Milton, "knowledge is dialectical; it proceeds by contraries." Rather than seeing this as congruent with a providential understanding, Kahn emphasizes the way in which the tract "illustrates the tensions between the concept of truth as fixed and absolute and truth as something we know rhetorically or dialectically."[18] Christopher Hill, in contrast, stresses rational consensus rather than dialectical conflict: "*Areopagitica* starts from the assumption that, given freedom of debate, the reason which is common to all men is likely to lead them to recognize the same truths."[19] Such readings privilege rational human action and neglect or diminish the role of divine providence, and yet for Milton the dialectical expansion of knowledge described by Kahn and Hill comes about as a result of both divine providence and human agency.

These two elements come together in a short passage in which Milton provides an account of reason: "many there be that complain of divin Providence for suffering *Adam* to transgresse, foolish tongues! when God gave him reason, he gave him freedom to choose, for reason is but choos-ing; he had bin else a meer artificial *Adam*, such an *Adam* as he is in the

motions" (II, 527). According to Milton, the autonomy that saves Adam
from the status of mere puppet is no derogation of divine providence.
Milton's aphoristic identification of reason with choosing – echoed in
Paradise Lost as "reason also is choice" (3.108) – seems to allow for a choice
between various alternatives, but the act of choosing itself creates a dyadic
structure: all unchosen alternatives constitute a set poised against that
which is chosen. Finally, as Stanley Fish writes, "there is only one choice –
to be or not to be allied with divinity."[20] Consequently, there is a polarity –
the contest between Christ and Antichrist, truth and falsehood, virtue and
vice, good and evil – structuring all decisions made by reason. In contrast to
speculative or contemplative versions of reason, Milton here insists on the
active and ethical nature of reason: it does not merely eventuate in decision,
it *is* decision. This barely submerged polarity subtending reason as choice
creates a polemical dynamic, accordingly reason becomes a matter of
taking sides. The scriptural text that best captures this dynamic is
Matthew 12:30: "He who is not with me is against me, and he who does
not gather with me scatters."[21] Compare, for example, an early eighteenth-
century description of reason: "It compares Things one with another, and
chooses them, if they are good; or neglects them, if they are indifferent; or
shuns them, if they are bad."[22] Though Milton acknowledges the existence
of things indifferent, his account of reason as choice focuses attention on
ethically relevant choice. The possibility of benign neglect, of indifference,
is for Milton consistently associated with the lukewarm neutrality of the
Laodiceans. The choosing that concerns him is strenuous and consequential.

Of course, the choices of autonomous reason are clearly not infallible.
What redeems the claims of reason is, in Milton's account, trial. The
metaphor of a purifying trial does seemingly carry with it the assumption
of freedom of choice and its epistemological efficacy; that is, if we think of
a trial as a practice institutionalized within a court and oriented toward
reaching a verdict. In this case, the individual acts as judge and evaluates the
case for or against something or one. But there is an alternative: trial as
ordeal and purgation. In this sense, the range and robustness of human
choice is reduced and attenuated, the individual is in the dock and what is
required is perseverance, the ability to "stand." Trial in both senses is
adversarial; the important point is that while the individual tries (tests,
evaluates, judges) things encountered in the world, the world tries the
individual. Milton's argument for polemic, then, has a residue of the
providential justification of trial by combat.[23] What finally guarantees
the triumph of truth is not freely exercised human choice but that the
truth itself is "strong next to the Almighty" (II, 562). This claim for a truth

that is loose and working in the world is theological without raising the interpretive difficulties entailed by a narrow scripturalism.

Though it is true that Milton does not ground his defense of polemic on the authority of scriptural citations, allusions to and quotations of the Bible are a fundamental element in his argument. The importance of scripture is visible, for instance, in Milton's invocation of Dionysius Alexandrinus, a bishop of the early church and noted controversialist. As Milton explains it, Dionysius was asked by "a certain Presbyter" how he dared to risk exposing himself to the heretical books that he undertook to confute:

> The worthy man loath to give offence fell into a new debate with himselfe what was to be thought; when suddenly a vision sent from God, it is his own Epistle that so averrs it, confirm'd him in these words: Read any books what ever that come to thy hands, for thou art sufficient both to judge aright, and to examine each matter. To this revelation he assented the sooner, as he confesses, because it was answerable to that of the Apostle to the Thessalonians, Prove all things, hold fast that which is good. (II, 511–12)

There is a wonderful circularity to this episode. I Thessalonians 5:21 and I John 4:1 both urge a process of adjudication which, in a Protestant context, was almost inevitably interpreted as an evaluation of scriptural conformity.[24] Indeed, Dionysius does precisely this, testing his vision against the standard of scripture and finding in its conformity proof that it too is a genuine revelation. Scripture and revelatory vision are in harmony, but there is nonetheless something vertiginous in their mutually confirming exhortations to judgment. Judgemental reading has the sanction of both scripture and direct revelation, but the precise process that allows the godly reader to decide whether a book is good or evil cannot be reduced to a strict formula or a mechanical procedure and defies routinization.

The episode is, however, even more complicated. Milton's choice of a scriptural warrant for Dionysius is not supported by his source. Dionysius actually invokes the apostolic voice "which says to the more able: 'Approve yourselves bankers of repute.'" As Ernest Sirluck points out, "This 'apostolic' injunction . . . had long before Milton's day been rejected as apocryphal, and no longer appeared in scripture" (II, 512 n. 90). This silent emendation replaces an apocryphal sentence with the canonical text of I Thessalonians 5:21, a passage that was frequently used to justify the reading and writing of polemic. The injunction to prove all things was not usually understood as a skeptical imperative but as an assertion about the need to make teaching and behaviour conform to the dictates of scripture. As the preacher Henry Smith glosses the passage: "Hee doeth not bid vs take a taste of all sinnes and vanities, as SALOMON did, to try them, for they are tried alreadie: but that wee should set the word of GOD always before vs like a rule, and beleeue nothing but that alone which it teacheth, loue nothing but that which it prescribeth, hate nothing but that which it forbiddeth, and doo nothing but that which it commaundeth: and then wee *Trye all things* by the *word of GOD*."[25] Milton, needless to say, is not committed to the sort of austere scripturalism advocated by Smith, but his argument does draw powerfully on the resources of biblical language and ideas.

Milton's substitution gives what might best be described as polemical reading the sanction of scripture. Secure and canonical scripture provides an essential framework for Milton's argument not least because it is the guarantor of the identity of Protestantism against the corruptions of Rome.[26] Though Milton manages to avoid the exegetical pedantry common in religious controversy, his commitment to scripture as the sole external arbiter acknowledged by all Protestants is unwavering.[27] Scripture properly interpreted is, for Milton, a constant source of truth that insures against a devolution into "a muddy pool of conformity and tradition" (II, 543).

But scripture is not the only source of truth mentioned in the story of Dionysius. Dionysius is the beneficiary of a "vision sent from God," and *Areopagitica* hints that direct revelation may also aid the "champions of Truth," "Those whom God hath fitted for the special use of these times with eminent and ample gifts" (II, 548, 567). Unlike the ignorant censors who "let passe nothing but what is vulgarly receiv'd already" and cannot abide "one sentence of a ventrous edge, utter'd in the height of zeal, and who knows whether it might not be the dictat of a divine Spirit," their revelation depends upon an inspirational epistemology: "the Truth inspires," and "when she gets a free and willing hand, opens herself faster, then the pace of method and discours can overtake her" (II, 534, 521). In his enthusiasm for the quickening pace of change, Milton reveals an impatience if not outright hostility toward *method*, a term that, whether associated with Ramus or Descartes, alludes to a rigorously procedural rationality.[28] The Pauline language of divine gifts or talents and edification merges with a humanist elitism: "That this is not therefore the disburdening of a particular fancie, but the common grievance of all those who had prepar'd their minds and studies above the vulgar pitch to advance truth in others" (II, 539). It will be remembered that Milton uses his membership in such an elite – "the industry of a life wholly dedicated to studious labours, and those naturall endowments haply not the worst for two and fifty degrees of northern latitude" (II, 489–90) – in order to justify his address to Parliament.

In *Areopagitica*, Milton envisions an intellectual elite – ranging from directly inspired prophets to humanistically trained scholars – working together to restore the dismembered body of truth. But the precise quality of this truth remains elusive; because new truth is constantly being revealed, no definitive account is possible. Each new revelation of truth may radically reconfigure the constellation of existing knowledge, requiring a reformation of what was thought to be established doctrine. Clearly, Milton describes the discovery of truth as a provisional project, one in which revisions will be necessary and in which, short of Christ's return to earth, no absolute certainty is possible.

But alongside the clear logic of this position, which renders all knowledge precarious and subject to fundamental revision, is a slightly different argument, one in which the recovery of truth is a cumulative process, a progressive aggregation of solid truths. Milton admits that when God "shakes a Kingdome with strong and healthfull commotions to a generall reforming," there will appear "sectaries and false teachers":

> But yet more true it is, that God then raises to his own work men of rare abilities, and more then common industry not only to look back and revise what hath been taught heretofore, but to gain furder and goe on, some new enlighten'd steps in the discovery of truth. For such is the order of Gods enlightening his Church, to dispense and deal out by degrees his beam, so as our earthly eyes may best sustain it. (II, 566)

This same optimism about the cumulative recovery, by steps and degrees, of truth appears in Milton's contention that now "God is decreeing to begin some new and great period in his Church, ev'n to the reforming of Reformation it self" (II, 553). This element of Milton's argument bears stressing because it provides a very different rationale for unlicensed printing than does the relaxed ecumenical pluralism that is frequently evinced.

The claim for pluralism has tended to focus on a series of images that seem to suggest that certain truth is unavailable and that therefore a diversity of views should not simply be tolerated but encouraged, since each may contain truth. Often cited in support of this position is Milton's invocation of "old Proteus." Expanding on the robustness of truth, Milton writes, "Give her but room, and do not bind her when she sleeps, for then she speaks not true, as the old Proteus did, who spake oracles only when he was caught and bound, but rather then turns herself into all shapes except her own, and perhaps tune her voice according to the time, as *Micaiah* did before *Ahab*, untill she be adjur'd into her own likenes" (II, 563). Rather than suggesting that truth is fundamentally protean, this passage argues quite the opposite: the figure of *old* Proteus, taken from classical mythology, is deliberately contrasted with the prophet Micaiah. The compelled oracles of Proteus represent a pagan world, while the confirmed prophecy of Micaiah is held forth as an example of the complex revelation of truth. It is useful to recall that when first asked by Ahab whether he should go to war, Micaiah had indeed tuned his voice according to the time, offering an ambiguous endorsement of the judgment of the 400 prophets: "Go and prosper: for the Lord shall deliver it into the hand of the king" (I Kings 22:15). To which, Ahab responds, "How many times shall I *adjure* [emphasis added] thee that thou tell me nothing but *that which is* true in the name of the Lord?" (22:16). Micaiah then accurately predicts the king's defeat and death. The point is that though truth cannot be caught and bound, for it then becomes something else, it can be adjured, put on oath.[29]

Nonetheless, the claim that truth can be "adjured into her own likeness," seems immediately to be undercut by the question that follows: "Yet is it not impossible that she may have more shapes then one?" (II, 563). The apparently solid personification of Truth the warrior seems put in doubt by this suggestion of multiplicity. And yet the terms of the claim do not amount to antinomianism or even a radical fallibilism. Milton immediately locates this variability by answering his own question with another question: "What is all the rank of things indifferent, wherein Truth may be on this side, or the other, without being unlike herself?" This expression suggests not that truth can be on both sides but that there is a range of things indifferent in which the precise location of truth is obscure. Milton does not imagine the rank of things indifferent as a neutral zone; instead, he allows that for each contested issue truth may be either *pro* or *contra* without being "unlike herself." Milton, may, as Ernest Sirluck contends, enormously enlarge "the scope of indifferency" (II, 170) but this does not mean that Milton is advocating an expansive area in which the truth is strictly unavailable.

Milton is clearly eager to undercut the certitude of those claiming to pronounce on matters indifferent: "How many other things might be tolerated in peace, and left to conscience, had we but charity, and were it not the chief strong hold of our hypocrisie to be ever judging one another" (II, 563). And yet he is deliberately vague on what these other things might be; a subsequent allusion to "neighboring differences, or rather indifferences ... whether in some point of doctrine or discipline" reveals that matters not only of ecclesiology but also of theology are found in the rank of things indifferent. However, Milton does not claim that these things are impervious to rational argument and thus that the relevant parties must simply agree to differ. Further discussion and debate might yield agreement on some of the controverted issues. "Neighboring differences" is Milton's description of a lively dissensus that avoids the stark polarity of enmity, and Milton's ability to imagine such a possibility is one aspect of *Areopagitica* that supports a liberal interpretation: "Yet if all cannot be of one mind, as who looks they should be? this doubtles is more wholsome, more prudent, and more Christian that many be tolerated, rather then all compell'd" (II, 565). However, the Christian liberty in things indifferent that Milton here celebrates is a Protestant prerogative as the next sentence makes clear.

"I mean not tolerated Popery, and open superstition," writes Milton, "which as it extirpats all religions and civill supremacies, so it should be extirpat" (II, 565). Rather than being a mere aside or a defensive concession, this assertion is central to Milton's entire argument. The polemical writing that Milton is eager to defend depends upon the existence of a discernible and definable enemy. The established perfidy of popery and open superstition must be extirpated. The martial metaphors and the celebration of discursive violence that run throughout the tract come to a chilling point in the participle *extirpat.* Here the continuity between polemic and physical warfare is made explicit. Milton's treatment of popery almost perfectly exemplifies Schmitt's conceptualization of the political as that which pertains to the friend–enemy antithesis. "The distinction of friend and enemy denotes," according to Schmitt, "the utmost degree of intensity of a union or separation, of an association or dissociation." The unconditional rejection of popery, the common enemy, is further evidence of the essential unity of the reformed churches. Moreover, the enemy presents an existential threat that can only be addressed by violence: "as it extirpats . . . so it should be extirpat."[30] It is, then, unsurprising that at this juncture in the argument rhetorical violence and the force of persuasion give way to physical violence and the force of repression. Milton also observes the need to outlaw "that also which is impious or evil absolutely either against faith or manners" (II, 565). These strictures make it clear that while Milton was perfectly ready to concede that the recovery of truth was an incremental process, he is convinced that some errors have been established with certainty: "we are to send our thanks and vows to heav'n, louder then most of Nations, for that great measure of truth which we enjoy, especially in those main points between us and the Pope" (II, 549).

A shared spirit unites the reformed churches, and it is, in its constant movement toward further improvement and correction, essentially opposed to the "iron yoke of outward conformity" (II, 563). Milton fears that "The ghost of a linnen decency yet haunts us" and that "A rigid externall formality" will only encourage "a grosse conforming stupidity" (II, 564). Divisions based on such considerations do untold damage to the cause of the godly. A single spirit animates the reformed churches, in spite of their minor differences, and will eventuate in the building up of the true church.

This language of edification is used to describe the incremental recovery of truth:

> To be still searching what we know not, by what we know, still closing up truth to truth as we find it (for all her body is *homogeneal,* and proportionall) this is the golden rule in *Theology* as well as Arithmetick, and makes up the best harmony in a Church; not the forc't and outward union of cold, and neutrall, and inwardly divided minds. (II, 551)

Compulsion, coldness, neutrality, and uncertainty (an "inwardly divided" mind) are all the attributes of a false church; liberty, zeal, commitment, and convincement are the marks of a true church. Since we tend to associate religious zeal with intolerance, skepticism and neutrality with tolerance, Milton's simultaneous promotion of fierce conviction and (limited) toleration of dissent strikes us as contradictory. Toleration is not, for Milton, an end in itself: allowing the clash of controversial voices furthers the project of reform. Milton, here, invokes the "golden rule," but he does not use it to argue for the "mean" or middle, a rhetoric that locates truth in moderation and balance.[31] Rather the concept of proportion is what allows for the constant extension of truth, a dynamic process that incorporates radical and dissonant voices and will continue until Christ's second coming.

Knowledge in *Areopagitica* is described as being brought about by social interactions – both harmonious and conflictual – and at the center of this process are the book and the printing press. The book can, for Milton, function as a figure for all communication: "what ever thing we hear or see, sitting, walking, travelling, or conversing may be fitly call'd our book, and is of the same effect that writings are" (II, 528). At the same time, Milton reveals an interest in the physical aspects of the book, remarking on "wet sheets," "dangerous Frontispices," the improving effect of "the fairest Print," and the fact that "Sometimes 5 *Imprimaturs* are seen together dialogue-wise in the Piatza of one Title page" (II, 528, 524, 530, 504). Moreover, Milton consistently emphasizes the "labour of book-writing" (II, 532). This is, of course, construed largely in terms of authorial labor, but such labor is not performed by the individual in isolation but within the context of a social world in which the writer seeks the judgment of "his judicious friends" (II, 332). Once in print, the book encounters other books, provoking contradiction and support, and thus having effects that ramify widely.

While recognizing this discursive network, Milton does not make an "argument for a process of social authorship" that would acknowledge the contributions of all the agents involved in the process of making a book.[32] Milton concedes that "the trade of book-selling" is "an honest profession to which learning is indetted" (II, 570), but he pointedly avoids the sort of praise for the art or science of printing that appears in the writings of Foxe. On an empirical level Milton lacked Foxe's extensive experience in the printing house, but more importantly, even at his most optimistic, Milton does not share Foxe's appreciation of the "common" sort, an appreciation that led Foxe to include the stories of commoners alongside those of kings and queens. Foxe's confidence in the abilities of the common reader contributes to his sense that the advent of print is an epochal event. Milton, however, refers to printers themselves only twice in *Areopagitica*, and in neither case is he particularly positive.[33] First, discussing the diffi- culty of making revisions to a text after it has been licensed, he suggests that printers are not especially courageous: "The Printer dares not go beyond his licenc't copy" (II, 532). Second, he endorses the parliamentary order that commanded "that no book be Printed, unlesse the Printers and the Authors name, or at least the Printers be register'd" (II, 569). If this is an acknow- ledgment of the printer's role in the "process of social authorship," it is construed entirely in the negative sense of liability.

Milton's resistance to a full-blown celebration of the press comes about, at least in part, as a result of his distaste for the "*Sophisms* and *Elenchs* of marchandize" (II, 570). He is well aware that the conservatism of the book trade can in fact trammel and impede the recovery of truth, but his concern is not limited to the baleful consequences of monopoly. This is best seen in his stinging portrait of the country minister who limits himself to "an English concordance and a *topic folio*" as well as "the infinite helps of interlinearies, breviaries, *synopses*, and other loitering gear" (II, 546). The objection to such popular aids to learning is that they trap the user into "treading the constant round of certain common doctrinall heads." What such ministers practice is not learning but mere "book-craft." Closely allied to such "loitering gear" are the countless conventional and pedestrian sermons printed: "But as for the multitude of Sermons ready printed and pil'd up, on every text that is not difficult, our London trading St. *Thomas* in his vestry, and adde to boot St. *Martin*, and St. *Hugh*, have not within their hallow'd limits more vendible ware of all sorts ready made" (II, 546–47).

Milton's attack on monopolies evinces a more general mistrust of the market itself: "Truth and understanding are not such wares as to be monopoliz'd and traded in by tickets and statutes, and standards" (II, 535). There is no hint here of the "market place of ideas," the aggregation of preferences that produces consensus.[34] Indeed, when Milton conceives of books as commodities – and as Joseph Loewenstein astutely notes, "the book was, for Milton, the leading instance of commodification"[35] – he invariably betrays his distaste for shop-soiled merchandise. Though Milton is attentive to the material book, he is ambivalent about commerce and prefers a more heroic idiom that insists on the agonistic aspect of debate.

The closest that Milton comes to the Foxean perspective on the technology of the press is in his discussion of the history of censorship. Pre-publication licensing was, he explains, "first establisht and put in practice by Anti-christian malice and mystery on set purpose to extinguish, if it were possible, the light of Reformation, and settle falsehood" (II, 548). By focusing on the emergence of restriction, this account conspicuously avoids the notion that the press itself is allied with the Reformation. Another example of language reminiscent of Foxe appears in Milton's scornful reference to papal censorship: "As if S. *Peter* had bequeath'd them the keys of the Presse" (II, 503). But the uncontainable press imagined by Milton is only by implication allied with reform; indeed, the futility of restriction, captured in the chimerical keys of the press, hints at the possibility of unrestrained production, an endless proliferation of print that includes the good and the bad, the true and the false. Milton conspicuously avoids making the press itself into a figure of freedom and never indulges in the sort of technological optimism found in Bacon, whose celebration of the "force and virtue and consequences" of "mechanical discoveries" identifies technology with modernity.[36]

Milton's attitude toward the collaborations of print is illuminated by a remark he makes in *Colasterion: A Reply to a Nameles Answer against " The Doctrine and Discipline of Divorce"* (1645). In deriding his anonymous detractor, Milton accuses the author of "bearing us in hand as if hee knew both Greek and Ebrew, and is not able to spell it; which had hee bin, it had bin either writt'n as it ought, or scor'd upon the Printer" (II, 724–25). Either, Milton claims, these misspellings originate with the author and manifest ignorance or are the fault of the printer and should have been included in a list of errata prepared by the assiduous author. The dilemma – either confess ignorance or admit indolence – does not allow the opponent a dignified retreat. Such opportunistic and apparently trivial point-scoring suggests a severe view of the author's responsibilities: errors in the press are not trivial consequences of transmission but manifest proof of authorial insufficiency.

Milton was, of course, directly familiar with the fallibility of print. *Areopagitica* itself shows what may be the signs of surreptitious printing. Unregistered, unlicensed, and without a printer's imprint, and therefore in contravention of the Licensing Order of June 16, 1643, that the text inveighs against, *Areopagitica* is a closely printed quarto that uses a battered typeface and contains, despite several stop-press corrections, a number of errors.[37] Most famous is an exhortation to the "true wayfaring Christian" that is usually emended to read "warfaring." The editorial rationale for emendation has relied preeminently on the fact that all four extant presentation copies of the work have been corrected by hand to read, "warfaring." Along with this evidence, there is the claim that "Christian warfare" is a concept used by Milton, while "Christian pilgrimage" is not.[38] Placed within the context of the argument of *Areopagitica*, "warfaring" is, indeed, more congruent than "wayfaring," but a definitive argument cannot be made for either reading. Indeed, it is precisely because "wayfaring" makes sense that it was set in type – the ease with which a Miltonic *r* could be mistaken for a *y* would be quite irrelevant if the word in question was *playhouse*. Granted that both readings make sense, "warfaring Christian" is the *lectio difficilior* offering a hard and uncomfortable concept; in contrast, "wayfaring Christian" is a mundane example of *contemptus mundi* likely the result of the compositor's reversion to traditional categories.[39] This error in the print and its subsequent scribal correction point to the fact that print as a collaborative medium inevitably involves the transformation of an author's text by other intentions (or inattentions), and yet for Milton, this is no cause for celebration.

Such transformations are inevitably and unsurprisingly construed by Milton as corruptions in need of correction. Indeed, some of the most famous language in *Areopagitica* promotes the view that books are themselves transparent, though fragile and corruptible, vessels: "For Books are not absolutely dead things, but doe contain a potencie of life in them to be as active as that soule was whose progeny they are: nay they do preserve as in a violl the purest efficacie and extraction of that living intellect that bred them" (II, 492).[40] An initial emphasis on the liveliness of books imagined as agents with quasi-souls of their own modulates into a more familiar image of the book as a vial containing the quintessence of the author's intellect. Milton then develops the conceit, claiming that "a good Booke is the pretious life-blood of a master spirit, imbalm'd and treasur'd up on purpose to a life beyond life" (II, 493). These metaphors certainly tend to instrumentalize both the press and printers; theirs is a necessary job but they do not add anything and in many cases they may lose something. Such an attitude is also evident in Milton's apparently casual alternation between *printing* and *writing.*

Though Milton's concern with printing and its regulation is manifest, he often speaks more generally of writing. It is, for instance, preferable, according to Milton, to have an individual "openly by writing publish to the world what his opinion is," rather than go "privily from house to house" (II, 548). The assertion that "writing is more publick than preaching" makes it clear that the operative distinction here is between the oral and the written rather than the divide between writing and printing.[41] Indeed, Milton here provides an excellent example of what Harold Love has termed scribal publication. Writing is the public act, and print is merely one mode for the dissemination of writing. The same privileging of writing itself is visible in Milton's declaration that, "When a man writes to the world, he summons up all his reason and deliberation to assist him" (II, 532). Milton, then, has a tendency to emphasize the authorial labor of writing and, correspondingly, to forget the efforts of printers and publishers. Put another way, Milton's aristocratic classicism leads him to dismiss the "print revolution" as a non-event.[42] For Milton, the culture of the book precedes the press and is perfectly embodied in his exemplar Isocrates, "who from his private house wrote that discourse to the Parlament of *Athens,* that perswades them to change the forme of *Democraty* which was then establisht" (II, 489).

Milton's ambivalent attitude toward print technology stems from his awareness that it has encouraged the creation of a market in cultural goods. Unlike Foxe, for whom the simultaneous appearance of print and Reformation was a striking coincidence that was understood as evidence of God's providence, Milton writes from the position of one who has seen both a more fully developed and variegated print culture and the continued uneven progress of Reformation itself. Though *Areopagitica* defends the efflorescence of printed polemic, the emphasis is decidely on polemic rather than print. The mundane productions of the press – the epitomes, concordances, glossaries, and manuals – that seem least polemical in orientation are derided as so much detritus, and consequently print is rendered almost incidental. The famous passage describing London as a "mansion house of liberty" illustrates the point:

The shop of warre hath not there more anvils and hammers waking, to fashion out the plates and instruments of armed Justice in defence of beleaguer'd Truth, then there be pens and heads there, sitting by their studious lamps, musing, searching, revolving new notions and idea's wherewith to present, as with their homage and their fealty the approaching Reformation: others as fast reading, trying all things, assenting to the force of reason and convincement. (II, 554)

The manufacture of armaments is here compared to the production of written texts. Though the clamorous industry of the armourers invites comparison with the work of the printers in their shops, Milton does not in fact make this connection. Instead he seems intent on urging the genuine contribution to the war effort made by scholars. As Nigel Smith notes, Milton frequently presents "polemical controversy as heroic action."[43] *Areopagitica* is not an exercise in dispassionate political philosophy – it is an impassioned defense of zealous writing born out of a conviction that in the struggle to come God would grant victory to the righteous.

Of course, Milton was soon to be disappointed in his hopes for a continuous Reformation, but Milton was not the only one to experience defeat. The trauma of civil war and regicide led many to question the idea of a providentially ordained progressive revelation of truth. To many it may indeed have seemed that "all the windes of doctrin were let loose to play upon the earth" (II, 561). Robert Heath, a minor poet of Royalist sympathies, provides an epigram, "On the Invention of Printing and Guns," that could be interpreted as a response to *Areopagitica*'s confident celebration of discursive combat. The association between guns and the press has a long history – both inventions are routinely invoked as examples of modern achievement – but Heath is not interested in the debate between the ancients and the moderns. Like Milton, he pursues the association between controversy in learning and combat in the field, but his account emphasizes the fragility of learning:

> A souldier found at first the way to Print,
> And 'twas a German Munk did Guns invent:
> Thus like arm'd *Pallas*, learning doth depend
> On arms, nor can they without this, defend.[44]

This etiological fable giving print a military and artillery a religious origin is laden with irony, but the concluding couplet offers stark realism. Heath exposes the pretensions and vunerability of learning and, at the same time, insists that arms require learning in order to be effective. The invocation of Athena, patron of a once glorious city, by a Royalist in the dark days of 1650 is a grim insistence that entire cultures fall prey to barbarism, that learning and civility will go down to defeat if not supported by armed force. Rather than see guns and the press as harbingers of modern progress, Heath imagines them as technological twins locked together in a world of conflict.[45] Stressing the precariousness of learning and the threat of contingency, Heath, in a time of adversity, embraces the notion of a contestatory culture in which wisdom and reason must go armed.

The restoration of monarchy in 1660 did not introduce a general pacification of this contestatory culture, but it did quickly change the terms in which argument itself could be justified. Two late seventeenth-century appropriations of *Areopagitica*, William Denton's "An Apology for the Liberty of the Press" (1681) and Charles Blount's *A Just Vindication of Learning: Or, an Humble Address to the High Court of Parliament in behalf of the Liberty of the Press* (1679), suggest that the experience of protracted civil war limited the appeal of Milton's argument for polemic. Both of these tracts have been discussed by George Sensabaugh as evidence of Milton's contribution to the "attempted Whig revolution."[46] Though Sensabaugh judges them pale imitations of *Areopagitica*, they do indicate that "*Areopagitica* at the very least converted two men, and their adaptions of it perhaps convinced others of the iniquity of licensing acts and of the desirability of freedom of thought and expression." While the influence of *Areopagitica* is a fascinating problem that deserves more study, I am principally interested in the way in which these two adaptations provide evidence of the ways in which *Areopagitica* could be read in the Restoration. The elements of the tract that get taken up as well as those parts of the argument that are silently abandoned not only illuminate the conditions of controversy that prevailed in 1679–81 but also throw into relief Milton's initial intervention in 1644.

The immediate impetus for both tracts was the lapse of the Licensing Act in 1679. Like Milton, both Denton and Blount argue against pre-publication licensing; and like Milton, both admit the need for post-publication censorship in some form. However, on this point, Denton, having mentioned the extant libel laws, echoes Milton, "For it is most just and reasonable, that all and every State should consider how Books as well as men do behave themselves, and punish or not punish accordingly," while Blount restricts himself to an account of the available laws against treason, heresy, libel, and popish books.[47] Despite broad agreement on the basic question of licensing and a common debt to *Areopagitica*, the two writers present very different arguments. Denton, a physician who had served both Charles I and Charles II, was an earnest Protestant, and he focuses attention on the Roman Catholic origins of licensing, devoting the bulk of his account to a recapitulation of the history already told by Milton. Blount takes a much wider perspective; as his title suggests, he places the debate over licensing within the larger context of learning itself. His opening sentence makes a universal appeal: "All civilized People, as well Ancient as Modern, have ever had that veneration and deference for Learning, that almost no Nation, dis-engaged from Barbarism, wants its publick Donations either of magnificent Structures or plentiful Revenues, for the encouragement of Literature and Learned men" (A4ʳ). Though Blount also uses the language of anti-popery, confessional categories are not really central to his argument. The Whig triumvirate of "Liberty, Property, and Religion" are identified as "great matters" (C1ᵛ), but the emphasis is decidedly on the first two terms. Indeed, Blount favors religious toleration for all sects whose opinions do not "disturb the publick Interest" (C3ᵛ). In fact, Blount, by drawing on the work of Jeremy Taylor, an Anglican divine, develops a language of interest that is alien to Milton.[48] Blount uses this language of interest in both a negative and a positive fashion. On the one hand, he extolls "Liberty of the Press, *whereby whoever opposes the Publick Interest, are exposed and rendred odious to the people*" (A2ᵛ). On the other hand, he complains of that "Dead-weight *of Interest which opposes us; and will not be converted, for that it is not for its Interest so to be*" (A3ʳ). Though Blount uses the language of interest analytically, he also considers interest as a historical phenomenon. In this mode, the emergence of interest marks a decline: "there was never any such Inquisition upon Learning known in the World, till *Slavery supplanted Liberty, and Interest Religion*" (B2ʳ). The claim is reiterated in a slightly modified quotation of Jeremy Taylor's *A Discourse of the Liberty of Prophesying*: "Faction and Heresie were things unknown in the World, till the increase of Interest, and abatement of Christian Simplicity; when the Churches Fortune grew better, her sons worse, and her Fathers worst of all" (C3ʳ).[49] Though Blount regrets the dominance of interest, he is also able to consider it with equanimity as part of the political world. Again, he quotes Taylor: "Why should I hate men because their Understandings have not been brought up like mine, have not had the same Masters, have not met with the same Books, nor the same Company, or have not the same Interest, or are not so Wise, or are much Wiser, and therefore do not determine their School-questions to the sense of my Sect or Interest?" (C4ʳ). Blount silently dispenses with an important adjectival phrase in Taylor's text: "why then should I hate such persons whom God loves, and who love God, who are partakers of Christ, and Christ hath a title to them, who dwell in Christ, and Christ in them" (B1ᵛ). As a consequence, his rendition of Taylor's argument for toleration – which itself employs an unMiltonic pastoral language – is far more secular than its original.

Blount's distance from Milton is evident in yet another passage that he adopts from Taylor:

Certainly 'tis very unreasonable for men to press and pretend every Opinion in matters of Religion, as necessary in so high a degree, that if they spoke Truth, or indeed two of them in 500 Sects, which are now in the World (and for ought I know there may be 5000.) it is 500. to one that but every man is Damn'd; for every Sect Damns all but it self, and yet that is Damn'd of 499. and it is excellent Fortune then if that escape. (c3ᵛ)[50]

Though Milton would certainly have conceded the unreasonableness of insisting on the necessity of "every Opinion," it is hard to imagine him endorsing this probabilistic line of argument. The religious variance that for Blount makes all dogmatism improbable and unreasonable is for Milton evidence of the need for religious polemic that reveals robust truth and exposes feeble error. Blount, in contrast, is making the argument that religious controversy is endless and unproductive, and he shows a marked preference for confining religion to the private sphere as something we can agree to disagree on, but for Milton every Christian has a positive duty to proselytize.

Blount's more secular stance, which distinguishes him from both Milton and Taylor, is visible in his version of the passage treating the licensing of books by deceased authors. *Areopagitica* describes the licenser taking offense at a single sentence "utter'd in the height of zeal, and who knows whether it might not be the dictat of a divine Spirit" (II, 534). Blount instead worries: "if there be found in the Book any one Opinion that thwarts the *Licenser's* Humour, whether it be of a Vacuum, Motion, Air, or never so inconsiderable a Subject; the sense of that great man shall to all posterity be lost" (b3ᵛ). The religious idiom of zeal and inspiration has here been replaced by the language of experimental science; the great man in question more obviously a Robert Boyle than a John Milton.[51]

Blount's deism is well known, and it is unsurprising that his appropriation of *Areopagitica* lacks Milton's millennial enthusiasm and his commitment to religious polemic. Denton, however, initially appears to be much closer to Milton. Like Milton, he is motivated by a fierce Protestantism that structures his argument around the fundamental opposition between popery and reform. Denton's account of the unity of Protestantism goes beyond the anticipatory claim made in *Areopagitica*, drawing instead on Milton's later work, *A Treatise of Civil Power in Ecclesiastical Causes* (1659), which locates Protestant unity in an agreement that scripture is the only external authority for religious beliefs.[52] Protestants are, according to

Denton, unified by their appeal to scripture: "*The* Protestant Clergy, *I doubt not but will acknowledge that it is* evers [sic] Man's duty and concern *to be a good Christian, and as Christians their undeniable right* to try Spirits and to examine by the Scriptures, whether the things our Priests do teach us, are so in truth or no" (A3ʳ). The resort to I John 4, as I have noted, is common; what distinguishes Denton's version is his assertion of an "*undeniable right.*" This language is especially prominent in a subsequent formulation: "For that such Prohibition would discourage Learning, and hinder Discoveries, and put a damp upon searching and inquisitive Brains and Abilities, and impeach that natural Right and Liberty, which belongs to every Individual" (A2ᵛ). This passage echoes the description of Milton's visit with Galileo, but the idiom is strikingly different. Denton uses a language of individual rights that does not appear in *Areopagitica.* There are, certainly, passages that suggest an individual liberty; perhaps most famous is the plea: "Give me the liberty to know, to utter, and to argue freely according to conscience, above all liberties" (II, 560). Whether a demand or request, this formulation operates on the assumption that the liberty in question is to be conferred by parliamentary authority. Entirely absent is the claim that the individual possesses a natural right to free inquiry.[53]

Both Denton and Blount soften *Areopagitica*'s argument in favor of religious polemic. This is done by omitting the bellicose rhetoric trumpeting the virtue of spiritual warfare and by intruding language concerning rights and interests foreign to the original text. There is a final and telling way in which these two tracts differ from *Areopagitica*: both celebrate the invention of the printing press. Denton concludes with an "Observation concerning Printing it self" in which he reports that during the troubles associated with German Reformation "it was suggested unto *Clement the 7ᵗʰ*. that the occasion of them all was from the *new Invention of Printing,*" which a marginal note explains was "By Faust and Guttenburg" (A4ᵛ). Denton endorses this possibility, describing how "men being better enlightened by *printed Books,* began to call in question the present Faith." Blount also celebrates Faust and Gutenberg, "who by their Ingenuity discovered and made known to the World that Profound Art of Printing, which hath made Learning not only Easie, but Cheap" (B1ʳ). Milton, as we have seen, does not discuss the invention of print, and he would, in all likelihood, have found Blount's praise of the cheap and easy learning made possible by print profoundly misguided.

Denton and Blount's endorsement of an earlier Foxean line on the significance of print technology is striking because it is accompanied by a refusal of the apocalyptic vocabulary that Milton shares with Foxe. As a consequence, Denton and Blount seem more securely part of a modern liberal understanding in which religion becomes a private interest and technological achievement a secure sign of progress. Milton, in contrast, belongs to an earlier moment, a moment in which religious polemic was not merely tolerated but actively encouraged. Such encouragement depended on faith, a faith that also decreed the final end of polemic. The notion of such an end, however distant, is what separates Milton from his secular, liberal epigones. The religious polemic of early modern England unfolded under the shadow of the decisive apocalyptic battle that would end history; the eternal discussion of liberal politics exists in a world without end.

CHAPTER 6

Institutionalizing polemic: the rise and fall of Chelsea College

The good old times were always on his lips: meaning the days when polemic theology was in its prime, and rival prelates beat the drum ecclesiastic with Herculean vigour, till the one wound up his series of syllogisms with the very orthodox conclusion of roasting the other.

Thomas Love Peacock, *Nightmare Abbey*

Early in the nineteenth century, Thomas Faulkner, a bookseller and amateur local historian, published an account of Chelsea that included a description of an all but forgotten episode in the district's past, the endowment and construction of King James I's College at Chelsea, an institution dedicated to the pursuit of controversial divinity. Faulkner described Matthew Sutcliffe, who gave generously to the College and served as its first provost, as a man of "piety and christian feeling" and yet concluded: "he might, in our opinion, have bestowed his fortune on foundations of much greater general utility, as he was, in fact, fomenting disputes, and, as it were, building a nursery for controversy."[1] Indeed, from the standpoint of "general utility," as elaborated over the course of the eighteenth century, it is hard to see the value of a college devoted to religious controversy. Hume, for example, concluded that Chelsea was "an institution quite superfluous,"[2] and though Faulkner does not share Hume's antipathy toward religion, he too finds religious polemic to be a supererogatory endeavor: "The necessity, likewise, of Sutcliffe's design, is continually diminishing, inasmuch as the Protestant faith is constantly acquiring fresh strength, and everyday affords clearer proof of the fallacy of the doctrines of the Church of Rome" (154). Both Faulkner and Hume, despite their differences, evince impatience with the very idea of religious polemic. Reflecting upon the reign of James I, Hume flatly states: "Scholastic learning and polemical divinity retarded the growth of all true knowledge" (155). Hume's assessment is unsurprising: theological controversy, often linked to the bugbear of scholasticism, served the Enlightenment imagination as an image of sterile and intractable debate – it and its attendant wars of religion defined the pre-modern and were precisely what needed to be overcome in order to usher in the age of reason. Though confidence in such progressive historical narratives has waned, the general repudiation of polemic that they entail has not been much examined.

Asked, in a late interview, why he refused to engage in polemical exchanges, Foucault dismissed such writing as unproductive, adding: "Perhaps, someday, a long history will have to be written of polemics, polemics as a parasitic figure on discussion and an obstacle to the search for truth."[3] It is ironic to find Foucault sounding so much like Hume, and yet at the same time, Foucault at least acknowledges that a history of polemic needs to be written. Such a history would reveal that polemic itself has been transvalued: once a laudable endeavor, now a thoroughly compromised activity. In the chapter that follows, I will develop the argument made concerning Milton's promotion of polemic by examining the emergence of the concept and its institutionalization. The practice of polemic pre-dates both Chelsea College and the emergence in English of the word *polemic.* What is important about these developments is that they mark a new awareness of and commitment to the practice of polemic. At the same time, the relatively short life of Chelsea College suggests that the moment in which an English institution devoted exclusively to religious polemic appeared both viable and desirable was brief. Like Milton's *Areopagitica,* Chelsea College serves as a vivid reminder of the days when polemic theology was in its prime. Unlike *Areopagitica,* the obscure institution has never been lauded as a harbinger of things to come (though one could plausibly argue that it was an early modern think tank). Indeed, the few accounts of the college that exist tend to focus on the institution's failure, creating the impression that the venture was either doomed from the start or rendered otiose by history itself. Things might, of course, have been otherwise, and my central concern is to consider Chelsea College, not as a dead-end, but as a vital indicator of the prominence of polemic in seventeenth-century England.

The attempt to create an enduring and independent institution, a perpetual corporation, dedicated to the pursuit of religious controversy is an important indication of the place occupied by polemic in early modern English culture. "An institution is, first and foremost," according to Roland Mousnier, "a guiding idea, the idea of a definite purpose of public good which is to be realized, by way of procedures that have been provided for and laid down, through an obligatory form of behavior,"[4] and Chelsea College is, I argue, the institutional embodiment of polemic as a "public good," a form of writing that follows distinct procedures in pursuit of a robust defense of the English church and state. The creation of the College is an assertion that such writing is obligatory and too important to be left to the vagaries of independent writers and publishers. As Mousnier points out, it is the presence of such a guiding idea and a set of procedures that makes a group of persons an institution. However, in what follows my main focus will not be on personnel but on the way in which the institution of Chelsea College registered a series of intellectual and cultural changes.

Though the institutional history of Chelsea College is relatively short, it is nonetheless important not only because it reveals an earlier moment's commitment to polemic but also because it can help us to better understand the shifting place of polemic in subsequent periods. Though Chelsea College provides an unprecedented example of the institutionalizing of polemic, the institution itself was before long to become the object of polemical debate. This chapter tells the story of Chelsea's foundation and its eventual demise, but it also examines the way in which the idea of Chelsea animated writers even as the institution itself failed. Chelsea College had both supporters and detractors, and the debate over the institution became, at times, a debate over the proper constitution of knowledge and the appropriate forms of higher education. With the passage of time, the defunct college came to emblematize a now obsolete form of polemical engagement. Andrew Marvell, himself an accomplished polemicist, was, in 1676, to deride the "Divines in Mode ... the great Animadverters of the times" as "Men that seem to be members only of *Chelsey* Colledge, nothing but broken Windows, bare Walls, and rotten Timber."[5] Marvell here scorns his opponents as at once driven by a time-serving desire to be *au courant* and yet hopelessly outmoded, like the bare ruins of Chelsea College. By this time, Chelsea College was only a memory, but still a memory of some potency. Before Chelsea College became the stuff of casual insult, it had been, in the words of Samuel Purchas, "*a Towre of Sion* intended against the Towre of *Babylon*."[6]

While polemic in the late sixteenth and throughout much of the seventeenth century was a reputable form of writing, the untidy proliferation of printed polemic caused deep unease. Not only did bishops and magistrates worry about the welter of polemical opinion, English controversialists themselves were regularly accused by their Catholic opponents of lacking a consistent doctrine. A relevant example of this line of attack is provided by Edward Knott, a Jesuit, who writes of the English polemicists, "when they speak or write, but in the name or persons of particular men, one of them will not thinke, that himselfe, or his cause is much preiudiced, if any other of them be found guilty of error; and in such cases, it is vsuall for them to say, what care I if Doctor *Morton* say this, or Doctour *White* say that?" Knott adds that for this reason "some Catholickes affirme" that it would be a good "if the pretended Colledge of Chelsy, or any other, were founded by Protestants expressly for writing books of controuersie, by common consent."[7] As Knott suggests, King James's College at Chelsea was, in part, an attempt to replace an ad hoc system for the production of polemic with a central institution directly under royal control. Earlier networks of clerical and lay patronage, as well as the efforts of entrepreneurial publishers and the writers they supported, had proceeded within the constraints of an inconsistent governmental system of censorship but without systematic, official direction. Chelsea College was intended as a central clearing-house for polemic, a place for a group of intellectuals committed to the pursuit of public argument and relieved of pastoral or teaching obligations. At the same time, the institution held forth the promise of a united front in the discursive war against popery.

Though James I was the institution's royal patron, Matthew Sutcliffe appears to have been the instigator of the project. An Elizabethan clergyman who authored a book on warfare as well as numerous controversial works written against both puritans and Catholics, Sutcliffe served as the first provost of the College and gave generously to its foundation. Indeed, in his will Sutcliffe claims credit for having established the foundation:

> The Colledge of Chelsey procured, founded, and built almost all at my charge, principally for the mainteinance of the true, Catholique, Apostolique, and Christian faith; and next for the practice, setting forth, and increase of true, and sound Learning ag[ain]st the pedantry, Sophistry, and Novelties of the Jesuites, and other the Popes factors, and followers; and thirdly against the trechery of pelagianizing Arminians, and others, that draw towards Popery, and Babilonian slavery, endeavouring to make a rent in Gods Church, and a peace between heresy, and Gods true faith, between Christ and Antichrist.[8]

Sutcliffe goes on to leave various lands in trust to John Prideaux and Thomas Clifford for the maintenance of the College "if this work be not hindred, or stopped by wicked men or corrupt minds." This proviso, along with his allusion to "pelagianizing Arminians," reveals that Sutcliffe died aware that his establishment was in jeopardy, threatened by a shifting religious and political climate.

However, Sutcliffe is not the only figure given credit for the institution. Arthur Wilson, a dramatist and historian, attributes the plan to Archbishop Richard Bancroft: "whose *design* was to answer all *Popish Books*, or others, that vented their *malignant spirits* against the *Protestant Religion*, either the *Errors* of those that strook at *Hierarchy*, so that they should be two-edged

Fellows" (H3ʳ). Bancroft is indeed a likely supporter of such an endeavor, having on several occasions exploited the press in the pursuit of religious conformity.[9] On the other hand, a London letter-writer in 1610 describes "a certain Project which is here in hand, for the erecting a Colledge at Chelsey, for the studying and handling Controversies in Religion," adding that the king's support was gained by the "solicitation" of Matthew Sutcliffe.[10] On balance, the evidence favors Sutcliffe, but it is plausible to assume that Bancroft favored the project. Both men shared a commitment to the established English church, printed polemic, and, to varying degrees, Calvinism. Chelsea College was, as D. E. Kennedy writes, "a late-Elizabethan edifice, a citadel designed by masters of sixteenth-century ecclesiastical warfare."[11]

Though Chelsea College had its roots in the sixteenth century, it did not come to fruition until James I, in the wake of the Gunpowder Plot and in the midst of the Oath of Allegiance controversy, decided to grant it a charter and land. In addition, an Act of Parliament gave the new institution the right to bring water from the river Lea to London, a privilege that proved worthless when a competing scheme to supply water to London engineered by Hugh Middleton succeeded. The king further committed himself to reviving the "King's silver," a poll tax to be paid upon taking the Oath of Allegiance, in order to defray the costs of construction. This last measure, had it been pursued, would have been especially appropriate since James undoubtedly saw the defense of the Oath as central to the College's mission. Certainly James took a personal interest in the foundation, and he is said to have laid the cornerstone.[12]

James also nominated the provost and the fellows of the College, a group exhibiting, according to Kenneth Fincham and Peter Lake, "a broad spectrum of theological opinion."[13] Though James did not allow any one particular theological position to dominate, his appointment of Matthew Sutcliffe as provost gave the institution a notably Calvinist leader. In addition to the provost, James I appointed seventeen regular fellows and two historians, William Camden and John Hayward. Their inclusion indicates that the society was not exclusively clerical; indeed it points to a desire to unite matters of state and religion in order to better promulgate James I's Erastian policies. Additional evidence that the College encouraged the writing of history is found in an undated Latin petition for the admittance of the antiquarian Henry Spelman.[14] The common denominator amongst these figures is a commitment to a national church governed by a godly monarch and administered by bishops.

Despite its auspicious beginnings, the College was soon facing financial difficulties, and in 1616 King James wrote to the Archbishop of Canterbury instructing him to begin a campaign seeking charitable contributions for the College. Furthermore, Sutcliffe alienated the king by coming out strongly against what he saw as the encroachments of Arminianism, and in 1621 his vehement opposition to the Spanish match earned him a brief imprisonment. However, late in James I's reign the College was providing support to at least one writer: Samuel Purchas, listed as a fellow in 1629, remarks that his work on *Purchas His Pilgrimes* (1625) was made possible by "the opportunities of His Majesties Colledge at *Chelsie*, where these foure last Summers I have retired my selfe."[15] The College, then, was not flourishing but nor was it defunct in James's final year. After 1625, even sporadic royal patronage appears to have dried up. Charles I, unlike his father, took no active interest in the pursuit of religious controversy. Where James had seen an opportunity to clarify doctrine, convince the mistaken, and ultimately reunite Christendom, Charles saw only a social problem, a source of confusion and contention. Despite this the College was not dissolved: a report on the state of Chelsea College prepared in 1629 lists a group of fifteen fellows.[16]

Charles I's neglect did encourage others to propose alternative uses for the College's land and buildings. In 1636, during an outbreak of plague, Sir Francis Kynaston petitioned the king for permission to move his own academy, the Museum Minervae, onto the College grounds. Kynaston, an esquire of the body to Charles I, was the rector of this newly founded academy. Situated in Kynaston's own house in Covent Garden, the Museum was intended to furnish an education in "the sciences of Navigation, Riding, Fortification, Architecture, Painting, and such like being most useful accomplishments of a gentleman."[17] Admission was to be limited to the armigerous, with exceptions possible for the descendants of benefactors. The Museum's curriculum presents a fascinating blend of new science and finishing-school subjects: medicine, astronomy, and geometry are included alongside music, modern languages, weapons training, and wrestling. Despite the evident risks of dilettantism posed by such a curriculum, one of the Museum's members managed to publish an early contribution to the study of parasitology: *A Most Certaine and True Relation of a Strange Monster or Serpent Found in the Left Ventricle of the Heart of Iohn Pennant, Gentleman, of the Age of 21. Yeares. By Edward May Doctor of Philosophy and Physick, and Professor Elect of Them, in the Colledge of the Academy of Noble-men, Called the Musæum Minervæ* (London, 1639). Nonetheless, an educational project more at odds with Chelsea College's original mandate would be hard to devise. Unsurprisingly, Daniel Featley, Sutcliffe's successor as Provost of Chelsea, was vehemently opposed to giving Kynaston and his students even temporary use of the College. In a long remonstrance addressed to Archbishop Laud, Featley avers that "the Whole College was not at my disposing for there is a com[m]on Librarie in w[hi]ch there are some hundreds of bookes vnchained, as also an vpper roome where the pattents & all muniments of the college are kept w[hi]ch may not be com[m]itted into the hands of strangers that are not sworne to the College."[18] Featley's arguments apparently dissuaded Laud from pursuing the issue, for no further action was taken.

In the same year, 1636, Laud received a letter from George Cottington, charging that rents due to the College were being misappropriated by those who "pretend to be members" and urging the archbishop "please to move his Maj[esty] that all these particulars may be established upon the reparac[i]on of St. Paul's Church; and there continue untill altercations and controversies in religion be necessary in a Christian Commonwealth, or untill Oxford and Cambridge (the two prime Seminaries of learning in Christendome) shall grow barren of able divines."[19] Unlike Kynaston who saw Chelsea as an attractive location for his own school of connoisseurs and virtuosi, Cottington maintained a focus on religious matters. However, by suggesting that Chelsea's revenue be directed to the rebuilding of St. Paul's, he identified himself as a proponent of decorous worship as opposed to strident controversy who preferred literal to literary edification. Such a position, perfectly congruent with Laud's own, was undoubtedly tailored to win the support of the archbishop.[20] Laud's sympathetic endorsement appears in his own hand on the outside of the letter: "Geo. Cottington's letter concerning controversy college." Expropriating Chelsea College's income and devoting it to the refurbishment of St. Paul's Church undoubtedly appealed to Laud; however, he was himself soon to be occupied with more pressing matters.

The next proposal concerning Chelsea came from a very different direction. During a visit to England, Comenius, a Protestant Czech who had been influenced by Francis Bacon's call for educational reform, petitioned Parliament for aid in establishing a Universal Didactic College. He did so in consultation with and supported by Samuel Hartlib, himself a German refugee from the Thirty Years' War, who, after graduating from Cambridge, remained in England. Comenius attended on Parliament in the fall of 1641, having been told that the Parliament intended to appoint a commission to hear his plan. In addition, "they communicated also beforehand their plans for assigning to us some college with its revenues"; the list of possibilities included Chelsea, "inventories of the last named and of its revenues were communicated to us." The signs were auspicious, and

Comenius was optimistic: "nothing seemed more certain than that the plan
of the great Verulam respecting the opening of a Universal College, wholly
devoted to the advancement of the sciences could be carried out."[21]
Comenius's hopes of parliamentary action were dashed; however, while
in England he wrote *Via Lucis*, a work that includes a description of his
planned college and that would eventually be published in 1668 with an
extensive dedication to the Royal Society.

   Though Comenius left England disappointed, his ally Samuel Hartlib
maintained a steady interest in Chelsea College. Hartlib is usually given
credit for "An Humble Memorandum Concerning Chelsea College," which
was printed as an appendix to *The Reformed Spirituall Husbandman* (1652).
This text urges Parliament to not only confirm the original patent but to
grant additional funds "to maintain more Fellowes not onely to oppose
Popery (for which at first it was founded) but also to maintain an
Evangelicall Intelligence and Brotherly Correspondency with forreign
Divines." To further this endeavor, the College should admit one fellow
"of every severall Nation of different Language, where the Protestant
Religion is professed."[22] Hartlib's scheme is an interesting hybrid dedicated
to both polemic and communication. Imagining Chelsea as a center for
international Protestantism, Hartlib moves away from the original model's
commitment to the defense of a national church and yet does not abandon
the discursive war against the Rome.

   Hartlib's manuscript notes reveal that a modified Chelsea College was
part of his scheme for a London university. In one account of this
university, he lists fourteen colleges, the ninth "For Controversies and
Pacification or Chelsy to be that Colledge."[23] This retooled institution
would have, somewhat paradoxically, simultaneously pursued discursive
war and peace. The third item on the same list, "For Education or an
Academy of Nobility and Gentry," is none other than the Museum
Minervae, for another set of notes on the same subject lists "One of these
Colledges or Houses for an Academy as Sir Francis Keniston."[24] This
alternative version of the planned university includes "One of the
Colledges de Propaganda fide of [Iews?] et Gentiles correspondence with
forraigne churches or rather Chelsy Colledge."[25] Hartlib's plans for
Chelsea show the degree to which a figure dedicated to the reform of
education and the study of practical and technical subjects could remain
deeply committed to the idea of an institution for polemic. And yet,
Hartlib's concern for "correspondence" and "Pacification" reveals serious
reservations about the efficacy of undiluted polemic, especially when based
on a narrowly national model of the church.

By the late 1630s, the College had become an attractive target for a variety of projectors who saw in it an opportunity to realize their own visions for the advancement of learning. The proposals made by Kynaston, Comenius, and Hartlib all indicate that Chelsea was a weak, if not moribund, institution. During the Civil Wars and the Commonwealth, the College buildings gradually fell into disrepair. In 1651, the Council of State directed the committee on prisoners to ascertain whether the College belonged to the state or to private individuals: "if to the State, they are to make use of it; if to particular persons, they are to treat with them, that it may be made use of for the accommodation of some of the Scots prisoners."[26] In 1652 a House of Commons commission surveyed the property and described a "brick building, 130 feet in length, from east to west, and 33 in breadth; consisting of a kitchen, two butteries, two larders, a hall, and two large parlours below stairs; on the second story, four fair chambers, two with drawing-rooms, and four closets; the same on the third story; and on the fourth a very large gallery, having at each end a little room, with turrets covered with slate."[27] The commission concluded: "the discontinuance of the corporation, being determined, and the aforesaid premises not being employed to the uses they were given, wee conceive the same to be in the present possession of the Commonwealth."[28] Thomas Fuller, writing in 1655, treats the College as defunct. Indeed, Fuller interrupts the chronological flow of his *Church History of Britain* in order to offer the first extended historical analysis of Chelsea College: "1. As intended and designed. 2. As growing and advanced. 3. As hindered and obstructed. 4. As decaying, and almost, at the present, ruined." The history of Chelsea College is, for Fuller, an exemplary episode: it perfectly embodies the trajectory expected, according to the canons of humanist historiography, of a historical subject and its focus on dispute and contention makes it an appropriate and edifying emblem for a troubled time. Fuller came to bury Chelsea College not to praise it, and in offering an elegy for the dead College, he was attempting to lay the belligerent ghosts of the recent past.

Not only was the College itself a source of disagreement, the causes of its collapse were also subject to debate. Fuller adduces no fewer than nine numbered reasons for the project's failure but refuses to judge between them, remarking

Thus I have opened my wares with sundry sorts of commodities therein, assigning those reasons which I have either read or heard from prime men of several interests, and am confident that in the variety, yea, contrariety of judgments nowadays, even those very reasons, which are cast away by some as weak and frivolous, will be taken up, yea, preferred by others as most satisfactory and substantial.

Chelsea College provides Fuller with an opportunity to ostentatiously demonstrate his own neutrality; his disavowal of partisan purpose is signaled by his willingness to let the variety of causes stand before the discerning reader, though a marginal note flags the fifth (the hostility of the bishops) and the sixth (the jealousy of the universities) as signifying "nothing to discreet men." Moreover, his remark about the "contrariety of judgments nowadays" suggests that he has little real confidence that his readers will come to any agreement concerning the causes of Chelsea College's failure.

While Fuller himself ostentatiously withholds judgment, the very magnitude of his inventory of alleged impediments creates the impression that the College was doomed from the start. A suit in Chancery contesting the ownership of property bequeathed to Chelsea provides an opportunity for Fuller's wit: "As this Colledge was intended for Controversies: so now there is a controversie about the Colledge."²⁹ Fuller's not so subtle insinuation is that there is something peculiarly appropriate, even perhaps inevitable, about such a turn of events. A similar assessment was made by Arthur Wilson, who, writing in 1653, suggested that King James withdrew his support for the project because he recognized that "nothing begets more contention than, *opposition,* and such *Fuellers* would be apt to inflame, rather than quench the *heat* that would arise from those *embers*: For Controversies are often (for the most part) the exuberancies of Passion; and the *Philosopher* saith, men are drunk with *disputes,* and in that *inordinateness* take the next thing that comes to hand to throw at one anothers faces."³⁰ James I is, one suspects, being made to deliver what is in fact Wilson's own assessment of controversial writing. His insistence that such writing is essentially without rules, akin to a barroom brawl, reveals a sensibility constitutionally opposed to the institutionalizing of polemic. Indeed, Wilson's description of controversy insists that it is recklessly violent and passionately opportunistic, essentially hostile to all regulation. An institution devoted to polemic is, from Wilson's perspective, a stark contradiction destined for collapse.

Despite such criticisms, the College was not without defenders. The most visible support took the form of a series of works produced by the publishing establishment of Nicholas Bourne in order to promote the College and its original purpose. Bourne was, along with Nicholas Butter, one of the first publishers of newsbooks in England, and his career reveals a consistent interest in the cause of international Protestantism. Though this suggests a general sympathy with the program pursued by Chelsea College, the connection is further solidified by Bourne's personal relationship with

Featley, an active press licenser from 1617–25, for whom Bourne acted as publisher. Taken together these facts suggest that Bourne's role in the publication of three important texts defending Chelsea College was not accidental.

The first of these texts appeared in an edition of John Stow's *Survey of London* published by Bourne in 1633. This is the second edition edited by Anthony Munday (an earlier expansion of Stow's work was published in 1618), and it reveals a consistent attempt to rework the conservative and nostalgic orientation of its original. According to J. F. Merritt, the changes made by Munday "introduced a more positive, forward-looking account of what was now clearly a Protestant city." Though there is evidence throughout of Munday's Protestant sympathies, Munday also included a new section on church-building in London that "provides the clearest evidence that Munday intended to build in a more specifically Protestant agenda to the *Survey*."[31] However, Munday did not work alone. Bourne's edition gives the following account of itself on its title page: "Begunne first by the paines and industry of Iohn Stow, in the yeere 1598. Afterwards inlarged by the care and diligence of A.M. in the yeere 1618. And now completely finished by the study and labour of A.M.H.D. and others, this present year 1633." Munday was helped by Edmund Howes, a chronicler who also extended Stow's *Annales* and his *Abridgement*, and Humfrey Dyson (H.D.), a notary public and book collector who had an interest in political affairs.[32] In addition, Nicholas Bourne, the publisher, undoubtedly exerted some influence; he may, for example, have been responsible for the insertion of "The fatall Vesper," a polemical pamphlet (originally printed in 1623) describing the catastrophic collapse of a Catholic chapel in the French ambassador's residence that killed over ninety people.[33]

The insertion that concerns Chelsea College was made while the book was in press and may therefore not be the work of Munday who died before the volume appeared. The relevant section is an irregular signature of four leaves signed "(YY)" and inserted between 2Y5 and 2Y6. The insertion has continuous pagination, running 527–34, but the immediately following section repeats these page numbers, indicating a late addition. The new material consists of the parliamentary Act granting the College the right to construct water conduits and "A briefe Declaration of the reasons that moved his Maiestie and the State to erect a Colledge of Divines, and other Learned men, at Chelsey," which includes King James's letter to the Archbishop of Canterbury as well as the archbishop's letter to the bishops and is described as having been "published by

Authority in the yeere 1616" ([yy1ʳ]). The text explains the rationale for the College in the following terms:

> to make a sufficient defence for the truth of Religion, and honour of the State, and a strong and continuall opposition against the continued lies, slanders, errors, heresies, sects, idolatries, and blasphemies of our Adversaries, it was necessary to unite our forces, and to appoint speciall men, that without other distraction might attend the cause of Religion and the State, being furnished with Directions, Instructions, Counsell, Bookes, Presses, competent maintenance, and other necessaries. (530)

The writer confesses that the work "hath hitherto proceeded slowly," but calls on the public for support: "This common business requireth common help" (533, 534). The pitch is sharpened by the assertion that "It is not sufficient for true Christians to professe true Religion, but they must with zeale maintaine it, and with heart abhorre, and with hand supresse idolatry and superstition" (532). This attack on idolatry and superstition is typical anti-popery, but in this particular case the reprinting of the 1616 letter with its harsh language and the description of Chelsea College are a response to the perceived threat of Laudianism.

As J. F. Merritt makes clear, this edition was in part a defense of the Protestant regime's record on church building, an attempt to counter the charge that Protestant worship, after the stripping of the altars, was a bare and pitiful thing.[34] Of further significance is the fact that Henry Holland's account of the monuments of St. Paul's Cathedral, which had appeared in the 1618 edition of Stow's *Survey*, was also published, not by Bourne, as a single volume in 1633. The preface of this volume explains that the new edition has been motivated by the news that "his Maiesties gracious Commission about the Decayes and for the repayring of the famous Church is on foot, and in agitation" (A3ʳ). This set of developments may help to account for the sudden insertion of a section on Chelsea College into Bourne's edition of Stow. The recent "agitation" on behalf of St. Paul's, which would lead George Cottington to suggest that Chelsea's assets be devoted to the repairing of the cathedral, may have made the supporters of Chelsea eager to reassert the virtues of an institution that some contemporaries understood as offering a very different sort of edification. Bourne's working relationship with Daniel Featley, the Provost of Chelsea College, may well explain the inclusion of a defense of the institution.

The likelihood that Bourne was at least in part responsible for this inclusion is increased by his subsequent publication, in 1646, of the very same material (without the parliamentary Act) in pamphlet form as *A Briefe Declaration of The Reasons that moved King James of blessed memory, and the State, to erect a Colledge of Divines, and other Learned Men at Chelsey.* Featley himself died on April 17, 1645, and his demise represents a crucial juncture in the institution's history. In this same year Cambridge University petitioned Parliament for the grant of books that Archbishop Bancroft had left to Chelsea College with the proviso that they should go to the University should the College fail. At this moment, Bourne, either on his own or at another's suggestion, published in pamphlet form the earlier defense of Chelsea. The connection between Bourne's establishment and Chelsea College is further solidified by the subsequent publication of *The Glory of Chelsey Colledge Revived* in 1662 by Jane Bourne, Nicholas's widow.

    The Glory of Chelsey Colledge Revived seems, from our present perspective, to be a quixotic enterprise. Dedicated to Charles II, John Darley's description of the College is ostensibly an effort to enlist the restored king's aid in completing the project begun by his grandfather. In the very front of the pamphlet, there appears an elaborate engraving, depicting "The Modell of Chelsey Colledge as it was intended to be built" (fig. 20). This image, accompanied by a short poem, stresses the importance of intentions unrealized. In the body of the pamphlet Darley quotes Fuller's contention that "such must needs be sad who consider the disproportion betwixt what was performed, and what was projected," adding in square brackets: "as in the Synopsis of the Model in the Frontispiece may be observed" ($D2^r$). Charles II is an especially appropriate patron, Darley claims, because God has singled him out to be the "Repairer of decayed Persons and Places" ($A1^v$). In making this argument, however, Darley elides the difference between the restoration of a damaged edifice and the fulfillment of thwarted plans, between a conservative recovery of the past and the progressive realization of an idea. This blurring is designed to make the project palatable to Charles II; however, the appeal to Charles II is not sustained throughout the text.

    The pamphlet pursues two related arguments that make the dedicatory appeal appear both superficial and unrealistic. In his Epistle to the Reader, Darley admits that he was partially moved by a desire to "clear the innocency of Dr. Featley ... somewhat blotted by Dr. Fuller's pen" ($A3^v$). Indeed, Darley, though constantly professing his admiration for the good doctor, contests Fuller's account on several points. The precise insult Fuller had offered to Featley's reputation is unclear, but there is no doubt that Featley and Fuller pursued distinctly different approaches to

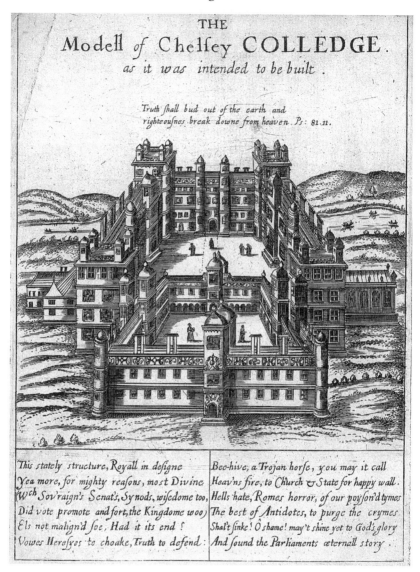

THE
Modell *of* Chelfey COLLEDGE.
as it was intended to be built.

Truth ſhall bud out of the earth and
righteouſnes break downe from heaven. Pſ: 81.11.

This ſtately ſtructure, Royall in deſigne	Bee-hive, a Trojan horſe, you may it call
Yea more, for mighty reaſons, moſt Divine	Heav'ns fire, to Church & State for happy wall.
Wᶜʰ Sov'raign's Senat's, Synods, wiſedome too,	Hells hate, Romes horror, of our poyſon'd tymes
Did vote promote and fort, the Kingdome woo)	The beſt of Antidotes, to purge the crymes
Els not malign'd foe, Had it its end ?	Shal't ſinke! O ſhame! may't ſhine yet to God's glory
Vowes Hereſyes to choake, Truth to defend:	And ſound the Parliaments æternall ſtory.

Fig. 20 Frontispiece, John Darley, *The Glory of Chelsey Colledge Revived* (1662)

matters of religion. Featley, after all, had made his reputation as a fierce
polemicist, while Fuller, himself no stranger to controversy, maintained a
studied pose of moderation, declaring it "the silken string running through
the pearl-chain of all virtues."[35] Fuller's noncommittal stance on the subject

of Chelsea was undoubtedly read by Darley as a sign of culpable weakness, if not outright hostility toward the institution. From the perspective of an unreconstructed polemicist such as Darley – who simultaneously cites Matthew 12:30 ("He that is not with me is against me") and the infamous curse of Meroz from Judges 5:23 ("Curse ye Meroz (saith the Angel) for they came not to help the Lord"), both texts that deny the possibility of neutrality[36] – Fuller's delicate balancing-act could only appear to be temporizing.

Darley's commitment to the polemical mode is also evident in his second argument, an extended attack on the idea of religious toleration. That this argument needs to be made suggests the implausibility of the plea to Charles II for the revival of Chelsea, for it was Charles II and his Catholic family that presented the most obvious threat of an open toleration of Catholic religion. Indeed, Darley's pamphlet is a classic example of polemic, attacking the "moderate" Fuller and renewed claims being made for toleration in the Restoration; rather than being incidental to the larger program of rehabilitation, these arguments are central. Though it appears belated, the claim that Chelsea College was in 1662 no longer a viable project misses an important point: in Darley's hands Chelsea College functions less as a practical plan than as a polemical idea, a standard to be raised in the battle against the papists. Indeed, though he begins by asserting his desire to see the original design realized, the vast majority of the tract is devoted to what has been rather than to what might be. In giving his version of the project's history, Darley constructs a broad Protestant tradition behind Chelsea College. The title page promises to reveal "How this design was by the Renowned King *James*, and the three Estates of his first Parliament, highly applauded; As also by the most Illustrious Prince Henry, and King *Charles* the First of ever blessed Memory, with the Right Reverend the Bishops, &c." The poem that accompanies the engraving of the plan expresses the wish that the College may "shine yet to God's glory / And sound the Parliaments aeternall story." In a section that quotes extensively from *A Briefe Declaration*, Darley expands on the assertion that the College had the support of "King & State," declaring that Chelsea was the work of "the intire representative body, with the head of Church and State" (B3ᵛ). In addition to the approval of the political nation, Chelsea had, according to Darley, the support of a broad range of Protestant opinion.

This Protestant consensus is displayed by quoting extensively from "Stow," Daniel Featley, Joseph Hall, and Richard Baxter. The Civil Wars, according to Darley, are not attributable to an excess of polemic but rather to a failure to support Chelsea College. Darley quotes Joseph Hall's comments in *The Peace-Maker*: "It is great pitty that the late Chelseyan Project was suffered so foully to fall to the ground; whereof had not the Judicious King seen that great use that might have been made of it, he had not condescended to so Gracious Privileges as his Majesty was pleased to inrich it withall."[37] Darley quickly promotes Hall as a Cassandra, who "foreseeing the Calamities which turbulent spirits in malecontents would bring by storm, through Civil Warrs and intestine Contentions" (c3^r), urged that Chelsea College be established on a firm footing. Had the project been promoted, the fellows might have "effected so much by their wisdom, as with a *Caduceus* to have stilled the furious spirits of very many bad ones, and so charmed them to have worshipped the blessed Peace of God" (c4^r). Claiming Hall as a supporter was an especially astute move, since Hall, a staunch defender of episcopacy, had consistently identified himself as a moderate.[38] Though Hall was able to speak the language of moderation convincingly, he never abandoned a strong anti-papal position. Baxter, a presbyterian, presents a more extreme picture of mid-century Protestantism, and unsurprisingly he too was fierce in his denunciation of all things Catholic. While Featley was no presbyterian, his own anti-Catholic rhetoric sounds strikingly like that of Baxter. Darley's strategy is to insist that Protestant identity is founded and maintained by its rejection of Roman Catholicism.

These various writers all bolster Darley's argument against toleration. Commenting on a line from *A Briefe Declaration* (1633) – "Some suppose that Christianitie and Poperie may stand together, and themselves as Newters stand betweene both, or as Mediators would reconcile both" (a3^r) – Darley first quotes extensively from Featley's *Vertumnus Romanus* (1642) on the opposition between Christ and Belial and then adds: "No toleration then of false and true religion together" (B4^v). Fear that Charles II would soon declare just such a toleration clearly animates Darley's account of Chelsea. Reviewing Fuller's list of impediments, Darley considers an obstacle not mentioned by Fuller: "the Papists their conjuring up again their Project for Toleration" (D4^v). Darley goes on to describe the various attempts made under James I to secure toleration for Catholics, asserting that these attempts impeded the progress of Chelsea College. He concludes, however, that James, though willing to entertain such proposals for political reasons, was never close to accepting the possibility of toleration.

Darley's own list of impediments also includes the rebuilding of St. Paul's: "the design for the repairing of *Pauls* Church likewise quite eclipsed and damped the building of *Chelsey* College" (E2ʳ). Darley here sets himself in opposition to Laud's program of "beautification," and reproduces a familiar opposition between word-centered religion and ceremonial worship. Archbishop Laud is criticized for rejecting Featley's plea for support: Laud failed to realize that it was incumbent upon him to "have looked upon *Chelsey* college as a grand business of Christ's, as well as to be zealous for the re-edifying of *Pauls*" (F3ʳ). The archbishop was "so immoveably fixed upon the repairing of the dead and decaying walls of *Pauls* Church" that he failed to notice "the Chaos of Heresies, Sects and Schisms, by Satan's Panurgy, and by the madness of the people . . . for want of that publick armature, sword and spear of the spirit, the spiritual sword of God's word in the mouths of his more select Ministers" (F3ᵛ). Compared to the "pure spiritual consideration and intention" of Chelsea College, St. Paul's is a "Carnal Church," and "the specious repairing whereof could not be without immense charge, did much dazle the Archbishops eyes" (F3ᵛ). Darley here repeats a familiar argument that associated Laud's program for the restoration of beauty and decorum with a return to idolatry, the carnal worship of the Catholics.

His denigration of St. Paul's, which suggests an austere view of the value of church worship, is accompanied by a sanctifying of polemic ("the sword of God's word" from Ephesians 6:17). Darley asserts, with rousing militancy, "we" will not sleep,

until we have obtained this *Chelsey* College to be set upon its own *Basis*, and to be the place for the Lord to dwell amongst us, as between the Cherubims, and for the most honourable and glorious service of his most sanctifying and saving Truth . . . (F3ᵛ)

Comparing Chelsea College to the mercy seat on the Ark of the Covenant suggests that it, as opposed to St. Paul's Cathedral, should serve as the center of national religious life. Chelsea College is identified very precisely as the place where God will deliver instruction to the chosen people: "I wil declare my selfe vnto thee, and from above the Merciseat between the two Cherubims, which are vpon the Arke of the Testimonie, I will tel thee all things which I wil giue thee in commandement vnto the children of Israel" (Exodus 25:22). Darley offers a variation on the figural interpretation of the Ark as the Church Militant that reduces the church to Chelsea College and leaves little room for alternative ecclesiological structures and pastoral practices.[39] This intense fixation on the physical location of Chelsea College has the perverse effect of rendering all other forms of edification otiose. On the one hand, the figure of the Ark insists that contemporary Protestant polemic is based on divine law and reveals a lingering attraction to theocracy – a desire to establish godly forms of governance here and now "set upon its own *Basis*." On the other hand, what Darley calls "Spiritual Polemicks" (C4^v) do not need to be housed in bricks and mortar – "sanctifying and saving Truth" is equally at home in pulpit and press.

The attempt to institutionalize polemic at Chelsea reaches one culmination in the transformation of the College itself into a polemical pamphlet. The frontispiece gives a detailed rendering of Chelsea College as it was intended, and the pamphlet's endpaper displays a "Catologue of Books sold by *J. Bourn*," a list that includes "Several pieces of the Reverend Dr *Daniel Featley* against the Papists and against the Anabaptists," as well as Stow's *Survey of London* and several works on commercial subjects. That this catalogue contains works cited by Darley is not in itself surprising; however, it does underscore the connection between print and polemic – a connection that is further reinforced by the plan, early in Chelsea's troubled history, to include printing presses on the site. The description in Stow's *Survey* mentions "Bookes, Presses, competent maintenance, and other necessaries" ([YY2^v]); the concluding section, explaining why the College was located in Chelsea, also alludes to the printing of books:

That this place was thought most fit to receive directions from our Superiou[r]s, to consult with men of best experience, to obtaine intelligence from forraigne parts, to print Bookes, and to disperse them; And lastly, to obtain the favour of the State and City. ([YY4^v])

Undoubtedly, such a press would have been, and perhaps was, resisted by the Stationers' Company, which jealously guarded its monopoly on print. Nonetheless, the plan itself points to an important connection made between print and polemic. Access to a press was considered crucial for the pursuit of polemical warfare, and the establishment of a house press would have streamlined the production of controversial books by dispensing with the task of negotiating with London's publishers and printers. While the failure of this aspect of the plan explains Featley's association with Nicholas Bourne, Bourne's own consistent support of the College suggests a commitment that was more than commercial.

Darley's plea for the revival of Chelsea College went unheeded, as he knew it would: in his Epistle to the reader, he explains that he has published at the request of friends "not so much in full hope of effecting what I would, as being unwilling to refuse them, and desirous of making trial" (A3^r–A3^v). The institution's final chapter suggests that Darley's fervent defense of the College and "Spiritual Polemicks" was a determinedly unfashionable gesture. In the mid 1660s, the newly founded Royal

Society petitioned the king for the College buildings and land. This request was not immediately met, but letters patent granting Chelsea College to the Royal Society were eventually issued by Charles II on April 8, 1669. It thus appears that Thomas Sprat was somewhat premature, when, in his *History of the Royal Society* published in 1667, he described "the *College* at *Chelsey*, which the *King* has bestow'd on them; where they have a large Inclosure, to serve for all *Experiments* of *Gardning* and *Agriculture*: and by the neighbourhood of the *River* they have excellent opportunity of making all *Trials* that belong to the Water."[40] The site that had served successive writers as the real and imagined location of a spiritual garrison, a place committed to the polemical pursuit of religious truth, is transformed by Sprat into a bucolic garden, ideally situated for the practical experiments of the gentlemen virtuosi of the Royal Society.

Of course, Sprat, and the Royal Society more generally, were instrumental in pursuit of what J. G. A. Pocock has called the Restoration "polemic against enthusiasm."[41] Restoration culture eagerly pursued polemic while ostentatiously repudiating its earlier form, what Sprat, for example, punningly derides as "holy speculative Warrs."[42] Claiming to reserve judgment on the ultimate utility of religious controversy, he nonetheless identifies it as a hindrance to the study of nature. Not surprisingly, Sprat's seemingly innocuous attempt to create a broad base of support for the new Society provoked a number of hostile responses, one of which was Henry Stubbe's *A Censure upon Certaine Passages Contained in the History of the Royal Society, As being Destructive to the Established Religion and Church of England* (1670). This book, which quotes large passages from Sprat only to subject them to withering analysis, is the classic form of printed polemic, similar in technique and form to books of religious polemic being published fully a century earlier.

Though polemic in its various forms did not vanish like a mist before the bright sun of a restored monarchy, the word *polemic* and its variants quickly became pejorative. The speed of this transformation can be seen by comparing early uses of *polemical* to post-Restoration appearances of the word. A funeral sermon by William Loe, printed in 1645, praises the accomplishments of "that learned and polemicall divine, Daniel Featley." Apparently, there is, for Loe, no contradiction between learning and polemic. Another illuminating example appears in an elegy for John Prideaux, another member of Chelsea College, printed in 1656: "But thou art gone (Brave Soul) & with thee all / The gallantry of Arts Polemical."[43] *Gallantry* is not a word that we readily connect with polemical writing, and yet the juxtaposition here is evidence not of linguistic incompetence but of a deep connection that existed between controversial writing and the chivalric arts of war. These eulogistic examples unreservedly celebrate the achievements of the polemicist as a soldier in the wars of truth. By the beginning of the next century such unabashedly celebratory uses of the word are hard to come by.

Though pejorative examples are many, I will settle for two particularly revealing occurrences. The first appears in a curious and massive compendium of heraldic lore by Randle Holme: *The Academy of Armory* (1688). In a section on Grammar, Holme provides the following definition of "Argumentation": "to Dispute, Debate, Reason or Argue, that is when from something already known and granted, we endeavour to prove some other: termed also Demonstration, Sophistry, Chop Logick, Polemic."[44] The concluding list of increasingly negative terms betrays a fundamental impatience with argumentation. Holme is merely an extreme and unsophisticated example of an increasing frustration with what is construed as merely verbal disagreement, a frustration voiced earlier in a philosophical idiom by both Bacon and Hobbes. The second example emerges out of a more explicitly Baconian tradition. In his *Lexicon Technicum* (1704), John Harris, a fellow of the Royal Society, includes an entry for *Polemical*, defining it as "a word used in Reference to that part of Theology which relates to Controversie; which because of the Wars, Jars, and Squabbles that usually arise about controverted points is called *Polemical Divinity.*" While Harris is certainly correct about the word's association with theological controversy, his folk etymology construes the word as a recognition that theological controversy leads directly to war. However, the practitioners of polemical divinity did not see their activity as a prelude to war; it *was* war itself. Though neither of these examples rejects polemic outright, the implications are clear enough: polemical writing is both refractory and retrograde.

The new pejorative understanding of polemic indicates that conflict over polemic itself has emerged. The increasing prevalence of negative, as opposed to neutral or positive, uses of the word point to a major cultural shift. Though it is tempting to see Chelsea College at the beginning and the Royal Society at the end of the seventeenth century as milestones delimiting a cultural watershed, it would be unwise to overestimate the speed of this change. The Restoration put a premium on wit, irony, and politeness and still managed to be raucously polemical. It remained, in Mark Goldie's assessment, "a persecuting society," and in such circumstances, religious polemic continued to find an audience.[45] Furthermore, resistance to polemic is surely as old as polemic itself. Despite these necessary qualifications, a long-term process of change is discernible: religious polemic gradually relinquishes the prestige and cultural centrality that had made it the focus of King James's College at Chelsea. This is in part a consequence of the reaction against enthusiasm, but it is also a result of the proliferation of secular political theory. During the sixteenth and early seventeenth centuries, religious polemic invariably involved political claims. The questions it addressed were fundamental to the salvation of the individual and the safety of the state. Indeed, the language of religion was the most prominent and prestigious idiom that addressed questions of society and community, identity and enmity. Religious language was not politics allegorized – such a claim assumes the separate nature of religion and politics. Instead what can, after the fact, be analytically separated out into politics and religion shared a domain. This situation was radically transformed by the emergence of an explicitly secular political theory that understands religion (and the conflict that it generates) as something to be quarantined if not suppressed. Though England remained, as J. C. D. Clark reminds us, a confessional state, wars of religion end and with them one strong rationale for religious polemic as a public good.[46]

Epilogue: polite learning

Scholarship is polite argument.
Philip Rieff

The history of Chelsea College suggests that the cultural ascendancy of religious polemic was short: the Restoration marks the passing of the heroic age of religious polemic in England. Of course, polemic did not disappear, nor did religiously inflected arguments about the proper political order. Defenders of the English church remained vocal and even vociferous; the language of anti-Catholicism continued to be a potent political force; and nonconformists of various stripes made impassioned arguments for accommodation and toleration. Nonetheless, religious discourse could no longer claim the centrality that it once had. In the sixteenth century, arguments about the polity are invariably constructed in religious terms; by the end of the seventeenth century, this religious dimension is no longer inescapable. The emergence of secular political thought does not entail a general decline in religious conviction or sentiment, but it does involve a process of differentiation that reorganizes knowledge and reshapes the cultural landscape. In fact, no violent prolepsis is required to see in the Restoration world the beginnings of the segregation of scientific, moral, and aesthetic cultural spheres described by Weber as a hallmark of modernity.[1]

Despite a reputation for obscenity and frivolity, Restoration literary culture was also marked by a new emphasis on "polite learning." That civility and politeness might cohabit with obscenity and mockery is not as contradictory as it appears. The Stuart Restoration was marked, in Steven Zwicker's phrase, by "cultural miscellany and miscegenation."[2] This promiscuous mixing brought low and high forms of art and literature together, but aesthetic hybridity was not accompanied by a relaxation of social hierarchy. While the return of the monarch was not the occasion for a general cultural and social clampdown, many felt that the difficulties of the mid-century had been compounded, if not caused, by impolite learning in the form of religious and political extremism. In retrospect, religious enthusiasm seemed directly linked to fanaticism in all its varieties; and fanaticism was conveniently, but no less decisively, tied to the lower orders – the tub-preachers, the soldiers, the women, and the apprentices – who had briefly made a claim for inclusion in the political nation. Politeness was the proper antidote for enthusiasm, and though Restoration culture did exhibit the raucous mixing described by Zwicker, it retained a strong commitment to both social and aesthetic decorum. Obscenity and irony were licensed by class privilege and could, consequently, serve to reinforce rather than confuse or confute social hierarchies.

Politeness performed a similar social service, encouraging fine discriminations in terms of breeding and taste. Though politeness, as the gentrification of courtesy, can be situated within the long-term civilizing process identified by Norbert Elias, this particular social ideal can also be located more precisely as a response to recent English political history.[3] Indeed, the premium placed on polite sociability in late seventeenth-century England is, at least in part, an immediate reaction to the experience of civil war.[4] This emergent form of sociability, unlike the bibulous conviviality celebrated in Cavalier poetry, was emphatically literate; social exchange, of course, remained predominately oral, but books, newspapers, periodicals, plays, and poems increasingly provided the basis for polite conversation.

These altered circumstances made possible the career of Jacob Tonson, the most famous Restoration publisher and the first stationer fully devoted to English poetry and drama. Tonson had predecessors, such as Nicholas Ling and Humphrey Moseley, who made a specialty of English literature, but for these earlier stationers poetry and drama were never an exclusive preoccupation.[5] In contrast, Keith Walker describes Tonson "as the founder of literary publishing in English."[6] "The most notable development in the London trade at the end of the 17th century," writes D. F. McKenzie, "is Jacob Tonson's brilliant definition and exploitation of the market for 'polite' literature."[7] He stands out as the first publisher to display a commitment to literature as a discernible field, a specialization that was, according to Joseph Loewenstein, the result of "a pressure to niche marketing that had never before been as powerful as it became in the 1680s."[8] The list he acquired is quite remarkable: not only did he publish the writings of contemporaries, such as Pope, Dryden, and Congreve, he systematically acquired the rights to earlier poets and dramatists, such as Spenser, Donne, Shakespeare, Suckling, and Waller, in order to publish new editions geared toward the Restoration market. Of his many new editions, the most famous single volume is undoubtedly the 1688 *Paradise Lost*.

The Tonson *Paradise Lost* is a remarkable book. A deluxe edition with engraved illustrations, it presents Milton's epic in a material form appropriate for a national treasure. Unlike prior editions, which had been humble and unprepossessing, Tonson's folio ostentatiously proclaims luxury. The aesthetic elements of this volume are more than a reflection of the high value Tonson placed on Milton's text; they also serve to rehabilitate the republican Milton, a notorious defender of regicide and advocate of austere virtue. The newly commissioned engravings that precede each book, like the prefatory arguments that summarize the action, perform an introductory function. These illustrations owe more to the iconography of Counter-Reformation Europe than to the iconophobia of seventeenth-century English puritanism, and while they are not strictly accurate renditions of the narrative, they do present vivid and memorable images.[9] A similar desire to soften Milton's hard ideological edge undoubtedly played a role in Tonson's decision to invite Dryden to contribute a prefatory poem. Dryden's own poetic eminence, his royalism, and his admiration for Milton made him a perfect choice.

Dryden did not disappoint. Appearing below an engraved portrait of Milton, Dryden's short poem effortlessly achieves all that Tonson could have desired:

> *Three* Poets, *in three distant Ages born,*
> Greece, Italy, *and* England *did adorn.*
> *The* First *in loftiness of thought surpass'd,*
> *The* Next *in Majesty; in both the* Last.
> *The force of* Nature *cou'd no farther goe:*
> *To make a* Third *she joynd the former two.*

A literary history in miniature, Dryden's epigram identifies Milton as the culminating figure in an epic triumvirate that begins with Homer and Virgil and thus fixes a safely dead Milton among the antique busts of a specifically literary tradition that transcends the minutiae of local politics. Milton, who studiously emulated the classics, is rewarded with a place in the pantheon; however, this elevation is also, at least potentially, an embalming that effaces Milton's deep commitment to a literature of engagement. A combination of Homeric sublimity and Virgilian majesty, Milton the epic poet breathes the pure air of Parnassus.

Dryden's hand in the 1688 edition is not the only political complexity concerning the book. The Tonson edition also garnered considerable support in Tory Oxford, in good part, according to Nicholas von Maltzahn, because of that university's new emphasis on "liberal humanist schooling, in which a regard for classical texts was encouraged by new standards of politeness, to be promoted especially in the cultivation of the gentry."[10] In particular, Tonson's edition benefited from the attention of Francis Atterbury and Henry Aldrich, both at Christ Church. In addition, the list of subscribers supporting the publication reveals a wide range of political positions. This consensus forming around Milton was far from robust and certainly not unanimous, but Tonson's edition does suggest that segments of Whig and Tory opinion could agree together that, as von Maltzahn writes, "Milton the poet needed redeeming from Milton the controversialist, that the English classic needed reclaiming from its republican but also apparently Puritan author" (p. 169). Though von Maltzahn's account of the volume is convincing, it does little to illuminate Tonson's role in the project. A consideration of party politics before the Glorious Revolution needs to be joined by an attention to Tonson's own long-term project. He famously purchased half the rights to *Paradise Lost* on August 17, 1683, when still a relatively young bookseller. This acquisition was the start of a series aimed at gaining a deep list in what would come to be seen as the classics of English literature.[11] Of these, the purchase of the rights to Shakespeare's plays in 1707 is a clear indication of Tonson's ambitious vision.

Having commissioned Nicholas Rowe as editor, Tonson published in 1709 a multi-volume set in octavo, the first printing of Shakespeare's plays that breaks with the textual tradition established by the Folios and quartos.[12] Though Rowe was untroubled by the finer points of editorial scholarship, his edition is, nonetheless, the first that shows evidence of serious editorial intervention. Working almost exclusively from the 1685 Folio, Rowe focused on producing a clean and legible text; his principal innovations were an attempt to regularize act and scene divisions, the addition of location notes and stage directions, and the inclusion of a biography of Shakespeare. The first two of these changes reveal a sensibility attuned to the requirements of the playhouse, and yet they also indicate a desire to translate that experience for the solitary and leisured reader. The same might be said of the new engravings that prefaced each play. These images, as with those in the 1688 *Paradise Lost*, add value and distinction, but they also perform a mediating function, offering representations of what is clearly Restoration stage practice in a way that serves to make Shakespeare's scenes seem familiar. For example, the engraving that illustrates *Hamlet* depicts the closet scene: a startled prince, in a luxuriant wig and three-quarter-length coat, reacts to the appearance of an armor-clad ghost, while Gertrude, tricked out in the fashionable garb of a Restoration lady and seated in a high-backed chair, looks at her son in amazement.

These depictions of current theatrical practice, as well as the absence of explanatory glossing, support Ronald McKerrow's assertion that "Rowe's editions are the last in which Shakespeare is treated as a contemporary."[13] Nonetheless, it would be a mistake to conclude that the edition presents its readers with an entirely theatrical and contemporary Shakespeare.

The aspect of the edition that militates against a seamless assimilation of Shakespeare by present readers is its sanctification of Shakespeare as author. Tonson's edition continues and extends a process that begins with the First Folio's posthumous monumentalizing of Shakespeare. Notably, the new edition was supplied with a frontispiece depicting a portrait of Shakespeare upon a pedestal, flanked by two muses who place laurel garlands above his head, and surmounted by a winged angel blowing a trumpet. In contrast to the plain portrait in the Folio, a new image of Shakespeare, based on the Chandos portrait, is here surrounded by the paraphernalia of classicism, which insists upon cultural and temporal distance. Much the same effect is achieved by the inclusion of "Some Account of the Life &c. of Mr William Shakespear." Not only does the biography unequivocally establish that its subject is dead and by definition non-contemporaneous, it also frequently acknowledges the paucity of verifiable information concerning Shakespeare, a gesture that invariably draws attention to the historical gap between the early eighteenth century and the Tudor–Stuart period.[14]

Tonson's edition, then, acknowledges the continuing vitality of Shakespeare's theatrical legacy while positioning him as a literary classic. Indeed, Tonson's attempt to secure literary status on behalf of dramatic writing is a distinctive aspect of his larger project.[15] Tonson's commitment to English poetry and drama is perfectly exemplified by his adoption in 1710, immediately after the publication of the Rowe edition, of a new shop sign: The Shakespeare's Head. Having moved his establishment from the vicinity of Gray's Inn to the Strand, Tonson retired his old sign, The Judge's Head, and adopted a new image, one that proclaimed his fealty to a specifically literary tradition. While Shakespeare's printed image has been frequently analyzed, the shift registered by this change in sign has not occasioned much commentary.[16] Tonson was not the first English bookseller to identify himself with a sign depicting a specific English author: Robert Pollard's shop was identified as The Ben Jonson's Head from 1655 to 1659, and Francis Kirkman operated out of The John Fletcher's Head from 1661 to 1672.[17] Tonson, however, was the first to elevate Shakespeare to iconic status, turning his image into an emblem representing polite literature in general. Tonson's innovation soon had imitators: over the course of the eighteenth century, bookshops boasting the Shakespeare's

Head would appear in Boston, Providence, and New York. That emblematic signs, initially devised to attract a quasi-literate clientele, are pressed into service by booksellers committed to the primacy of the printed word is richly ironic. Though Tonson's promotion of Shakespeare, Milton, and other literary luminaries, is divorced from narrow partisan purposes, his systematic support of and attention to a specifically literary market has political implications. Tonson was, of course, a Whig, and his political commitments undoubtedly informed his publishing strategies. Yet, as a Restoration bookseller, he saw an opportunity to sell polite literature to a broad market. While Tonson did on several occasions print books that were of an explicitly political nature, his willingness to print the works of Aphra Behn, Dryden, and Roger L'Estrange indicates that his list was not constrained by narrow political orientation.

Certainly party politics were overlooked by Jacob Tonson's great-nephews, Richard and Jacob Tonson, when they, as part of a larger syndicate, published Johnson's edition of Shakespeare in 1765. Long considered a key figure in the professionalization of authorship, Johnson, a conservative Tory, provides a fitting, and final, exemplification of the way in which polite learning emerges as a repudiation of the polemical. By the middle of the eighteenth century, whether Whig or Tory, members of polite society could agree on certain things, and Shakespeare, apparently, was one of them. Johnson's Preface opens with a meditation on antiquity; quick to condemn as superstitious the automatic veneration of antiquity, Johnson is well aware that the approbation of antiquity is often merely a disapprobation of the present. Furthermore, he concedes that since "time has sometimes co-operated with chance," the mere preservation of a thing is no guarantee of its value. Nonetheless, Johnson goes on to defend the notion that longevity is a reliable, if not infallible, indicator of literary value. Turning to Shakespeare, Johnson writes, "The poet, of whose works I have undertaken the revision, may now begin to assume the dignity of an ancient, and claim the privilege of established fame and prescriptive veneration."[18] That Shakespeare's reputation has withstood the depredations of time is undeniable, but that that should command a compulsory respect or, indeed, worship is at least contestable.

Johnson's classicism, his reflexive attraction to the antique, is not, however, the crucial point. He goes on, in typical neoclassical fashion, to develop the notion of the general or universal as against the specific or local:

The effects of favour and competition are now at an end; the tradition of his friendships and his enmities has perished; his works support no opinion with arguments, nor supply any faction with invectives; they can neither indulge vanity nor gratify malignity, but are read without any other reason than the desire of pleasure, and are therefore praised only as pleasure is obtained; yet, thus unassisted by interest or passion, they have past through variations of taste and changes of manners, and, as they devolved from one generation to another, have received new honours at every transmission.

This elegiac description of the serene Shakespearean text, resting in peace, insists that the polemical aspect of literature, its ability to furnish a faction with invectives, is local and ephemeral, and not, finally, part of the literary text's essential identity. According to Johnson, Shakespeare is now a classic because he is no longer polemical. This elevation of Shakespeare to the status of English classic makes explicit the repudiation of polemic that was only implicit in Tonson's refashioning of Milton. In both cases, a classic is understood to exist beyond the heat and strife of controversy. Against passions and interests (the stuff of polemic), Johnson counterpoises pleasure, specifically the pleasure of reading (the stuff of aesthetic experience).

Though Johnson's career as literary drudge and celebrity was made possible by the increasing prominence of polite learning in the eighteenth century, Johnson was himself acutely aware of the way in which passions and interests continued to shape the world of letters. Indeed, Johnson does not deny that Shakespeare was involved in faction, but he does claim that such affiliations are no longer relevant. In fact, Johnson's keen awareness of partisanship undoubtedly helped to motivate his espousal of the classic as something universal and rational. Johnson's conviction that the true poet does not "number the streaks of the tulip" is, in part, a bid to place literature beyond the rancor of party politics. The same belief led him to conclude that Shakespeare depicts a general humanity and disregards the peculiarities of place and time. "His story requires Romans or kings," according to Johnson, "but he thinks only on men." The espousal of literary transcendence is no indicator that Johnson himself transcended his own political circumstances or that he was apolitical.[19] Though Johnson positioned himself as the Olympian champion of a disinterested literature, many of his contemporaries were quick to see the malevolent influence of party in his critical pronouncements.[20]

The only partial success of Johnson's attempt to claim the high ground of disinterested judgment is attested to by Robert Potter's remarks on Johnson's *Lives of the Poets*. Potter, an Anglican clergyman and translator of Greek drama, was distressed by "the spirit of party," which he found "warmly diffused throughout the work." But the most egregious example was to be found in Johnson's account of Milton. Johnson's aspersions were, according to Potter, "disgusting"; and yet Potter himself is far from offering a defense of the good old cause:

> not that I am inclined to defend the religious or political principles of our great poet; I know too well the intolerant spirit of that liberty, which worked its odious purposes through injustice, oppression, and cruelty; but it is of little consequence to the present and future ages whether the author of Paradise Lost was Papist or Presbyterian, Royalist or Republican; it is the poet that claims our attention . . .[21]

This assessment of Milton sounds surprisingly close to Johnson's own account of Shakespeare: both Johnson and Potter advocate a form of historical amnesia concerning the polemical context of early modern English literature. The polemical engagements of the dead author are precisely beside the point: what matters is literary edification, the pleasure and instruction offered by an imaginative engagement with the essentially human.

Despite widespread differences in time, temperament, profession, and politics, Tonson, Johnson, and Potter all agree that the literary is antithetical to the polemical. Such general agreement does not, of course, mean that the genre of the polemic or the mode of the polemical disappear. The ideal separation between proper literature and polemic proved elusive in practice, and yet a change is evident. The printing press and religious controversy together transformed early modern English literary culture, making dispute visible in an entirely new way and to an unprecedented degree, but the unruly passions that played themselves out over the middle years of the seventeenth century provoked a cultural backlash of enduring consequence. The myth of the Restoration, that it was a time in which religious passions were exhausted and cooler heads prevailed, no longer convinces, but the myth is not simply the wishful thinking of liberal and Whiggish scholars. Its roots can be found in the political and cultural struggles of the Restoration itself, in the need to legitimate a return to the old order of church and state. The ascendancy of polite learning that I have briefly described was in part a response to this set of circumstances. However, it was also encouraged by the long-term development of a market in print books.

The promulgation of polite learning is one way in which publishers responded to a fractious reading public. At the same time, the emphasis on polite learning, on belles-lettres, was accompanied by the development of criticism, writing intended to guide and instruct the new audiences taking shape in the Restoration world. The word *criticism*, used in the modern sense as writing that evaluates aesthetic and literary productions, only appears in the Restoration. Dryden, in the passage cited by the *OED* as the first example of this usage, predictably makes the claim that criticism was "first instituted by Aristotle." Nonetheless, there is a world of difference between the ancient and continuous tradition of poetics and the specifically modern field of criticism.

The emergent field of criticism institutionalizes a new sort of controversy. Whereas previous readers had been exposed to voluminous religious and political controversy, arguments about poetic and dramatic judgment and taste now became prominent. The obtrusive novelty of criticism led some to suspect that it was an innovation of the booksellers. As the eighteenth century progresses, it becomes possible to imagine that Grub Street is not simply encouraging combatants but actually making up entire combats. For example, Henry Fielding's *The Author's Farce* (1732) contains a bookseller, aptly named Bookweight, who operates a literary sweatshop and exhorts his workers in revealing terms:

Fie upon it, gentlemen! What, not at your pens? Do you consider, Mr. Quibble, that it is above a fortnight since your Letter from a Friend in the Country was published? Is it not high time for an Answer to come out? At this rate, before your Answer is printed your Letter will be forgot. I love to keep a controversy up warm. I have had authors who have writ a pamphlet in the morning, answered it in the afternoon, and compromised the matter at night.[22]

This description of manufactured disagreement, despite its humor, contains a deeply conservative idea: print controversy is ubiquitous but superficial, an invented animosity that inevitably ends in compromise. This ludic understanding of print controversy, though it has antecedents in the sixteenth and seventeenth centuries, reveals a sensibility untroubled by the possibility of genuine enmity. Grub Street and its controversies provide raucous entertainment without fundamentally threatening the world of polite learning.

However, the emerging field of literary criticism is not devoid of serious or consequential disputes. Indeed, the peculiar bitterness of literary polemic is notorious. Critics claim to articulate and defend the values made available by the literary text, and unsurprisingly their claims are widely perceived to have political and religious motivations. Like the religious polemicists of the sixteenth century, the literary critics of the eighteenth century are committed to interpretive labor oriented toward public debate. However, I do not intend a quasi-Arnoldian argument claiming literary critics as the clerical custodians of a new scripture. My point is more modest. The volatile mixture of religious controversy and print technology introduced a new polemical element into the literary culture of early modern England, and the invention of polemic in turn produced a reaction in the form of polite learning, the category that directly precedes the fully modern understanding of literature as sweetness and light.[23]

Notes

INTRODUCTION: THE DISORDER OF BOOKS

1 For an account that positions Swift's book as part of the "last battle" in a long-running war between the Ancients (literary practitioners) and the Moderns (scientists), see Richard Foster Jones, *Ancients and Moderns: A Study of the Rise of the Scientific Movement in Seventeenth-Century England*, 2nd edn. (St. Louis: Washington University Press, 1961). For the argument that the battle is in fact attributable to a tension within Renaissance humanism between rhetorical imitation and philological investigation, see Joseph M. Levine, *The Battle of the Books: History and Literature in the Augustan Age* (Ithaca: Cornell University Press, 1991).

2 Jonathan Swift, *A Tale of a Tub*, ed. D. Nichol Smith and A.C. Guthkelch (Oxford: Clarendon Press, 1958), 223.

3 Though Swift, perhaps ironically, focuses on the restrictive aspect of chaining books, the practice was an effort to secure their accessibility not limit their circulation.

4 Myles Davies, *Eikon Mikro-Biblike Sive Icon Libellorum, or, a Critical History of Pamphlets* (London: 1715), 1.

5 This does not mean that manuscript polemic does not exist. For the preeminent Elizabethan example, see *Leicester's Commonwealth: The Copy of a Letter Written by a Master of Art of Cambridge (1584) and Related Documents*, ed. D.C. Peck (Athens, OH: Ohio University Press, 1985). As Harold Love has demonstrated, a lively manuscript culture, especially focused on political questions, flourished alongside print up through the seventeenth century. It is also true that the practice of writing manuscript libels was widespread; see Pauline Croft, "Libels, Popular Literacy and Public Opinion in Early Modern England," *Historical Research: The Bulletin of the Institute of Historical Research* 68 (1995), Pauline Croft, "The Reputation of Robert Cecil: Libels, Political Opinion and Popular Awareness in the Early Seventeenth Century," *Transactions of the Royal Historical Society* 6th ser. 1 (1991), Adam Fox, "Ballads, Libels and Popular Ridicule in Jacobean England," *Past and Present* 145 (1994).

6 Qtd. in M.H. Black, "The Printed Bible," in *The Cambridge History of the Bible*, ed. S.L. Greenslade (Cambridge University Press, 1963), 432. Black also points out that Luther criticized the greed and incompetence of printers. This

theme is treated in Elizabeth L. Eisenstein, *Print Culture and Enlightenment Thought* (Chapel Hill: Hanes Foundation, 1986), I, 304; Elizabeth L. Eisenstein, *Printing as a Divine Art: Celebrating Western Technology in the Age of the Hand Press, Harold Jantz Memorial Lecture* (Oberlin, OH: Oberlin College Library, 1996); Paul Needham, "Haec Sancta Ars: Gutenberg's Invention as a Divine Gift," *Gazette of the Grolier Club* 42 (1990).

7 For two important exceptions, see Jean-Francois Gilmont, ed., *The Reformation and the Book* (Aldershot: Ashgate, 1998) and Ian Green, *Print and Protestantism in Early Modern England* (Oxford University Press, 2000).

8 Thomas Babington Macaulay, *The Works of Lord Macaulay*, 6 vols., rpt. AMS Press, 1980 edn. (London: Longmans, Green, 1898), I, 448, 46.

9 Merritt Roe Smith and Leo Marx, eds., *Does Technology Drive History?: The Dilemma of Technological Determinism* (Cambridge, MA: MIT Press, 1994). Smith and Marx suggest that such "mini-fables" attest to a widespread awareness of technological determinism (x). Of course, they do not suggest that folk belief is a warrant for technological determinism itself.

10 Elizabeth L. Eisenstein, *The Printing Press as an Agent of Change*, 2 vols. (Cambridge University Press, 1979), I, 310.

11 Perry Anderson, *Lineages of the Absolutist State* (London: Verso, 1974), 22 n. 11. More recently Eisenstein has objected to the charge of technological determinism, Elizabeth L. Eisenstein, "An Unacknowledged Revolution Revisited," *American Historical Review* 107 (2002).

12 For a solid introduction to the expansive literature on technological determinism, see Smith and Marx, eds., *Does Technology Drive History?*

13 Lucien Febvre and Henri-Jean Martin, *The Coming of the Book: The Impact of Printing 1450–1800*, trans. David Gerard (London: Verso, 1976), 12. *The Coming of the Book* has, however, been criticized for focusing on production and serial history at the expense of consumption and cultural history. See, for example, Roger Chartier, "Frenchness in the History of the Book: from the History of Publishing to the History of Reading," *Proceedings of the American Antiquarian Society* 97 (1987). While Febvre and Martin largely avoid hypostasizing print, their insistence on the importance of the larger social context at times risks dissolving the specificities of print. For instance, Benedict Anderson, drawing on Febvre and Martin, posits the existence of something called "print-capitalism" – a category that conflates a particular technology (or productive force) with an entire mode of production; Benedict Anderson, *Imagined Communities: Reflections on the Origin and Spread of Nationalism*, rev. edn. (London: Verso, 1991).

14 Adrian Johns, *The Nature of the Book: Print and Knowledge in the Making* (University of Chicago Press, 1998), 33.

15 Johns poses this question and comes down in favor of history conditioning print in a recent exchange with Eisenstein. However, at the bottom of the same page he offers a more balanced formulation: "Print is conditioned by history as well as conditioning it"; Adrian Johns, "How to Acknowledge a Revolution," *American Historical Review* 107 (2002): 124. Johns is also more nuanced about

the characteristics of the press than his polemical account of Eisenstein's work would suggest. He frequently pillories her for her unwarranted assumption that the press has "inherent" or "intrinsic" properties, and yet his assertion "that the uniformity exhibited by printed material was as much a product of social actions as the inherent properties of the press" (121) appears to acknowledge the existence of "inherent properties" even as it curtails their effects.

16 Brian Cummings, *The Literary Culture of the Reformation: Grammar and Grace* (Oxford University Press, 2002). Cummings's learned account of the way in which writing and grammar both shaped and were shaped by the crisis of Reformation has much to teach us about the period's contentious struggle for meaning. Cummings provides an enormously rich and convincing argument for the profound imbrication of theological and literary discourses in the period. Where our treatments diverge most significantly is on the question of print, which is not central to Cummings's treatment.

17 For print and the imposition of uniformity in religion, see John N. Wall Jr., "The Reformation in England and the Typographical Revolution: 'By This Printing . . . The Doctrine of the Gospel Soundeth to All Nations,'" in *Print and Culture in the Renaissance*, ed. Gerald P. Tyson and Sylvia S. Wagonheim (Newark: University of Delaware Press, 1986). For a perceptive account of the tendency to see print as either enforcing uniformity *or* promoting diversity, see Wendy Wall, *The Imprint of Gender: Authorship and Publication in the English Renaissance* (Ithaca: Cornell University Press, 1993).

18 David Scott Kastan, "'The Noyse of the New Bible': Reform and Reaction in Henrician England," in *Religion and Culture in Early Modern England*, ed. Claire McEachern and Deborah Shuger (Cambridge University Press, 1997), 22.

19 Evelyn B. Tribble, *Margins and Marginality: The Printed Page in Early Modern England* (Charlottesville: University Press of Virginia, 1993), 55. Though Tribble's emphasis on print's cultural productivity is useful, the uncertain identity of "*the* institution" invoked in this sentence points to a generalizing tendency in her account of the social world.

20 William Barlow, *An Answer to a Catholike English-Man* (London: 1609), B1^v.

21 This is one reason for insisting that concepts are not simply words; it allows for a situation in which a concept is designated by a cluster of words. The site of a particular word is what reveals its conceptual specificity.

22 The *OED* claims that the English word comes by way of the French *polemique*. The term does not appear in classical Latin, and it seems to have had only limited circulation in the medieval period. Du Cange does not list it; however, the *Dictionary of Medieval Latin from British Sources* (Oxford University Press) will cite at least one example, which turns out to come from the pen of none other than John Wyclif, see W. W. Shirley, ed., *Fasciculi Zizaniorum Magistri Johannis Wyclif Cum Tritico* (London: Longman, Brown, Green, Longmans, and Robert, 1858), 463. I would like to thank the editor, David Howlett, for his assistance on this point. The fascicle containing P has yet to be published.

23 Simon Birckbek, *The Protestants Evidence* (London: 1634), L1^v–L2^r. Birckbek at one point uses the phrase "when he is out of his polemick controversies" to

describe Bellarmine (13ᵛ). In the preface, Birckbek acknowledges the assistance of Daniel Featley (A5ʳ–A6ʳ).

24 Joseph Mede, *The Name Altar, or Thysiasterion, Anciently Given to the Holy Table* (London: 1637). The first example in the *OED* is William Drummond's lament of 1638: "Unhappy we! amidst our many diverse contentions, furious polemicks, endless variances ... debates and quarrels." Drummond is responding to the Bishops' War and his opinion of "furious polemicks" is low.

25 Sir Edward Dering, *A Collection of Speeches Made by Sir Edward Dering, Knight and Baronet, in Matter of Religion* (London: 1642).

26 Robert Greville Brooke, *A Discourse Opening the Nature of That Episcopacie, Which Is Exercised in England* (1641).

27 Joseph Hall, *A Recollection of Such Treatises as Haue Bene Heretofore Seuerally Published, and Are Now Reuised, Corrected, Augmented* (London: 1615).

28 John Lewis, *Vnmasking of the Masse-Priest* (London: 1624), A2ᵛ.

29 Daniel Featley, *Cygnea Cantio: Or, Learned Decisions, and Most Prudent and Pious Directions for Students in Divinitie; Delivered by Our Late Soveraigne of Happie Memorie, King Iames, at White Hall a Few Weekes before His Death* (London: 1629).

30 John Foxe, *Actes and Monuments of Matters Most Speciall and Memorable Happening in the Church* (London: 1632), ()1ʳ.

31 Cf. Peter Heylyn, *Theologia veterum, or, The summe of Christian theologie, positive, polemical, and philological, contained in the Apostles creed, or reducible to it according to the tendries of the antients both Greeks and Latines* (London: 1654) and George Leyburn, *Holy characters containing a miscelany of theolocicall* [sic] *discovrses that is theology, positiue, scholasticall, polemicall, and morall* (Douai: 1662).

32 *Diatelesma. The Moderne History of the World, expressing the principall Passages of the Christian Countries in the last six Moneths, whether Politicall, or Polemicall brought downe from Aprill last to this present* (London: 1637). Cf. *The Continvation of the Actions, Passages, and Occurences, both Politike and Polemicall, in the upper Germanie* (London: 1637). This sense of *polemic* is still available in the late seventeenth century: Elisha Coles, *An English Dictionary* (London: 1676) defines *Polemicks* as "treatises of war, also disputations" (Ff3ʳ).

33 Abraham Gibson, *Christiana-Polemica, or a Preparative to Warre* (London: 1619).

34 Thomas Fuller, *The Holy State* (London: 1642), 12ᵛ. Fuller's description is a fascinating condensation of conventional wisdom concerning theological controversy; it is also evidence that the controversialist has become a recognizable type. Tellingly, Fuller's account of this character is followed by his life of William Whitaker, an Elizabethan divine known for his controversial writings.

35 Josias Nichols, *The Plea of the Innocent: Wherein Is Auerred; That the Ministers & People Falslie Termed Puritanes, Are Iniuriouslie Slaundered for Enemies or Troublers of the State* ([Middelburg]: 1602), D4ʳ.

36 Job Throkmorton?, *A Petition Directed to Her Most Excellent Maiestie, Wherein Is Deliuered 1 A Meane Howe to Compound the Ciuill Dissention in the Church of*

England. 2 A Proofe That They Who Write for Reformation, Doe Not Offend against the Stat. Of 23.Eliz.C. And Therefore Till Matters Bee Compounded, Deserue More Fauour ([Middelburg]: 1592), A2^r.

37 Matthew Sutcliffe, *An Answere to a Certaine Libel Supplicatorie* (London: 1592), B3^r.

38 George Hakewill, *An Answer to a Treatise Written by Dr. Carier, by Way of Letter to His Maiestie* (London: 1616), A2^r–A2^v.

39 On this point, see the examples cited by Michael C. Questier, *Conversion, Politics and Religion in England, 1580–1625* (Cambridge University Press, 1996), 17–18.

40 In *The Epistle*, Marprelate writes that Whitgift "left the cause you defend in the plaine field / and for shame threw downe his weapons with a desperate purpose to runne away / and leaue the cause / as he like a coward hath done: For this dozen yeares we neuer saw any thing of his in printe for the defence of his cause / and poore M. Cartwright doth content himselfe with the victorie / which the other will not (though in deed he hath by his silence) seeme to grant" (C2^r).

41 See Pierre Bourdieu, "The Forms of Capital," in *Handbook of Theory and Research for the Sociology of Education*, ed. John G. Richardson (New York: Greenwood Press, 1986). Interestingly, a printed book also registers social capital: "The volume of the social capital possessed by a given agent thus depends on the size of the network of connections he can effectively mobilize and on the volume of the capital (economic, cultural or symbolic) possessed in his own right by each of those to whom he is connected" (249).

42 William Winstanley, *Histories and Observations Domestic and Foreign* (London: Will. Whitwood, 1683), A5^v–A6^r. Unless otherwise noted, Shakespeare quotations are from William Shakespeare, *The Complete Works of Shakespeare*, ed. David Bevington (New York: Longman, 1997). The joke, in the one case, and the derision, in the other, only work if the audience or readership can both acknowledge that this notion is silly and at the same time believe that others more rural and less sophisticated might find it credible. On this point I am in disagreement with Johns, who somewhat exaggerates the skepticism provoked by print. Concerning those who produced and read scientific books, he may well be right, but in the wider culture the case seems more complex. I think it fair to say that there were very few Mopsas for whom print conferred an irrefragable authority; indeed, print revealed the ubiquity of contentious, and sometimes mutually exclusive, truth claims. Nonetheless, print created the impression that the writer was not alone, that the claims made in the book had the implicit, sometimes explicit, endorsement of the publisher, the writers of commendatory verses and epistles, the dedicatee, and, possibly, a host of anonymous but sympathetic readers. An MS. text also attests to a value judgment: somebody thought it worth writing out or copying. The point is that in purely formal terms an MS. text does not entail more than one hand.

43 Carl Schmitt, *The Concept of the Political*, trans. George Schwab (New Brunswick, NJ: Rutgers University Press, 1976), 26. I do not intend an endorsement of Schmitt's metaphysics of violence. As F. R. Ankersmit has

pointed out, "Schmitt's Hobbesianism requires him to construct a political reality that is effectively *founded* on enmity and brokenness, thereby transforming enmity and brokenness into metaphysical principles." *Aesthetic Politics: Political Philosophy Beyond Fact and Value* (Stanford University Press, 1996), 127.

44 Though this awareness resembles the concerns of the traditional envoi (for example, Chaucer's conclusion to *Troilus and Criseyde*), it is in fact a significant departure. Originally a concluding dedication to a patron, by the fifteenth century the envoi shows an increasing concern with the fate of the little book being sent out into a potentially hostile world. While the fifteenth-century envoi marks "an uneasiness that reflected the replacement of a personal relationship between author and patron with an increasingly anonymous literary market," its depiction of the "envy of a critical public" owes more to the *topos* of envy than it does to the notion of a socially or ideologically variegated public; Bernd Engler, "Literary Form as Aesthetic Program: the Envoy in English and American Literature," *REAL: The Yearbook of Research in English and American Literature* 7 (1990): 74, 75.

45 For a fascinating attempt to "appropriate the term for different purposes," see Peter Lake and Michael Questier, "Puritans, Papists, and the 'Public Sphere' in Early Modern England: the Edmund Campion Affair in Context," *Journal of Modern History* 72 (2000). However, the use of scare-quotes in the title and the admission that they have "no particular theoretical or linguistic stake in the term" (625) suggest that Lake and Questier are less than fully committed to a Habermasian vocabulary. In any case, the article provides a sophisticated account of the conditions of public debate in the Elizabethan period. For an excellent exploration of the early modern public sphere, see the work of David Norbrook, especially "*Areopagitica*, Censorship, and the Early Modern Public Sphere," in *The Administration of Aesthetics: Censorship, Political Criticism, and the Public Sphere*, ed. Richard Burt (Minneapolis: University of Minnesota Press, 1994) and "Rhetoric, Ideology and the Elizabethan World Picture," in *Renaissance Rhetoric*, ed. Peter Mack (New York: St. Martin's Press, 1994).

46 David Zaret, "Religion, Science, and Printing in the Public Spheres in Seventeenth-Century England," in *Habermas and the Public Sphere*, ed. Craig Calhoun (Cambridge, MA: MIT Press, 1992), 213. This critique has been expanded into an important book, David Zaret, *Origins of Democratic Culture: Printing, Petitions, and the Public Sphere in Early-Modern England* (Princeton University Press, 2000).

47 Remarkably, these invocations frequently ignore Habermas's critical account of the demise of the public sphere: "When the laws of the market governing the sphere of commodity exchange and of social labor also pervaded the sphere reserved for private people as a public, rational–critical debate had a tendency to be replaced by consumption, and the web of public communication unraveled into acts of individuated reception, however uniform in mode." Jürgen Habermas, *The Structural Transformation of the Public Sphere: An Inquiry into a Category of Bourgeois Society*, translated by Thomas Burger with the assistance of Frederick Lawrence (Cambridge, MA: MIT Press, 1991), 161.

48 Annabel Patterson, "Rethinking Tudor Historiography," *South Atlantic Quarterly* 92 (1993): 205. Patterson's more recent thoughts on the history of liberalism can be found in Annabel Patterson, *Early Modern Liberalism* (Cambridge University Press, 1997).

49 Chantal Mouffe, *The Return of the Political* (New York: Verso, 1993), 2.

50 Walter Ong, *The Presence of the Word: Some Prolegomena for Cultural and Religious History* (Minneapolis: University of Minnesota Press, 1981), 328.

51 Elsewhere Ong writes, "Print encourages a sense of closure, a sense that what is found in a text has been finalized, has reached a state of completion." Walter Ong, *Orality and Literacy: The Technologizing of the Word*, rev. edn. (New York: Routledge, 1997), 132.

52 For honor culture, see Mervyn James, "English Politics and the Concept of Honour, 1485–1642," in *Society, Politics and Culture*, Past and Present Publications (Cambridge University Press, 1986). On education, see Thomas Whitfield Baldwin, *William Shakespere's Small Latine & Lesse Greeke* (Urbana: University of Illinois Press, 1944), Lisa Jardine and Anthony Grafton, *From Humanism to the Humanities: Education and the Liberal Arts in Fifteenth and Sixteenth Century Europe* (Cambridge, MA: Harvard University Press, 1986).

53 Reinhart Koselleck, *Critique and Crisis: Enlightenment and the Pathogenesis of Modern Society* (Cambridge, MA: MIT Press, 1988), 17.

54 The solution to the wars of religion, according to Koselleck, was, at least on the Continent, the absolutist state. Stephen Toulmin makes a similar argument for seeing Cartesian philosophy as an response to the "doctrinal contradictions that had been a prime occasion for the religious wars." *Cosmopolis: The Hidden Agenda of Modernity* (University of Chicago Press, 1990), 62.

55 The most prominent and convincing exponent of the view that the English Civil War was the last of the wars of religion is John Morrill; see John Morrill, "The Religious Context of the English Civil War," *Transactions of the Royal Historical Society* 34 (1984).

56 The currency and contextual engagement of polemic is its defining attribute for Quentin Skinner. Indeed, Skinner has done much to turn the attention of intellectual historians to the topic of polemic by his insistence on an "understanding of past political thought as political argument." James Tully, ed., *Meaning and Context: Quentin Skinner and His Critics* (Princeton University Press, 1988), 205.

57 Foxe, with good reason, becomes a locus classicus for the claim that print is God's gift to the Reformation. His own brief disquisition on the benefit of printing is in part a translation, acknowledged in a marginal note, of Matthaeus Judex, *De Inventione Typographia* (Copenhagen: 1566). It first appears in the edition of 1570 (STC 11223) on p. 837 and is reproduced in subsequent editions. I am grateful to Dr. Thomas Freeman for information on this point. Foxe offered additional thoughts on the value of print in the preface to his edition of the works of Tyndale, Frith, and Barnes. There he suggests of the premature reformation of Wyclif and Huss: "But by reason the Arte of

Printing was not yet inuented, their worthy bookes were the sooner abo-
lyshed"; John Foxe, ed., *The Whole Workes of W. Tyndale, Iohn Frith, and
Doct. Barnes* (London: John Day, 1572). Thankfully, writes Foxe, "it so pleased
the goodnes of our God to prouide a remedy for that mischiefe, by multiplying
good bookes by the Printers penne, in such sort, as no earthly power was able
after that (though they did their best) to stoppe the course thereof, were he
neuer so myghtie, and all for the fartheraunce of Christes Church" (A3ᵛ).

58 Mark U. Edwards Jr., *Printing, Propaganda, and Martin Luther* (Berkeley:
University of California Press, 1994), 173.

59 See Hugh Trevor-Roper, "Toleration and Religion after 1688," in *From
Persecution to Toleration: The Glorious Revolution and Religion in England*, ed.
Ole Peter Grell, Jonathan I. Israel, and Nicholas Tyacke (Oxford: Clarendon
Press, 1991), John Feather, "The Book Trade in Politics: the Making of the
Copyright Act of 1710," *Publishing History* 8 (1980), Mark Rose, *Authors and
Owners: The Invention of Copyright* (Cambridge, MA: Harvard University
Press, 1993).

60 Thomas Williamson, *The Sword of the Spirit to Smite in Pieces That
Antichristian Goliah, Who Daily Defieth the Lords People the Host of Israel*
(London: Printed by Edw. Griffin, 1613), John Wilson, *The English
Martyrologe Conteyning a Summary of the Liues of the Glorious and Renowned
Saintes of the Three Kingdomes, England, Scotland, and Ireland* (Saint-Omer:
Printed at the English College Press, 1608).

61 Patrick Collinson, *From Iconoclasm to Iconophobia: The Cultural Impact of the
Second English Reformation* (University of Reading, 1986).

62 Robert Darnton, "What Is the History of Books?," *Daedalus* 111, no. 3 (1982).
For a critical review, see Thomas Adams and Nicolas Barker, "A New Model
for the Study of the Book," in *A Potencie of Life: Books in Society*, ed. Nicolas
Barker (London: British Library, 1993).

63 Peter Lake, "Anti-Popery: the Structure of a Prejudice," in *Conflict in Early
Stuart England: Studies in Religion and Politics, 1603–1642*, ed. Richard Cust
and Ann Hughes (London: Longman, 1989). For a less sophisticated but
still useful analysis, see Carol Z. Wiener, "The Beleaguered Isle: a Study
of Elizabethan and Early Jacobean Anti-Catholicism," *Past and Present*
51 (1971). For more recent work on the topic, see Michael Questier,
"Practical Antipapistry During the Reign of Elizabeth I," *Journal of British
Studies* 36 (1997), Alexandra Walsham, *Church Papists: Catholicism, Conformity
and Confessional Polemic in Early Modern England* (Woodbridge: The Boydell
Press for the Royal Historical Society, 1993).

64 Just how adept various religious groups were at exploiting the potential of
print is debated among historians of religion. In particular, the thesis that
the Marian regime failed to exploit the potential of literacy and printing
has met with sharp criticism at the hands of revisionist historians, such as
Eamon Duffy, *The Stripping of the Altars: Traditional Religion in England
1400–1580* (New Haven: Yale University Press, 1992), 525–43, and Christopher
Haigh, *English Reformations: Religion, Politics, and Society under the Tudors*

(Oxford: Clarendon Press, 1993), 216, 23. Furthermore, as Geoffrey Parker has suggested, the Counter-Reformation was so successful in good part because Catholics "made full use of all the media available to them: pictures, prints, plays and songs as well as catechisms, schools, sermons and visitations," Geoffrey Parker, "Success and Failure During the First Century of the Reformation," *Past and Present* 136 (1992): 74. For recent work on the Catholic exploitation of the press, see T. A. Birrell, "English Counter-Reformation Book Culture," *Recusant History* 22 (1994), Alexandra Walsham, "'Domme Preachers'? Post-Reformation English Catholicism and the Culture of Print," *Past and Present* 168 (2000).

65 Foxe, ed., *The Whole Workes of W. Tyndale, Iohn Frith, and Doct. Barnes*, A2ʳ.

66 Thomas Cartwright, *A Replye to an Answere Made of M. Doctor Whitgifte* (Hemel Hempstead?: 1573), A4ʳ.

67 This is in contrast to the medieval scribal custom of highlighting quotations by underlining. For a brief account of the development of quotation marks within different national contexts that stresses the importance of print, see C. J. Mitchell, "Quotation Marks, National Compositorial Habits and False Imprints," *The Library* 6th ser. 5 (1983). A much more wide-ranging account is provided by M. B. Parkes, *Pause and Effect: An Introduction to the History of Punctuation in the West* (Berkeley: University of California Press, 1993). An interesting consideration of the relationship between quotation marks and notions of intellectual property can be found in Margreta De Grazia, "Sanctioning Voice: Quotation Marks, the Abolition of Torture, and the Fifth Amendment," in *The Construction of Authorship: Textual Appropriation in Law and Literature*, ed. Martha Woodmansee and Peter Jaszi (Durham, NC: Duke University Press, 1994).

68 Mitchell, "Quotation Marks, National Compositorial Habits and False Imprints," 363.

69 It may be that the printer's complaint only provoked Whitgift and Bynneman to even greater displays of typographic ingenuity; their *Defense of the Aunswere to the Admonition against the Replie of T. C.* (London, 1574) is even more sophisticated than *The Answere*.

70 John Whitgift, *Defense of the Aunswere to the Admonition against the Replie of T. C.*, 312.

71 In a persuasive attempt to dislodge two of the metaphysical pieties regarding the impact of print (print is permanent, print encourages closure), Donald McKenzie emphasizes the continuities between speech, manuscript and print, arguing that printers endeavored to recreate in print "the social space of dialogue," "Speech–Manuscript–Print," in *New Directions in Textual Studies*, ed. Dave Oliphant and Robin Bradford. Intro. Larry Carver (Austin: Harry Ransom Humanities Research Center, 1990), 104. He concludes that "Dialogic and inter-textual functions seem to have been the dominant ones in the commonest forms of print; they are certainly the ones most evident in the pamphlets, and they are those that most approximate the element of presence in speech and writing as the more traditional discourse" (108).

72 Qtd. in Matthew Parker, *Correspondence of Matthew Parker, D. D., Archbishop of Canterbury*, ed. John Bruce and Thomas Thomason Perowne (Cambridge: Parker Society, 1853), 417. I would like to thank Benedict Robinson for drawing my attention to this passage.

73 William Barlow, *A Sermon Preached at Paules Crosse* (London: 1601), c6^r.

74 The long history of medieval heresy, as well as strident academic controversy, is enough to contradict any account of the period as without cultural conflict. Nonetheless, the Reformation and print produced a new level of conflict. For a helpful account of the space of the page, see Tribble, *Margins and Marginality*, esp. pp. 11–17 which discusses the *Glossa ordinaria*.

75 Michel Foucault, "Polemics, Politics, and Problemizations: an Interview with Michel Foucault," in *The Foucault Reader*, ed. Paul Rabinow (New York: Pantheon Books, 1984), 381.

76 The vogue for dialogue in literary studies owes a great deal to English translations of Bakhtin, especially M. M. Bakhtin, *The Dialogic Imagination: Four Essays*, ed. Michael Holquist (Austin: University of Texas Press, 1981). But variations on the dialogue concept mark many contemporary theories, for instance, Rorty's conceptualization of the history of philosophy as an interminable conversation, the therapeutic dialogue of psychoanalysis, the question-and-answer dynamic of Gadamer's hermeneutics, and Habermas's ideal speech situation. It is even possible to see Althusser's theory of interpellation as a dystopian inversion of the dialogue ideal.

77 See Aaron Fogel, "Coerced Speech and the Oedipus Dialogue Complex," in *Rethinking Bakhtin: Extensions and Challenges*, ed. Gary Saul Morson and Caryl Emerson (Evanston: Northwestern University Press, 1989). For a recent attempt to synthesize Gadamer and Foucault that emphasizes dialogue, see Hans Herbert Kögler, *The Power of Dialogue: Critical Hermeneutics after Gadamer and Foucault*, trans. Paul Hendrickson (Cambridge, MA: MIT Press, 1996).

78 William Fulke, *A Retentive to Stay Good Christians, in Trve Faith and Religion, against the Motiues of Richard Bristow* (London: 1580), vi^v.

79 Mark Goldie, "Ideology," in *Political Innovation and Conceptual Change*, ed. Terence Ball, James Farr, and Russell L. Hanson (Cambridge University Press, 1989), 279.

80 Alastair Fowler, *Kinds of Literature: An Introduction to the Theory of Genre and Modes* (Cambridge, MA: Harvard University Press, 1982).

81 For a classic version of such an argument, see Walter J. Ong, *Ramus, Method, and the Decay of Dialogue: From the Art of Discourse to the Art of Reason* (Cambridge, MA: Harvard University Press, 1958).

82 Peter Burke, "The Renaissance Dialogue," *Renaissance Studies* 3 (1989): 6–7.

83 Virginia Cox, *The Renaissance Dialogue: Literary Dialogue in Its Social and Political Contexts, Castiglione to Galileo* (Cambridge University Press, 1992), 6. For an argument that links seventeenth-century philosophical dialogues with the emergence of a public sphere, see Timothy Dykstal, *The Luxury of Skepticism: Politics, Philosophy, and Dialogue in the English Public Sphere, 1660–1740* (Charlottesville: University Press of Virginia, 2001).

84 Ian Green, *The Christian's ABC: Catechisms and Catechizing in England c.1530–1740* (Oxford: Clarendon Press, 1996).

85 George Gifford, *A Briefe Discourse of Certaine Pointes of the Religion, Which Is among the Common Sort of Christians, Which May Be Termed the Countrie Diuinitie* (London: 1581).

86 All three are reproduced in Dickie Spurgeon, ed., *Three Tudor Dialogues* (Delmar, NY: Scholars' Facsimiles & Reprints, 1978).

87 See Andrew McRae, *God Speed the Plough: The Representation of Agrarian England, 1500–1600* (Cambridge University Press, 1996). See also, Sarah A. Kelen, "Plowing the Past: 'Piers Protestant' and the Authority of Medieval Literary History," *Yearbook of Langland Studies* 13 (1999).

88 *A Dialogve, Concerning the Strife of Our Churche* (London: Printed by Robert Waldegrave, 1584), A3^r–A3^v.

89 Richard Bancroft, *A Sermon Preached at Paules Crosse the 9 of Februarie, Being the First Sunday in the Parleament, Anno. 1588* (London: 1588). For Marprelate, see chapter 2.

90 Deakins's survey of Tudor prose dialogues, marked by a desire to recuperate the dialogue form, proposes a distinction between "genre" and "anti-genre" before concluding that there are only five examples of the former and 230 plus of the latter; Roger Deakins, "The Tudor Prose Dialogue: Genre and Anti-Genre," *Studies in English Literature, 1500–1800* 20 (1980). For an older, but still representative, version of the idealizing account of Renaissance dialogue, see Joel B. Altman, *The Tudor Play of Mind: Rhetorical Inquiry and the Development of Elizabethan Drama* (Berkeley: University of California Press, 1978).

91 Hans Robert Jauss, *Question and Answer: Forms of Dialogic Understanding*, trans. Michael Hays (Minneapolis: University of Minnesota Press, 1989), 210.

92 C. S. Lewis, *English Literature in the Sixteenth Century* (Oxford: Clarendon Press, 1954), 409.

93 Thomas Lodge, *Catharos. Diogenes in His Singularitie.* (London: 1591), A2^v.

94 See, e.g., Bancroft, *A Sermon Preached at Paules Crosse the 9 of Februarie, Being the First Sunday in the Parleament, Anno. 1588*, which lists four principal causes of schism: contempt of bishops, ambition, self-love, and covetousness (14–23). In the passage on self-love, Bancroft quotes St. Bernard on the dire consequences of those who seek "to hunt after commendation by singularitie of knowledge" (21). The very same list of causes is repeated in *A Myrror for Martinists* (1590), A4^r, with one alteration: self-love is transformed into "false loue." The author of *An Almond for a Parrot* accuses the presbyterians of "the pride of singularity" and later identifies singularity as "the eldest childe of heresy" (D1^r, D2^r), and Thomas Nashe claims "they set their self-love to study to invent new sects of singularity"; Thomas Nashe, *The Works of Thomas Nashe*, ed. Ronald B. McKerrow (Oxford: Basil Blackwell, 1958), 67.

95 Peter de la Primaudaye, *The Second Part of the French Academie*, trans. Thomas Bowes (London: G. Bishop, R. Newbery, R. Barker, 1594).

96 For this identification see Alice Walker, "The Reading of an Elizabethan: Some Sources of the Prose Pamphlets of Thomas Lodge," *Review of English Studies* 8 (1932).

97 Bowes excoriates a recent writer who has defended stage plays as "rare exercises of vertue" (B4^v), a direct quotation of Nashe's *Pierce Penilesse* (F3^r). For discussion of Nashe's allegory, see Donald J. McGinn, "The Allegory of the 'Beare' and the 'Foxe' in Nashe's *Pierce Penilesse*," *PMLA* (1946), Anthony G. Petti, "Political Satire in *Pierce Penilesse His Suplication to the Divill*," *Neophilologus* 45 (1961). Another influential beast fable is Spenser's *Prosopopia. Or Mother Hubberds Tale* (1591). Attempting to decipher such topical allegory presents intractable difficulties. For a treatment that displays all the virtues and vices of such attempts, see Edwin Greenlaw, "Spenser and the Earl of Leicester," *PMLA* 25 (1910).

98 Roger Ascham, *The Scholemaster or Plaine and Perfite Way of Teachyng Children, to Vnderstand, Write, and Speake, the Latin Tong* (London: John Day, 1570).

99 Robert Greene, *A Notable Discouery of Coosenage* (London: 1591), A2^r, Nashe, *The Works of Thomas Nashe*, II, 237.

100 Richard Helgerson, *The Elizabethan Prodigals* (Berkeley: University of California Press, 1976), 79–104.

101 Thomas Lodge, *Wits Miserie, and the Worlds Madnesse: Discouering the Deuils Incarnat of This Age* (London: 1596), B3^r; Robert Greene, *A Quip for an Vpstart Courtier: Or, a Quaint Dispute Between Veluet Breeches and Clothbreeches* (London: 1592), B4^r, C2^v, D3^r, H3^r.

102 Gifford, *A Brief Discourse*, A1^v. For a discussion, see Dewey D. Wallace, "George Gifford, Puritan Propaganda and Popular Religion in Elizabethan England," *Sixteenth Century Journal* 9 (1978).

103 Edwin Haviland Miller, "Deletions in Robert Greene's *A Quip for an Upstart Courtier* (1592)," *Huntington Library Quarterly* 15 (1951–52), Edwin Haviland Miller, "The Editions of Robert Greene's *A Quip for an Upstart Courtier* (1592)," *Studies in Bibliography* 6 (1954). For an argument that there were three states of the first edition, see I. A. Shapiro, "The First Edition of Greene's *Quip for an Upstart Courtier*," *Studies in Bibliography* 14 (1961).

104 Walsham, *Church Papists: Catholicism, Conformity and Confessional Polemic in Early Modern England.*

105 Patrick Collinson, *The Puritan Character: Polemics and Polarities in Early Seventeenth-Century English Culture* (Los Angeles: The William Clark Memorial Library, 1989). For the distortions imposed by polemic, see T. N. Corns, W. A. Speck, and J. A. Downie, "Archetypal Mystification: Polemic and Reality in English Political Literature, 1640–1750," *Eighteenth-Century Life* (1981–82). While polemical identities are constructed, their relationship to reality is complex. They are factitious not fictitious. As I hope to show, polemic is *real* though its claims may be false, and it contributes to the self-understanding of various actors. One cannot simply peel away the accretions of mere polemic in order to reveal reality in all its generous splendor. Too

frequently an insistence on the exaggerations and distortions of polemic leads to its dismissal.

106 For an ambitious attempt to assess the relationship between print and Protestantism, see Green, *Print and Protestantism in Early Modern England.* Green bases his analysis on a sample of 737 religious best or steady sellers and, unsuprisingly, finds strong evidence for a consensual vision of religion. There are two points to be made here. First, the sample virtually precludes polemics, which were rarely reprinted, and thus underrepresents an important set of books about religion. A very different perspective would be provided if one were to calculate the ratio of "steady sellers" to other more ephemeral texts. I am not denying the significance of a core set of books that found a steady market, only observing that their significance relative to polemic cannot be decided without analyzing polemic itself. Second, as recent historians of reading have insisted, the serial data of publication numbers is not an adequate basis for the construction of a cultural map or mentality. We need evidence of the often unpredictable and usually multiple ways in which a given book was actually read, and this evidence is invariably provided by writing (in letters and commonplace books, in the margins of books, and, most obviously, in new books themselves).

107 For this argument, see Stuart Clark, *Thinking with Demons: The Idea of Witchcraft in Early Modern Europe* (Oxford University Press, 1997), esp. 31–79.

108 Pierre Saint-Amand, *The Laws of Hostility: Politics, Violence, and the Enlightenment,* trans. Jennifer Curtiss Gage (Minneapolis: University of Minnesota Press, 1996), 11. Pierre Bourdieu, *In Other Words: Essays Towards a Reflexive Sociology,* trans. Matthew Adamson (Stanford University Press, 1990), 103.

1 "FOXE'S" BOOKS OF MARTYRS: PRINTING AND POPULARIZING THE *ACTES AND MONUMENTS*

1 Thucydides, *The History of the War Fought between Athens and Sparta,* ed. Rex Warner (London: Penguin, 1956), 13.

2 Katherine Firth, *The Apocalyptic Tradition in Reformation Britain, 1530–1645* (Oxford University Press, 1979), 110.

3 Charles Whibly, "Chroniclers as Antiquaries," in *The Cambridge History of English Literature,* ed. A. W. Ward and A. R. Waller (Cambridge University Press, 1918), 332.

4 For an excellent account of the proliferation of competing martyrologies, see Brad S. Gregory, *Salvation at Stake: Christian Martyrdom in Early Modern Europe* (Cambridge, MA: Harvard University Press, 1999).

5 For this point, see Glyn Parry, "John Foxe, 'Father of Lyes', and the Papists," in *John Foxe and the English Reformation,* ed. David Loades (Aldershot: Scolar Press, 1997). See also Annabel Patterson, *Reading Holinshed's Chronicles* (University of Chicago Press, 1994).

6 For medieval English historiography, see Antonia Gransden, *Historical Writing in England: c. 1307 to the Early Sixteenth Century*, 2 vols., vol. II (London: Routledge & Kegan Paul, 1982) and "Propaganda in English Medieval Historiography," *Journal of Medieval History* 1 (1975). On English humanist history, see F. J. Levy, *Tudor Historical Thought* (San Marino, CA: Huntington Library, 1967). The best recent work on English historical scholarship is D. R. Woolf, *The Idea of History in Early Stuart England: Erudition, Ideology, and "the Light of Truth" from the Accession of James I to the Civil War* (University of Toronto Press, 1990), *Reading History in Early Modern England* (New York: Cambridge University Press, 2000), and *The Social Circulation of the Past: English Historical Culture, 1500–1730* (Oxford University Press, 2003).

7 The polemical status of *Actes and Monuments* once again becomes an issue in religious history written in the nineteenth century and later. For the controversy surrounding the publication of the Victorian editions, see D. Andrew Penny, "John Foxe's Victorian Reception," *The Historical Journal* 40 (1997). More recently, Christopher Haigh has identified the object of his criticism as the "Foxe–Dickens approach"; Christopher Haigh, *English Reformations: Religion, Politics, and Society under the Tudors* (Clarendon Press, 1993), 2. Nonetheless, Haigh often finds himself in the peculiar position of having to rely on *Actes and Monuments* as source (see *English Reformations*). For a helpful consideration of the methodology of *Actes* and its place within present histories of the Reformation, see Patrick Collinson, "Truth and Legend: the Veracity of John Foxe's Book of Martyrs," in *Elizabethan Essays* (London: The Hambledon Press, 1994).

8 Thomas Nashe, *The Works of Thomas Nashe*, ed. Ronald B. McKerrow (Oxford: Basil Blackwell, 1958).

9 For Perne's contemporary reputation, see Patrick Collinson, "Perne the Turncoat: an Elizabethan Reputation," in *Elizabethan Essays*.

10 V. Norskov Olsen, *John Foxe and the Elizabethan Church* (Berkeley: University of California Press, 1973), 152–55. For more on the Admonition Controversy, see chapter 2 below.

11 *A Booke of Certaine Canons, Concernyng Some Parte of the Discipline of the Church of England* (London: 1571), A3^v.

12 Laud is the striking exception that proves the rule, and even his resistance was guarded. When faced, at his trial in 1644, with the accusation that he had illegimately suppressed good books including *Actes and Monuments*, Laud defended himself by arguing that his unwillingness to license an abridgement was motivated by a desire to preserve the large book: "But since *the Book of Martyrs* was named, I shall tell *your Lordships* how careful I was of it. It is well known, how easily *Abridgements*, by their Brevity and their Cheapness, in short time work out the Authors themselves. Mr. *Young* the Printer laboured me earnestly and often for an *Abridgement of the Book of Martyrs*. But I still withstood it ... upon these two Grounds. The one, lest it should bring the large Book it self into disuse. And the other, lest if any Material thing should be left out, that should have been charged as done of purpose by me; as now I see it

is in other Books"; William Laud, *The History of the Troubles and Trial of William Laud* (London: 1695), 2z1ʳ. Laud here demonstrates a sophisticated understanding of both the economics and the politics of abridgement. Elsewhere, Laud reveals a distinct suspicion of the book when he concedes having said of Jewel's *Works* and *Actes and Monuments*, that "it were better they should not have these Books in Churches, than so to abuse them" (2Uʳ). In his own defense, Laud makes three points: first, he suggests that his opponents have misunderstood Jewel and Foxe; second, he claims that though they "were very worthy men in their Time, yet everything they say is not by and by *the Doctrine of the Church* of England"; third, his speech was provoked by his antagonists who had "picked diverse things out of those Books which they could not master, and with them distempered both themselves and their Neighbours" (2Uᵛ).

13 John R. Knott, *Discourses of Martyrdom in English Literature, 1563–1694* (Cambridge University Press, 1993), 2. For later Protestant disputes over Foxe, see William M. Lamont, *Godly Rule: Politics and Religion, 1603–60* (London: Macmillan, 1969).

14 Roy Strong, *The Cult of Elizabeth* (Berkeley: University of California Press, 1977), 127. In a similar vein: "After the Bible, Foxe's works were the most widely read books in sixteenth-century England," Philip Corrigan and Derek Sayer, *The Great Arch: English State Formation as Cultural Revolution*, rev. edn. (Oxford: Blackwell, 1991), 57. This claim appears to have been well established by 1964, when Patrick Collinson observed: "If as we are often told, 'Foxe's Book of Martyrs' for long had an influence in this country second only to that of the English Bible, it is perhaps not inappropriate that its history should have curiously resembled that of the Bible itself"; Patrick Collinson, "Review of William Haller, *Foxe's Book of Martyrs and the Elect Nation*," *Journal of Ecclesiastical History* 15 (1964).

15 Christopher Hill, *Intellectual Origins of the English Revolution* (Oxford: Clarendon Press, 1965), 291. This claim is repeated in Christopher Hill, *Intellectual Origins of the English Revolution Revisited* (Oxford: Clarendon Press, 1997), 258. It should be pointed out that Hill himself recognized that "Foxe's is no narrow patriotism. The English Church was part of the international Church, even though in most other countries that Church was oppressed. Englishmen had international as well as patriotic duties" (179).

16 Richard Helgerson, *Forms of Nationhood* (University of Chicago Press, 1992), 253.

17 William Haller, *Foxe's Book of Martyrs and the Elect Nation* (London: Jonathan Cape, 1963), 245.

18 An important earlier source for this argument is Louis B. Wright, *Religion and Empire: The Alliance between Piety and Commerce in English Expansion, 1558–1625* (Chapel Hill: University of North Carolina Press, 1943). For a recent disavowal of the connection between Foxe's book and the early modern ideology of British empire, see David Armitage, *The Ideological Origins of the British Empire, Ideas in Context* (Cambridge University Press, 2000).

19 For a recent and helpful survey, see Patrick Collinson, "John Foxe and National Consciousness," in *John Foxe and His World*, ed. Christopher Highley and John N. King (Aldershot: Ashgate, 2002).

20 See Richard Bauckham, *Tudor Apocalypse*, vol. VIII, *The Courtenay Library of Reformation Classics* (Oxford: The Sutton Courtenay Press, 1978), 86–87, Paul Christianson, *Reformers and Babylon* (University of Toronto Press, 1978), 41, Firth, *The Apocalyptic Tradition*, 106–10. A notable exception to this trend is Pocock, who claims that Haller "has not been displaced," despite "often-justified criticisms"; J. G. A. Pocock, "A Discourse of Sovereignty: Observations on the Work in Progress," in *Political Discourse in Early Modern Britain*, ed. Nicholas Phillipson and Quentin Skinner (Cambridge University Press, 1993), 381 n. 17.

21 Bauckham, *Tudor Apocalypse*, 85.

22 As Haller himself puts it: "The intention in the following pages is not to inquire whether Foxe told the truth about the past or whether his beliefs and opinions about religion and the Church are correct and just. The intention is rather to relate the human circumstances that led to the composition and publication of his book, to explain what the book appears to have conveyed to the people of its own time, and to suggest what seems to have been its effect on the public mind in that and the immediately succeeding age" (15). Despite the imprecise and dated invocation of "the public mind," this is a broad agenda that includes more than the technical viability of "apocalyptic nationalism."

23 This does *not* entail a denigration of Foxe's own work. He was an indefatigable editor and an energetic writer whose work eminently deserves scholarly attention. The point is simply that, as much recent work has revealed, we can learn a great deal by broadening our focus to include not only authors and their texts, but also the material forms in which those texts circulated, the publisher and printers that fashioned those forms, and the booksellers and readers who handled them.

24 A notable and early exception is Mark Breitenberg, "The Flesh Made Word: Foxe's *Actes and Monuments*," *Renaissance and Reformation* 24 (1989). But see now the work of Thomas Freeman who has been a staunch advocate of returning to the original editions. A helpful introduction to the issues can be found in Thomas Freeman, "Texts, Lies, and Microfilm: Reading and Misreading Foxe's 'Book of Martyrs,'" *Sixteenth Century Journal* 30 (1999).

25 Warren Wooden, *John Foxe* (Boston: Twayne, 1983), 105–09.

26 See Patrick Collinson, *The Elizabethan Puritan Movement* (Berkeley: University of California Press, 1967), Peter Lake, *Anglicans and Puritans? Presbyterianism and English Conformist Thought from Whitgift to Hooker* (London: Unwin Hyman, 1988).

27 Oliver writes that "whatever the motive may have been, the 1576 edition is decidedly the poorest and cheapest that was ever printed"; Leslic M. Oliver, "The *Actes and Monuments* of John Foxe: a Study of the Growth and Influence of a Book" (PhD, Harvard University, 1945), 65. He suggests that the price was cut but acknowledges that there is no direct evidence that Day actually reduced the retail price.

28 Qtd. in J. F. Mozley, *John Foxe and His Book* (New York: Farrar, Straus & Giroux, 1940), 138.

29 The bibliographical term, "preliminaries," refers to the gathering(s) that appear before the sequence of signatures that make up the main body of the book. Usually, these gatherings were produced last and signed with a symbol, such as ¶, that is not part of the sequence used for the rest of the book. Thus, a distinction between preliminaries and main text is part of the process of production; however, this does not mean that preliminaries, as something sitting outside the book, are somehow dispensable.

30 Michel Foucault, "What Is an Author?," in *Textual Strategies: Perspectives in Post-Structuralist Criticism*, ed. Josué V. Harari (Ithaca: Cornell University Press, 1977), 159.

31 For an incisive account of this tendency, see Debra Belt, "The Poetics of Hostile Response, 1575–1610," *Criticism* 33 (1991).

32 Qtd. in Hans H. Wellisch, "The Oldest Printed Indexes," *The Indexer* 15 (1986): 80.

33 *The Printing Press as an Agent of Change* (Cambridge University Press, 1979), I, 100. For an account of the way in which the sales appeal of indexes led to their systematization in books of natural philosophy, see Ann Blair, "Annotating and Indexing Natural Philosophy," in *Books and the Sciences in History*, ed. Marina Frasca-Spada and Nick Jardine (Cambridge University Press, 2000). Blair also makes the argument that the rise of indexes was in part a response to the information overload that accompanied the spread of print.

34 Qtd. in Evelyn B. Tribble, *Margins and Marginality: The Printed Page in Early Modern England* (Charlottesville: University Press of Virginia, 1993), 23.

35 Qtd. in Claire McEachern, "'A Whore at the First Blush Seemeth Only a Woman': John Bale's *Image of Both Churches* and the Terms of Religious Difference in the Early English Reformation," *The Journal of Medieval and Renaissance Studies* 25 (1995).

36 See, in particular, "The Book as an Expressive Form," chapter 1 of *Bibliography and the Sociology of Texts* (London: British Library, 1986), 1–20. Elsewhere, McKenzie argues that "every book tells a story quite apart from that recounted by its text." This claim can be extended, he suggests, to "all recorded texts as collaborative creations – the product of social acts involving the complex interventions of human agency acting on material forms"; D. F. McKenzie and Bibliographical Society (Great Britain), *'What's Past Is Prologue': The Bibliographical Society and the History of the Book* (London: Hearthstone Publications, 1993).

37 For an illuminating account of the functions of the commonplace in Tudor and Stuart England, see Mary Thomas Crane, *Framing Authority: Sayings, Self, and Society in Sixteenth-Century England* (Princeton University Press, 1993). In addition, see Peter Beal, "Notions in Garrison: the Seventeenth-Century Commonplace Book," in *New Ways of Looking at Old Texts: Papers of the Renaissance English Text Society, 1985–1991*, ed. W. Speed Hill (Binghamton,

NY: Medieval and Renaissance Texts and Studies in conjunction with Renaissance English Text Society, 1993).

38 Pollard notes that the comprehensive index to Calvin's *Institution of a Christian Man* responded to the needs of Protestant polemicists: *Institution* "was the armory from which every controversialist drew his weapons, and that the weapons might be ready for use at any moment, a good index was a necessity"; Alfred W. Pollard, "Indexes," *Living Age* 257 (1908). On the other hand, Knight suggests that William Prynne's *Histrio-mastix* might have escaped the notice of the authorities if not for its polemical index; G. Norman Knight, "Book Indexing in Great Britain: a Brief History," *The Indexer* 6 (1968). In Prynne's case the index, designed to guide the reader, exposes the book to hostile scrutiny.

39 Kevin Dunn draws attention to the neglected preface but significantly focuses exclusively on those written by authors; Kevin Dunn, *Pretexts of Authority: The Rhetoric of Authorship in the Renaissance* (Stanford University Press, 1994).

40 Francis Bacon, *The Works of Francis Bacon*, ed. Robert Leslie Ellis, James Spedding, and Douglas Denon Heath (London: Longmans, 1870), VI, 498.

41 Glanvill and Swift are qtd. in Henry B. Wheatley, *How to Make an Index* (London: Elliot Stock, 1902). Alexander Pope, *The Dunciad Variorum*, Bk. I, lines 234–35. Swift's scorn for indexes was probably increased by William Wotton's claim that they are one of the several benefits of printing, see William Wotton, *Reflections Upon Ancient and Modern Learning* (London: 1694).

42 Oliver Ormerod, *The Picture of a Papist: or, a Relation of the Damnable Heresies. Together with a Discourse of the Late Treason. Whereunto is Annexed Pagano-Papismus* (London, 1605). The even-handed Ormerod wrote a companion volume entitled *The Picture of a Puritane: or, a Relation of the Opinions and Practises of the Anabaptists in Germanie, and of the Puritanes in England. Whereunto is Annexed Puritano-papismus* (London, 1605).

43 James is qtd. in J. P. Sommerville, *Royalists and Patriots: Politics and Ideology in England, 1603–1640*, 2nd edn. (London: Longman, 1999), 197. John Harington, *A New Discourse of a Stale Subject, Called the Metamorphosis of Ajax*, ed. Elizabeth Story Donno (New York: Columbia University Press, 1962), 263.

44 Lake, *Anglicans and Puritans?*, 18.

45 Olsen, *John Foxe and the Elizabethan Church*, 156. For a more recent account of Foxe's attitudes toward church discipline, see Catharine Davies and Jane Facey, "A Reformation Dilemma: John Foxe and the Problem of Discipline," *Journal of Ecclesiastical History* 39 (1988).

46 Qtd. in Olsen, *John Foxe and the Elizabethan Church*, 153.

47 Lake, *Anglicans and Puritans?*, 22.

48 For the chronology of sixteenth-century, English presbyterianism see Collinson, *The Elizabethan Puritan Movement*.

49 Elizabeth Evenden and Thomas S. Freeman, "John Foxe, John Day and the Printing of the 'Book of Martyrs,'" in *Lives in Print: Biography and the Book Trade from the Middle Ages to the Twenty-first Century*, ed. Robin Myers, Michael Harris, and Giles Mandelbrote (London: British Library, 2002), 45.

Evenden and Freeman suggest that the book embodies another sort of monumentality: "Day, aware that he didn't have long to live, was determined that this book would be a monument to his memory" (45). I would add that Foxe himself was to die four years later at the age of 70 and may well have recognized that the '83 edition was likely to be his final version of the book. In any case, the relatively advanced age of the edition's two prime movers, John Foxe and John Day, may help to explain the conservative and conciliatory aspects of this edition.

50 By the "language of national election," I mean a specific vocabulary that stressed the unique role of England in the maintenance of true religion. Obviously, such a language does not suggest that everyone in England is elect, nor does it imply that *only* the English are elect. This language was not entirely a post-Reformation invention. For an account of late medieval claims that England enjoyed a special status with God, see John W. McKenna, "How God Became an Englishman," in *Tudor Rule and Revolution: Essays for G. R. Elton from His American Friends*, ed. Delloyd J. Guth and John W. McKenna (Cambridge University Press, 1982).

51 On the ubiquity of abridged chronicles, see D. R. Woolf, "Genre into Artifact: the Decline of the English Chronicle in the Sixteenth Century," *Sixteenth Century Journal* 19 (1988).

52 Such a conjecture is supported by a cryptic entry, dated June 2, 1589, in the records of the court of the Stationers' Company. The Court of Assistants determines that the Company as a whole accepts the financial liability for any claims or damages by John Windet, the printer of the *Abridgement*, and Timothy Bright that may result from "anie promise or Agreemente" made by the Master and the Wardens of the Company "before anie the Lordes of her maiesties privie Councell or otherwise touchinge anie thinge or matter that was moved in or aboute the late Controversie or striffe touchinge the abridgement of the Booke of Martyrs"; W. W. Greg and E. Boswell, eds., *Records of the Court of the Stationers' Company* (London: The Bibliographical Society, 1930), 31–32. See also the ruling recorded earlier (January 16, 1588/9), holding the partners in Richard Day's privilege responsible for the legal costs incurred for the "defence of the book of m'tyrs" (30). For a brief account, Leslie M. Oliver, "The Seventh Edition of John Foxe's *Actes and Monuments*," *The Papers of the Bibliographical Society of America* 37 (1943).

53 At the request of Whitgift, the Bishop of London wrote to the Archdeacon of St. Albans, praising Bright's book as "small in price yet of great worth" and urging the Archdeacon "to recommend the same to the Clergy and Laity in your Diocese" (qtd. in Lady Margaret Hoby, *Diary of Lady Margaret Hoby, 1599–1605*, ed. Dorothy M. Mead [London: G. Routledge & Sons, 1930], 253). The letter goes on to explain in detail how copies of the book can be ordered. For a recent, and illuminating, account of Whitgift's role, see Damian Nussbaum, "Whitgift's 'Book of Martyrs': Archbishop Whitgift, Timothy Bright and the Elizabethan Struggle over John Foxe's Legacy," in *John Foxe: An Historical Perspective*, ed. David Loades (Aldershot: Ashgate, 1999).

54 Thomas Mason, *Christs Victorie over Sathans Tyrannie* (London: 1615), A3^r–A3^v.

55 Richard Grafton, *A Chronicle at Large* ... *Of the Affayres of Englande from the Creation of the Worlde, Vnto the First Yere of Queene Elizabeth* (London: 1569), ¶2^r.

56 Obviously, such a schematic narrative places emphasis on the providential story of the nation. This sort of history was criticized by those who desired a thicker description and a closer attention to secondary causes. *The Advancement of Learning*, for example, pours scorn on abridged histories: "As for the corruptions and moths of history, which are Epitomes, the use of them deserveth to be banished, as all men of sound judgment have confessed; as those that have fretted and corroded the sound bodies of many excellent histories, and wrought them into base and unprofitable dregs," Bacon, *The Works of Francis Bacon*, VI, 189.

57 For an account of the development of Foxe's scheme of periodization, see Palle J. Olsen, "Was John Foxe a Millenarian?," *Journal of Ecclesiastical History* 45 (1994).

58 Nussbaum's assertion that the volume is "a robust apologetic of the English church's purity in the face of puritan attacks" is certainly correct, but this apologetic motive does not mitigate the book's celebratory rhetoric (153). Only a restrictive understanding of apologetic would claim that it is solely the product of defensiveness and anxiety. The triumphalism that I detect in the book is a matter of rhetoric, a rhetoric well suited to a number of polemical purposes; it is not evidence of a generalized Elizabethan optimism.

59 Patrick Collinson, *The Birthpangs of Protestant England: Religious and Cultural Change in the Sixteenth and Seventeenth Centuries* (New York: St. Martin's Press, 1988) and Patrick Collinson, "Biblical Rhetoric: the English Nation and National Sentiment in the Prophetic Mode," in *Religion and Culture in Renaissance England*, ed. Claire McEachern and Deborah Shuger (Cambridge University Press, 1997).

60 For an account of British nationalism that stresses the importance of Protestantism, see Linda Colley, *Britons: Forging the Nation, 1707–1837* (New Haven: Yale University Press, 1992).

61 This image first appears in the '70 edition of *Actes* illustrating the year 1534 (3B2^r). In this edition another woodcut introduces Henry VIII's reign: a less dynamic image of the king in state surrounded by his councilors (2Aa1^r). In the '83 edition this woodcut is dropped and the image of Henry in triumph assumes pride of place (2Aa2^r). Coming immediately after the title page of the second volume, it serves as an iconic introduction to both Henry VIII's reign and the volume.

62 The Online Variorum Edition prepared by the British Academy John Foxe Project in association with Sheffield University includes the complete texts of the 1563, 1570, 1576, and 1583 editions, allowing readers to quickly discern the changes made between these editions. In addition, the Project has sponsored a series of colloquia that have resulted in several volumes (Christopher Highley and John N. King, eds., *John Foxe and His World* [Aldershot: Ashgate, 2002],

David Loades, ed., *John Foxe and the English Reformation* [Aldershot: Scolar Press, 1997], David Loades, ed., *John Foxe: An Historical Perspective* [Aldershot: Ashgate, 1999]) that have done a great deal to illuminate the publication history of the book.

63 For an excellent survey of these abridgements, see David Scott Kastan, "Little Foxes," in *John Foxe and His World*, ed. Christopher Highley and John N. King (Aldershot: Ashgate, 2002). For more on Taylor, see Bernard Capp, *The World of John Taylor the Water-Poet, 1578–1653* (Oxford University Press, 1994), esp. 121–40. Though Taylor cannot, as Capp acknowledges, be claimed as typical, the popularity of his rendition of *Actes and Monuments* deserves greater attention than it has received. In a recent essay on Foxe and "national consciousness," Patrick Collinson discusses Bright, Mason, and Cotton, but omits Taylor; Collinson, "John Foxe and National Consciousness." Unlike Cotton with his loose aggregation of edifying tales, Taylor was decidedly interested in the "grand edifice of apocalyptic nationalism" (34). As Capp points out, Taylor's "summary of Foxe went even further than the original, damning the papacy as 'absolute, and only Antichrist'" (122). Foxe, in contrast, argued for a dual Antichrist comprised of the pope and the Turk. In addition, Taylor placed his versification of *Actes* in the penultimate position in his *Workes*; the final item is "Gods Manifold Mercies in these Miracvlovs Deliverances of our Church of *England*, from the yeare 1565 vntill this present, 1630 particularly and briefly Described"; John Taylor, *All the Workes of Iohn Taylor, the Water Poet* (London: 1630), 142.

64 Ian Green's sample of 727 religious books that each went through at least five editions within 30 years of initial publication excludes *Actes and Monuments* but includes both Cotton and Taylor; Ian Green, *Print and Protestantism in Early Modern England* (Oxford University Press, 2000), 610, 63.

65 Thomas Fuller, *The Holy State* (London: 1642), Rr3ᵛ.

2 MARTIN MARPRELATE AND THE FUGITIVE TEXT

1 For an illuminating account of the strategic uses of anonymity in print, see Marcy L. North, *The Anonymous Renaissance: Cultures of Discretion in Tudor–Stuart England* (University of Chicago Press, 2003).

2 Waldegrave is an important player in the production of the tracts, and it seems plausible to suggest that he was responsible for some of Marprelate's extensive knowledge of the London printing world. For an account of his career, see Katherine S. Van Eerde, "Robert Waldegrave: the Printer as Agent and Link between Sixteenth-Century England and Scotland," *Renaissance Quarterly* 34 (1981). Valentine Simmes, however, seems not to have had any ideological commitment to the project. Indeed, later in life he was involved in the printing of "Popish books." See William Craig Ferguson, *Valentine Simmes: Printer to Drayton, Shakespeare, Chapman, Greene, Dekker, Middleton, Daniel, Jonson, Marlowe, Marston, Heywood, and Other Elizabethans* (Charlottesville: Bibliographical Society of the University of Virginia, 1968), 9.

3 Collinson rightly regrets that the "academic parlour game of hunt the disguised author" has distracted scholars from studying the pamphlets themselves but is perhaps too dismissive when he asserts that such an investigation is "in itself a rather sterile exercise," "Ecclesiastical Vitriol: Religious Satire in the 1590s and the Invention of Puritanism," in *The Reign of Elizabeth I: Court and Culture in the Last Decade*, ed. John Guy (Cambridge University Press in assn. with the Folger Institute, 1995), 157.

4 See Matthew Sutcliffe, *An Answere to a Certaine Libel Supplicatorie* (London, 1592) and *An Answere unto a Certaine Calumnious Letter Published by M. Job Throkmorton* (London, 1595). Michel Foucault, "What Is an Author?," in *Textual Strategies: Perspectives in Post-Structuralist Criticism*, ed. Josué V. Harari (Ithaca: Cornell University Press, 1977).

5 Benger seems to acknowledge this when, after endorsing Carlson's identification of Throkmorton, he writes, "In fact it is likely that all the satires were to some degree a collaborative project, even though the distinctive style suggests one presiding genius as writer-in-chief"; John Benger, "The Authority of the Writer and Text in Radical Protestant Literature 1540 to 1593 with Particular Reference to the Marprelate Tracts" (PhD dissertation, University of Oxford, 1989), 182.

6 Ibid., 173.

7 Carlson has "come as close to a definitive answer as we are likely to get," according to Peter Lake, who, nonetheless, remains "unconvinced that Penry could not have collaborated with Throkmorton"; Peter Lake, "Puritan Identities," *Journal of Ecclesiastical History* 35 (1984). Alternatively, Patrick Collinson suggests the authorship of "George Carleton, perhaps as one of a consortium including Throkmorton"; Collinson, "Ecclesiastical Vitriol," 158. See also Patrick Collinson, *The Elizabethan Puritan Movement* (Berkeley: University of California Press, 1967), 394–96. An early advocate of "composite authorship," John Dover Wilson, argued that Roger Williams, Throkmorton, and Penry all had a hand in writing the pamphlets, but he then went on to assign, in typical New Bibliographic fashion, various pamphlets and sections of pamphlets to particular authors, "Martin Marprelate and Shakespeare's Fluellen: a New Theory of the Authorship of the Marprelate Tracts," *The Library* 3rd ser. 3 (1912).

8 Huntington MS. EL 2148 87^r.

9 The obvious exception is Leland H. Carlson, *Martin Marprelate, Gentleman: Master Job Throckmorton Laid Open in His Colors* (San Marino, CA: Huntington Library, 1981). The only other full-length treatment is William Pierce, *An Historical Introduction to the Marprelate Tracts* (London: Archibald Constable, 1908). See also Edward Arber, *An Introductory Sketch to the Martin Marprelate Controversy, 1588–1590* (London: Archibald Constable, 1895), Benger, "The Authority of the Writer and Text," and Joseph Black, "Pamphlet Wars: the Marprelate Tracts and 'Martinism,' 1588–1688" (PhD dissertation, University of Toronto, 1996).

10 For an excellent example, see Arber: "While one regrets the frequent narrow-mindedness, and sometimes the ignorant fanaticism that characterized so

many of the Puritans; as a whole, they were in the right. They saved England from a perpetual tyranny. They were essentially a law-abiding class. In time, they learnt the hard lesson of toleration. Let their great acts and greater long-suffering be remembered with gratitude for ever!" (*An Introductory Sketch*, 14). The same vision is succinctly registered in the claim that, "It is in the matter of Civil Rights that the *MARTIN MARPRELATE* tracts are so important in our history" (9). Alternatively, one might note the subtitle of William Pierce's *An Historical Introduction to the Marprelate Tracts: A Chapter in the Evolution of Religious and Civil Liberty in England*. Arber and Pierce both published their work on Marprelate at the close of the nineteenth century and in the first decade of the twentieth, before the experience of the Great War, and both assumed that the modern English constitution was the *telos* of all prior history. It is perhaps worth remembering in this context that Herbert Butterfield's *The Whig Interpretation of History* (London: G. Bell), which set out to demolish such just-so histories, was first published in 1931.

11 All citations of the Marprelate tracts are from the facsimile editions in *The Marprelate Tracts [1588–1589]* (Leeds: The Scolar Press, 1967).

12 For popular print see Margaret Spufford, *Small Books and Pleasant Histories: Popular Fiction and Its Readership in Seventeenth-Century England* (London: Methuen, 1981), Tessa Watt, *Cheap Print and Popular Piety, 1550–1640* (Cambridge University Press, 1991). On the importance of ephemeral print, see D. F. McKenzie, "Speech–Manuscript–Print," in *New Directions in Textual Studies*, ed. Dave Oliphant and Robin Bradford. Intro. Larry Carver (Austin: Harry Ransom Humanities Research Center, 1990).

13 For an excellent account of John Dee's reading practices, see William H. Sherman, *John Dee: The Politics of Reading and Writing in the English Renaissance* (Amherst: University of Massachusetts Press, 1997). See also, Lisa Jardine and Anthony Grafton, "'Studied for Action': how Gabriel Harvey Read His Livy," *Past and Present* 129 (1990).

14 By political inertness I mean simply that print does not entail any particular political ideology; this does not, however, preclude the possibility that the practices of print are deeply connected to a number of thoroughly political issues such as literacy and the creation and distribution of knowledge. I am most eager to avoid an account that sees an incipient democracy in print as well as one that sees in print the austere fixity of a peculiarly modern form of authoritarianism.

15 John N. Wall, Jr., "The Reformation in England and the Typographical Revolution: 'by This Printing ... The Doctrine of the Gospel Soundeth to All Nations,'" in *Print and Culture in the Renaissance*, ed. Gerald P. Tyson and Sylvia S. Wagonheim (Newark: University of Delaware Press, 1986), 208.

16 Qtd. in J. E. Neale, *Elizabeth I and Her Parliaments 1584–1601* (London: Jonathan Cape, 1957), 70.

17 Keith Thomas writes: "For us, black letter is quite difficult to read by comparison with the 'roman' type which gradually superseded it. But for contemporaries it was the other way around: they found black letter easier. For that reason

black letter was long retained for emphasis: it can be seen in James Harrington's political treatise, *Oceana* (1656), and it was long used for proclamations and Acts of Parliament. Black letter was the type for the common people"; Keith Thomas, "The Meaning of Literacy in Early Modern England," in *The Written Word: Literacy in Transition*, ed. Gerd Baumann (Oxford University Press, 1986), 99. See also Charles C. Mish, "Black Letter as a Social Discriminant in the Seventeenth Century," *PMLA* 68 (1953).

18 Myron P. Gilmore, *The World of Humanism* (New York: Harper & Bros., 1952), 189.

19 Peter Lake, *Anglicans and Puritans? Presbyterianism and English Conformist Thought from Whitgift to Hooker* (London: Unwin Hyman, 1988), Donald J. McGinn, *The Admonition Controversy* (New Brunswick: Rutgers University Press, 1949).

20 Thomas Cooper, *An Admonition to the People of England (1589)*, ed. Edward Arber (London: Archibald Constable, 1895), 105. For an account of the various states of the text see Pierce, *An Historical Introduction*, 172.

21 Patrick Collinson's *The Elizabethan Puritan Movement* devotes several sympathetic pages to the Marprelate Controversy (391–96) and acknowledges that, "here, at last, was the appeal to 'the people'" (393). However, he appears to agree with Josias Nichols in concluding that the episode "damaged the failing cause at this critical moment" (391). In a review article, Peter Lake asserts that "how far [the Marprelate tracts] represented an attempt to appeal for support for a failing Presbyterian cause to a wider audience remains an open question" (Lake, "Puritan Identities," 122). This important question is not addressed in his subsequent *Anglicans and Puritans?*, which characterizes Marprelate's style as marking "the final abandonment of the claim to inclusion within the magic circle of protestant respectability which had been at the very least implicit in previous presbyterian contributions to the debate" (84). In Lake's view, "Marprelate's rather loose talk about the shedding of blood by episcopal tyranny and the need for martyrdom in the cause of Christ seemed to betray a mind at the end of its tether." As for the popular audience, Lake suggests that the "ill-starred" Hacket–Coppinger conspiracy can be seen as "the effect of a Marprelate-style hysteria on uneducated, indeed, decidedly deranged minds" (85). Of course, Lake is not actually claiming that Marprelate caused the Hacket–Coppinger conspiracy; rather they are both symptoms of the desperation and frustration created by the imminent collapse of the presbyterian movement.

22 Perhaps this is only to say that the Marprelate episode has not been well served by present historiographical traditions. The Marprelate writings are certainly on the fringe of what count as the major developments within religious history, and they fail to offer anything especially innovative in terms of political theory.

23 See, in general, David Loades, *Politics, Censorship and the English Reformation* (New York: Pinter Publishers, 1991), Leona Rostenberg, *The Minority Press and the English Crown* (Nieuwkoop: B. De Graaf, 1971). For an excellent account of Marprelate's position within a long tradition of Protestant satire, see Benger, "The Authority of the Writer and Text."

24 Collinson, *The Elizabethan Puritan Movement,* 78.

25 In fact, Skinner draws attention to a tradition of anti-clerical polemic that precedes the Reformation; see *The Foundations of Modern Political Thought II: The Age of Reformation* (Cambridge University Press, 1978), 27. For a detailed account of Marprelate's more immediate predecessors, see Benger, "The Authority of the Writer and Text."

26 According to Lake, early religious polemic operated according to the standards of logic and proof inculcated at the universities. Of the debate between Whitgift and Cartwright, he writes: "In particular they sniped consistently at one another's logic. The whole protestant enterprise was based on the application of the authority of scripture directly to contemporary doctrinal and moral issues. Syllogisms were formed on the basis of what were taken to be unimpeachable scriptural premises and thus general rules and injunctions were teased out of the bare word of God"; Lake, *Anglicans and Puritans?,* 15.

27 Recent work has done much to recover the early modern practice of "ballading" or "libelling," and there is no doubt that such practices informed the production of the Marprelate tracts. See Alastair Bellany, "A Poem on the Archbishop's Hearse: Puritanism, Libel, and Sedition after the Hampton Court Conference," *Journal of British Studies* 34 (1995), Alastair Bellany, "'Raylinge Rymes and Vaunting Verse': Libellous Politics in Early Stuart England, 1603–1628," in *Culture and Politics in Early Stuart England,* ed. Kevin Sharpe and Peter Lake (Stanford University Press, 1993), Pauline Croft, "Libels, Popular Literacy and Public Opinion in Early Modern England," *Historical Research: The Bulletin of the Institute of Historical Research* 68 (1995), Pauline Croft, "The Reputation of Robert Cecil: Libels, Political Opinion and Popular Awareness in the Early Seventeenth Century," *Transactions of the Royal Historical Society* 6th ser. 1 (1991), Adam Fox, "Ballads, Libels and Popular Ridicule in Jacobean England," *Past and Present* 145 (1994). However, Collinson surely overstates the case when he argues that instead of seeing "the Marprelate Tracts as 'books', published products of the printing press appealing to 'readers' . . . we should rather see the Tracts as more or less *accidentally* serving to fix in imperishable print an otherwise more ephemeral and localized polemic, part oral, part written down, flourishing primarily in the word spoken and sung, secondarily in handwritten form, and only exceptionally printed, for an exceptional reason" [emphasis mine]; Collinson, "Ecclesiastical Vitriol," 163.

28 The Marprelate tracts have recently been analyzed by Evelyn B. Tribble, *Margins and Marginality: The Printed Page in Early Modern England* (Charlottesville: University Press of Virginia, 1993), 101–16. While Tribble offers a novel reading of the tracts, she wants to collocate the opposition between main text and margin to that between Marprelate and the bishops. Thus Tribble assumes that the initial interruption is made by the bishops and that the response "positions the bishops as 'malapert' intruders in [Martin's] own discourse" (110). The same identification is made in the reading of the second exchange between main text and margin which, we are told,

"marginalizes the bishops; they literally stand by the main text, which he has reclaimed as his own domain" (111).

29 Ibid., 112.

30 Pierce, in his edition of the tracts, notes that 1401 is the last page of Bridges's *Defence* (306), and Carlson suggests that 812 refers to the number of pages in Whitgift's *The Defense of the Aunswere to the Admonition*, Carlson, *Martin Marprelate, Gentleman*, 395 n. 43.

31 Raymond A. Anselment, *"Betwixt Jest and Earnest": Marprelate, Milton, Marvell, Swift and the Decorum of Religious Ridicule* (University of Toronto Press, 1979), 34.

32 Marprelate uses what Pierce identifies as west country dialect in *Hay Any Worke*: "cha bin" for "I have been" (E4^v) and "chwarnt tee / ti vorehead zaze hard as horne" for "I warrant thee, thy forehead is as hard as horn" (G1^r). See Pierce, *The Marprelate Tracts*, 257 n. 4 and 272 n. 3.

33 Margaret Spufford writes of cheap print: "The whole point of this literature is that it is useless. It is truly a pass-time, as the advertisements recommended, and truly a relaxation, and it does not serve any other ends polemic or political" (*Small Books and Pleasant Histories*, 249). The consistent neutrality of cheap print may be suspected, but it is clear that Marprelate uses the language of the pamphlets in an attempt to gain the same audience. For an illuminating account of the "interface between hot protestantism and cheap print," see Peter Lake, "Protestants, Puritans and Cheap Print," in Peter Lake and Michael Questier, *The Antichrist's Lewd Hat: Protestants, Papists and Players in Post-Reformation England* (New Haven: Yale University Press, 2002), 3–183.

34 The variety found within the tracts seems well suited to what Chartier describes as "a style of reading at ease only with brief and self-enclosed sequences set off from one another and readers content with a minimal level of coherence"; Roger Chartier, *The Order of Books*, trans. Lydia G. Cochrane (Stanford University Press, 1994), 14.

35 Thomas Wilson, *The Rule of Reason* (London, 1552), H6^r.

36 Bellany, "'Raylinge Rymes and Vaunting Verse,'" 292.

37 See Bellany, "A Poem on the Archbishop's Hearse," Collinson, "Ecclesiastical Vitriol," Croft, "The Reputation of Robert Cecil," Richard Cust, "News and Politics in Early Seventeenth-Century England," *Past and Present* 112 (1986), Fox, "Ballads, Libels and Popular Ridicule," Martin Ingram, "Ridings, Rough Music and Mocking Rhymes in Early Modern England," in *Popular Culture in Seventeenth-Century England*, ed. Barry Reay (London: Croom Helm, 1985), C. J. Sisson, *Lost Plays of Shakespeare's Age* (Cambridge University Press, 1936).

38 Collinson, *The Elizabethan Puritan Movement*, 394. For archival material that was not published in the period, see Albert Peel, ed., *The Seconde Parte of a Register. Being a Calender of Manuscripts under That Title Intended for Publication by the Puritans About 1593, and Now in Dr. William's Library, London*, 2 vols. (Cambridge University Press, 1915).

39 For an illuminating account of one such local contention, in which individuals were named from the pulpit and hostile auditors took notes at sermons in

order defame the preacher, see Patrick Collinson, "Cranbrook and the Fletchers: Popular and Unpopular Religion in the Kentish Weald," in *Godly People: Essays on English Protestantism and Puritanism* (London: Hambledon Press, 1983).

40 E. J. Ashworth points out that one of the things that distinguishes late sixteenth-century logic textbooks from their late medieval and early sixteenth-century predecessors is that "the syllogism is presented as the focal point of valid inference"; E. J. Ashworth, "Traditional Logic," in *The Cambridge History of Renaissance Philosophy*, ed. Charles B. Schmitt, Quentin Skinner, Eckhard Kessler, and Jill Kraye (Cambridge University Press, 1988), 164. In contrast, as Jardine writes, "A humanist treatment of logic is characterised by the fundamental asumption that *oratio* may be persuasive, even compelling, without its being formally valid (or without the formal validity of the argument being ascertainable)"; Lisa Jardine, "Humanist Logic," in *The Cambridge History of Renaissance Philosophy*, ed. Schmitt et al., 175.

41 The close association between incumbent and office could also be used to repress criticism. See, for instance, Coke's belief "that to libel a public person was also to libel the government of the king"; Bellany, "A Poem on the Archbishop's Hearse," 156.

42 A complete examination of this process would also entail a consideration of Marprelate's reaction to the players and the pamphlet writers.

43 In using these terms, I am following Lake: "The term 'puritan' is used to refer to a broader span of opinion, encompassing those advanced protestants who regarded themselves as 'the godly,' a minority of genuinely true believers in an otherwise lukewarm or corrupt mass ... The term 'conformist' is used to refer not to all those who can in some sense be said to have conformed to the rites and ceremonies of the English church, but only to those men who chose to make a polemical fuss about the issues of church government and ceremonial conformity and who sought to stigmatize as puritans, those less enthusiastic about such issues than themselves"; Lake, *Anglicans and Puritans?*, 7.

44 On the "people" and popularity, see Christopher Hill, "The Many-Headed Monster," in *Change and Continuity in Seventeenth-Century England* (New Haven: Yale University Press, 1991).

45 Regarding the Marprelate tracts, the Earl of Hertford was reported to have remarked, "as they shoote at Bishopps now, so will they doe at the Nobilitie also, if they be suffred" (Arber, *Introductory Sketch*, 114). This same logic is famously epitomized by King James's aphorism: "No bishop, no king," William Barlow, *The Summe and Substance of the Conference* (London: 1604), F2^{v} and M1^{v}.

46 The potential contradiction between scriptural literalism and antinomian inspiration suggests that the term *Anabaptist* – based on their widespread adherence to adult baptism accompanied by a profession of faith – was used to unite a variety of heterogeneous beliefs and practices. As A. G. Dickens points out: "So-called Anabaptists can be found to represent Arianism, Socinianism, Pelagianism, Manichaeism, Docetism, Millenarianism,

mysticism and communism. Their varied programmes embrace almost every imaginable reform from pacifism to polygamy"; A. G. Dickens, *The English Reformation* (New York: Schocken Books, 1964), 236.

47 Lake, *Anglicans and Puritans?*, 24.

48 This aspect of the charge has no necessary connection to questions of religion. We find it, for instance, in William Barlow's disquisition on the Earl of Essex's rebellion: "That is a very diuine Speech, *All popularitie and trust in men is vayne*"; William Barlow, *A Sermon Preached at Paules Crosse* (London: 1601), D5ᵛ.

49 See, esp. chapter 2, "The Common-law Mind: Custom and the Immemorial," of J. G. A. Pococock, *The Ancient Constitution and the Feudal Law: A Study of English Historical Thought in the Seventeenth Century*, A Reissue with a Retrospect (Cambridge University Press, 1987).

50 J. P. Sommerville, *Royalists and Patriots: Politics and Ideology in England, 1603–1640*, 2nd edn. (London: Longman, 1999), 197. But see also W. D. J. Cargill Thompson, "Sir Francis Knollys' Campaign against the *Jure Divino* Theory of Episcopacy," in *The Dissenting Tradition: Essays for Leland Carlson*, ed. C. Robert Cole and Michael E. Moody (Athens, OH: Ohio University Press, 1975). For the development of the *jure divino* theory, see W. D. J. Cargill Thompson, "Anthony Marten and the Elizabethan Debate on Episcopacy," in *Essays in Modern English Church History: In Memory of Norman Sykes*, ed. G. V. Bennett and J. D. Walsh (Oxford University Press, 1966), W. D. J. Cargill Thompson, "A Reconsideration of Richard Bancroft's Paul's Cross Sermon of 9 February 1588/9," *Journal of Ecclesiastical History* 20 (1969).

51 In response to Cartwright, Whitgift had denied that "there are more lawful kinds of government than three" and had asserted that "both the scripture and philosophy alloweth of the monarchy as simply the best"; John Whitgift, *The Works of John Whitgift*, ed. J. Ayre (Cambridge: Parker Society, 1851–53), 197. See also Lake, *Anglicans and Puritans?*, 55–56. However, as Collinson observes, John Aylmer, another of Marprelate's favorite targets, in *An Harborowe for Faithfull and Trewe Subiectes* (London, 1589), H3ʳ, defined the "regiment of England" as "mixte"; Patrick Collinson, *De Republica Anglorum, or, History with the Politics Put Back* (Cambridge University Press, 1989), 25.

52 Tribble, considering this episode, argues that: "Martin's attempt to contain the violence of his words, to establish interpretive authority over his meaning . . . fails in the face of a consistent movement on the part of the authorities to define his language as dangerous" (*Margins and Marginality*, 116).

53 This would hardly be surprising if we accept Carlson's attribution of this pamphlet of 1592 to Job Throkmorton (*Martin Marprelate, Gentleman*, 117).

54 Francis Bacon, *Francis Bacon: A Critical Edition of the Major Works*, ed. Brian Vickers (Oxford University Press, 1996), 3.

55 See Joseph Black, "The Rhetoric of Reaction: the Martin Marprelate Tracts (1588–89), Anti-Martinism, and the Uses of Print in Early Modern England," *Sixteenth Century Journal* 28 (1997): n. 5, and Collinson, *The Elizabethan Puritan Movement*, 393.

56 The entire letter is transcribed in Andrew Forret Scott Pearson, *Thomas Cartwright and Elizabethan Puritanism, 1535–1603* (Cambridge University Press, 1925), 451–52.

57 Josias Nichols, *The Plea of the Innocent* ([Middelburg], 1602), D5^r. Nichols is an important source, but it is worth considering Peter Clark's conclusion that "Nicholls never became a full-blooded Presbyterian," Peter Clark, "Josias Nicholls and Religious Radicalism, 1553–1639," *Journal of Ecclesiastical History* 28 (1977): 141.

58 For instance, Cartwright, in response to Sutcliffe's accusation that he sympathized with Marprelate, maintained that "the first time that euer I heard of *Martin Marprelate*, I testified my great misliking & grief, for so naughtie, and so disorderly a course as that was." And yet Sutcliffe's demand to know why Cartwright has not publicly repudiated Martin and Penry is met with evasion: "I aske againe what office of charge I haue to publish condemnation vpon euery vnlawfull and vnciuill writing that cometh abroad? And yet I haue witnesses, that euen publikely when I was allowed to preach, I condemned all dealing in that kinde"; Thomas Cartwright, *A Brief Apologie of Thomas Cartwright against All Such Slaunderous Accusations as It Pleaseth Mr Sutcliffe in Seuerall Pamphlettes Most Iniuriously to Loade Him With* (Middelburg: 1596), C2^v.

59 Anselment, *"Betwixt Jest and Earnest"*, 36.

60 *A Revelation of the Apocalyps* (Amsterdam, 1611), S1^r.

61 The reasons for this failure may include the shift from iconoclasm to iconophobia described by Patrick Collinson, *From Iconoclasm to Iconophobia: The Cultural Impact of the Second English Reformation* (University of Reading, 1986). The argument that the 1580s saw a crucial shift in puritan attitudes toward all forms of art could be used to claim that Marprelate with his comfortable use of literary forms is a representative of a residual puritan culture preaching to a new breed of iconophobes. Of course, one might as easily make the claim that Marprelate is evidence that the shift to "iconophobia" was never as complete as Collinson suggests.

62 The best introduction to the historiographical debates surrounding the term *puritanism* is Peter Lake, "Defining Puritanism – Again?," in *Puritanism: Transatlantic Perspectives on a Seventeenth-Century Anglo-American Faith*, ed. Francis J. Bremer (Boston: Massachusetts Historical Society, 1993). Lake synthesizes the view that would see puritanism as defined by a specific puritan piety and style with the view that emphasizes the polemical creation of the category (an argument that, in its extreme form, denies the existence of anything specifically "puritan"). As Lake explains, it is a mistake "in analyzing both the linguistic usages and the conceptual categories of the godly (and the polemical images devised by their enemies to denounce them) to posit too sharp a division between the artifice and artificiality of the merely literary and the supposed reality of the social" (18). For a fascinating genealogy of the concept *Puritanism*, see Glyn J. R. Parry, "The Creation and Recreation of Puritanism," *Parergon* n.s. 14 (1996). Parry argues that the Restoration attack on "Puritanism" as "a fanatic delusion of the lower

orders" reponsible for the civil wars has continued to shape the historiographical tradition.

63 Peter Lake, *Moderate Puritans and the Elizabethan Church* (Cambridge University Press, 1982), 3.

64 Gabriel Harvey, *Foure Letters, and Certaine Sonnets* (London: 1592), E3^r.

65 R. W., *Martine Mar-Sixtus* (London: 1591), A4^v.

66 To Marprelate's legacy one must also add the subsequent Marpriest tracts by Richard Overton. See Christopher Hill, "Radical Prose in Seventeenth-Century England: from Marprelate to the Levellers," *Essays in Criticism* 32 (1982), Nigel Smith, "Richard Overton's Marpriest Tracts: Towards a History of Leveller Style," *Prose Studies* 9 (1986). The most extensive treatment of Marprelate's afterlife is provided by Joseph Black's dissertation, "Pamphlet Wars"; for an account of the traces of Martinism in Shakespeare's *1 Henry IV*, see Kristen Poole, "Saints Alive! Falstaff, Martin Marprelate, and the Staging of Puritanism," *Shakespeare Quarterly* 46 (1995).

3 "WHOLE HAMLETS": Q1, Q2, AND THE WORK OF DISTINCTION

1 The argument that follows shares a number of claims with the recent work of Leah S. Marcus, *Unediting the Renaissance: Shakespeare, Marlowe, Milton* (New York: Routledge, 1996). However, despite our agreement on several aspects of Q1 and Q2, our arguments are fundamentally different. In her chapter, "Bad Taste and Bad Hamlet," Marcus seeks "to recast the discussion about Q1 *Hamlet* entirely by considering the text and its 'betters' in terms of the differing expectations created by orality and writing as competing forms of communication within the Renaissance playhouse" (137). Unlike Marcus's focus on the theatre and its developing aesthetic, my argument is about the market for printed books. Nonetheless, we agree that Q2 promoted a more literate understanding of the theatrical text. For recent work on the literary status of early printed play texts, see Douglas Brooks, *From Playhouse to Printing House: Drama and Authorship in Early Modern England* (Cambridge University Press, 2000), Lukas Erne, *Shakespeare as Literary Dramatist* (Cambridge University Press, 2003), and Zachary Lesser, "Walter Burre's *The Knight of the Burning Pestle*," *English Literary Renaissance* 29 (1999).

2 The problem presented by Q1, as Horace Howard Furness sees it, is "whether, in the Quarto of 1603, we have the first draught of Shakespeare's tragedy, which the author afterwards remodelled and elaborated until it appears as we now have it . . . or is the First Quarto merely a maimed and distorted version 'of the true and perfect coppie'?" *A New Variorum Edition of Shakespeare: Hamlet*, ed. Horace Howard Furness (New York: Dover, 1963), II, 14. However, the dichotomy between growth and decline, perfection and corruption, has since been complicated by theories focusing on the shaping influence of the playhouse. These take two principal forms: arguments claiming Q1 as a theatrical abridgement and those identifying the text as an actor's memorial reconstruction. Indeed, these two possibilities are not incompatible; for a recent attempt to

combine them, see Kathleen Irace, "Origins and Agents of QI *Hamlet*," in *The Hamlet First Published (QI, 1603)*, ed. Thomas Clayton (Newark: University of Delaware Press, 1992).

3 See Marcus, *Unediting the Renaissance*, 132–76, Annabel Patterson, *Shakespeare and the Popular Voice* (Oxford: Basil Blackwell, 1989), Robert Weimann, *Shakespeare and the Popular Tradition in the Theater* (Baltimore: Johns Hopkins University Press, 1978).

4 Ronald B. Bond, ed., *Certain Sermons or Homilies (1547) and a Homily against Disobedience and Wilful Rebellion (1570)* (University of Toronto Press, 1987), 190.

5 See Gerald D. Johnson, "Nicholas Ling, Publisher 1580–1607," *Studies in Bibliography* 37 (1985).

6 William Shakespeare, *Hamlet*, ed. Harold Jenkins, The Arden Shakespeare (London: Methuen, 1982), 15.

7 Most recently Lukas Erne has proposed a variation on this story: "Ling and Trundle seem to have licensed but not entered their manuscript and had it printed without anyone realizing that Roberts had once entered a different version. Having found out about Ling and Trundle's unintentional breach, Roberts could have caused them trouble but preferred to negotiate an advantageous deal with his neighbours in Fleet Street, selling to Ling and Trundle his longer and better manuscript and having them pay him to print it"; Erne, *Shakespeare as Literary Dramatist*, 81. In this version, the technical right resides with Roberts who presses his advantage in order to sell the manuscript and secure a print job. This Roberts is a shrewd operator actively pursuing his own interests rather than the upstanding citizen outmaneuvered by Ling found in Jenkins's account.

8 The classic example of an attempt to supply this missing moment is Alfred W. Pollard, *Shakespeare Folios and Quartos: A Study in the Bibliography of Shakespeare's Plays, 1594–1685* (London: Methuen, 1909). Pollard popularized the notion that Roberts had cooperated with the acting company to register a "blocking" entry that would prevent unauthorized publication (73). For a scathing critique of this hypothesis, see Peter W. M. Blayney, "The Publication of Playbooks," in *A New History of Early English Drama*, ed. John D. Cox and David Scott Kastan (New York: Columbia University Press, 1997).

9 Harold Love, *The Culture and Commerce of Texts: Scribal Publication in Seventeenth-Century England* (Amherst: University of Massachusetts Press, 1998), 36. Love goes on to make a distinction between publication in the strong and weak sense. The "strong" sense designates "the provision of large numbers of copies"; the "weak" sense construes "publication as an activity carried out by a special kind of person called a publisher" (37–38). The threat of tautology that haunts the "weak" sense of the word is not entirely dissipated by Love's taxonomy of three modes of publication (author, entrepreneur, and user).

10 Edward Arber, ed., *A Transcript of the Registers of the Company of Stationers*, 5 vols. (London: 1875–79), III, 212.

11 For an incisive account of the taxonomy of the First Folio, see Thomas L. Berger, "'Opening Titles Miscreate': Some Observations on the Titling of Shakespeare's 'Works,'" in *The Margins of the Text*, ed. D. C. Greetham (Ann Arbor: University of Michigan Press, 1997).

12 Paul Werstine, "Narratives about Printed Shakespeare Texts: 'Foul Papers' and 'Bad' Quartos," *Shakespeare Quarterly* 41 (1990).

13 Gerald D. Johnson, "John Trundle and the Book Trade 1603–1626," *Studies in Bibliography* 39 (1986): 180.

14 Qtd. in Bernard Capp, *The World of John Taylor the Water-Poet, 1578–1653* (Oxford University Press, 1994), 53.

15 Johnson, "John Trundle and the Book Trade 1603–1626," 177.

16 Pierre Bourdieu, *Distinction: A Social Critique of the Judgement of Taste*, trans. Richard Nice (Cambridge, MA: Harvard University Press, 1984), 231.

17 Peter Burke describes a gradual process of "withdrawal" on the part of the upper classes, *Popular Culture in Early Modern Europe* (New York University Press, 1978). On the dangers of the category see, Pierre Bourdieu, "Did You Say 'Popular'?," in *Language and Symbolic Power*, ed. John B. Thompson (Cambridge, MA: Harvard University Press, 1991). Chartier declares "This book has been constructed, then, primarily in opposition to this now classic use of the notion of popular culture," *The Cultural Uses of Print in Early Modern France*, trans. Lydia G. Cochrane (Princeton University Press, 1987), 3. Chartier's critique of the opposition between *populaire* and *savant* and the reductions that attend it is compelling, and my own examination of early modern English culture also finds "fluid circulation, practices shared by various groups, and blurred distinctions." However, it does not follow that the term *popular* is devoid of content. Robert Scribner sensibly suggests that "we must study the processes of cultural formation, differentiation and subordination," but professes indifference as to what such a project is called: "history of popular culture, people's history, total history, cultural history, history of mentalities – the enterprise is the same"; Robert Scribner, "Is a History of Popular Culture Possible?," *History of European Ideas* 10 (1989): 184, 187. For an account of "important divisions within 'popular' culture that historians, like educated contemporaries, have sometimes overlooked," see Capp, *The World of John Taylor*.

18 Johnson, "Nicholas Ling," 203.

19 Fredson Bowers, *On Editing Shakespeare* (Charlottesville: University Press of Virginia, 1966), 109.

20 This phrase is used to describe "auspices" in Alfred Harbage, rev. S. Schoenbaum, and Sylvia Stoler Wagonheim, *Annals of English Drama: 975–1700* (New York: Routledge, 1989).

21 Blayney, "The Publication of Playbooks," 389.

22 My point is simply that an attention to the general field of print locates printed plays not in relationship to their origin but in relationship to adjacent printed matter such as dialogues, ballads, poetry, and prose romance.

23 The classic account is J. W. Saunders, "The Stigma of Print: a Note on the Social Bases of Tudor Poetry," *Essays in Criticism* 1 (1951). See also chapter 4, p. 146.

24 Francis Beaumont, *The Knight of the Burning Pestle*, ed. Michael Hattaway (New York: W. W. Norton, 1969), 3.

25 For an excellent account of Burre's attempt to fashion an audience of literary wits for printed drama, see Lesser, "Walter Burre's *The Knight of the Burning Pestle*."

26 Roslyn L. Knutson attempts to recast the old narrative of the "War of the Theatres," suggesting that it is informed by a capitalist notion of competition that transforms "popularity" into "rivalry"; Roslyn L. Knutson, "Falconer to the Little Eyases: a New Date and Commercial Agenda for the 'Little Eyases' Passage in *Hamlet*," *Shakespeare Quarterly* 46 (1995).

27 Janice Lull, "Forgetting *Hamlet*: the First Quarto and the Folio," in *The Hamlet First Published (Q1, 1603)*, ed. Thomas Clayton (Newark: University of Delaware Press, 1992), 141. The case for memorial reconstruction was first made by G. I. Duthie, *The "Bad" Quarto of Hamlet* (Cambridge University Press, 1941). The most recent and exacting study concludes that it is possible that Q1 is a memorial reconstruction, "but if so, a very good one," Laurie E. Maguire, *Shakespearean Suspect Texts: The 'Bad' Quartos and Their Contexts* (Cambridge University Press, 1996), 255. See also, William Shakespeare, *The First Quarto of Hamlet*, The New Cambridge Shakespeare: The Early Quartos, ed. Kathleen O. Irace (Cambridge University Press, 1998).

28 Giorgio Melchiori, "*Hamlet*: the Acting Version and the Wiser Sort," in *The Hamlet First Published (Q1, 1603)*, ed. Thomas Clayton (Newark: University of Delaware Press, 1992), 208. An earlier and similar argument can be found in W. W. Greg's assertion that "In composition Shakespeare must have had in mind readers as well as spectators; he must have written for the closet as well as for the stage"; W. W. Greg, "Hamlet's Hallucination," *Modern Language Review* 12 (1917): 420.

29 Erne, *Shakespeare as Literary Dramatist*.

30 Gabriel Harvey, *Gabriel Harvey's Marginalia*, ed. G. C. Moore Smith (Stratford-upon-Avon: Shakespeare's Head Press, 1913), 232.

31 Melchiori, "*Hamlet*: the Acting Version and the Wiser Sort," 208.

32 Stephen Orgel, "Acting Scripts, Performing Texts," in *Crisis in Editing: Texts of the English Renaissance*, ed. Randall M. McLeod (New York: AMS Press, 1994).

33 Barbara Mowat, "The Form of *Hamlet*'s Fortunes," *Renaissance Drama* 19 (1988).

34 J. Dover Wilson, *The Manuscript of Shakespeare's Hamlet and the Problems of Its Transmission: An Essay in Critical Bibliography*, 2 vols. (Cambridge University Press, 1934). For evidence that the editorial tradition established by Wilson no longer commands loyalty, see *Hamlet*, ed. G. R. Hibbard and *William Shakespeare: The Complete Works*, ed. Stanley Wells and Gary Taylor, both of which present a *Hamlet* once again based on F. Further evidence of dissension will soon be provided by the Arden3 *Hamlet*, edited by Ann Thompson and Neil Taylor, which will present all three early versions in two volumes.

35 William Shakespeare, *Hamlet, Prince of Denmark*, ed. Philip Edwards, The New Cambridge Shakespeare (Cambridge University Press, 1985), 30.

36 Wilson, *The Manuscript of Shakespeare's Hamlet*, I, 12.

37 The most famous example is probably the recent Oxford edition of the complete works which gives its readers *The History of King Lear* and *The Tragedy of King Lear*. Here generic terms become evidence of an essential difference between the two texts. Another example is provided by Leah S. Marcus, who finds that "the two quartos of *Faustus* offer distinctive patterns of signification that can be correlated with specific phases of English religious and political history"; Leah S. Marcus, "Textual Indeterminacy and Ideological Difference: the Case of *Doctor Faustus*," *Renaissance Drama* n.s. 20 (1989): 22. For a skeptical response to Marcus, see Christopher Marlowe, *Doctor Faustus: A- and B-Texts (1604, 1616)*, ed. David Bevington and Eric Rasmussen (Manchester University Press, 1993), 92. Paul Werstine both displays and questions this tendency: "While, like other revisionists, I have been intent upon asserting continuities within each of the early printed texts and discontinuities between them, there are no grounds for privileging the alleged integrity of each of Q2 and F to the host of aesthetic forms that critics have produced from their reading of the combined Q2 / F text"; Paul Werstine, "The Textual Mystery of *Hamlet*," *Shakespeare Quarterly* 39, no. 1 (1988): 23. Werstine goes on to point out that the "divergent aesthetic patterns" that he has isolated are, in fact, "radically unstable, and threaten . . . to collapse into the combination with each other so familiar from the editorial tradition" (24). However, Werstine's argument takes a curious turn when he claims that "The only imaginable grounds for privileging Q2 and F with unassailable integrity would be evidence that each is independently linked to Shakespeare." This would seem to overlook the possibility of a sociological account of the two texts; however, even such an account would stop short of granting "unassailable integrity" – a hyperbolic phrase – to a socially produced text. See also Luke Wilson, whose examination of the relationship between Q2 and F concludes that "There is no single *Hamlet*, but neither are there two entirely independent *Hamlet*s"; Luke Wilson, "*Hamlet*: Equity, Intention, Performance," *Studies in the Literary Imagination* 24 (1991): 103.

38 However, for a trenchant defense of editorial eclecticism (or "judicious consolidation") as the only way to recover authorial intentions, see Ann R. Meyer, "Shakespeare's Art and the Texts of *King Lear*," *Studies in Bibliography* 47 (1994).

39 Brooks, *From Playhouse to Printing House*, David Scott Kastan, *Shakespeare and the Book* (Cambridge University Press, 2001), Julie Stone Peters, *Theatre of the Book, 1480–1880: Print, Text, and Performance in Europe* (Oxford University Press, 2000). In addition, see the forthcoming volume by Zachary Lesser.

40 Steven Urkowitz, "'Well-Sayd Olde Mole': Burying Three *Hamlet*s in Modern Editions," in *Shakespeare Study Today*, ed. Georgianna Ziegler (New York: AMS Press, 1986), 69.

41 A. C. Bradley, *Shakespearean Tragedy* (London: Macmillan, 1904), 147.

42 For an attempt to see the play as compatible with Calvinist doctrine see Charles K. Cannon, "'As in a Theater': *Hamlet* in the Light of Calvin's Doctrine of Predestination," *Studies in English Literature 1500–1900* 11 (1971). For the Lutheran alternative, Raymond B. Waddington, "Lutheran Hamlet," *English Language Notes* 27 (1989).

43 There is a long tradition of *Hamlet* criticism that sees the play as political commentary engaged with the problem of succession; for an early version, see Lillian Winstanley, *Hamlet and the Scottish Succession: Being an Examination of the Play of Hamlet to the Scottish Succession and the Essex Conspiracy* (Cambridge University Press, 1921). The *Hamlet*–James I connection continues to be popular; see Alvin Kernan, *Shakespeare, the King's Playwright: Theater in the Stuart Court, 1603–1613* (New Haven: Yale University Press, 1995), 24–49, Eric Mallin, *Inscribing the Time: Shakespeare and the End of Elizabethan England* (Berkeley: University of California Press, 1995), 106–66. For an illuminating account that takes up succession, gender politics, and editorial practice, see Katherine Eggert, *Showing Like a Queen: Female Authority and Literary Experiment in Spenser, Shakespeare, and Milton* (Philadelphia: University of Pennsylvania Press, 2000), 100–30.

44 William Barlow, *The Summe and Substance of the Conference* (London: 1604).

45 King James I, *By the King* (London: 1603) STC 8336; King James I, *By the King* (London: 1603) STC 8343.

46 See Patrick Collinson, "The Jacobean Religious Settlement: the Hampton Court Conference," in *Before the Civil War*, ed. Howard Tomlinson (London: Macmillan, 1983), M. H. Curtis, "The Hampton Court Conference and Its Aftermath," *History* 46 (1961), Kenneth Fincham and Peter Lake, "The Ecclesiastical Policy of King James I," *Journal of British Studies* 24 (1985), F. Shriver, "Hampton Court Revisited: James I and the Puritans," *Journal of Ecclesiastical History* 33 (1982).

47 For an account of the king's treatment of the nonconforming clergy at the beginning of his reign, see B. W. Quintrell, "The Royal Hunt and the Puritans, 1604–1605," *Journal of Ecclesiastical History* 31 (1980).

48 Barlow, *The Summe and Substance of the Conference*, A2^v.

49 Qtd. in H. C. Porter, *Reformation and Reaction in Tudor Cambridge* (Cambridge University Press, 1958), 373.

50 For an excellent introduction to philosophical skepticism, see Burnyeat, who labels the interpretation of Pyrrhonism that insulates the "non-theoretical judgements of everyday life" from skepticism, "in honour of Montaigne," the "country gentleman's interpretation"; M. F. Burnyeat, "The Sceptic in His Place and Time," in *Philosophy in History*, ed. J. B. Schneewind, Quentin Skinner, and Richard Rorty (Cambridge University Press, 1985), 231.

51 Margreta De Grazia, "Soliloquies and Wages in the Age of Emergent Consciousness," *Textual Practice* 9 (1995). For an earlier consideration of this moment see Hardin Craig, "Hamlet's Book," *Huntington Library Bulletin* 6 (1934).

52 Lull, "Forgetting *Hamlet*: the First Quarto and the Folio," 144.

53 The standard account is Richard H. Popkin, *The History of Scepticism: From Erasmus to Descartes* (New York: Harper & Row, 1968). For an account that stresses the importance of Pyrrhonism in the development of late sixteenth- and early seventeenth-century political thought in Europe, see Richard Tuck, *Philosophy and Government 1572–1651* (Cambridge University Press, 1993).

54 Catherine Belsey, "The Case of Hamlet's Conscience," *Studies in Philology* 76 (1979): 132.

55 Thomas Hobbes, *Leviathan*, ed. C. B. MacPherson (New York: Penguin Books, 1968), 366, Richard Hooker, *The Folger Library Edition of the Works of Richard Hooker*, ed. W. Speed Hill, 7 vols. (Cambridge, MA: Harvard University Press, 1977–98), III, 396. In an earlier discussion, Hobbes argues that originally *conscience* referred to an intersubjective event, a knowing with, but that by a metaphorical extension it came to be used for "secret facts" and "secret thoughts." Finally, people "vehemently in love with their new opinions, (though never so absurd,) and obstinately bent to maintain them, gave those their opinions also that reverenced name of Conscience" (132).

56 Robert Some, *Three Questions, Godly, Plainly, and Briefly Handled* (Cambridge: 1596), 43–44.

57 Michael MacDonald, "Ophelia's Maimed Rites," *Shakespeare Quarterly* 37 (1986): 316. MacDonald provides a valuable corrective to Roland Mushat Frye, *The Renaissance Hamlet: Issues and Responses in 1600* (Princeton University Press, 1984), who argues that a contemporary audience would have "endorsed Laertes's view both emotionally and ethically" (298).

58 Michael MacDonald and Terence R. Murphy, *Sleepless Souls: Suicide in Early Modern England* (Oxford University Press, 1990), 60.

59 Robert Parsons, *Three Conversions* (?1603), 304.

60 Popular pelagianism, the persistent belief that good behaviour would win salvation, was a constant source of frustration for Protestant ministers seeking to bring the gospel to the people. For a helpful account of George Gifford's evangelical strategies, see Dewey D. Wallace, "George Gifford, Puritan Propaganda and Popular Religion in Elizabethan England," *Sixteenth Century Journal* 9 (1978).

61 This question-begging parodies an argument made in the notorious case of Sir James Hale and recorded by Plowden. Yet the concern is not, finally, the quiddities and quillities of the law; the story of Hale, a Protestant who drowned himself, registered in both Foxe's *Actes* and Holinshed's *Chronicle*, was a provocation to religious polemic. See MacDonald and Murphy, *Sleepless Souls*, 61–63.

62 For an account, see Johann P. Sommerville, "The 'New Art of Lying': Equivocation, Mental Reservation, and Casuistry," in *Conscience and Casuistry in Early Modern Europe*, ed. Edmund Leites (Cambridge University Press, 1988).

63 The bibliography on the place of the dead and death in early modern culture is enormous and growing: an excellent place to start is Peter Marshall, *Beliefs and the Dead in Reformation England* (Oxford University Press, 2002). Marshall stresses the role played by "beliefs about the dead in promoting among

contemporaries a heightened awareness of, and reflectiveness about, the historical consequences of religious change" (315). The play's graveyard scene is a provocation to just such an awareness and reflectiveness.

64　James Pilkington, *A Godlie Exposition Upon Certeine Chapters of Nehemiah* (Cambridge: 1585), B7^v.

65　The claim that Q2 is, in some sense, the more anti-clerical text is supported by Ophelia's shifting personification of hypocrisy: the "cunning Sophister" (C2^r) becomes "some vngracious pastors" (C3^v).

66　Norman T. Burns, *Christian Mortalism from Tyndale to Milton* (Cambridge, MA: Harvard University Press, 1972).

67　John E. Booty, ed., *The Book of Common Prayer, 1559: The Elizabethan Prayer Book* (Charlottesville: Published for the Folger Shakespeare Library by the University Press of Virginia, 1976), 311.

68　Thomas Browne, *Religio Medici* (London: 1643), G8^r–G8^v.

69　Ernst Bloch, *The Principle of Hope*, trans. Neville Plaice, Stephen Plaice, and Paul Knight, 3 vols. (Oxford: Basil Blackwell, 1986), III, 1028.

70　Q1 does not contain Hamlet's first-person description of his sea voyage with its emphasis on the guidance of providence; instead Horatio, after receiving a letter, relates these events to the Queen (H2^v).

71　Q2's "special providence" invokes divine intervention but without the doctrinal spin. Q1's formulation points toward the close connection made between predestination and providence in Calvinist theology and practice. See Alexandra Walsham, *Providence in Early Modern England* (Oxford University Press, 1999), esp. 15–20. Walsham stresses the elasticity of providential thinking as a common Christian inheritance that shaped the thinking of an enormous variety of post-Reformation believers. What might be called unproblematic providentialism does not sit very well with either Q1 or Q2 *Hamlet*. Q1 with its hint of sectarian thinking points toward confessional divisions; Q2, in contrast, offers a much fuller account of a less determinate providence, a providence easily assimilated to a variety of doctrinal positions, but this very expansiveness and indeterminacy makes providence a problem in need of interpretation.

72　Hugh Latimer, *Sermons*, ed. G. E. Corrie (Cambridge: Parker Society, 1845), 44.

73　It is worth noting that the ghost in Q1 makes no reference to the ritual preparation for death mentioned by the ghost in Q2: "Cut off euen in the blossomes of my sinne, / Vnhvzled, disappointed, vnanueld" (D3^r). For an illuminating discussion of the significance of these terms, see Stephen Greenblatt, *Hamlet in Purgatory* (Princeton University Press, 2001).

74　Such a reading is in disagreement with Janice Lull's conclusion that "By selectively forgetting parts of *Hamlet* that allude to Protestant ideology, Q1 reinterprets the play, making it affirm the very warrior values that the F version calls into question," "Forgetting *Hamlet*."

75　Stephen Greenblatt's recent survey of purgatorial allusions is illuminating, but I am not convinced by his claim that the play evinces a general nostalgia for the lost world of Catholic ritualism. Greenblatt, operating under the influence of

Haigh and Duffy, gives an excellent account of the pull of memory and the claims of the dead, but is less compelling on the problem of revenge and violence more generally. That said, Greenblatt's reading helps reveal the marked contrast between Q1 and Q2 in terms of the religious language used in the texts.

76 See Peter Iver Kaufman, *Prayer, Despair, and Drama: Elizabethan Introspection* (Chicago: University of Illinois Press, 1996), 103–43.

77 For a brief survey, see Alan Sinfield, "Hamlet's Special Providence," *Shakespeare Survey* 33 (1980): 89.

78 Robert G. Hunter, *Shakespeare and the Mystery of God's Judgments* (Athens: University of Georgia Press, 1976), 105.

79 Sinfield, "Hamlet's Special Providence," 95–96.

80 This should not be taken anachronistically as an expression of agnosticism; as Roland Mushat Frye points out, "The reference to death as silence is common in Scripture," *Shakespeare and Christian Doctrine* (Princeton University Press, 1963), 53.

81 For a treatment of the several references to doomsday in *Hamlet*, see David Kuala, "*Hamlet* and the Image of Both Churches," *Studies in English Literature 1500–1900* 24 (1984).

82 Anthony Scoloker?, *Daiphantvs, or the Passions of Loue* (London: 1604).

83 Philip Sidney, *Sir Philip Sidney*, ed. Katherine Duncan-Jones (Oxford University Press, 1989), 244.

84 Henslowe's diary records a performance of "hamlet" at Newington Butts on June 9, 1594, Philip Henslowe, *Henslowe's Diary*, ed. R. A. Foakes and R. T. Rickert (Cambridge University Press, 1961), 21. Presumably, this is the *Hamlet* referred to by both Thomas Nashe in his preface to Robert Greene's *Menaphon* (1589) and Thomas Lodge in *Wit's Miserie, and the Worlds Madnesse* (1596). For an energetic if not entirely convincing argument claiming that this early *Hamlet* was penned by Shakespeare, see Eric Sams, *The Real Shakespeare: Retrieving the Early Years, 1564–1594* (New Haven: Yale University Press, 1995).

4 PRINTING DONNE: POETRY AND POLEMIC IN THE EARLY SEVENTEENTH CENTURY

1 See life of Lucius Cary, Viscount Falkland, John Aubrey, *Aubrey's Brief Lives*, ed. Oliver Lawson Dick (Ann Arbor: University of Michigan Press, 1957), 56.

2 For an incisive and recent account that acknowledges Donne's interest in polemic, see Daniel W. Doerksen, "Polemicist or Pastor?: Donne and Moderate Calvinist Conformity," in *John Donne and the Protestant Reformation* (Detroit: Wayne State University Press, 2003).

3 For studies that emphasize the cultural consequences of James's published writings, see Leah S. Marcus, *Puzzling Shakespeare: Local Reading and Its Discontents* (Berkeley: University of California Press, 1988) and Jonathan Goldberg, *James I and the Politics of Literature: Jonson, Shakespeare, Donne, and Their Contemporaries* (Baltimore: Johns Hopkins University Press, 1983).

For a response to Marcus and Goldberg that places less emphasis on the cultural power of the monarch, see Curtis Perry, *The Making of Jacobean Culture: James I and the Renegotiation of Elizabethan Literary Practice* (Cambridge University Press, 1997). On the specifically religious poetry spurred by the arrival of James I, see James Doelman, *King James I and the Religious Culture of England* (Woodbridge: D. S. Brewer, 2000).

4 See chapter 6, which discusses the king's founding of Chelsea College, an institution dedicated to the pursuit of controversial divinity.

5 See Arthur F. Marotti, *Manuscript, Print, and the English Renaissance Lyric* (Ithaca: Cornell University Press, 1995), Arthur F. Marotti, *John Donne, Coterie Poet* (Madison: University of Wisconsin Press, 1986), Ted-Larry Pebworth, "John Donne, Coterie Poetry, and the Text as Performance," *Studies in English Literature* 29 (1989). For an attempt to correct this view, see Ernest W. Sullivan II, *The Influence of John Donne: His Uncollected Seventeenth-Century Printed Verse* (Columbia: University of Missouri Press, 1993).

6 J. W. Saunders, "The Stigma of Print: a Note on the Social Bases of Tudor Poetry," *Essays in Criticism* 1 (1951). For a vigorous, if not entirely persuasive, dissent, see Steven W. May, "Tudor Aristocrats and the Mythical 'Stigma of Print,'" *Renaissance Papers* (1980). For a positive, though balanced, assessment of Saunders, see Daniel Traister, "Reluctant Virgins: the Stigma of Print Revisited," *Colby Quarterly* 26 (1990).

7 John Donne, *Letters to Severall Persons of Honour* (London: 1651).

8 For a consideration of the conceptual space imagined in this letter, see Richard B. Wollman, "The 'Press and the Fire': Print and Manuscript Culture in Donne's Circle," *Studies in English Literature* 33 (1993).

9 Annabel Patterson, "All Donne," in *Soliciting Interpretation: Literary Theory and Seventeenth-Century English Poetry*, ed. Elizabeth D. Harvey and Katherine Eisaman Maus (University of Chicago Press, 1990). For an illuminating account that places more emphasis on theology than psychology, see Brian Cummings, *The Literary Culture of the Reformation: Grammar and Grace* (Oxford University Press, 2002), 365–417. "Far from sudden epiphany, Donne's lycanthropy," writes Cummings, "is a work of controversy . . . Donne's conversion was controversial through and through" (377–78).

10 Annabel Patterson, *Reading between the Lines* (Routledge: New York, 1993). A similar point is made by Phebe Jensen, "'The Obedience Due to Princes': Absolutism in *Pseudo-Martyr*," *Renaissance and Reformation* 19 (1995).

11 Evelyn M. Simpson, *A Study of the Prose Works of John Donne* (Oxford: Clarendon Press, 1924), 166.

12 Isaak Walton's "The life and death of Dr. Donne" first appeared in John Donne, *LXXX Sermons* (London: 1640).

13 An extreme example is provided by Dennis Flynn, who argues that Donne intended "to satirize the religious controversy by parodying the practices of partisan writers such as Coke"; Dennis Flynn, "Irony in Donne's *Biathanatos and Pseudo-Martyr*," *Recusant History* 12 (1973): 66. It is also possible to read *Pseudo-Martyr* as a covert attack on the pretensions of royal absolutism: "The

attack on overblown claims to authority of the Catholic Church that takes place throughout the work, then, can be read as an exercise in political criticism applicable as well to the ideology of royal absolutism," Marotti, *John Donne, Coterie Poet,* 191.

14 An excellent introduction to this debate is provided in a series of articles by Thomas Clancy, S. J., "English Catholics and the Papal Deposing Power, 1570–1640, Parts I and II," *Recusant History* 6 (1961–62), "English Catholics and the Papal Deposing Power, 1570–1640, Part III," *Recusant History* 7 (1963–64).

15 Cummings, *The Literary Culture of the Reformation,* 379.

16 Donne, *Letters to Severall Persons of Honour.*

17 John Donne, *Ignatius His Conclave,* ed. T. S. Healy, S. J. (Oxford: Clarendon Press, 1969).

18 M. C. Questier, "Loyalty, Religion and State Power in Early Modern England: English Romanism and the Jacobean Oath of Allegiance," *The Historical Journal* 40, no. 2 (1997): 311. Questier convincingly argues that the required oath was not the innocently moderate measure described by many historians. Though the oath did not require a repudiation of the pope's power of excommunication, it did "turn a denial of the deposing power into what could plausibly be regarded as a rejection of the papal primacy" (320).

19 For Gallicanism and Ultramontanism, see J. H. M. Salmon, "Catholic Resistance Theory, Ultramontanism, and the Royalist Response, 1580–1620," in *Cambridge History of Political Thought, 1450–1700,* ed. J. H. Burns and Mark Goldie (Cambridge University Press, 1991), J. H. M. Salmon, "Gallicanism and Anglicanism in the Age of the Counter-Reformation," in *Renaissance and Revolt: Essays in the Intellectual and Social History of Early Modern France,* ed. J. H. M. Salmon (Cambridge University Press, 1987).

20 John Boys, *An Exposition of the Dominicall Epistles and Gospels Used in Our English Liturgie* (London: 1610) STC 3459.3, 13ᵛ.

21 John Donne, *Pseudo-Martyr,* ed. Anthony Raspa (University of Toronto Press, 1993). Throughout I quote from this edition.

22 A king who enthusiastically engaged in polemic and debate certainly dignified these activities. For an account of the consequences, see Lori Anne Ferrell, *Government by Polemic: James I, the King's Preachers, and the Rhetorics of Conformity, 1603–1625* (Stanford University Press, 1998).

23 Sydney Anglo, *Images of Tudor Kingship* (London: Seaby, 1992), 351.

24 Chapter 3 is dedicated to the proposition that "The Roman Religion doth by many erroneous doctrines misencourage and excite men to this vicious affectation of danger" (37). In it Donne considers three chief doctrinal errors: the diminishment of secular magistracy, the doctrine of merits, and purgatory.

25 Bald cites two letters to Goodyer requesting the return of "certain heads which I purposed to enlarge"; R. C. Bald, *John Donne, a Life* (Oxford University Press, 1970), 218–19.

26 Donne's awareness of the ideological work performed by an index might serve as a commentary on the changes made to the index of *Actes and Monuments* between the 1576 and 1583 editions, see above chapter 1.

27 See Sir Edward Coke, *The Fift Part of the Reports* (London: 1606). It opens with a section "Of the Kings Ecclesiasticall Law," fols. 1–41. For an unauthorized publication of a speech by Coke that was subsequently suppressed, see Robert Pricket, *The Lord Coke His Speech and Charge. With a Discouerie of the Abuses and Corruption of Officers* (London: 1607). Parsons responds in Robert Parsons, *An Answere to the Fifth Part of Reportes Lately Set Forth by Syr Edward Cooke Knight, the Kinges Attorney Generall* ([St. Omer]: 1606), Robert Parsons, *A Quiet and Sober Reckoning With M. Thomas Morton* ([St. Omer]: 1609). *A Quiet and Sober Reckoning* dedicates chapter 8 to an attack on Coke (529–624).

28 Raspa points out that these conjugate leaves, Sigs. ¶1 and ¶2, are found in a variety of different places in various copies of the book (lxvi–lxx).

29 For an earlier, less hesitant, formulation, see Anthony Raspa, "Time, History and Typology in John Donne's *Pseudo-Martyr*," *Renaissance and Reformation* 11 (1987).

30 An exception is Healy, who points out that "the standard critical comment about *Pseudo-Martyr*, that it is a charitable work filled with irenic sweetness, is something of an exaggeration" (*Ignatius His Conclave*, xviii n. 2).

31 Donne, *Letters to Severall Persons of Honour*, 29.

32 For a useful introduction to Counter-Reformation political theory, see Quentin Skinner, *The Foundations of Modern Political Thought II: The Age of Reformation* (Cambridge University Press, 1978), 135–73. For an account of "designation theory" see J. P. Sommerville, *Royalists and Patriots: Politics and Ideology in England, 1603–1640*, 2nd edn. (London: Longman, 1999), 24–29.

33 Jean Bodin, *The Six Bookes of a Common-Weale*, trans. Richard Knolles (London: 1606), 84. See also Julian H. Franklin, "Sovereignty and the Mixed Constitution: Bodin and His Critics," in *The Cambridge History of Political Thought, 1470–1700*, ed. J. H. Burns with Mark Goldie (Cambridge University Press, 1991).

34 A general skepticism about the existence in the early seventeenth century of a cohesive body of political thought that can usefully be labeled *absolutism* is part of the general trend that would downplay or deny the existence of genuine ideological conflict in the pre-Civil War years. An excellent introduction to the range of ideas expressed by seventeenth-century invocations of absolute monarchy is James Daly, "The Idea of Absolute Monarchy in Seventeenth-Century England," *The Historical Journal* 21 (1978). A short and helpful account of the development of absolutist ideas is J. H. Burns, "The Idea of Absolutism," in *Absolutism in Seventeenth-Century Europe*, ed. John Miller (New York: St. Martin's Press, 1990). For the claim that the idea of absolutism is a late-appearing precipitate of anti-French sentiment and English self-congratulation, see the comparative account of Nicholas Henshall, *The Myth of Absolutism: Change and Continuity in Early Modern European Monarchy* (London: Longman, 1992). A full-scale assault on the idea, which claims that it is the product of a "whig hermeneutic," is provided by Glenn Burgess, *Absolute Monarchy* (New Haven: Yale University Press,

1996). Sommerville, *Royalists and Patriots*, offers a robust defense of the claim that there was a discernible absolutist line of thinking in early seventeenth-century England.

35 For a short and helpful discussion of the debate over Cowell's book, see Sommerville, *Royalists and Patriots*, 113–19.

36 J. R. Tanner, ed., *Constitutional Documents of the Reign of James I, 1603–1625* (Cambridge University Press, 1960).

37 A. L. Rowse, *Ralegh and the Throkmortons* (London: Macmillan, 1962).

38 For an account of Hall's writing, see Richard A. McCabe, *Joseph Hall: A Study in Satire and Meditation* (Oxford: Clarendon Press, 1982).

39 Geoffrey Keynes, *A Bibliography of Dr. John Donne, Dean of Saint Paul's* (Oxford: Clarendon Press, 1973), 171.

40 R. C. Bald, *Donne and the Drurys* (Cambridge University Press, 1959), 63.

41 This letter was first published in *Poems* (1635), T5^r–T5^v and then in *Letters* (1651), Hh3^r–Hh4^r.

42 Frank Manley provides a representative assessment when he writes: "He regretted publishing them almost as soon as they appeared and felt ashamed and humiliated at having degraded himself by becoming a professional poet"; John Donne, *John Donne: "The Anniversaries,"* ed. Frank Manley (Baltimore: Johns Hopkins University, 1963). Harold Love alludes to "a small number of highly reluctant appearances in print" (147), an assessment that depends upon the subsequent expressions of regret.

43 Donne, *Letters* (1651), Kk4^r. The alternative version is found on Hh3^r–Hh4^r. Gosse suggests that they are the same letter and blames the variations on scribal corruption; Edmund Gosse, *The Life and Letters of John Donne*, 2 vols. (London: William Heinemann, 1899), I, 301–03. But it seems more likely that a process of revision is at work.

44 Ben Jonson, *Ben Jonson*, ed. C. H. Herford and Percy Simpson (Oxford: Clarendon Press, 1925), 133.

45 Louis Martz was the first to realize that the poem conforms to the meditative structure commended by Ignatius Loyola, a reading that locates the poem squarely in the Counter-Reformation tradition. As he explains: "The Petrarchan tradition has here combined with the great tradition of methodical religious meditation which formed the spearhead of the Counter-Reformation"; Louis L. Martz, "Donne in Meditation: the *Anniversaries*," *English Literary History* 14 (1947): 249. Martz's verdict, somewhat softened in later accounts, was that this was not a successful marriage: the contempt of the world articulated in the meditations and the glorification of Elizabeth Drury espoused in the eulogies failed to form a cohesive whole. Donne had sinned conspicuously against the ideal of organicism so cherished by the New Critics. Martz went so far as to opine that "One can omit all the rest of the poem and simply read through the Meditations consecutively; the sequence is consistent and, with a brief conclusion, would form a complete – and a rather good – poem" (259). This critical judgment also has the effect of claiming that the good bits of the poem are indelibly marked as the property of the Counter-Reformation. Martz's

negative verdict on the poem's aesthetic achievement was not new, but the rationale offered was. Barbara Kiefer Lewalski, in response to Martz, made a strong bid to recuperate Donne's *Anniversaries* by situating them within the context of a fully developed Protestant poetics; Barbara Kiefer Lewalski, *Donne's "Anniversaries" and the Poetry of Praise: The Creation of a Symbolic Mode* (Princeton University Press, 1973). In contrast to Martz's charge of formal deficiency, Lewalski found "coherent symbolic meaning and method as well as their careful logical articulation" (7). This claim was itself dependent upon her recovery of a distinctly Protestant discourse that combined meditation and sermon and that made use of typological symbolism. The poems, according to Lewalski, emerged out of a Protestant and English context rather than the Catholic and European one delineated by Martz. At the same time as Lewalski sought to normalize the poems by showing their congruence with an established body of writing, she also argued that they "defined a significant new kind of poetry of praise which exploited the rich potentialities for symbolization and figurative expression available in the matrix of English Protestantism at the turn of the century" (335). Lewalski is, above all, eager to vindicate the poetic resources of Protestantism against the naïve claim that it is "inherently anti-literary" (6). For Lewalski, the figure of Elizabeth Drury is an instance of typological symbolism, a specifically Protestant reconfiguration of the ancient hermeneutic technique of typology, according to which Elizabeth, as a regenerate Christian, contains within herself the image of God. Lewalski's alignment of the poem with a doctrinal Calvinism has, in turn, been severely criticized by Edward Tayler, who resists the confessionalization of the poem by placing it squarely in an Aristotelean–Thomist tradition that precedes both the Protestant typological symbolism described by Lewalski and the Jesuit meditations delineated by Martz. That Donne meant an Aristotelian and Thomist *idea* as opposed to an Augustinian and Platonic one might well be granted without conceding that this restrictive *idea* provides the interpretive key to the poem. *An Anatomy* becomes in Tayler's treatment a document, perhaps one of the last, that testifies to the vibrancy and vitality of what used to be called the medieval synthesis; Edward Tayler, *Donne's Idea of a Woman: Structure and Meaning in "The Anniversaries"* (New York: Columbia University Press, 1991).

46 There has been a long-running debate over the degree to which these "companion" poems form a single whole. Marjorie Nicolson makes an influential case for treating them as a unit; Marjorie Nicolson, *The Breaking of the Circle: Studies in the Effect of the "New Science" Upon Seventeenth Century Poetry* (Evanston: Northwestern University Press, 1950).

47 Hall has been criticized for accommodating "Donne's symbolic method more closely than seems warranted to the Petrarchan or Neoplatonic stance"; Lewalski, *Donne's "Anniversaries" and the Poetry of Praise*, 225.

48 This use of *Religion* is an excellent example of what John Bossy has described as the emergence in the first third of the seventeenth century of an abstract and general notion of religion that arose in response to the proliferation of religions

in the wake of the Reformation; John Bossy, "Some Elementary Forms of Durkheim," *Past and Present* 95 (1982): 6.

49 This passage has become a touchstone. It provides a title for Victor Harris, *All Coherence Gone: The Seventeenth-Century Controversy on the Decay of Nature* (University of Chicago Press, 1949). It furnishes an epigraph for Stephen Toulmin, *Cosmopolis: The Hidden Agenda of Modernity* (University of Chicago Press, 1990). For Steven Shapin it is the most eloquent expression of "Unease in the face of infinity, of shaken systems of traditional cosmological knowledge, and of the decentering of the earth"; Steven Shapin, *The Scientific Revolution* (University of Chicago Press, 1996), 28. For Jonathan Dollimore it is a recognition that "Relational identity has ... given way to anarchic egotism"; Jonathan Dollimore, *Radical Tragedy: Religion, Ideology and Power in the Drama of Shakespeare and His Contemporaries*, 2nd edn. (Durham, NC: Duke University Press, 1993), 158.

50 John Donne, *The Poems of John Donne*, ed. H. J. C. Grierson (Oxford: Clarendon Press, 1912), II, 190.

51 "She could not transubstantiate / All states to gold" (B5^r). "If vnder all, a Vault infernall be, / (Which sure is spacious, except that we / Inuent another torment, that there must / Millions into a strait hote roome be thrust) / Then solidnes, and roundnes haue no place" (B2^v). The parenthetical claim is, to paraphrase, that there is ample room for hell within the earth as long as we do not continue to invent new torments such as purgatory.

52 Lewalski, *Donne's "Anniversaries" and the Poetry of Praise*, 222.

53 John Davies, *The Muses Sacrifice* (London: 1612), P6^r.

54 For a helpful account, see Brian Vickers, "The 'Songs and Sonnets' and the Rhetoric of Hyperbole," in *John Donne: Essays in Celebration*, ed. A. J. Smith (London: Methuen, 1972).

55 Lewalski takes it at face-value: "John Davies of Hereford explicitly identified the *Anniversary* poems as the literary model he was attempting to imitate but could not hope to equal in his own elegy" (*Donne's "Anniversaries" and the Poetry of Praise*, 309).

56 Davies elsewhere criticizes proverbial claims about the sufficiency of the will: "In Matters great, to will it doth suffize; / I blush to heare how lowd this *Prouerb* lyes: / For, they that owe great summes by Bond or Bill, / Can neuer cansell them with meere *Good-will*"; John Davies, *The Scourge of Folly* (London: 1611), FI^r.

57 Perhaps the three most familiar examples in prose are John Lyly, *Euphues: The Anatomy of Wit* (1578); Thomas Nashe, *The Anatomie of Absurditie* (1589); Phillip Stubbes, *The Anatomie of Abuses* (1583). A seventeenth-century example is Joseph Hall?, *The Anathomie of Sinne* (1603).

58 In this passage, Davies follows Puttenham closely but with some important variations. Chapters 3 and 4 of *The Arte of English Poesie* (London, 1589) are entitled "How Poets were the first priests, the first prophets, the first Legislators and politicians in the world" and "How the Poets were the first Philosophers, the first Astronomers and Historiographers and Oratours and

Musitiens of the world." Davies, for his part, asserts: "Then, Poets were the first Philosophers; / first State-obseruers, and Historians: First Metaphickes, and Astronomers, / Yea, the first Great-clarks, and Astrologians" ($A2^r$).

59 For this group see David Norbrook, *Poetry and Politics in the English Renaissance*, rev. edn. (Oxford University Press, 2002), 195–214, Michelle O'Callaghan, *The "Shepheard's Nation": Jacobean Spenserians and Early Stuart Political Culture* (Oxford University Press, 2000).

60 Davies contributed "An Eclogue between yong Willy the singer of his natiue Pastorals, and old Wernocke his friend" ($G3^r$–$G7^r$), a Spenserian complaint about the decay of true poetry. Interestingly, here Davies writes, "Swaines, that con no skill of holy-rage, / Bene foe-men to faire skils enlawrel'd Queene" ($G4^v$).

61 The nature of Davies's own religious convictions presents something of a puzzle. It is frequently claimed that he was a Roman Catholic, but the sole authority for this assertion (repeated by the *DNB*) is Arthur Wilson's brief autobiography. Wilson's narrative, entitled "Observations of God's provid-ence, in the tract of my life," catalogs the various escapes that lead him to become a convinced Protestant. Crucial to this narrative is his early exposure to the threat of Catholicism. His father, we are told, intended to set him up as apprentice to a merchant, but when it was discovered that the merchant was a papist, an alternative was sought. A place was found at the Exchequer but first Arthur needed to learn Court and Chancery hands and so was sent to John Davies. Unfortunately, Davies was "also a papist, with his wife & familie," and consequently young Arthur "often debated which was the true religion." After acquiring the needed hands, Wilson was taken on, at the Exchequer, by Sir Henry Spiller, "who also, with his familie, were some of them absolute, & others of them church-papists." Despite this Arthur "still stood indifferent." Unwilling to embrace Catholicism, he remained troubled by the charge that Protestantism was a novelty. "But it was not God's will that I should live long in those doubts." And so the narrative continues. The personal narrative of spiritual awakening combines with Wilson's politically motivated desire to depict the reign of James I as especially tolerant of Roman Catholicism to provide an inducement to revision. But simply because Wilson had strong motives for misremembering the past does not mean that he in fact did so. It does, however, suggest that some caution is needed concerning his pronounce-ments about Davies of Hereford. For the ambivalent evidence provided by his works, see the introductory comments in John Davies, *The Complete Works of John Davies of Hereford*, ed. Alexander B. Grosart (New York: AMS Press [rpt.], 1967), xviii–xix.

62 Arnold Stein, "Donne's Obscurity and the Elizabethan Tradition," *English Literary History* 13 (1946): 110.

63 George Chapman, *Ouids Banquet of Sence* (London: 1595), $A2^r$–$A2^v$.

64 Reprinted in G. Gregory Smith, ed., *Elizabethan Critical Essays*, 2 vols. (Oxford University Press, 1904), I, 53, and II, 327.

65 Though there is growing critical consensus that the label "metaphysical" bestows a misleading unity on a varied tradition, there is evidence – in the copious references to "strong lines" and "hard conceits" – that seventeenth-century observers of the poetic scene realized new poetic fashions were emerging. For a helpful survey of allusions, see George Williamson, "Strong Lines," *English Studies* 18 (1936). A criticism of Williamson's attempt to identify "strong lines" with "metaphysical poetry" is provided by Gregory T. Dime, "The Difference between 'Strong Lines' and 'Metaphysical Poetry,'" *Studies in English Literature* 26 (1986). Though Dime is certainly right to point out that what a seventeenth-century critic meant by "strong lines" is not synonymous with what we mean by "metaphysical poetry," he does concede that the debate over strong lines "consistently centers on the issue of excessive brevity and abstruse ideas – in short, on the question of difficulty or obscurity" (51–52). The crucial point is that the new poetics was understood by its critics as rejection of the euphonious style and rhetorical method of the Elizabethans. Elizabethan poetry could, in retrospect, be invested with an aesthetic and moral clarity that it might never have had. For an excellent account of the manuscript circulation of Sidney's works, see H. R. Woudhuysen, *Sir Philip Sidney and the Circulation of Manuscripts, 1558–1640* (Oxford: Clarendon Press, 1996).

66 Dudley North, *A Forest of Varieties* (London: 1645), A3^v. For a brief introduction, see L. A. Beaurline, "Dudley North's Criticism of Metaphysical Poetry," *Huntington Library Quarterly* 25 (1962).

67 It is, of course, ironic that Sidney's accessibility was in large part the consequence of the posthumous printing of poems that had during his lifetime circulated in manuscript.

68 Lewalski covers a number of other responses. For a Jesuit response, see Josephine Evetts-Secker, "*Fuga Saeculi* or Holy Hatred of the World: John Donne and Henry Hawkins," *Recusant History* 14 (1977). For a manuscript response, possibly by Elizabeth Isham, see Karl Josef Höltgen, "Unpublished Early Verses 'on Dr. Donnes Anatomy,'" *Review of English Studies* 22 (1971).

69 Donne, *Letters to Severall Persons of Honour*, CC2^v.

70 Harold Love, *The Culture and Commerce of Texts: Scribal Publication in Seventeenth-Century England* (Amherst: University of Massachusetts Press, 1998), 146.

71 Marotti, *Manuscript, Print*, 1. An important exception to this trend, Woudhuysen expresses a desire "to stress that there was no absolute separation of the handwritten and the printed" (*Sir Philip Sidney and the Circulation of Manuscripts*, 25).

5 *AREOPAGITICA* AND "THE TRUE WARFARING CHRISTIAN"

1 For an essay that describes Milton's "aesthetic polemic" – and also gives a good survey of relevant Milton scholarship – see James Egan, "Creator–Critic: Aesthetic Subtexts in Milton's Antiprelatical and Regicide Polemics," *Milton Studies* 30 (1993).

2 See the still helpful George Frank Sensabaugh, *That Grand Whig, Milton* (Stanford University Press, 1952). For a more recent account, see Nicholas von Maltzahn, "The Whig Milton, 1667–1700," in *Milton and Republicanism*, ed. David Armitage, Armand Himy, and Quentin Skinner (Cambridge University Press, 1995).

3 J. G. A. Pocock, *Virtue, Commerce, and History: Essays on Political Thought and History, Chiefly in the Eighteenth Century* (Cambridge University Press, 1985), 263.

4 Christopher Hill, *Some Intellectual Consequences of the English Revolution* (Madison: University of Wisconsin Press, 1980), 64.

5 A more recent, and more complex, account of Restoration cultural dynamics can be found in J. G. A. Pocock, "Within the Margins: the Definitions of Orthodoxy," in *The Margins of Orthodoxy: Heterodox Writing and Cultural Response, 1660–1750*, ed. Roger D. Lund (Cambridge University Press, 1995). The notion that the Restoration marks a cultural watershed dividing a religious past from a secular present has come in for serious criticism in recent scholarship. See, for example, Tim Harris, Paul Seaward, and Mark Goldie, eds., *The Politics of Religion in Restoration England* (Oxford: Basil Blackwell, 1990). The introduction by Tim Harris provides an especially helpful review of the historiography. For a response to the revisionist tendency, most dramatically displayed by J. C. D. Clark, to downplay the significance of the Restoration, see Alan Houston and Steve Pincus, eds., *A Nation Transformed: England after the Restoration* (Cambridge University Press, 2001).

6 Daniel Defoe's *The Shortest Way* (1702) serves to illustrate both these points. This attack on High Church policies was presented ironically; the fact that at least one reader read it straight suggests that the literal proposal was not so ludicrous as to be immediately recognized as irony. Harold Love identifies this development as the consequence of the eclipse of the scribal lampoon by printed satire. Discussing Swift's satire, Love observes that its force stems from "his involvement in the historical project of translating script values into the medium of print," and adds: "The emergence of the ironic mode in satire was itself an effect of this transference"; Harold Love, *The Culture and Commerce of Texts: Scribal Publication in Seventeenth-Century England* (Amherst: University of Massachusetts Press, 1998), 308. While Love's case for the continued importance and vitality of scribal culture is deeply persuasive, he tends to reify the scribal mode and invest it with an essential set of values. Manuscript is, for Love, "the medium of frankness"; at the same time, "in a seventeenth-century context it was script and not print that was the critical, subversive medium" (309, 292–93). Throughout the book, Love makes numerous fine distinctions between scribal and print production, but here he seems to operate with blunt instruments. This is not to suggest that print is "the critical, subversive medium" in the seventeenth century, rather it is to express skepticism about the possibility of allocating such a title to either medium in isolation.

7 For the emergence of the term *polemic*, see chapter 6.

8 On the expansion of print in the 1640s, see Sharon Achinstein, *Milton and the Revolutionary Reader* (Princeton University Press, 1994), 27–70, Nigel Smith, *Literature and Revolution in England, 1640–1660* (New Haven: Yale University Press, 1994), 23–58. For a skeptical assessment, see D. F. McKenzie, "The London Book Trade in 1644," in *Bibliographia: Lectures 1975–1988 by Recipients of the Marc Fitch Prize for Bibliography*, ed. John Horden (Leeds: Leopard's Head Press, 1992). For a helpful account of the politics of censorship in the early 1640s, see Cyprian Blagden, *The Stationers' Company: A History, 1403–1959* (London: George Allen & Unwin, 1960), 130–52, Michael Mendle, "De Facto Freedom, De Facto Authority: Press and Parliament, 1640–1643," *Historical Journal* 38 (1995).

9 Ernest Sirluck, editor of vol. II, provides an excellent account of the tract's polemical tactics in John Milton, *Complete Prose Works of John Milton*, 8 vols., gen. ed. Don M. Wolfe (New Haven: Yale University Press, 1953–82), II, 170–78. I cite Milton's prose from this edition throughout.

10 For an insightful account of the polemical mode of *Of Reformation*, see Michael Lieb, "Milton's *Of Reformation* and the Dynamics of Controversy," in *Achievements of the Left Hand: Essays on the Prose of John Milton*, ed. Michael Lieb and John T. Shawcross (Amherst: University of Massachusetts Press, 1974).

11 *Complete Prose Works*, I, 868–69.

12 It also entails a qualified dissent from readings that emphasize the republican language of *Areopagitica*, such as David Norbrook, "*Areopagitica*, Censorship, and the Early Modern Public Sphere," in *The Administration of Aesthetics: Censorship, Political Criticism, and the Public Sphere*, ed. Richard Burt (Minneapolis: University of Minnesota Press, 1994), Nigel Smith, "*Areopagitica*: Voicing Contexts, 1643–5," in *Politics, Poetics, and Hermeneutics in Milton's Prose*, ed. David Loewenstein and James Grantham Turner (Cambridge University Press, 1990). For an excellent critique of liberal readings (and their authoritarian counterparts), see William Kolbrener, *Milton's Warring Angels: A Study of Critical Engagements* (Cambridge University Press, 1997), 11–27.

13 Stanley Fish, "Driving from the Letter: Truth and Indeterminacy in Milton's *Areopagitica*," in *Re-membering Milton: Essays on Texts and Traditions*, ed. Mary Nyquist and Margaret W. Ferguson (New York: Methuen, 1987), 251, and Annabel Patterson, *Censorship and Interpretation: The Conditions of Writing and Reading in Early Modern England* (Madison: University of Wisconsin Press, 1984), 112. Fish cannot be accused of underestimating the religious conviction that animates *Areopagitica*; my dissent from his otherwise compelling reading concerns what I take to be his exaggeration of Milton's antinomianism. An emphasis on the tract's endless flight from the indeterminacy of the letter obscures an important strand of apocalypticism that sees history as something more than another temptation. A slightly expanded version of this essay appears in Stanley Fish, *How Milton Works* (Cambridge, MA: The Belknap Press of Harvard University Press, 2001), 187–214.

14 Fish, "Driving from the Letter," 244.

15 Milton himself considers this problem when he quotes Bacon: "*such authoriz'd books are but the language of the times*" (II, 534). Elsewhere he raises the possibility that Truth "perhaps tunes her voice according to the time" (II, 563). For an ingenious, but ultimately unconvincing, argument that Milton's refusal to tolerate popery is simultaneously politically expedient and ironic, see Joseph Anthony Wittreich, "Milton's *Areopagitica*: Its Isocratic and Ironic Contexts," *Milton Studies* 4 (1972). The myriad attempts to discount or palliate Milton's stance on popery spring from a well-intentioned inability to countenance the strength of theological opprobrium. The pressure to explain away Milton's anti-popery comes from modern readers, not the text or its historical situation.

16 Patterson, *Censorship and Interpretation*, 112.

17 "On the New Forcers of Conscience under the Long Parliament," line 20, in John Milton, *John Milton*, ed. Stephen Orgel and Jonathan Goldberg (Oxford University Press, 1990), 84.

18 Victoria Kahn, *Machiavellian Rhetoric: From the Counter-Reformation to Milton* (Princeton University Press, 1994), 175, 74. See also Michael Wilding's assertion: "His method is truly dialectical"; Michael Wilding, "Milton's *Areopagitica*: Liberty for the Sects," *Prose Studies* 9 (1986): 35.

19 Christopher Hill, *Milton and the English Revolution* (London: Faber and Faber, 1977), 150.

20 Fish, *How Milton Works*, 567.

21 Milton cites this text in *An Apology Against a Pamphlet, Complete Prose Works*, I, 911–12.

22 David L. Jacobson, ed., *The English Libertarian Heritage: From the Writings of John Trenchard and Thomas Gordon in the Independent Whig and Cato's Letters* (New York: Bobbs-Merrill, 1965), 30. In Milton's "Letter to a Friend," he uses similar language when he considers the possibility that his love of learning may "proceed from a principle bad, good, or natural," *Complete Prose Works*, I, 319–21. "Natural" serves here as *tertium quid* analogous to "indifferent" in the example from Trenchard and Gordon. The important difference is that Milton is not here discussing reason. Revealingly, Milton goes on to condemn the "unprofitable sin of curiosity" because it transforms one into "the most pusillanimous, and unweaponed creature in the world, the most unable and unfit to do that which all mortals most aspire to, either to defend and be useful to his friends, or to offend his enemies ..." This an especially vivid expression of Milton's polemical consciousness, which construes the world as divided between friends and enemies and sees discursive combat as the height of aspiration. I am grateful to Steve Fallon for pointing this passage out to me.

23 Milton's military metaphors – "a revolutionary figuration of true discourse" – are emphasized by Barker, but his reading of *Areopagitica* concludes by focusing on the way in which the text prefigures "the modern regime of discourse" in which violence is occluded by the subject's "pre-constitution in docility";

Francis Barker, "In the Wars of Truth: Violence, True Knowledge and Power in Milton and Hobbes," in *Literature and the English Civil War*, ed. Thomas Healy and Jonathan Sawday (Cambridge University Press, 1990), 100–01. Such a reading shares the whiggishness of liberal readings that insist on seeing *Areopagitica* as an anticipation of fully modern arguments with their attendant concepts and categories.

24 For discussion, see above pp. 39–40. I John 4:1 ("Beloved, believe not every spirit, but try the spirits whether they are of God: because many false prophets are gone out into the world") is invoked later in the tract when Milton imagines the order of discursive battle in the "mansion house of liberty": "there be pens and heads there, sitting by their studious lamps, musing, searching, revolving new notions and ideas wherewith to present, as with their homage and their fealty the approaching Reformation: others as fast reading, *trying all things*, assenting to the force of reason and convincement" (II, 534, emphasis added). Mueller notes that these passages are part of an apocalyptic tradition that sees the presence of false prophets as a sign of the approach of the final days; Janel Mueller, "Embodying Glory: the Apocalyptic Strain in Milton's *Of Reformation*," in *Politics, Poetics, and Hermeneutics in Milton's Prose*, ed. David Loewenstein and James Grantham Turner (Cambridge University Press, 1990), 11.

25 Henry Smith, *Vpon Part of the 5. Chapter of the First Epistle of Saint Paul to the Thessalonians* (London: 1591). Smith is using the Geneva translation's *try*; Milton's *prove* has the sanction of the King James Bible.

26 This is one reason for the anxiety provoked in the godly sort by the Apocrypha. The very category introduces a threat to the integrity and sufficiency of scripture by making it clear that some extra-scriptural authority is required to separate the apocryphal from the canonical. Hooker, in his attack on the scripturalism of the puritans, makes this very point, suggesting that it is pertinent to ask, "How the books of holy scripture contain in them all necessary things, when of things necessary the very chiefest is to know what books we are bound to esteem holy, which point is confessed impossible for the scripture itself to teach"; Richard Hooker, *Of the Laws of Ecclesiastical Polity*, ed. Arthur Stephen McGrade (Cambridge University Press, 1989), 112.

27 For a latter statement of this view, see *A Treatise of Civil Power in Ecclesiastical Causes* (1659). "First, it cannot be deni'd, being the main foundation of our protestant religion, that we of these ages, having no other divine rule or autoritie from without us warrantable to one another as a common ground but the holy scripture" (5). Cf. "in controversies, there is no arbitrator except Scripture, or rather each man is his own arbitrator, so long as he follows Scripture and the Spirit of God" qtd. in Hill, *Milton and the English Revolution*, 247.

28 This passage should be compared to Milton's earlier praise for Selden's "exquisite reasons and theorems almost mathematically demonstrative" (II, 513). For discussion of this passage and Selden's influence on *Areopagitica*, see Smith, "*Areopagitica*: Voicing Contexts, 1643–5," esp. 106–08.

29 For a different view, see Victoria Kahn, who focuses on the fact that this passage reveals – by invoking the false prophecy of the 400 prophets – "the way in which divine inspiration may be feigned" (*Machiavellian Rhetoric*, 178).

30 Carl Schmitt, *The Concept of the Political*, trans. George Schwab (New Brunswick, NJ: Rutgers University Press, 1976), 26. I cite Schmitt because his formulations illuminate the world of early modern polemic. Not entirely coincidentally, Schmitt himself identifies and celebrates as the best example of the high points in politics "in which the enemy is, in concrete clarity, recognized as the enemy ... Cromwell's enmity towards papist Spain" (67).

31 This position reveals the distance between Milton and the early Tudor reformers described by Verkamp as "mainline Protestants" who believed in the efficacy of the "indifferent mean" or *via media*. The metaphor of the *via media* crucially depends on the location of two poles – usually popery and Anabaptism – between which to steer. Curiously, the road thus conceived is actually a figure of stasis or balance construed as the simultaneous repudiation of opposing extremes and is itself repudiated by Milton's vision of a forward motion toward the recovery of an as yet unrecognized truth.

32 This is the claim made by Dobranski in a fascinating essay on the imagery of printing that appears in *Areopagitica*; Stephen B. Dobranski, "Letter and Spirit in Milton's *Areopagitica*," *Milton Studies* 32 (1995): 143. While Milton's account of the discovery of knowledge is certainly social, it seems implausible to claim that "Milton's puns and allusions [on the subject of print] *force* readers to acknowledge *all* the agents in the bookmaking process" (146; emphasis added). The Milton described here sounds suspiciously like D. F. McKenzie. I am sympathetic with Dobranski's account of the importance of the material book and am convinced by his claim that Milton was especially attentive to matters of print. I am not convinced, however, by the attempt to transform this awareness into an endorsement of "social authorship."

33 The only time, so far as I am aware, that Milton names an individual printer is in his references to Vlacq in *A Second Defence of the English People* and in *Pro Se Defensio* (*Complete Prose Works*, IV, pt. 1, 572–73, 576–78; V, pt. 2, 729–31). In these passages Milton excoriates Vlacq – who had, shortly after soliciting work from Milton, printed Alexander More's *Cry of the King's Blood* – for his inconstancy: "For he [Vlacq] says, I am a printer. 'What concern are these great controversies to printers except as they are their work?' Acute, to be sure, and typographical! No one would concede more to printers than I would in this respect" (IV, pt. 2, 730).

34 For the argument that *Areopagitica* "is a landmark, in its way, in the formation of this market ideology," see Christopher Kendrick, "Ethics and the Orator in *Areopagitica*," *English Literary History* 50 (1983). Kendrick argues that despite Milton's explicit "protest against the commodification of human activity," "the commodity places its shadowy imprint on much of the imagery of the tract, and as a result market ideology comes to be inscribed most intimately within Milton's argument and to motivate its very figuration" (677–78). For a related argument, see Sandra Sherman,

"Printing the Mind: the Economics of Authorship in *Areopagitica*," *English Literary History* 60 (1993).

35 Joseph Loewenstein, *The Author's Due: Printing and the Prehistory of Copyright* (University of Chicago Press, 2002), 318. Loewenstein provides a valuable corrective to readings that have wanted to see in the tract an argument for authorial copyright, see esp. 171–91.

36 For Bacon the consequences of technology are "to be seen nowhere more conspicuously than in those three which were unknown to the ancients, and of which the origin, though recent is obscure and inglorious; namely, printing, gunpowder, and the magnet," three discoveries that have "changed the whole face and state of things throughout the world"; Francis Bacon, *The Works of Francis Bacon*, ed. Robert Leslie Ellis, James Spedding, and Douglas Denon Heath (London: Longmans, 1870), IV, 114.

37 Sirluck gives a short bibliographic account (II, 482–83). See also Shawcross, who observes that "the type is so poor that broken types and the like do not allow for any certain identification"; John T. Shawcross, "A Survey of Milton's Prose Works," in *Achievements of the Left Hand: Essays on the Prose of John Milton*, ed. Michael Lieb and John T. Shawcross (Amherst: University of Massachusetts Press, 1974), 304. Shawcross raises the possibility that Augustine Matthewes, who did not have a license to print, may have been responsible.

38 See Sirluck (II, 515 n. 102).

39 While this crux appears to offer a stark choice between pilgrimage and conflict, Thomas Watson, an ejected minister, gives the following homiletic advice in 1663: "Our life is a wayfaring life, and a warfaring life; there is a duel fought every day between the two Seeds: A Believer will not let sin have peaceable possession: If he cannot keep sin out, he will keep sin under"; Thomas Watson, *A Divine Cordial* (London: 1663), E3^r.

40 McKenzie uses this quotation to exemplify the notion of the book as transparent container that he intends to critique; D. F. McKenzie, *Bibliography and the Sociology of Texts* (London: British Library, 1986), 23–24. Stephen M. Fallon, in contrast, argues for Milton's "monistic conception of the book as the 'precious life-blood of a master spirit'"; Stephen M. Fallon, *Milton Among the Philosophers: Poetry and Materialism in Seventeenth-Century England* (Ithaca: Cornell University Press, 1991), 122. Loewenstein perceptively notes "the distinctively physiological character of the aftereffect of writing, its potency embalmed as a nearly material immortality" in this passage, but also observes that "the tactical project of denigrating the industrial mediation of the press inhibits the representation of the book as independent and fully embodied" (*The Author's Due*, 174–75).

41 This point merits attention because many critics have tended to elide "writing" and "print publication." This may in fact have been Milton's intention, but the obvious consequence is to diminish the role of the printing press.

42 In this regard, Milton is in sympathy with those contemporary historians of the book who have sought to revise the claim that the advent of print institutes a radical cultural break.

43 Smith, *Literature and Revolution in England, 1640–1660*, 190.
44 Robert Heath, *Clarastella* (London: 1650), 37.
45 The association of the printing press and artillery is commonplace in the sixteenth century. For example, in Samuel Daniel's *The Civil Wars*, Nemesis instructs Pandora to disrupt the Western world by sowing contention: "And better to effect a speedy end, / Let there be found two fatall instruments, / The one to publish, th'other to defend / Impious contention, and proud discontents"; Samuel Daniel, *The Poeticall Essayes* (London: 1599), 95^v.
46 Sensabaugh, *That Grand Whig, Milton*, 65.
47 William Denton, *Jus Cæsaris Et Ecclesiæ Vere Dictæ* (London: 1681), 6–7. "An Apology for the Liberty of the Press" appears at the end of this volume with its own pagination. Charles Blount, *A Just Vindication of Learning: Or, an Humble Address to the High Court of Parliament in Behalf of the Liberty of the Press* (London: 1679).
48 While Milton frequently refers to the public good, "publik interest" appears only in *The Readie & Easie Way* (*Complete Prose Works*, VII, 461). *Interest* and its cognates do appear in a variety of other formulations, but these occasional uses do not amount to a systematic or consistent engagement with the political language of interest that was taking shape at the time. See J. A. W. Gunn, "'Interest Will Not Lie': a Seventeenth-Century Political Maxim," *Journal of the History of Ideas* 29 (1968), J. A. W. Gunn, *Politics and the Public Interest in the Seventeenth Century* (London: Routledge & Kegan Paul, 1969), Albert O. Hirschman, *The Passions and the Interests: Political Arguments for Capitalism before Its Triumph* (Princeton University Press, 1977).
49 Jeremy Taylor claims that the restraint of prophesying and the attempt to control conscience "came in with the retinue and traine of Antichrist, that is, they came as other abuses and corruptions of the Church did, by reason of the iniquity of times, and the cooling of the first heats of Christianity, and the encrease of interest, and the abatements of Christian simplicity, when the Churches fortune grew better, and her Sonnes grow worse, and some of her Fathers worst of all"; Jeremy Taylor, *Treatises* (London: 1650), CI^v.
50 Cf. ibid., D3^v–D4^r.
51 Blount here alludes to the controversies over Boyle's experiments with the air-pump. For an account, see Steven Shapin and Simon Schaffer, *Leviathan and the Air-Pump: Hobbes, Boyle, and the Experimental Life* (Princeton University Press, 1985).
52 In the opening section of *Jus Cæsaris Et Ecclesiæ Vere Dictæ* Denton quotes from *A Treatise of Civil Power in Ecclesiastical Causes* by "J. M." See n. 27 above.
53 Despite the echoes of Selden detected by Nigel Smith (see n. 28 above), Milton's tract does not make extensive use of natural law arguments.

6 INSTITUTIONALIZING POLEMIC: THE RISE AND FALL
OF CHELSEA COLLEGE

1 Thomas Faulkner, *An Historical and Topographical Description of Chelsea and Its Environs* (London: 1810), 146. An earlier version of this work appeared as *An*

Historical and Descriptive Account of the Royal Hospital, and the Royal Military Asylum at Chelsea: To Which is prefixed an Account of King James's College at Chelsea (London, 1805).

2 David Hume, *History of England*, vol. V (London: 1778), 132.

3 Michel Foucault, "Polemics, Politics, and Problemizations: an Interview with Michel Foucault," in *The Foucault Reader*, ed. Paul Rabinow (New York: Pantheon Books, 1984), 382.

4 Roland Mousnier, *The Institutions of France under the Absolute Monarchy, 1598–1789*, trans. Brian Pearce (University of Chicago Press, 1979), vii.

5 Andrew Marvell, *Mr. Smirke; or, the Divine in Mode: Being Certain Annotations Upon the Animadversions on the Naked Truth: Together with a Short Historical Essay, Concerning General Councils, Creeds, and Impositions, in Matters of Religion* (London: 1676), F1^r.

6 Samuel Purchas, *The Kings Towre, and Trivmphant Arch of London* (London: 1623), F6^v.

7 Edward Knott, *Charity Mistaken* ([St. Omer]: 1630), F7^v.

8 Bodleian MS. Tanner 142 f. 52.

9 Gladys Jenkins, "The Archpriest Controversy and the Printers, 1601–1603," *The Library* 5th ser. 2 (1947–48), Henry R. Plomer, "Bishop Bancroft and a Catholic Press," *The Library* n.s. 8 (1907).

10 Qtd. in John Nichols, *Progresses of James I*, 4 vols. (London: 1828), II, 313.

11 D. E. Kennedy, "King James I's College of Controversial Divinity at Chelsea," in *Grounds of Controversy: Three Studies in Late Sixteenth and Early Seventeenth Century English Polemics*, ed. D. E. Kennedy (Parkville, Vic., Australia: History Department, University of Melbourne, 1989), 118. Kennedy's essay, the only extended treatment of the College by a modern historian, provides a wealth of information. Though Kennedy is certainly correct about the origins of Chelsea College, he tends to overdraw the Elizabethan aspects of the College, depicting it as the remnant of an earlier age increasingly out of step with political and religious developments in Stuart England.

12 Alfred Beaver, *Memorials of Old Chelsea: A New History of the Village of Palaces* (London: Elliot Stock, 1892), 260.

13 Kenneth Fincham and Peter Lake, "The Ecclesiastical Policy of King James I," *Journal of British Studies* 24 (1985): 187.

14 Bodleian MS. Tanner 142 ff. 80–81.

15 Samuel Purchas, *Purchas His Pilgrimes* (London: 1625), ¶6^r.

16 Faulkner, *An Historical and Topographical Description of Chelsea and Its Environs*, 147.

17 *The Constitutions of the Musaeum Minervae* (London: 1636), ¶¶^{v}.

18 MS. Tanner 142 f. 69.

19 Ibid., f. 61.

20 Peter Lake, "The Laudian Style: Order, Uniformity and the Pursuit of the Beauty of Holiness in the 1630s," in *The Early Stuart Church, 1603–1642*, ed. Kenneth Fincham (Stanford University Press, 1993).

21 Qtd. Robert Fitzgibbon Young, *Comenius in England* (Oxford University Press, 1932), 53–55.

22 John Dury, *The Reformed Spirituall Husbandman: With an Humble Memorandum Concerning Chelsy Colledge* (London: 1652), F3ʳ– F3ᵛ.

23 Hartlib MS. 47/9/21a.

24 Ibid., 16b.

25 This Latin phrase suggests that Hartlib was aware that the Roman Catholic Church had formally constituted a Congregation *de Propaganda Fide* in 1622.

26 Chelsea Hospital, *Papers Illustrative of the Origin and Early History of the Royal Hospital at Chelsea Compiled in the Secretary's Office of That Institution* (London: 1872), 92.

27 Qtd. in Faulkner, *An Historical and Topographical Description of Chelsea and Its Environs*, 151.

28 Chelsea Hospital, *Papers Illustrative of the Origin and Early History of the Royal Hospital at Chelsea*, 92.

29 Thomas Fuller, *The Church History of Britain; from the Birth of Jesus Christ, Untill the Year M. Dc. Xlviii* (London: 1655), 51, 55.

30 Arthur Wilson, *The History of Great Britain, Being the Life and Reign of King James the First* (London: 1653), H3ʳ.

31 J. F. Merritt, "The Reshaping of Stow's 'Survey': Munday, Strype, and the Protestant City," in *Imagining Early Modern London: Perceptions and Portrayals of the City from Stow to Strype, 1598–1720*, ed. J. F. Merritt (Cambridge University Press, 2001), 56, 59. For more on Munday's reshaping of Stow, see Tracey Hill, *Anthony Munday and Civic Culture: Theatre, History and Power in Early Modern London, 1580–1633* (Manchester University Press, 2004), 175–83.

32 For more on Dyson, see Nigel Ramsay, *Oxford Dictionary of National Biography* (Oxford University Press, 2004); available from http://www.oxforddnb.com/view/article/37380.

33 The reprinted pamphlet appears on pp. 380–86; the original is W. C., *The Fatall Vesper: or, A True and Punctual Relation* (London: 1623). For an illuminating account of the episode, see Alexandra Walsham, "'The Fatall Vesper': Providentialism and Anti-Popery in Late Jacobean London," *Past and Present* 144 (1994).

34 J. F. Merritt, "Puritans, Laudians, and the Phenomenon of Church Building in Jacobean London," *Historical Journal* 41 (1998).

35 Thomas Fuller, *The Holy State* (London: 1642). Fuller is quoting Joseph Hall, *Christian Moderation* (London: 1640). Fuller's commitment to moderation should not be taken at face value. It certainly did not save him from the wrath of Peter Heylyn who subjected *The Church History* to withering criticism. For an illuminating account, see Robert Mayer, "The Rhetoric of Historical Truth: Heylyn Contra Fuller on *The Church History of Britain*," *Prose Studies* 20 (1997).

36 John Darley, *The Glory of Chelsey Colledge Revived* (London: 1662), C2ᵛ. The Curse of Meroz was the text of a fast sermon preached by Stephen Marshall in 1641 urging military action against the Irish Catholics as a religious duty. The sermon was printed: *Meroz Cursed. Or, a Sermon, Preached to the Honourable House of Commons, at Their Late Solemn Fast, Febr. 23. 1641* (London: 1642). Edward Symmons was compelled to answer, having discovered the baleful effects of Marshall's sermon when interviewing captured parliamentarian

soldiers; see Symmons, *Scripture Vindicated from the Mis-Apprehensions, Mis-Interpretations, and Mis-Applications of Mr. Stephen Marshall, in His Sermon Preached before the Commons House of Parliament, Feb. 23. 1641. And Published by Order of That House* (Oxford: 1645). A sermon preached in 1680 at the Guildhall chapel by Edmond Hickeringill sets out self-consciously to rehabilitate a text that had become decidedly unfashionable through its association with rebellion and dissent: "I have chosen a Text, very seldom (if at all) insisted upon in these Times, and never before by me at any time. But yet about Forty years ago, this Text (I have heard) was the Common Theam in Pulpits, and Usher'd in (as well as promoted) the late Bloody Civil Wars," *Curse Ye Meroz, or the Fatal Doom* (London: 1680), B1^r.

37 Darley, *The Glory of Chelsey Colledge Revived*, C4^r, Joseph Hall, *The Peace-Maker* (London: 1647), K7^r–K7^v.

38 For an excellent account of the way in which Hall's professed moderation operated to polarize as opposed to unify, see Peter Lake, "The Moderate and Irenic Case for Religious War: Joseph Hall's *Via Media* in Context," in *Political Culture and Cultural Politics in Early Modern England*, ed. Susan D. Amussen and Mark A. Kishlansky (Manchester University Press, 1995).

39 For example, "The portable Arke in the Old Testament, and the flying woman in the New, are images of the militant Church in this world; the one was drawne by beasts from place to place, the other was carried with the wings of an Eagle from Country to Country: neither of them was fixed," Daniel Featley, *Clavis Mystica: A Key Opening Divers Difficult and Mysterious Texts of Holy Scripture* (London: 1636), Dd1^r.

40 Thomas Sprat, *History of the Royal Society*, ed. Jackson I. Cope and Harold Whitmore Jones (St. Louis: Washington University Studies, 1959), 434.

41 J. G. A. Pocock, *Virtue, Commerce, and History: Essays on Political Thought and History, Chiefly in the Eighteenth Century* (Cambridge University Press, 1985), 236. For a more recent reiteration, see J. G. A. Pocock, "Within the Margins: the Definitions of Orthodoxy," in *The Margins of Orthodoxy: Heterodox Writing and Cultural Response, 1660–1750*, ed. Roger D. Lund (Cambridge University Press, 1995). See also, Michael Heyd, "The Reaction to Enthusiasm in the Seventeenth Century: Towards an Integrative Approach," *Journal of Modern History* 53 (1981), George Williamson, "The Restoration Revolt against Enthusiasm," *Studies in Philology* 30 (1933).

42 *History of the Royal Society*, 25.

43 R. Fletcher, *Ex Otio Negotium* (London: 1656), 171.

44 Randle Holme, *The Academy of Armory* (Chester: 1688), 254.

45 Mark Goldie, "The Theory of Religious Intolerance in Restoration England," in *From Persecution to Toleration: The Glorious Revolution and Religion in England*, ed. Ole Peter Grell, Jonathan I. Israel, and Nicholas Tyacke (Oxford: Clarendon Press, 1991).

46 J. C. D. Clark, *English Society, 1688–1832: Ideology, Social Structure, and Political Practice during the Ancien Régime* (Cambridge University Press, 2nd edn, 2000). The Peace of Westphalia that concluded the Thirty Years' War in

1648 is frequently cited as the termination of European wars of religion. See, for example, Stephen Toulmin, *Cosmopolis: The Hidden Agenda of Modernity* (University of Chicago Press, 1990), 90–91. In the English context, the series of wars fought against the Dutch beginning in 1652 decisively demonstrated that war policy was to be shaped by commercial interests not religious sympathies.

EPILOGUE: POLITE LEARNING

1 Max Weber, "Science as a Vocation," in *From Max Weber: Essays in Sociology*, ed. H. H. Gerth and C. Wright Mills (Oxford University Press, 1946).
2 Steven N. Zwicker, "Irony, Modernity, and Miscellany: Politics and Aesthetics in the Stuart Restoration," in *Refiguring Revolutions: Aesthetics and Politics from the English Revolution to the Romantic Revolution*, ed. Kevin Sharpe and Steven N. Zwicker (Berkeley: University of California Press, 1998), 181.
3 Norbert Elias, *The Civilizing Process*, trans. Edmund Jephcott (Oxford: Blackwell, 1994). For a critique of Elias that argues for a religious, as opposed to courtly, origin for civility, see Dilwyn Knox, "*Disciplina*: the Monastic and Clerical Origins of European Civility," in *Renaissance Society and Culture: Essays in Honor of Eugene F. Rice, Jr.*, ed. John Monfasani and Ronald G. Musto (New York: Italica Press, 1991), Dilwyn Knox, "Erasmus' *De Civilitate* and the Religious Origins of Civility in Protestant Europe," *Archiv für Reformationsgeschichte* 86 (1995). Knox provides an important corrective to Elias's influential account, yet his attempt to isolate a single origin for European civility seems unnecessarily reductive. However one assesses the long-term causes of civility, the language of politeness comes to prominence after 1660.
4 For an excellent analysis of politeness and sociability in Restoration and post-1688 England, see Lawrence E. Klein, "Sociability, Solitude, and Enthusiasm," *Huntington Library Quarterly* 60 (1998).
5 For Ling, see above pp. 113–14, 117. For Moseley, see Ann Baynes Coiro, "Milton and Class Identity: the Publication of *Areopagitica* and the 1645 *Poems*," *Journal of Medieval and Renaissance Studies* 22 (1992), Arthur F. Marotti, *Manuscript, Print, and the English Renaissance Lyric* (Ithaca: Cornell University Press, 1995), 259–63.
6 Keith Walker, "Jacob Tonson, Bookseller," *The American Scholar* 61 (1992): 424. A similar argument is made by Harry M. Gelduld, *Prince of Publishers: A Study of the Work and Career of Jacob Tonson* (Bloomington: Indiana University Press, 1969). Tonson is also discussed in Margreta De Grazia, *Shakespeare Verbatim: The Reproduction of Authenticity and the 1790 Apparatus* (Oxford: Clarendon Press, 1991), 191–97, Joseph Loewenstein, *The Author's Due: Printing and the Prehistory of Copyright* (University of Chicago Press, 2002), 205–06, and Gary Taylor, *Reinventing Shakespeare* (New York: Weidenfeld & Nicolson, 1989).
7 D. F. McKenzie, "Typography and Meaning: the Case of William Congreve," in *Buch und Buchhandel in Europa im Achtzehnten Jahrhundert: The Book and*

the Book Trade in Eighteenth-Century Europe: Proceedings of the Fifth
Wolfenbüttler Symposium, November 3, 1977, ed. Giles Barber and Bernhard
Fabian (Hamburg: Dr. Ernst Hauswedell, 1981), 109.
8 Loewenstein, *The Author's Due*, 205.
9 A convincing case has been made for an element of political cartooning in the
1688 illustrations by Estella Schoenberg, "Seventeenth-Century Propaganda in
Book Illustrations," *Mosaic* 25 (1992). However, I am more interested in stressing the way in which the illustrations serve to transform the book into a
particular sort of aesthetic object. Obviously, these two interpretations
are not mutually exclusive. See also, Suzanne Boorsch, "The Illustrators of the
1688 *Paradise Lost*," *Metropolitan Museum Journal* 6 (1972), Nicholas von
Maltzahn, "Wood, Allam, and the Oxford Milton," *Milton Studies* 31
(1994), J. T. Shawcross, "The First Illustrations for *Paradise Lost*," *Milton
Quarterly* 9 (1975).
10 Maltzahn, "Wood, Allam, and the Oxford Milton."
11 It should be pointed out that Tonson was also eager to commission translations
of the classics into English.
12 For a general account, see Alfred Jackson, "Rowe's Edition of Shakespeare,"
The Library 4th ser. 10 (1929–30).
13 Ronald B. McKerrow, *The Treatment of Shakespeare's Text by His Earlier
Editors, 1709–1768* (London: Humphrey Milford, 1933), 15.
14 The importance of writers' biographies for the emergence of a modern understanding of literature has recently been discussed by Richard Terry, *Poetry and
the Making of the English Literary Past, 1660–1781* (Oxford University Press,
2001), esp. 63–92.
15 For Tonson's groundbreaking collaboration with Congreve, see McKenzie,
"Typography and Meaning: the Case of William Congreve."
16 See, for example, De Grazia, *Shakespeare Verbatim*, 78–86. The new shop and
sign are also discussed by Gelduld, *Prince of Publishers*, 15.
17 Given their seventeenth-century reputations, it is not surprising that Jonson
and Fletcher are put on signs before Shakespeare. For details, see W. W. Greg,
A Bibliography of the English Printed Drama to the Restoration, vol. III (London:
Printed for the Bibliographical Society at the University Press, Oxford, 1957),
1521, 1539.
18 Samuel Johnson, *The Yale Edition of the Works of Samuel Johnson*, ed. Arthur
Sherbo (New Haven: Yale University Press, 1968), VII, 61.
19 See J. C. D. Clark, "Religion and Political Identity: Samuel Johnson as a
Nonjuror," in *Samuel Johnson in Historical Context*, ed. Jonathan Clark and
Howard Erskine-Hill (New York: Palgrave, 2002). Though I am not convinced by the argument that Johnson was a nonjuror, Clark makes a strong
case for the importance of Johnson's political proclivities, especially
Jacobitism.
20 For a an account of hostile contemporary responses to Johnson, see J. C. D.
Clark, *Samuel Johnson: Literature, Religion and English Cultural Politics from
the Restoration to Romanticism* (Cambridge University Press, 1994).

21 Robert Potter, *An Inquiry into Some Passages in Dr. Johnson's Lives of the Poets: Particularly His Observations on Lyric Poetry, and the Odes of Gray* (London: 1783), 3.

22 Henry Fielding, *The Author's Farce*, ed. Charles B. Woods, Regents Restoration Drama Series (Lincoln, NE: University of Nebraska Press, 1966), 2.4.1–8.

23 The establishment of the literary as a category of cultural endeavor has attracted a great deal of scholarly attention. Notable recent contributions include Brean S. Hammond, *Professional Imaginative Writing in England, 1670–1740: 'Hackney for Bread'* (Oxford: Clarendon Press, 1997), Jonathan Brody Kramnick, *Making the English Canon: Print-Capitalism and the Cultural Past, 1700–1770* (Cambridge University Press, 1998), Trevor Ross, "The Emergence of 'Literature': Making and Reading the English Canon in the Eighteenth Century," *English Literary History* 63 (1996), Terry, *Poetry and the Making of the English Literary Past, 1660–1781*.

Works cited

PRIMARY WORKS

Arber, Edward, ed. *A Transcript of the Registers of the Company of Stationers*. 5 vols. Vol. III. London, 1875–9.

Ascham, Roger. *The Scholemaster or Plaine and Perfite Way of Teachyng Children, to Vnderstand, Write, and Speake, the Latin Tong.* London: John Day, 1570.

Aubrey, John. *Aubrey's Brief Lives*, edited by Oliver Lawson Dick. Ann Arbor: University of Michigan Press, 1957.

Bacon, Francis. *Francis Bacon: A Critical Edition of the Major Works*, edited by Brian Vickers. Oxford University Press, 1996.

The Works of Francis Bacon, edited by Robert Leslie Ellis, James Spedding, and Douglas Denon Heath. London: Longmans, 1870.

Bancroft, Richard. *A Sermon Preached at Paules Crosse the 9 of Februarie, Being the First Sunday in the Parleament, Anno. 1588.* London, 1588.

Barlow, William. *An Answer to a Catholike English-Man*. London, 1609.

A Sermon Preached at Paules Crosse. London, 1601.

The Summe and Substance of the Conference. London, 1604.

Beaumont, Francis. *The Knight of the Burning Pestle*, edited by Michael Hattaway. New York: W. W. Norton, 1969.

Birckbek, Simon. *The Protestants Evidence.* London, 1634.

Blount, Charles. *A Just Vindication of Learning: Or, an Humble Address to the High Court of Parliament in Behalf of the Liberty of the Press.* London, 1679.

Bodin, Jean. *The Six Bookes of a Common-Weale.* Translated by Richard Knolles. London, 1606.

Bond, Ronald B., ed. *Certain Sermons or Homilies (1547) and a Homily against Disobedience and Wilful Rebellion (1570).* University of Toronto Press, 1987.

A Booke of Certaine Canons, Concernyng Some Parte of the Discipline of the Church of England. London, 1571.

Booty, John E., ed. *The Book of Common Prayer, 1559: The Elizabethan Prayer Book.* Charlottesville: Published for the Folger Shakespeare Library by the University Press of Virginia, 1976.

Boys, John. *An Exposition of the Dominicall Epistles and Gospels Used in Our English Liturgie.* London, 1610.

Brightman, Thomas. *A Revelation of the Apocalyps.* Amsterdam, 1611.

Brooke, Robert Greville. *A Discourse Opening the Nature of That Episcopacie, Which Is Exercised in England,* 1641.

Browne, Thomas. *Religio Medici.* London, 1643.

Cartwright, Thomas. *A Brief Apologie of Thomas Cartwright against All Such Slaunderous Accusations as It Pleaseth Mr Sutcliffe in Seuerall Pamphlettes Most Iniuriously to Loade Him With.* Middelburg, 1596.

A Replye to an Answere Made of M. Doctor Whitgifte. Hemel Hempstead?, 1573.

Chapman, George. *Ouids Banquet of Sence.* London, 1595.

Chelsea Hospital. *Papers Illustrative of the Origin and Early History of the Royal Hospital at Chelsea Compiled in the Secretary's Office of That Institution.* London, 1872.

Coke, Sir Edward. *The Fift Part of the Reports.* London, 1606.

Colleton, John. *A Supplication to the King's Most Excellent Majestie.* English Secret Press, 1604.

Cooper, Thomas. *An Admonition to the People of England (1589),* edited by Edward Arber. London: Archibald Constable, 1895.

Cotton, Clement. *The Mirror of Martyrs.* London, 1613.

Daniel, Samuel. *The Poeticall Essayes.* London, 1599.

Darley, John. *The Glory of Chelsey Colledge Revived.* London, 1662.

Davies, John. *The Complete Works of John Davies of Hereford,* edited by Alexander B. Grosart. New York: AMS Press [rpt.], 1967.

The Muses Sacrifice. London, 1612.

The Scourge of Folly. London, 1611.

Davies, Myles. *Eikon Mikro-Biblike Sive Icon Libellorum, or, a Critical History of Pamphlets.* London, 1715.

Denton, William. *Jus Cæsaris Et Ecclesiæ Vere Dictæ.* London, 1681.

Dering, Sir Edward. *A Collection of Speeches Made by Sir Edward Dering, Knight and Baronet, in Matter of Religion.* London, 1642.

A Dialogve, Concerning the Strife of Our Churche. London: Printed by Robert Walde-graue, 1584.

Donne, John. *Ignatius His Conclave,* edited by T. S. Healy, S. J. Oxford: Clarendon Press, 1969.

John Donne: "The Anniversaries," edited by Frank Manley. Baltimore: Johns Hopkins University Press, 1963.

Letters to Severall Persons of Honour. London, 1651.

LXXX Sermons. London, 1640.

Poems of J. D. With Elegies on the Authors Death. London, 1633.

The Poems of John Donne, edited by H. J. C. Grierson. Oxford: Clarendon Press, 1912.

Pseudo-Martyr, edited by Anthony Raspa. University of Toronto Press, 1993.

Dury, John. *The Reformed Spirituall Husbandman: With an Humble Memorandum Concerning Chelsy Colledge.* London, 1652.

Faulkner, Thomas. *An Historical and Topographical Description of Chelsea and Its Environs.* London, 1810.

Featley, Daniel. *Clavis Mystica: A Key Opening Divers Difficult and Mysterious Texts of Holy Scripture*. London, 1636.

Cygnea Cantio: Or, Learned Decisions, and Most Prudent and Pious Directions for Students in Divinitie; Delivered by Our Late Soveraigne of Happie Memorie, King Iames, at White Hall a Few Weekes before His Death. London, 1629.

Fletcher, R. *Ex Otio Negotium*. London, 1656.

John Foxe, *Actes and Monuments of These Latter and Perilous Dayes, Touching Matters of the Church*. London, 1563.

The Ecclesiasticall History Contaynyng the Actes and Monuments. 2 vols. London, 1570.

The Ecclesiasticall History Contaynyng the Actes and Monuments. 2 vols. London, 1576.

Actes and Monuments of Matters Most Speciall in the Church. 2 vols. London, 1583.

Actes and Monuments of Matters Most Speciall in the Church. 2 vols. London, 1632.

Foxe, John, ed. *The Whole Workes of W. Tyndale, Iohn Frith, and Doct. Barnes*. London: John Day, 1572.

Fulke, William. *A Retentive to Stay Good Christians, in Trve Faith and Religion, against the Motiues of Richard Bristow*. London, 1580.

Fuller, Thomas. *The Holy State*. London, 1642.

The Church History of Britain; from the Birth of Jesus Christ, Untill the Year M. Dc. Xlviii. London, 1655.

Gibson, Abraham. *Christiana-Polemica, or a Preparative to Warre*. London, 1619.

Gifford, George. *A Briefe Discourse of Certaine Pointes of the Religion, Which Is among the Common Sort of Christians, Which May Be Termed the Countrie Diuinitie*. London, 1581.

Grafton, Richard. *A Manuell of the Chronicles of Englande*. London, 1565.

A Chronicle at Large ... Of the Affayres of Englande from the Creation of the Worlde, Vnto the First Yere of Queene Elizabeth. London, 1569.

Greene, Robert. *A Notable Discouery of Coosenage*. London, 1591.

A Quip for an Vpstart Courtier: Or, a Quaint Dispute Between Veluet Breeches and Clothbreeches. London, 1592.

Greg, W. W., and E. Boswell, eds. *Records of the Court of the Stationers' Company*. London: The Bibliographical Society, 1930.

Hakewill, George. *An Answer to a Treatise Written by Dr. Carier, by Way of Letter to His Maiestie*. London, 1616.

Hall, Joseph. *Christian Moderation*. London, 1640.

The Peace-Maker. London, 1647.

A Recollection of Such Treatises as Haue Bene Heretofore Seuerally Published, and Are Now Reuised, Corrected, Augmented. London, 1615.

Harington, John. *A New Discourse of a Stale Subject, Called the Metamorphosis of Ajax*, edited by Elizabeth Story Donno. New York: Columbia University Press, 1962.

Harvey, Gabriel. *Foure Letters, and Certaine Sonnets*. London, 1592.

Gabriel Harvey's Marginalia, edited by G. C. Moore Smith. Stratford-upon-Avon: Shakespeare's Head Press, 1913.

Heath, Robert. *Clarastella.* London, 1650.

Henslowe, Philip. *Henslowe's Diary,* edited by R. A. Foakes and R. T. Rickert. Cambridge University Press, 1961.

Hickeringill, Edmond. *Curse Ye Meroz, or the Fatal Doom.* London, 1680.

Hobbes, Thomas. *Leviathan,* edited by C. B. MacPherson. New York: Penguin Books, 1968.

Hoby, Lady Margaret. *Diary of Lady Margaret Hoby, 1599–1605,* edited by Dorothy M. Mead. London: G. Routledge & Sons, 1930.

Holme, Randle. *The Academy of Armory.* Chester, 1688.

Hooker, Richard. *The Folger Library Edition of the Works of Richard Hooker,* edited by W. Speed Hill. 7 vols. Cambridge, MA: Harvard University Press, 1977–98.

Of the Laws of Ecclesiastical Polity, edited by Arthur Stephen McGrade. Cambridge University Press, 1989.

Hospital, Chelsea. *Papers Illustrative of the Origin and Early History of the Royal Hospital at Chelsea Compiled in the Secretary's Office of That Institution.* London, 1872.

Hume, David. *History of England.* Vol. V. London, 1778.

Johnson, Samuel. *The Yale Edition of the Works of Samuel Johnson,* edited by Arthur Sherbo. Vol. VII. New Haven: Yale University Press, 1968.

Jonson, Ben. *Ben Jonson,* edited by C. H. Herford and Percy Simpson. Oxford: Clarendon Press, 1925.

Judex, Mathaeus. *De Inventione Typographia.* Copenhagen, 1566.

King James. *Proclamation* [STC 8336]. London, October 24, 1603.

Proclamation [STC 8343]. London, February 22, 1604.

Knott, Edward. *Charity Mistaken.* [St. Omer], 1630.

Kynaston, Francis. *The Constitutions of the Musaeum Minervae.* London, 1636.

Latimer, Hugh. *Sermons,* edited by G. E. Corrie. Cambridge: Parker Society, 1845.

Laud, William. *The History of the Troubles and Trial of William Laud.* London, 1695.

Lewis, John. *Vnmasking of the Masse-Priest.* London, 1624.

Lodge, Thomas. *Catharos. Diogenes in His Singularitie.* London, 1591.

Wits Miserie, and the Worlds Madnesse: Discouering the Deuils Incarnat of This Age. London, 1596.

Macaulay, Thomas Babington. *The Works of Lord Macaulay.* Rpt. AMS Press, 1980 edn. 6 vols. Vol. I. London: Longmans, Green, 1898.

Marlowe, Christopher. *Doctor Faustus: A- and B-Texts (1604, 1616),* edited by David Bevington and Eric Rasmussen. Manchester University Press, 1993.

Marprelate, Martin. *The Marprelate Tracts [1588–1589].* Leeds: The Scolar Press, 1967.

Marshall, Stephen. *Meroz Cursed. Or, a Sermon, Preached to the Honourable House of Commons, at Their Late Solemn Fast, Febr. 23. 1641.* London, 1642.

Marvell, Andrew. *Mr. Smirke; or, the Divine in Mode: Being Certain Annotations Upon the Animadversions on the Naked Truth: Together with a Short Historical Essay, Concerning General Councils, Creeds, and Impositions, in Matters of Religion.* London, 1676.

Mason, Thomas. *Christs Victorie over Sathans Tyrannie.* London, 1615.

May, Edward. *A Most Certaine and True Relation of a Strange Monster or Serpent Found in the Left Ventricle of the Heart of Iohn Pennant, Gentleman, of the Age of 21. Yeares.* London, 1639.

Mede, Joseph. *The Name Altar, or Thysiasterion, Anciently Given to the Holy Table.* London, 1637.

Milton, John. *Complete Prose Works of John Milton,* edited by Don M. Wolfe. 8 vols. New Haven: Yale University Press, 1953–82.

John Milton, edited by Stephen Orgel and Jonathan Goldberg. Oxford University Press, 1990.

Nashe, Thomas. *The Works of Thomas Nashe.* Edited by Ronald B. McKerrow. 5 vols. Oxford: Basil Blackwell, 1958.

Nichols, John. *Progresses of James I.* 4 vols. Vol. II. London, 1828.

Nichols, Josias. *The Plea of the Innocent: Wherein Is Auerred; That the Ministers & People Falslie Termed Puritanes, Are Iniuriouslie Slaundered for Enemies or Troublers of the State.* [Middelburg], 1602.

North, Dudley. *A Forest of Varieties.* London, 1645.

Parker, Matthew. *Correspondence of Matthew Parker, D. D., Archbishop of Canterbury,* edited by John Bruce and Thomas Thomason Perowne. Cambridge: Parker Society, 1853.

Parsons, Robert. *An Answere to the Fifth Part of Reportes Lately Set Forth by Syr Edward Cooke Knight, the Kinges Attorney Generall.* [St. Omer], 1606.

A Quiet and Sober Reckoning With M. Thomas Morton. [St. Omer], 1609.

Three Conversions, ?1603.

Peck, D. C., ed. *Leicester's Commonwealth: The Copy of a Letter Written by a Master of Art of Cambridge (1584) and Related Documents.* Athens, OH: Ohio University Press, 1985.

Peel, Albert, ed. *The Seconde Parte of a Register. Being a Calender of Manuscripts under That Title Intended for Publication by the Puritans About 1593, and Now in Dr. William's Library, London.* 2 vols. Cambridge University Press, 1915.

Pilkington, James. *A Godlie Exposition Upon Certeine Chapters of Nehemiah.* Cambridge, 1585.

Potter, Robert. *An Inquiry into Some Passages in Dr. Johnson's Lives of the Poets: Particularly His Observations on Lyric Poetry, and the Odes of Gray.* London, 1783.

Pricket, Robert. *The Lord Coke His Speech and Charge. With a Discouerie of the Abuses and Corruption of Officers.* London, 1607.

Primaudaye, Peter de la. *The Second Part of the French Academie.* Translated by Thomas Bowes. London: G. Bishop, R. Newbery, R. Barker, 1594.

Purchas, Samuel. *The Kings Towre, and Trivmphant Arch of London.* London, 1623.

Purchas His Pilgrimes. London, 1625.

Puttenham, George. *The Arte of English Poesie.* London, 1589.

Scoloker?, Anthony. *Daiphantvs, or the Passions of Loue.* London, 1604.

Shakespeare, William. *The Complete Works of Shakespeare,* edited by David Bevington. New York: Longman, 1997.

The First Quarto of Hamlet, The New Cambridge Shakespeare: The Early Quartos, edited by Kathleen O. Irace. Cambridge University Press, 1998.

Hamlet. London, 1603.

Hamlet. London, 1604.

Hamlet, The Arden Shakespeare, edited by Harold Jenkins. London: Methuen, 1982.

Hamlet, Prince of Denmark, The New Cambridge Shakespeare, edited by Philip Edwards. Cambridge University Press, 1985.

A New Variorum Edition of Shakespeare: Hamlet, edited by Horace Howard Furness. New York: Dover, 1963.

The Tragedy of Hamlet, The Oxford Shakespeare, edited by G. R. Hibbard. Oxford: Clarendon Press, 1987.

William Shakespeare, The Complete Works, edited by Stanley Wells, Gary Taylor, et al. Oxford: Clarendon Press, 1986.

Shirley, W. W., ed. *Fasciculi Zizaniorum Magistri Johannis Wyclif Cum Tritico*. London: Longman, Brown, Green, Longmans, and Robert, 1858.

Sidney, Philip. *Sir Philip Sidney*, edited by Katherin Duncan-Jones. Oxford University Press, 1989.

Smith, G. Gregory, ed. *Elizabethan Critical Essays*. 2 vols. Oxford University Press, 1904.

Smith, Henry. *Vpon Part of the 5. Chapter of the First Epistle of Saint Paul to the Thessalonians*. London, 1591.

Some, Robert. *Three Questions, Godly, Plainly, and Briefly Handled*. Cambridge, 1596.

Sprat, Thomas. *History of the Royal Society*, edited by Jackson I. Cope and Harold Whitmore Jones. London: Routledge & Kegan Paul, 1959.

Sutcliffe, Matthew. *An Answere to a Certaine Libel Supplicatorie*. London, 1592.

The Supplication of Certaine Masse-Priests Falsely Called Catholikes. London, 1604.

Swift, Jonathan. *A Tale of a Tub*, edited by D. Nichol Smith and A. C. Guthkelch. Oxford: Clarendon Press, 1958.

Symmons, Edward. *Scripture Vindicated from the Mis-Apprehensions, Mis-Interpretations, and Mis-Applications of Mr. Stephen Marshall, in His Sermon Preached before the Commons House of Parliament, Feb. 23. 1641. And Published by Order of That House*. Oxford, 1645.

Tanner, J. R., ed. *Constitutional Documents of the Reign of James I, 1603–1625*. Cambridge University Press, 1960.

Taylor, Jeremy. *Treatises*. London, 1650.

Taylor, John. *All the Workes of Iohn Taylor, the Water Poet*. London, 1630.

Throkmorton?, Job. *A Petition Directed to Her Most Excellent Maiestie, Wherein Is Deliuered 1 a Meane Howe to Compound the Ciuill Dissention in the Church of England. 2 a Proofe That They Who Write for Reformation, Doe Not Offend against the Stat. Of 23.Eliz.C. And Therefore Till Matters Bee Compounded, Deserue More Fauour*. [Middelburg], 1592.

Thucydides. *The History of the War Fought between Athens and Sparta*, edited by Rex Warner. London: Penguin, 1956.

W., R. *Martine Mar-Sixtus*. London, 1591.

Waldegrave, Robert. *A Dialogve, Concerning the Strife of Our Churche.* London, 1584.

A Dialogue. Wherein is Plainly Laide Open, the Tyrannicall Dealing of the L. Bishopps against Gods Children. [Rochelle], 1589.

Watson, Thomas. *A Divine Cordial.* London, 1663.

Whitgift, John. *The Defense of the Aunswere to the Admonition against the Replie of T.C.* London, 1574.

The Works of John Whitgift, edited by J. Ayre. Cambridge: Parker Society, 1851–53.

Williamson, Thomas. *The Sword of the Spirit to Smite in Pieces That Antichristian Goliah, Who Daily Defieth the Lords People the Host of Israel.* London: Printed by Edw. Griffin, 1613.

Wilson, Arthur. *The History of Great Britain, Being the Life and Reign of King James the First.* London, 1653.

Wilson, John. *The English Martyrologe Conteyning a Summary of the Liues of the Glorious and Renowned Saintes of the Three Kingdomes, England, Scotland, and Ireland.* Saint-Omer: Printed at the English College Press, 1608.

Wilson, Thomas. *The Rule of Reason.* London, 1552.

Winstanley, William. *Histories and Observations Domestic and Foreign.* London: Will. Whitwood, 1683.

Wotton, William. *Reflections Upon Ancient and Modern Learning.* London, 1694.

SECONDARY WORKS

Achinstein, Sharon. *Milton and the Revolutionary Reader.* Princeton University Press, 1994.

Adams, Thomas, and Nicolas Barker. "A New Model for the Study of the Book." In *A Potencie of Life: Books in Society*, edited by Nicolas Barker, 5–43. London: British Library, 1993.

Altman, Joel B. *The Tudor Play of Mind: Rhetorical Inquiry and the Development of Elizabethan Drama.* Berkeley: University of California Press, 1978.

Anderson, Benedict. *Imagined Communities: Reflections on the Origin and Spread of Nationalism.* Rev. edn. London: Verso, 1991.

Anderson, Perry. *Lineages of the Absolutist State.* London: Verso, 1974.

Anglo, Sydney. *Images of Tudor Kingship.* London: Seaby, 1992.

Ankersmit, F. R. *Aesthetic Politics: Political Philosophy Beyond Fact and Value.* Stanford University Press, 1996.

Anselment, Raymond A. *"Betwixt Jest and Earnest": Marprelate, Milton, Marvell, Swift and the Decorum of Religious Ridicule.* University of Toronto Press, 1979.

Arber, Edward. *An Introductory Sketch to the Martin Marprelate Controversy, 1588–1590.* London: Archibald Constable, 1895.

Armitage, David. *The Ideological Origins of the British Empire, Ideas in Context.* Cambridge University Press, 2000.

Ashworth, E. J. "Traditional Logic." In *The Cambridge History of Renaissance Philosophy*, edited by Charles B. Schmitt and Quentin Skinner, 143–72. Cambridge University Press, 1988.

Bakhtin, M. M. *The Dialogic Imagination: Four Essays.* Edited by Michael Holquist. Austin: University of Texas Press, 1981.

Bald, R. C. *Donne and the Drurys.* Cambridge University Press, 1959.

John Donne, a Life. Oxford University Press, 1970.

Baldwin, Thomas Whitfield. *William Shakespere's Small Latine & Lesse Greeke.* Urbana: University of Illinois Press, 1944.

Barker, Francis. "In the Wars of Truth: Violence, True Knowledge and Power in Milton and Hobbes." In *Literature and the English Civil War,* edited by Thomas Healy and Jonathan Sawday, 91–109. Cambridge University Press, 1990.

Bauckham, Richard. *Tudor Apocalypse.* Vol. VIII, *The Courtenay Library of Reformation Classics.* Oxford: The Sutton Courtenay Press, 1978.

Beal, Peter. "Notions in Garrison: the Seventeenth-Century Commonplace Book." In *New Ways of Looking at Old Texts: Papers of the Renaissance English Text Society, 1985–1991,* edited by W. Speed Hill. Binghamton, NY: Medieval and Renaissance Texts and Studies in conjunction with Renaissance English Text Society, 1993.

Beaurline, L. A. "Dudley North's Criticism of Metaphysical Poetry." *Huntington Library Quarterly* 25 (1962): 299–313.

Beaver, Alfred. *Memorials of Old Chelsea: A New History of the Village of Palaces.* London: Elliot Stock, 1892.

Bellany, Alastair. "A Poem on the Archbishop's Hearse: Puritanism, Libel, and Sedition after the Hampton Court Conference." *Journal of British Studies* 34 (1995): 137–64.

"'Raylinge Rymes and Vaunting Verse': Libellous Politics in Early Stuart England, 1603–1628." In *Culture and Politics in Early Stuart England,* edited by Kevin Sharpe and Peter Lake, 285–310. Stanford University Press, 1993.

Belsey, Catherine. "The Case of Hamlet's Conscience." *Studies in Philology* 76 (1979): 127–48.

Belt, Debra. "The Poetics of Hostile Response, 1575–1610." *Criticism* 33 (1991): 419–59.

Benger, John. "The Authority of the Writer and Text in Radical Protestant Literature 1540 to 1593 with Particular Reference to the Marprelate Tracts." PhD dissertation, University of Oxford, 1989.

Berger, Thomas L. "'Opening Titles Miscreate': Some Observations on the Titling of Shakespeare's 'Works.'" In *The Margins of the Text,* edited by D. C. Greetham, 155–72. Ann Arbor: University of Michigan Press, 1997.

Birrell, T. A. "English Counter-Reformation Book Culture." *Recusant History* 22 (1994): 113–22.

Black, Joseph. "Pamphlet Wars: the Marprelate Tracts and 'Martinism,' 1588–1688." PhD dissertation, University of Toronto, 1996.

"The Rhetoric of Reaction: the Martin Marprelate Tracts (1588–89), Anti-Martinism, and the Uses of Print in Early Modern England." *Sixteenth Century Journal* 28 (1997): 707–25.

Black, M. H. "The Printed Bible." In *The Cambridge History of the Bible,* edited by S. L. Greenslade, 408–75. Cambridge University Press, 1963.

Blagden, Cyprian. *The Stationers' Company: A History, 1403–1959.* London: George Allen & Unwin, 1960.

Blair, Ann. "Annotating and Indexing Natural Philosophy." In *Books and the Sciences in History,* edited by Marina Frasca-Spada and Nick Jardine, 69–89. Cambridge University Press, 2000.

Blayney, Peter W. M. "The Publication of Playbooks." In *A New History of Early English Drama,* edited by John D. Cox and David Scott Kastan, 383–422. New York: Columbia University Press, 1997.

Bloch, Ernst. *The Principle of Hope.* Translated by Stephen Plaice, Neville Plaice, and Paul Knight. 3 vols. Vol. III. Oxford: Basil Blackwell, 1986.

Boorsch, Suzanne. "The Illustrators of the 1688 *Paradise Lost.*" *Metropolitan Museum Journal* 6 (1972): 133–50.

Bossy, John. "Some Elementary Forms of Durkheim." *Past and Present* 95 (1982): 3–18.

Bourdieu, Pierre. "Did You Say 'Popular'?" In *Language and Symbolic Power,* edited by John B. Thompson. Cambridge, MA: Harvard University Press, 1991.

Distinction: A Social Critique of the Judgement of Taste. Translated by Richard Nice. Cambridge, MA: Harvard University Press, 1984.

"The Forms of Capital." In *Handbook of Theory and Research for the Sociology of Education,* edited by John G. Richardson, 241–58. New York: Greenwood Press, 1986.

In Other Words: Essays Towards a Reflexive Sociology. Translated by Matthew Adamson. Stanford University Press, 1990.

Bowers, Fredson. *On Editing Shakespeare.* Charlottesville: University Press of Virginia, 1966.

Bradley, A. C. *Shakespearean Tragedy.* London: Macmillan, 1904.

Breitenberg, Mark. "The Flesh Made Word: Foxe's *Acts and Monuments.*" *Renaissance and Reformation* 24 (1989): 381–407.

Brooks, Douglas. *From Playhouse to Printing House: Drama and Authorship in Early Modern England.* Cambridge University Press, 2000.

Burgess, Glenn. *Absolute Monarchy.* New Haven: Yale University Press, 1996.

Burke, Peter. *Popular Culture in Early Modern Europe.* New York University Press, 1978.

"The Renaissance Dialogue." *Renaissance Studies* 3 (1989): 1–12.

Burns, J. H. "The Idea of Absolutism." In *Absolutism in Seventeenth-Century Europe,* edited by John Miller, 21–42. New York: St. Martin's Press, 1990.

Burns, Norman T. *Christian Mortalism from Tyndale to Milton.* Cambridge, MA: Harvard University Press, 1972.

Burnyeat, M. F. "The Sceptic in His Place and Time." In *Philosophy in History,* edited by J. B. Schneewind, Quentin Skinner, and Richard Rorty, 225–54. Cambridge University Press, 1985.

Butterfield, Herbert. *The Whig Interpretation of History.* London: G. Bell, 1931.

Cannon, Charles K. "'As in a Theater': *Hamlet* in the Light of Calvin's Doctrine of Predestination." *Studies in English Literature 1500–1900* 11 (1971): 203–22.

Capp, Bernard. *The World of John Taylor the Water-Poet, 1578–1653*. Oxford University Press, 1994.

Carlson, Leland H. *Martin Marprelate, Gentleman: Master Job Throckmorton Laid Open in His Colors*. San Marino, CA: Huntington Library, 1981.

Chartier, Roger. *The Cultural Uses of Print in Early Modern France*. Translated by Lydia G. Cochrane. Princeton University Press, 1987.

"Frenchness in the History of the Book: From the History of Publishing to the History of Reading." *Proceedings of the American Antiquarian Society* 97 (1987): 299–329.

The Order of Books. Translated by Lydia G. Cochrane. Stanford University Press, 1994.

Christianson, Paul. *Reformers and Babylon*. University of Toronto Press, 1978.

Clancy, Thomas, S.J. "English Catholics and the Papal Deposing Power, 1570–1640, Part III." *Recusant History* 7 (1963–64): 2–10.

"English Catholics and the Papal Deposing Power, 1570–1640, Parts I and II." *Recusant History* 6 (1961–62): 114–40; 205–27.

Clark, J. C. D. *English Society, 1688–1832: Ideology, Social Structure, and Political Practice during the Ancien Régime*. 2nd edn. Cambridge University Press, 2000.

"Religion and Political Identity: Samuel Johnson as a Nonjuror." In *Samuel Johnson in Historical Context*, edited by Jonathan Clark and Howard Erskine-Hill, 79–145. New York: Palgrave, 2002.

Samuel Johnson: Literature, Religion and English Cultural Politics from the Restoration to Romanticism. Cambridge University Press, 1994.

Clark, Peter. "Josias Nichols and Religious Radicalism, 1553–1639." *Journal of Ecclesiastical History* 28 (1977): 133–51.

Clark, Stuart. *Thinking with Demons: The Idea of Witchcraft in Early Modern Europe*. Oxford University Press, 1997.

Coiro, Ann Baynes. "Milton and Class Identity: the Publication of *Areopagitica* and the 1645 *Poems*." *Journal of Medieval and Renaissance Studies* 22 (1992): 261–89.

Colley, Linda. *Britons: Forging the Nation, 1707–1837*. New Haven: Yale University Press, 1992.

Collinson, Patrick. "Biblical Rhetoric: the English Nation and National Sentiment in the Prophetic Mode." In *Religion and Culture in Renaissance England*, edited by Claire McEachern and Deborah Shuger, 15–45. Cambridge University Press, 1997.

The Birthpangs of Protestant England: Religious and Cultural Change in the Sixteenth and Seventeenth Centuries. New York: St. Martin's Press, 1988.

"Cranbrook and the Fletchers: Popular and Unpopular Religion in the Kentish Weald." In *Godly People: Essays on English Protestantism and Puritanism*, 399–428. London: Hambledon Press, 1983.

De Republica Anglorum, or, History with the Politics Put Back. Cambridge University Press, 1989.

"Ecclesiastical Vitriol: Religious Satire in the 1590s and the Invention of Puritanism." In *The Reign of Elizabeth I: Court and Culture in the Last*

Decade, edited by John Guy. Cambridge University Press in assn. with the Folger Institute, 1995.

The Elizabethan Puritan Movement. Berkeley: University of California Press, 1967.

From Iconoclasm to Iconophobia: The Cultural Impact of the Second English Reformation. University of Reading, 1986.

"The Jacobean Religious Settlement: the Hampton Court Conference." In *Before the Civil War,* edited by Howard Tomlinson, 27–51. London: Macmillan, 1983.

"John Foxe and National Consciousness." In *John Foxe and His World,* edited by Christopher Highley and John N. King, 10–34. Aldershot: Ashgate, 2002.

"Perne the Turncoat: an Elizabethan Reputation." In *Elizabethan Essays,* 179–217. London: The Hambledon Press, 1994.

The Puritan Character: Polemics and Polarities in Early Seventeenth-Century English Culture. Los Angeles: The William Clark Memorial Library, 1989.

"Review of William Haller, *Foxe's Book of Martyrs and the Elect Nation.*" *Journal of Ecclesiastical History* 15 (1964): 255–56.

"Truth and Legend: the Veracity of John Foxe's Book of Martyrs." In *Elizabethan Essays,* 151–77. London: Hambledon Press, 1994.

Corns, T. N., W. A. Speck, and J. A. Downie. "Archetypal Mystification: Polemic and Reality in English Political Literature, 1640–1750." *Eighteenth-Century Life* (1981–82): 1–27.

Corrigan, Philip, and Derek Sayer. *The Great Arch: English State Formation as Cultural Revolution.* Rev. edn. Oxford: Blackwell, 1991.

Cox, Virginia. *The Renaissance Dialogue: Literary Dialogue in Its Social and Political Contexts, Castiglione to Galileo.* Cambridge University Press, 1992.

Craig, Hardin. "Hamlet's Book." *Huntington Library Bulletin* 6 (1934): 17–37.

Crane, Mary Thomas. *Framing Authority: Sayings, Self, and Society in Sixteenth-Century England.* Princeton University Press, 1993.

Croft, Pauline. "Libels, Popular Literacy and Public Opinion in Early Modern England." *Historical Research: The Bulletin of the Institute of Historical Research* 68 (1995): 266–85.

"The Reputation of Robert Cecil: Libels, Political Opinion and Popular Awareness in the Early Seventeenth Century." *Transactions of the Royal Historical Society* 6th ser. 1 (1991): 43–69.

Cummings, Brian. *The Literary Culture of the Reformation: Grammar and Grace.* Oxford University Press, 2002.

Curtis, M. H. "The Hampton Court Conference and Its Aftermath." *History* 46 (1961): 1–16.

Cust, Richard. "News and Politics in Early Seventeenth-Century England." *Past and Present* 112 (1986): 60–90.

Daly, James. "The Idea of Absolute Monarchy in Seventeenth-Century England." *The Historical Journal* 21 (1978): 227–50.

Darnton, Robert. "What Is the History of Books?" *Daedalus* 111, no. 3 (1982): 65–83.

Davies, Catharine, and Jane Facey. "A Reformation Dilemma: John Foxe and the Problem of Discipline." *Journal of Ecclesiastical History* 39 (1988): 37–65.

De Grazia, Margreta. *Shakespeare Verbatim: The Reproduction of Authenticity and the 1790 Apparatus.* Oxford: Clarendon Press, 1991.

"Sanctioning Voice: Quotation Marks, the Abolition of Torture, and the Fifth Amendment." In *The Construction of Authorship: Textual Appropriation in Law and Literature,* edited by Martha Woodmansee and Peter Jaszi. Durham, NC: Duke University Press, 1994.

"Soliloquies and Wages in the Age of Emergent Consciousness." *Textual Practice* 9 (1995): 67–92.

Deakins, Roger. "The Tudor Prose Dialogue: Genre and Anti-Genre." *Studies in English Literature, 1500–1800* 20 (1980): 5–23.

Dickens, A. G. *The English Reformation.* New York: Schocken Books, 1964.

Dime, Gregory T. "The Difference between 'Strong Lines' and 'Metaphysical Poetry.'" *Studies in English Literature* 26 (1986): 47–57.

Dobranski, Stephen B. "Letter and Spirit in Milton's *Areopagitica.*" *Milton Studies* 32 (1995): 131–52.

Doelman, James. *King James I and the Religious Culture of England.* Woodbridge: D. S. Brewer, 2000.

Doerksen, Daniel W. "Polemicist or Pastor?: Donne and Moderate Calvinist Conformity." In *John Donne and the Protestant Reformation,* 12–34. Detroit: Wayne State University Press, 2003.

Dollimore, Jonathan. *Radical Tragedy: Religion, Ideology and Power in the Drama of Shakespeare and His Contemporaries.* 2nd edn. Durham, NC: Duke University Press, 1993.

Duffy, Eamon. *The Stripping of the Altars: Traditional Religion in England 1400–1580.* New Haven: Yale University Press, 1992.

Dunn, Kevin. *Pretexts of Authority: The Rhetoric of Authorship in the Renaissance.* Stanford University Press, 1994.

Duthie, G. I. *The "Bad" Quarto of Hamlet.* Cambridge University Press, 1941.

Dykstal, Timothy. *The Luxury of Skepticism: Politics, Philosophy, and Dialogue in the English Public Sphere, 1660–1740.* Charlottesville: University Press of Virginia, 2001.

Edwards, Mark U. Jr. *Printing, Propaganda, and Martin Luther.* Berkeley: University of California Press, 1994.

Egan, James. "Creator–Critic: Aesthetic Subtexts in Milton's Antiprelatical and Regicide Polemics." *Milton Studies* 30 (1993): 45–66.

Eggert, Katherine. *Showing Like a Queen: Female Authority and Literary Experiment in Spenser, Shakespeare, and Milton.* Philadelphia: University of Pennsylvania Press, 2000.

Eisenstein, Elizabeth L. *Print Culture and Enlightenment Thought.* Chapel Hill: Hanes Foundation, 1986.

Printing as a Divine Art: Celebrating Western Technology in the Age of the Hand Press, Harold Jantz Memorial Lecture. Oberlin, OH: Oberlin College Library, 1996.

The Printing Press as an Agent of Change. 2 vols. Cambridge University Press, 1979.

"An Unacknowledged Revolution Revisited." *American Historical Review* 107 (2002): 87–105.

Elias, Norbert. *The Civilizing Process.* Translated by Edmund Jephcott. Oxford: Blackwell, 1994.

Engler, Bernd. "Literary Form as Aesthetic Program: the Envoy in English and American Literature." *REAL: The Yearbook of Research in English and American Literature* 7 (1990): 61–97.

Erne, Lukas. *Shakespeare as Literary Dramatist.* Cambridge University Press, 2003.

Evenden, Elizabeth, and Thomas S. Freeman. "John Foxe, John Day and the Printing of the 'Book of Martyrs.'" In *Lives in Print: Biography and the Book Trade from the Middle Ages to the Twenty-first Century,* edited by Robin Myers, Michael Harris, and Giles Mandelbrote, 23–54. London: British Library, 2002.

Evetts-Secker, Josephine. "*Fuga Saeculi* or Holy Hatred of the World: John Donne and Henry Hawkins." *Recusant History* 14 (1977): 40–52.

Fallon, Stephen M. *Milton Among the Philosophers: Poetry and Materialism in Seventeenth-Century England.* Ithaca: Cornell University Press, 1991.

Feather, John. "The Book Trade in Politics: the Making of the Copyright Act of 1710." *Publishing History* 8 (1980): 19–44.

Febvre, Lucien, and Henri-Jean Martin. *The Coming of the Book: The Impact of Printing 1450–1800.* Translated by David Gerard. London: Verso, 1976.

Ferguson, William Craig. *Valentine Simmes: Printer to Drayton, Shakespeare, Chapman, Greene, Dekker, Middleton, Daniel, Jonson, Marlowe, Marston, Heywood, and Other Elizabethans.* Charlottesville: Bibliographical Society of the University of Virginia, 1968.

Ferrell, Lori Anne. *Government by Polemic: James I, the King's Preachers, and the Rhetorics of Conformity, 1603–1625.* Stanford University Press, 1998.

Fielding, Henry. *The Author's Farce,* edited by Charles B. Woods. Lincoln, NE: University of Nebraska Press, 1966.

Fincham, Kenneth, and Peter Lake. "The Ecclesiastical Policy of King James I." *Journal of British Studies* 24 (1985): 169–207.

Firth, Katherine. *The Apocalyptic Tradition in Reformation Britain, 1530–1645.* Oxford University Press, 1979.

Fish, Stanley. "Driving from the Letter: Truth and Indeterminacy in Milton's *Areopagitica,*" In *Re-membering Milton: Essays on Texts and Traditions,* edited by Mary Nyquist and Margaret W. Ferguson, 234–54. New York: Methuen, 1987.

　How Milton Works. Cambridge, MA: The Belknap Press of Harvard University Press, 2001.

Flynn, Dennis. "Irony in Donne's *Biathanatos* and *Pseudo-Martyr.*" *Recusant History* 12 (1973): 49–69.

Fogel, Aaron. "Coerced Speech and the Oedipus Dialogue Complex." In *Rethinking Bakhtin: Extensions and Challenges,* edited by Gary Saul Morson and Caryl Emerson, 173–96. Evanston: Northwestern University Press, 1989.

Foucault, Michel. "Polemics, Politics, and Problemizations: an Interview with Michel Foucault." In *The Foucault Reader*, edited by Paul Rabinow, 381–90. New York: Pantheon Books, 1984.

"What Is an Author?" In *Textual Strategies: Perspectives in Post-Structuralist Criticism*, edited by Josué V. Harari, 141–60. Ithaca: Cornell University Press, 1977.

Fowler, Alastair. *Kinds of Literature: An Introduction to the Theory of Genre and Modes*. Cambridge, MA: Harvard University Press, 1982.

Fox, Adam. "Ballads, Libels and Popular Ridicule in Jacobean England." *Past and Present* 145 (1994): 47–83.

Franklin, Julian H. "Sovereignty and the Mixed Constitution: Bodin and His Critics." In *The Cambridge History of Political Thought, 1470–1700*, edited by J. H. Burns with Mark Goldie, 298–328. Cambridge University Press, 1991.

Freeman, Thomas. "Texts, Lies, and Microfilm: Reading and Misreading Foxe's 'Book of Martyrs.'" *Sixteenth Century Journal* 30 (1999): 23–46.

Frye, Roland Mushat. *The Renaissance Hamlet: Issues and Responses in 1600*. Princeton University Press, 1984.

Shakespeare and Christian Doctrine. Princeton University Press, 1963.

Gelduld, Harry M. *Prince of Publishers: A Study of the Work and Career of Jacob Tonson*. Bloomington: Indiana University Press, 1969.

Gilmont, Jean-Francois, ed. *The Reformation and the Book*. Aldershot: Ashgate, 1998.

Gilmore, Myron P. *The World of Humanism*. New York: Harper, 1952.

Goldberg, Jonathan. *James I and the Politics of Literature: Jonson, Shakespeare, Donne, and Their Contemporaries*. Baltimore: Johns Hopkins University Press, 1983.

Goldie, Mark. "Ideology." In *Political Innovation and Conceptual Change*, edited by Terence Ball, James Farr, and Russell L. Hanson, 266–91. Cambridge University Press, 1989.

"The Theory of Religious Intolerance in Restoration England." In *From Persecution to Toleration: The Glorious Revolution and Religion in England*, edited by Ole Peter Grell, Jonathan I. Israel, and Nicholas Tyacke, 331–68. Oxford: Clarendon Press, 1991.

Gosse, Edmund. *The Life and Letters of John Donne*. 2 vols. London: William Heinemann, 1899.

Gransden, Antonia. *Historical Writing in England: c. 1307 to the Early Sixteenth Century*. 2 vols. Vol. II. London: Routledge & Kegan Paul, 1982.

"Propaganda in English Medieval Historiography." *Journal of Medieval History* 1 (1975): 363–82.

Green, Ian. *The Christian's ABC: Catechisms and Catechizing in England c. 1530–1740*. Oxford: Clarendon Press, 1996.

"'for Children in Yeeres and Children in Understanding': the Emergence of the English Catechism under Elizabeth and the Early Stuarts." *Journal of Ecclesiastical History* 37 (1986): 397–425.

Print and Protestantism in Early Modern England. Oxford University Press, 2000.

Greenblatt, Stephen. *Hamlet in Purgatory.* Princeton University Press, 2001.

Greenlaw, Edwin. "Spenser and the Earl of Leicester." *PMLA* 25 (1910): 535–61.

Greg, W. W. *A Bibliography of the English Printed Drama to the Restoration.* Vol. III. London: Printed for the Bibliographical Society at the University Press, Oxford, 1957.

"Hamlet's Hallucination." *Modern Language Review* 12 (1917): 393–421.

Gregory, Brad S. *Salvation at Stake: Christian Martyrdom in Early Modern Europe.* Cambridge, MA: Harvard University Press, 1999.

Gunn, J. A. W. "'Interest Will Not Lie': a Seventeenth-Century Political Maxim." *Journal of the History of Ideas* 29 (1968): 551–64.

Politics and the Public Interest in the Seventeenth Century. London: Routledge & Kegan Paul, 1969.

Habermas, Jürgen. *The Structural Transformation of the Public Sphere: An Inquiry into a Category of Bourgeois Society.* Translated by Thomas Burger with the assistance of Frederick Lawrence. Cambridge, MA: MIT Press, 1991.

Haigh, Christopher. *English Reformations: Religion, Politics, and Society under the Tudors.* Oxford: Clarendon Press, 1993.

Haller, William. *Foxe's Book of Martyrs and the Elect Nation.* London: Jonathan Cape, 1963.

Hammond, Brean S. *Professional Imaginative Writing in England, 1670–1740: 'Hackney for Bread'.* Oxford: Clarendon Press, 1997.

Harbage, Alfred, rev. S. Schoenbaum, and Sylvia Stoler Wagonheim. *Annals of English Drama: 975–1700.* New York: Routledge, 1989.

Harris, Tim, Paul Seaward, and Mark Goldie, eds. *The Politics of Religion in Restoration England.* Oxford: Basil Blackwell, 1990.

Harris, Victor. *All Coherence Gone: The Seventeenth-Century Controversy on the Decay of Nature.* University of Chicago Press, 1949.

Helgerson, Richard. *The Elizabethan Prodigals.* Berkeley: University of California Press, 1976.

Forms of Nationhood. University of Chicago Press, 1992.

Henshall, Nicholas. *The Myth of Absolutism: Change and Continuity in Early Modern European Monarchy.* London: Longman, 1992.

Heyd, Michael. "The Reaction to Enthusiasm in the Seventeenth Century: Towards an Integrative Approach." *Journal of Modern History* 53 (1981): 258–80.

Highley, Christopher, and John N. King, eds. *John Foxe and His World.* Aldershot: Ashgate, 2002.

Hill, Christopher. *Intellectual Origins of the English Revolution.* Oxford: Clarendon Press, 1965.

Intellectual Origins of the English Revolution Revisited. Oxford: Clarendon Press, 1997.

"The Many-Headed Monster." In *Change and Continuity in Seventeenth-Century England,* 181–204. New Haven: Yale University Press, 1991.

Milton and the English Revolution. London: Faber and Faber, 1977.

"Radical Prose in Seventeenth-Century England: from Marprelate to the Levellers." *Essays in Criticism* 32 (1982): 95–118.

Some Intellectual Consequences of the English Revolution. Madison: University of Wisconsin Press, 1980.

Hill, Tracey. *Anthony Munday and Civic Culture: Theatre, History and Power in Early Modern London, 1580–1633.* Manchester University Press, 2004.

Hirschman, Albert O. *The Passions and the Interests: Political Arguments for Capitalism before Its Triumph.* Princeton University Press, 1977.

Höltgen, Karl Josef. "Unpublished Early Verses 'on Dr. Donnes Anatomy.'" *Review of English Studies* 22 (1971): 302–06.

Houston, Alan, and Steve Pincus, eds. *A Nation Transformed: England after the Restoration.* Cambridge University Press, 2001.

Hunter, Robert G. *Shakespeare and the Mystery of God's Judgments.* Athens: University of Georgia Press, 1976.

Ingram, Martin. "Ridings, Rough Music and Mocking Rhymes in Early Modern England." In *Popular Culture in Seventeenth-Century England,* edited by Barry Reay, 166–97. London: Croom Helm, 1985.

Irace, Kathleen. "Origins and Agents of Q1 *Hamlet.*" In *The Hamlet First Published (Q1, 1603),* edited by Thomas Clayton, 90–122. Newark: University of Delaware Press, 1992.

Jackson, Alfred. "Rowe's Edition of Shakespeare." *The Library* 4th ser. 10 (1929–30): 455–73.

Jacobson, David L., ed. *The English Libertarian Heritage: From the Writings of John Trenchard and Thomas Gordon in the Independent Whig and Cato's Letters.* New York: Bobbs-Merrill, 1965.

James, Mervyn. "English Politics and the Concept of Honour, 1485–1642." In *Society, Politics and Culture,* Past and Present Publications, 308–415. Cambridge University Press, 1986.

Jardine, Lisa. "Humanist Logic." In *The Cambridge History of Renaissance Philosophy,* edited by Quentin Skinner, Charles B. Schmitt, Echhard Kessler, and Jill Kraye, 173–98. Cambridge University Press, 1988.

Jardine, Lisa, and Anthony Grafton. *From Humanism to the Humanities: Education and the Liberal Arts in Fifteenth and Sixteenth Century Europe.* Cambridge, MA: Harvard University Press, 1986.

"'Studied for Action': How Gabriel Harvey Read His Livy." *Past and Present* 129 (1990): 30–78.

Jauss, Hans Robert. *Question and Answer: Forms of Dialogic Understanding.* Translated by Michael Hays. Minneapolis: University of Minnesota Press, 1989.

Jenkins, Gladys. "The Archpriest Controversy and the Printers, 1601–1603." *The Library* 5th ser. 2 (1947–48): 180–86.

Jensen, Phebe. "'The Obedience Due to Princes': Absolutism in *Pseudo-Martyr.*" *Renaissance and Reformation* 19 (1995): 47–62.

Johns, Adrian. "How to Acknowledge a Revolution." *American Historical Review* 107 (2002): 106–25.

The Nature of the Book: Print and Knowledge in the Making. University of Chicago Press, 1998.

Johnson, Gerald D. "John Trundle and the Book Trade 1603–1626." *Studies in Bibliography* 39 (1986): 177–99.

"Nicholas Ling, Publisher 1580–1607." *Studies in Bibliography* 37 (1985): 203–14.

Jones, Richard Foster. *Ancients and Moderns: A Study of the Rise of the Scientific Movement in Seventeenth-Century England.* 2nd edn. St. Louis: Washington University Press, 1961.

Kahn, Victoria. *Machiavellian Rhetoric: From the Counter-Reformation to Milton.* Princeton University Press, 1994.

Kastan, David Scott. "Little Foxes." In *John Foxe and His World*, edited by Christopher Highley and John N. King, 117–29. Aldershot: Ashgate, 2002.

" 'The Noyse of the New Bible': Reform and Reaction in Henrician England." In *Religion and Culture in Early Modern England*, edited by Claire McEachern and Deborah Shuger. Cambridge University Press, 1997.

Shakespeare and the Book. Cambridge University Press, 2001.

Kaufman, Peter Iver. *Prayer, Despair, and Drama: Elizabethan Introspection.* Chicago: University of Illinois Press, 1996.

Kelen, Sarah A. "Plowing the Past: 'Piers Protestant' and the Authority of Medieval Literary History." *Yearbook of Langland Studies* 13 (1999): 101–36.

Kendrick, Christopher. "Ethics and the Orator in *Areopagitica*." *English Literary History* 50 (1983): 655–91.

Kennedy, D. E. "King James I's College of Controversial Divinity at Chelsea." In *Grounds of Controversy: Three Studies in Late Sixteenth and Early Seventeenth Century English Polemics*, edited by D. E. Kennedy, 99–126. Parkville, Vic., Australia: History Department, University of Melbourne, 1989.

Kernan, Alvin. *Shakespeare, the King's Playwright: Theater in the Stuart Court, 1603–1613.* New Haven: Yale University Press, 1995.

Keynes, Geoffrey. *A Bibliography of Dr. John Donne, Dean of Saint Paul's.* Oxford: Clarendon Press, 1973.

Klein, Lawrence E. "Sociability, Solitude, and Enthusiasm." *Huntington Library Quarterly* 60 (1998): 153–77.

Knight, G. Norman. "Book Indexing in Great Britain: a Brief History." *The Indexer* 6 (1968): 14–18.

Knott, John R. *Discourses of Martyrdom in English Literature, 1563–1694.* Cambridge University Press, 1993.

Knox, Dilwyn. "*Disciplina*: the Monastic and Clerical Origins of European Civility." In *Renaissance Society and Culture: Essays in Honor of Eugene F. Rice, Jr.*, edited by John Monfasani and Ronald G. Musto, 107–25. New York: Italica Press, 1991.

"Erasmus' *De Civilitate* and the Religious Origins of Civility in Protestant Europe." *Archiv für Reformationsgeschichte* 86 (1995): 7–54.

Knutson, Roslyn L. "Falconer to the Little Eyases: a New Date and Commercial Agenda for the 'Little Eyases' Passage in *Hamlet*." *Shakespeare Quarterly* 46 (1995): 1–31.

Kögler, Hans Herbert. *The Power of Dialogue: Critical Hermeneutics after Gadamer and Foucault.* Translated by Paul Hendrickson. Cambridge, MA: MIT Press, 1996.

Kolbrener, William. *Milton's Warring Angels: A Study of Critical Engagements.* Cambridge University Press, 1997.

Koselleck, Reinhart. *Critique and Crisis: Enlightenment and the Pathogenesis of Modern Society.* Cambridge, MA: MIT Press, 1988.

Kramnick, Jonathan Brody. *Making the English Canon: Print-Capitalism and the Cultural Past, 1700–1770.* Cambridge University Press, 1998.

Kuala, David. "*Hamlet* and the Image of Both Churches." *Studies in English Literature 1500–1900* 24 (1984): 241–55.

Lake, Peter. *Anglicans and Puritans? Presbyterianism and English Conformist Thought from Whitgift to Hooker.* London: Unwin Hyman, 1988.

"Anti-Popery: the Structure of a Prejudice." In *Conflict in Early Stuart England: Studies in Religion and Politics, 1603–1642,* edited by Richard Cust and Ann Hughes. London: Longman, 1989.

"Defining Puritanism – Again?" In *Puritanism: Transatlantic Perspectives on a Seventeenth-Century Anglo-American Faith,* edited by Francis J. Bremer, 3–29. Boston: Massachusetts Historical Society, 1993.

"The Laudian Style: Order, Uniformity and the Pursuit of the Beauty of Holiness in the 1630s." In *The Early Stuart Church, 1603–1642,* edited by Kenneth Fincham, 161–85. Stanford University Press, 1993.

"The Moderate and Irenic Case for Religious War: Joseph Hall's *Via Media* in Context." In *Political Culture and Cultural Politics in Early Modern England,* edited by Susan D. Amussen and Mark A. Kishlansky, 55–83. Manchester University Press, 1995.

Moderate Puritans and the Elizabethan Church. Cambridge University Press, 1982.

"Puritan Identities." *Journal of Ecclesiastical History* 35 (1984): 112–23.

Lake, Peter, and Michael Questier. *The Antichrist's Lewd Hat: Protestants, Papists and Players in Post-Reformation England.* New Haven: Yale University Press, 2002.

"Puritans, Papists, and the 'Public Sphere' in Early Modern England: the Edmund Campion Affair in Context." *Journal of Modern History* 72 (2000): 587–627.

Lamont, William M. *Godly Rule: Politics and Religion, 1603–60.* London: Macmillan, 1969.

Lesser, Zachary. "Walter Burre's *The Knight of the Burning Pestle.*" *English Literary Renaissance* 29 (1999): 22–43.

Levine, Joseph M. *The Battle of the Books: History and Literature in the Augustan Age.* Ithaca: Cornell University Press, 1991.

Levy, F. J. *Tudor Historical Thought.* San Marino, CA: Huntington Library, 1967.

Lewalski, Barbara Kiefer. *Donne's "Anniversaries" and the Poetry of Praise: The Creation of a Symbolic Mode.* Princeton University Press, 1973.

Lewis, C. S. *English Literature in the Sixteenth Century.* Oxford: Clarendon Press, 1954.

Lieb, Michael. "Milton's *Of Reformation* and the Dynamics of Controversy." In *Achievements of the Left Hand: Essays on the Prose of John Milton,* edited by Michael Lieb and John T. Shawcross, 55–82. Amherst: University of Massachusetts Press, 1974.

Loades, David. *Politics, Censorship and the English Reformation.* New York: Pinter Publishers, 1991.

Loades, David, ed. *John Foxe and the English Reformation.* Aldershot: Scolar Press, 1997.

John Foxe: An Historical Perspective. Aldershot: Ashgate, 1999.

Loewenstein, Joseph. *The Author's Due: Printing and the Prehistory of Copyright.* University of Chicago Press, 2002.

Love, Harold. *The Culture and Commerce of Texts: Scribal Publication in Seventeenth-Century England.* Amherst: University of Massachusetts Press, 1998.

Lull, Janice. "Forgetting *Hamlet*: the First Quarto and the Folio." In *The Hamlet First Published (Q1, 1603),* edited by Thomas Clayton, 137–50. Newark: University of Delaware Press, 1992.

MacDonald, Michael. "Ophelia's Maimed Rites." *Shakespeare Quarterly* 37 (1986): 309–17.

MacDonald, Michael, and Terence R. Murphy. *Sleepless Souls: Suicide in Early Modern England.* Oxford University Press, 1990.

Maguire, Laurie E. *Shakespearean Suspect Texts: The 'Bad' Quartos and Their Contexts.* Cambridge University Press, 1996.

Mallin, Eric. *Inscribing the Time: Shakespeare and the End of Elizabethan England.* Berkeley: University of California Press, 1995.

Maltzahn, Nicholas von. "The Whig Milton, 1667–1700." In *Milton and Republicanism,* edited by David Armitage, Armand Himy, and Quentin Skinner, 229–53. Cambridge University Press, 1995.

"Wood, Allam, and the Oxford Milton." *Milton Studies* 31 (1994): 155–77.

Marcus, Leah S. *Puzzling Shakespeare: Local Reading and Its Discontents.* Berkeley: University of California Press, 1988.

"Textual Indeterminacy and Ideological Difference: the Case of *Doctor Faustus.*" *Renaissance Drama* n.s. 20 (1989): 1–29.

Unediting the Renaissance: Shakespeare, Marlowe, Milton. New York: Routledge, 1996.

Marotti, Arthur F. *Manuscript, Print, and the English Renaissance Lyric.* Ithaca: Cornell University Press, 1995.

John Donne, Coterie Poet. Madison: University of Wisconsin Press, 1986.

Marshall, Peter. *Beliefs and the Dead in Reformation England.* Oxford University Press, 2002.

May, Steven W. "Tudor Aristocrats and the Mythical 'Stigma of Print.'" *Renaissance Papers* (1980): 11–18.

Mayer, Robert. "The Rhetoric of Historical Truth: Heylyn Contra Fuller on *The Church-History of Britain.*" *Prose Studies* 20 (1997): 1–20.

McCabe, Richard A. *Joseph Hall: A Study in Satire and Meditation.* Oxford: Clarendon Press, 1982.

McEachern, Claire. "'A Whore at the First Blush Seemeth Only a Woman': John Bale's *Image of Both Churches* and the Terms of Religious Difference in the Early English Reformation." *The Journal of Medieval and Renaissance Studies* 25 (1995): 245–69.

McGinn, Donald J. *The Admonition Controversy.* New Brunswick: Rutgers University Press, 1949.

"The Allegory of the 'Beare' and the 'Foxe' in Nashe's *Pierce Penilesse.*" *PMLA* (1946): 431–53.

McKenna, John W. "How God Became an Englishman." In *Tudor Rule and Revolution: Essays for G. R. Elton from His American Friends,* edited by Delloyd J. Guth and John W. McKenna, 25–43. Cambridge University Press, 1982.

McKenzie, D. F. *Bibliography and the Sociology of Texts.* London: British Library, 1986.

"The London Book Trade in 1644." In *Bibliographia: Lectures 1975–1988 by Recipients of the Marc Fitch Prize for Bibliography,* edited by John Horden, 131–52. Leeds: Leopard's Head Press, 1992.

"Speech–Manuscript–Print." In *New Directions in Textual Studies,* edited by Dave Oliphant and Robin Bradford. Intro. Larry Carver, 87–109. Austin: Harry Ransom Humanities Research Center, 1990.

"Typography and Meaning: the Case of William Congreve." In *Buch und Buchhandel in Europa im Achtzehnten Jahrhundert: The Book and the Book Trade in Eighteenth-Century Europe: Proceedings of the Fifth Wolfenbüttler Symposium, November 3, 1977,* edited by Giles Barber and Bernhard Fabian, 81–125. Hamburg: Dr. Ernst Hauswedell, 1981.

"What's Past Is Prologue": The Bibliographical Society and the History of the Book. London: Hearthstone Publications, 1993.

McKerrow, Ronald B. *The Treatment of Shakespeare's Text by His Earlier Editors, 1709–1768.* London: Humphrey Milford, 1933.

McRae, Andrew. *God Speed the Plough: The Representation of Agrarian England, 1500–1600.* Cambridge University Press, 1996.

Melchiori, Giorgio. "*Hamlet*: the Acting Version and the Wiser Sort." In *The Hamlet First Published (Q1, 1603),* edited by Thomas Clayton, 195–210. Newark: University of Delaware Press, 1992.

Mendle, Michael. "De Facto Freedom, De Facto Authority: Press and Parliament, 1640–1643." *Historical Journal* 38 (1995): 307–32.

Merritt, J. F. "Puritans, Laudians, and the Phenomenon of Church Building in Jacobean London." *Historical Journal* 41 (1998): 935–60.

"The Reshaping of Stow's 'Survey': Munday, Strype, and the Protestant City." In *Imagining Early Modern London: Perceptions and Portrayals of the City from Stow to Strype, 1598–1720,* edited by J. F. Merritt, 52–88. Cambridge University Press, 2001.

Meyer, Ann R. "Shakespeare's Art and the Texts of *King Lear.*" *Studies in Bibliography* 47 (1994): 128–46.

Miller, Edwin Haviland. "Deletions in Robert Greene's *A Quip for an Upstart Courtier* (1592)." *Huntington Library Quarterly* 15 (1951–52): 277–82.

"The Editions of Robert Greene's *A Quip for an Upstart Courtier* (1592)." *Studies in Bibliography* 6 (1954): 107–16.

Mish, Charles C. "Black Letter as a Social Discriminant in the Seventeenth Century." *PMLA* 68 (1953): 627–30.

Mitchell, C. J. "Quotation Marks, National Compositorial Habits and False Imprints." *The Library* 6th ser. 5 (1983): 359–84.

Morrill, John. "The Religious Context of the English Civil War." *Transactions of the Royal Historical Society* 34 (1984): 155–78.

Mouffe, Chantal. *The Return of the Political.* New York: Verso, 1993.

Mousnier, Roland. *The Institutions of France under the Absolute Monarchy, 1598–1789.* Translated by Brian Pearce. University of Chicago Press, 1979.

Mowat, Barbara. "The Form of *Hamlet*'s Fortunes." *Renaissance Drama* 19 (1988): 97–126.

Mozley, J. F. *John Foxe and His Book.* New York: Farrar, Straus & Giroux, 1940.

Mueller, Janel. "Embodying Glory: the Apocalyptic Strain in Milton's *Of Reformation.*" In *Politics, Poetics, and Hermeneutics in Milton's Prose,* edited by David Loewenstein and James Grantham Turner, 9–40. Cambridge University Press, 1990.

Neale, J. E. *Elizabeth I and Her Parliaments 1584–1601.* London: Jonathan Cape, 1957.

Needham, Paul. "Haec Sancta Ars: Gutenberg's Invention as a Divine Gift." *Gazette of the Grolier Club* 42 (1990): 106.

Nicolson, Marjorie. *The Breaking of the Circle: Studies in the Effect of the "New Science" Upon Seventeenth-Century Poetry.* Evanston: Northwestern University Press, 1950.

Norbrook, David. "*Areopagitica,* Censorship, and the Early Modern Public Sphere." In *The Administration of Aesthetics: Censorship, Political Criticism, and the Public Sphere,* edited by Richard Burt, 3–33. Minneapolis: University of Minnesota Press, 1994.

Poetry and Politics in the English Renaissance. Rev. edn. Oxford University Press, 2002.

"Rhetoric, Ideology and the Elizabethan World Picture." In *Renaissance Rhetoric,* edited by Peter Mack, 140–64. New York: St. Martin's Press, 1994.

North, Marcy L. *The Anonymous Renaissance: Cultures of Discretion in Tudor–Stuart England.* University of Chicago Press, 2003.

Nussbaum, Damian. "Whitgift's 'Book of Martyrs': Archbishop Whitgift, Timothy Bright and the Elizabethan Struggle over John Foxe's Legacy." In *John Foxe: An Historical Perspective,* edited by David Loades, 135–53. Aldershot: Ashgate, 1999.

O'Callaghan, Michelle. *The 'Shepheard's Nation': Jacobean Spenserians and Early Stuart Political Culture.* Oxford University Press, 2000.

Oliver, Leslie M. "*The Acts and Monuments* of John Foxe: a Study of the Growth and Influence of a Book." PhD, Harvard University, 1945.

"The Seventh Edition of John Foxe's *Acts and Monuments.*" *The Papers of the Bibliographical Society of America* 37 (1943): 243–60.

Olsen, Palle J. "Was John Foxe a Millenarian?" *Journal of Ecclesiastical History* 45 (1994): 600–24.

Olsen, V. Norskov. *John Foxe and the Elizabethan Church.* Berkeley: University of California Press, 1973.

Ong, Walter J. *Orality and Literacy: The Technologizing of the Word.* Rev. edn. New York: Routledge, 1997.

The Presence of the Word: Some Prolegomena for Cultural and Religious History. Minneapolis: University of Minnesota Press, 1981.

Ramus, Method, and the Decay of Dialogue: From the Art of Discourse to the Art of Reason. Cambridge, MA: Harvard University Press, 1958.

Orgel, Stephen. "Acting Scripts, Performing Texts." In *Crisis in Editing: Texts of the English Renaissance,* edited by Randall M. McLeod, 251–91. New York: AMS Press, 1994.

Parker, Geoffrey. "Success and Failure During the First Century of the Reformation." *Past and Present* 136 (1992): 43–82.

Parkes, M. B. *Pause and Effect: An Introduction to the History of Punctuation in the West.* Berkeley: University of California Press, 1993.

Parry, Glyn. "John Foxe, 'Father of Lyes', and the Papists." In *John Foxe and the English Reformation,* edited by David Loades, 295–305. Aldershot: Scolar Press, 1997.

Parry, Glyn J. R. "The Creation and Recreation of Puritanism." *Parergon* n.s. 14 (1996): 31–55.

Patterson, Annabel. "All Donne." In *Soliciting Interpretation: Literary Theory and Seventeenth-Century English Poetry,* edited by Elizabeth D. Harvey and Katherine Eisaman Maus, 37–67. University of Chicago Press, 1990.

Censorship and Interpretation: The Conditions of Writing and Reading in Early Modern England. Madison: University of Wisconsin Press, 1984.

Early Modern Liberalism. Cambridge University Press, 1997.

Reading between the Lines. Routledge: New York, 1993.

Reading Holinshed's Chronicles. University of Chicago Press, 1994.

"Rethinking Tudor Historiography." *South Atlantic Quarterly* 92 (1993): 185–208.

Shakespeare and the Popular Voice. Oxford: Basil Blackwell, 1989.

Pearson, Andrew Forret Scott. *Thomas Cartwright and Elizabethan Puritanism, 1535–1603.* Cambridge University Press, 1925.

Pebworth, Ted-Larry. "John Donne, Coterie Poetry, and the Text as Performance." *Studies in English Literature* 29 (1989): 61–75.

Penny, D. Andrew. "John Foxe's Victorian Reception." *The Historical Journal* 40 (1997): 111–42.

Perry, Curtis. *The Making of Jacobean Culture: James I and the Renegotiation of Elizabethan Literary Practice.* Cambridge University Press, 1997.

Peters, Julie Stone. *Theatre of the Book, 1480–1880: Print, Text, and Performance in Europe.* Oxford University Press, 2000.

Petti, Anthony G. "Political Satire in *Pierce Penilesse His Suplication to the Divill.*" *Neophilologus* 45 (1961): 139–50.

Pierce, William. *An Historical Introduction to the Marprelate Tracts.* London: Archibald Constable, 1908.

Plomer, Henry R. "Bishop Bancroft and a Catholic Press." *The Library* n.s. 8 (1907): 164–76.

Pocock, J. G. A. *The Ancient Constitution and the Feudal Law: A Study of English Historical Thought in the Seventeenth Century.* A Reissue with a Retrospect. Cambridge University Press, 1987.

"A Discourse of Sovereignty: Observations on the Work in Progress." In *Political Discourse in Early Modern Britain,* edited by Nicholas Phillipson and Quentin Skinner, 377–428. Cambridge University Press, 1993.

Virtue, Commerce, and History: Essays on Political Thought and History, Chiefly in the Eighteenth Century. Cambridge University Press, 1985.

"Within the Margins: the Definitions of Orthodoxy." In *The Margins of Orthodoxy: Heterodox Writing and Cultural Response, 1660–1750,* edited by Roger D. Lund, 33–53. Cambridge University Press, 1995.

Pollard, Alfred W. "Indexes." *Living Age* 257 (1908): 232–42.

Shakespeare Folios and Quartos: A Study in the Bibliography of Shakespeare's Plays, 1594–1685. London: Methuen, 1909.

Poole, Kristen. "Saints Alive! Falstaff, Martin Marprelate, and the Staging of Puritanism." *Shakespeare Quarterly* 46 (1995): 47–75.

Popkin, Richard H. *The History of Scepticism: From Erasmus to Descartes.* New York: Harper & Row, 1968.

Porter, H. C. *Reformation and Reaction in Tudor Cambridge.* Cambridge University Press, 1958.

Questier, Michael C. *Conversion, Politics and Religion in England, 1580–1625.* Cambridge University Press, 1996.

"Loyalty, Religion and State Power in Early Modern England: English Romanism and the Jacobean Oath of Allegiance." *The Historical Journal* 40, no. 2 (1997): 311–29.

"Practical Antipapistry During the Reign of Elizabeth I." *Journal of British Studies* 36 (1997): 371–96.

Quintrell, B. W. "The Royal Hunt and the Puritans, 1604–1605." *Journal of Ecclesiastical History* 31 (1980): 41–58.

Ramsay, Nigel. *Oxford Dictionary of National Biography.* Oxford University Press, 2004. Available from http://www.oxforddnb.com/view/article/37380.

Raspa, Anthony. "Time, History and Typology in John Donne's *Pseudo-Martyr.*" *Renaissance and Reformation* 11 (1987): 175–83.

Rose, Mark. *Authors and Owners: The Invention of Copyright.* Cambridge, MA: Harvard University Press, 1993.

Ross, Trevor. "The Emergence of 'Literature': Making and Reading the English Canon in the Eighteenth Century." *English Literary History* 63 (1996): 397–422.

Rostenberg, Leona. *The Minority Press and the English Crown.* Nieuwkoop: B. De Graaf, 1971.

Rowse, A. L. *Ralegh and the Throkmortons.* London: Macmillan, 1962.

Saint-Amand, Pierre. *The Laws of Hostility: Politics, Violence, and the Enlightenment.* Translated by Jennifer Curtiss Gage. Minneapolis: University of Minnesota Press, 1996.

Salmon, J. H. M. "Catholic Resistance Theory, Ultramontanism, and the Royalist Response, 1580–1620." In *Cambridge History of Political Thought, 1450–1700*, edited by J. H. Burns and Mark Goldie. Cambridge University Press, 1991.

"Gallicanism and Anglicanism in the Age of the Counter-Reformation." In *Renaissance and Revolt: Essays in the Intellectual and Social History of Early Modern France*, edited by J. H. M. Salmon. Cambridge University Press, 1987.

Sams, Eric. *The Real Shakespeare: Retrieving the Early Years, 1564–1594*. New Haven: Yale University Press, 1995.

Saunders, J. W. "The Stigma of Print: a Note on the Social Bases of Tudor Poetry." *Essays in Criticism* 1 (1951): 139–64.

Schmitt, Carl. *The Concept of the Political*. Translated by George Schwab. New Brunswick, NJ: Rutgers University Press, 1976.

Schoenberg, Estella. "Seventeenth-Century Propaganda in Book Illustrations." *Mosaic* 25 (1992): 1–24.

Scribner, Bob. "Is a History of Popular Culture Possible?" *History of European Ideas* 10 (1989): 175–91.

Sensabaugh, George Frank. *That Grand Whig, Milton*. Stanford University Press, 1952.

Shapin, Steven. *The Scientific Revolution*. University of Chicago Press, 1996.

Shapin, Steven, and Simon Schaffer. *Leviathan and the Air-Pump: Hobbes, Boyle, and the Experimental Life*. Princeton University Press, 1985.

Shapiro, I. A. "The First Edition of Greene's *Quip for an Upstart Courtier*." *Studies in Bibliography* 14 (1961): 212–18.

Shawcross, John T. "The First Illustrations for *Paradise Lost*." *Milton Quarterly* 9 (1975): 43–46.

"A Survey of Milton's Prose Works." In *Achievements of the Left Hand: Essays on the Prose of John Milton*, edited by Michael Lieb and John T. Shawcross, 291–391. Amherst: University of Massachusetts Press, 1974.

Sherman, Sandra. "Printing the Mind: the Economics of Authorship in *Areopagitica*." *English Literary History* 60 (1993): 323–47.

Sherman, William H. *John Dee: The Politics of Reading and Writing in the English Renaissance*. Amherst: University of Massachusetts Press, 1997.

Shriver, F. "Hampton Court Revisited: James I and the Puritans." *Journal of Ecclesiastical History* 33 (1982): 48–71.

Simpson, Evelyn M. *A Study of the Prose Works of John Donne*. Oxford: Clarendon Press, 1924.

Sinfield, Alan. "Hamlet's Special Providence." *Shakespeare Survey* 33 (1980): 89–97.

Sisson, C. J. *Lost Plays of Shakespeare's Age*. Cambridge University Press, 1936.

Skinner, Quentin. *The Foundations of Modern Political Thought II: The Age of Reformation*. Cambridge University Press, 1978.

Smith, Merritt Roe, and Leo Marx, eds. *Does Technology Drive History?: The Dilemma of Technological Determinism*. Cambridge, MA: MIT Press, 1994.

Smith, Nigel. "*Areopagitica*: Voicing Contexts, 1643–5." In *Politics, Poetics, and Hermeneutics in Milton's Prose*, edited by David Loewenstein and James Grantham Turner, 103–22. Cambridge University Press, 1990.

Literature and Revolution in England, 1640–1660. New Haven: Yale University Press, 1994.

"Richard Overton's Marpriest Tracts: towards a History of Leveller Style." *Prose Studies* 9 (1986): 39–66.

Sommerville, J. P. "The 'New Art of Lying': Equivocation, Mental Reservation, and Casuistry." In *Conscience and Casuistry in Early Modern Europe,* edited by Edmund Leites, 159–84. Cambridge University Press, 1988.

Royalists and Patriots: Politics and Ideology in England, 1603–1640. 2nd edn. London: Longman, 1999.

Spufford, Margaret. *Small Books and Pleasant Histories: Popular Fiction and Its Readership in Seventeenth-Century England.* London: Methuen, 1981.

Spurgeon, Dickie, ed. *Three Tudor Dialogues.* Delmar, NY: Scholars' Facsimiles & Reprints, 1978.

Stein, Arnold. "Donne's Obscurity and the Elizabethan Tradition." *English Literary History* 13 (1946): 98–118.

Strong, Roy. *The Cult of Elizabeth.* Berkeley: University of California Press, 1977.

Sullivan, Ernest W., II. *The Influence of John Donne: His Uncollected Seventeenth-Century Printed Verse.* Columbia: University of Missouri Press, 1993.

Taylor, Gary. *Reinventing Shakespeare.* New York: Weidenfeld & Nicolson, 1989.

Terry, Richard. *Poetry and the Making of the English Literary Past, 1660–1781.* Oxford University Press, 2001.

Thomas, Keith. "The Meaning of Literacy in Early Modern England." In *The Written Word: Literacy in Transition,* edited by Gerd Baumann, 97–131. Oxford University Press, 1986.

Thompson, W. D. J. Cargill. "Anthony Marten and the Elizabethan Debate on Episcopacy." In *Essays in Modern English Church History: In Memory of Norman Sykes,* edited by G. V. Bennett and J. D. Walsh, 44–75. Oxford University Press, 1966.

"A Reconsideration of Richard Bancroft's Paul's Cross Sermon of 9 February 1588/9." *Journal of Ecclesiastical History* 20 (1969): 253–66.

"Sir Francis Knollys' Campaign against the *Jure Divino* Theory of Episcopacy." In *The Dissenting Tradition: Essays for Leland Carlson,* edited by C. Robert Cole and Michael E. Moody, 39–77. Athens, OH: Ohio University Press, 1975.

Toulmin, Stephen. *Cosmopolis: The Hidden Agenda of Modernity.* University of Chicago Press, 1990.

Traister, Daniel. "Reluctant Virgins: the Stigma of Print Revisited." *Colby Quarterly* 26 (1990): 75–86.

Trevor-Roper, Hugh. "Toleration and Religion after 1688." In *From Persecution to Toleration: The Glorious Revolution and Religion in England,* edited by Ole Peter Grell, Jonathan I. Israel, and Nicholas Tyacke, 389–408. Oxford: Clarendon Press, 1991.

Tribble, Evelyn B. *Margins and Marginality: The Printed Page in Early Modern England.* Charlottesville: University Press of Virginia, 1993.

Tuck, Richard. *Philosophy and Government 1572–1651.* Cambridge University Press, 1993.

Tully, James, ed. *Meaning and Context: Quentin Skinner and His Critics.* Princeton University Press, 1988.

Urkowitz, Steven. "'Well-Sayd Olde Mole': Burying Three *Hamlets* in Modern Editions." In *Shakespeare Study Today,* edited by Georgianna Ziegler, 37–70. New York: AMS Press, 1986.

Van Eerde, Katherine S. "Robert Waldegrave: the Printer as Agent and Link between Sixteenth-Century England and Scotland." *Renaissance Quarterly* 34 (1981): 40–78.

Vickers, Brian. "The 'Songs and Sonnets' and the Rhetoric of Hyperbole." In *John Donne: Essays in Celebration,* edited by A. J. Smith, 132–74. London: Methuen, 1972.

Waddington, Raymond B. "Lutheran Hamlet." *English Language Notes* 27 (1989): 27–42.

Walker, Alice. "The Reading of an Elizabethan: Some Sources of the Prose Pamphlets of Thomas Lodge." *Review of English Studies* 8 (1932): 264–81.

Walker, Keith. "Jacob Tonson, Bookseller." *The American Scholar* 61 (1992): 424–30.

Wall, John N., Jr. "The Reformation in England and the Typographical Revolution: 'By This Printing . . . The Doctrine of the Gospel Soundeth to All Nations.'" In *Print and Culture in the Renaissance,* edited by Gerald P. Tyson and Sylvia S. Wagonheim, 208–21. Newark: University of Delaware Press, 1986.

Wall, Wendy. *The Imprint of Gender: Authorship and Publication in the English Renaissance.* Ithaca: Cornell University Press, 1993.

Wallace, Dewey D. "George Gifford, Puritan Propaganda and Popular Religion in Elizabethan England." *Sixteenth Century Journal* 9 (1978): 27–49.

Walsham, Alexandra. *Church Papists: Catholicism, Conformity and Confessional Polemic in Early Modern England.* Woodbridge: The Boydell Press for the Royal Historical Society, 1993.

"'Domme Preachers'? Post-Reformation English Catholicism and the Culture of Print." *Past and Present* 168 (2000): 72–123.

"'The Fatall Vesper': Providentialism and Anti-Popery in Late Jacobean London." *Past and Present* 144 (1994): 36–87.

Providence in Early Modern England. Oxford University Press, 1999.

Watt, Tessa. *Cheap Print and Popular Piety, 1550–1640.* Cambridge University Press, 1991.

Weber, Max. "Science as a Vocation." In *From Max Weber: Essays in Sociology,* edited by H. H. Gerth and C. Wright Mills, 129–56. Oxford University Press, 1946.

Weimann, Robert. *Shakespeare and the Popular Tradition in the Theater.* Baltimore: Johns Hopkins University Press, 1978.

Wellisch, Hans H. "The Oldest Printed Indexes." *The Indexer* 15 (1986): 73–82.

Werstine, Paul. "Narratives About Printed Shakespeare Texts: 'Foul Papers' and 'Bad' Quartos." *Shakespeare Quarterly* 41 (1990): 65–86.

"The Textual Mystery of *Hamlet.*" *Shakespeare Quarterly* 39, no. 1 (1988): 1–26.

Wheatley, Henry B. *How to Make an Index*. London: Elliot Stock, 1902.

Whibly, Charles. "Chroniclers as Antiquaries." In *The Cambridge History of English Literature*, edited by A. W. Ward and A. R. Waller, 313–38. Cambridge University Press, 1918.

Wiener, Carol Z. "The Beleaguered Isle: a Study of Elizabethan and Early Jacobean Anti-Catholicism." *Past and Present* 51 (1971): 27–62.

Wilding, Michael. "Milton's *Areopagitica*: Liberty for the Sects." *Prose Studies* 9 (1986): 7–38.

Williamson, George. "The Restoration Revolt against Enthusiasm." *Studies in Philology* 30 (1933): 571–603.

"Strong Lines." *English Studies* 18 (1936): 152–59.

Wilson, J. Dover. *The Manuscript of Shakespeare's Hamlet and the Problems of Its Transmission: An Essay in Critical Bibliography*. 2 vols. Cambridge University Press, 1934.

"Martin Marprelate and Shakespeare's Fluellen: a New Theory of the Authorship of the Marprelate Tracts." *The Library* 3rd ser. 3 (1912): 113–51, 241–76.

Wilson, Luke. "*Hamlet*: Equity, Intention, Performance." *Studies in the Literary Imagination* 24 (1991): 91–113.

Winstanley, Lillian. *Hamlet and the Scottish Succession: Being an Examination of the Play of Hamlet to the Scottish Succession and the Essex Conspiracy*. Cambridge University Press, 1921.

Wittreich, Joseph Anthony. "Milton's *Areopagitica*: Its Isocratic and Ironic Contexts." *Milton Studies* 4 (1972): 101–15.

Wollman, Richard B. "The 'Press and the Fire': Print and Manuscript Culture in Donne's Circle." *Studies in English Literature* 33 (1993): 85–97.

Wooden, Warren. *John Foxe*. Boston: Twayne, 1983.

Woolf, D. R. "Genre into Artifact: the Decline of the English Chronicle in the Sixteenth Century." *Sixteenth Century Journal* 19 (1988): 321–54.

The Idea of History in Early Stuart England: Erudition, Ideology, and "the Light of Truth" from the Accession of James I to the Civil War. University of Toronto Press, 1990.

Reading History in Early Modern England. New York: Cambridge University Press, 2000.

The Social Circulation of the Past: English Historical Culture, 1500–1730. Oxford University Press, 2003.

Woudhuysen, H. R. *Sir Philip Sidney and the Circulation of Manuscripts, 1558–1640*. Oxford: Clarendon Press, 1996.

Wright, Louis B. *Religion and Empire: The Alliance between Piety and Commerce in English Expansion, 1558–1625*. Chapel Hill: University of North Carolina Press, 1943.

Young, Robert Fitzgibbon. *Comenius in England*. Oxford University Press, 1932.

Zaret, David. *Origins of Democratic Culture: Printing, Petitions, and the Public Sphere in Early-Modern England*. Princeton University Press, 2000.

"Religion, Science, and Printing in the Public Spheres in Seventeenth-Century England." In *Habermas and the Public Sphere*, edited by Craig Calhoun, 212–35. Cambridge, MA: MIT Press, 1992.

Zwicker, Steven N. "Irony, Modernity, and Miscellany: Politics and Aesthetics in the Stuart Restoration." In *Refiguring Revolutions: Aesthetics and Politics from the English Revolution to the Romantic Revolution*, edited by Kevin Sharpe and Steven N. Zwicker, 181–95. Berkeley: University of California Press, 1998.

Index

absolutism 158
adiaphora 188–89
Admonition Controversy 58, 68–69, 87
An Admonition to Parliament 68, 101
Aldrich, Henry 225
Alexandrinus, Dionysius 185, 186
Anabaptist 100
Anderson, Perry 7
Anglo, Sidney 150
Anselment, Raymond 94
apocalypticism 182, 200
Aristotle 2
Arminianism 206
Ascham, Roger 49
Atterbury, Francis 225
Aubrey, John 145
Augustine
    On Christian Instruction 62
Aylmer, John 57

Bacon, Francis 192, 207
    *An Advertisement Touching the Controversies
        of the Church of England* 105
Bale, John
    The Image of Both Churches 62
Bancroft, Richard 40, 102, 105, 126–27,
        204–05, 213
    Davngerovs Positions 104
Barker, Christopher 125
Barlow, William 31, 34
    The Summe and Substance of the Conference
        126–27
Barrow, Henry 52–53
Bauckham, Richard 59
Baxter, Richard 215, 216
Beaumont, Francis
    The Knight of the Burning Pestle 118
Behn, Aphra 227
Bellarmine, Robert 151, 152, 158
Belsey, Catherine 129–30
The Ben Jonson's Head 226

Benger, John 81
Beza, Theodore 103
Bible
    Bishops' Bible 85
    Geneva Bible 39–40, 85, 141
    Great Bible 85
    King James Bible 159
Birckbek, Simon
    The Protestants Evidence 12
Blayney, Peter 118
Bloch, Ernst 138
Blount, Charles 182
    A Just Vindication of Learning 196–98
Blundeville, Thomas
    The Art of Logike 98, 99
Bodin, Jean 157
Book of Common Prayer 85–88, 126, 138
Bourdieu, Pierre 15, 55, 116
Bourne, Jane 213, 218
Bourne, Nicholas 13, 210–13, 218
Bowes, Thomas 48–50
Boys, John 149
Bradley, A. C. 124
Bradshaw, William 107
Bridges, John 105
    *A Defence of the Gouernment Established in
        the Church of England* 83–84, 95
A Briefe Declaration of The Reasons 213, 216
*A Briefe Discourse Against the Outwarde
        Apparell* 89
Bright, Timothy 61
    *An Abridgement of the Booke of Actes and
        Monumentes* 70–75
Brightman, Thomas 107
Brooke, Christopher 175
Brooke, Lord (Robert Greville) 12
Browne, Sir Thomas 138
Browne, William
    Britannia's Pastorals 175
    The Shepheards Pipe 175
burial rites 134–36, 138

Burke, Peter 36
Burre, Walter 118, 159
Butter, Nicholas 210
Bynneman, Henry 29

Calvinism 124, 205
    predestination 130, 139
Cambridge University 213
Camden, William 205
Campion, Thomas 175
Carey, John 169
Carier, Benjamin 14
Carlson, Leland
    *Martin Marprelate, Gentleman: Master Job
        Throckmorton Laid Open in His Colors* 81, 104
Cartwright, Thomas 15, 58, 68–69, 104, 106
    A Replye to an Answere 27
Cary, Elizabeth 173
Catholic Church 156
Catholicism 75, 150, 152, 153, 162, 216
Cecil, William, first Baron Burghley 106, 127
Chapman, George 175
Charles I 215
Charles II 213, 215, 216
Chaucer, Geoffrey 120
Chelsea College 4, 149, 201–21, 222
Clark, J. C. D. 221
Clifford, Thomas 204
Coke, Sir Edward 153
Colleton, John
    *A Supplication to the Kings Most Excellent
        Maiestie* 31
Collinson, Patrick 54, 74, 89, 97, 103
Comenius, Johannes Amos 207, 209
    Via Lucis 208
common law 102–04
Congreve, William 223
Conscience 129–30
Constantine 74
Cooper, Thomas 85, 87, 88–89, 104, 105
    Admonition to the People of England 101–02
copyright 181
Cottington, George 207, 212
Cotton, Clement
    Mirror for Martyrs 72, 76
Council of State 209
Counter-Reformation 163
Cowell, John
    The Interpreter 158
Cox, Virginia 36, 37
Crane, Elizabeth 80
Cranmer, Thomas 75
Cromwell, Thomas 75
Cummings, Brian 148
Cust, Richard 96

Daiphantvs, or the Passions of Loue 143
Darley, John 213–18
    The Glory of Chelsey Colledge Revived 213–18
Darnton, Robert 25
Davies, John, of Hereford 170, 175, 176, 177
    The Muses Sacrifice 170–75
Davies, Myles 3–4
    *Eikon Mikro-Biblike Sive Icon Libellorum, or,
        a Critical History of Pamphlets* 3
Day, John 64, 113
Day, Richard 64, 70, 71
Defoe, Daniel
    Essay on the Regulation of the Press 21
De Grazia, Margreta 128, 129
Dekker, Thomas
    The Whore of Babylon 116
Denton, William 182
    An Apology for the Liberty of the Press 196,
        198–200
Dering, Sir Edward 12
Descartes, René 186
designation theory 156
dialog 35
A Dialogve, Concerning the Strife of Our Churche
    38–42
*A Dialogue. Wherein is Plainly Laide Open,
    the Tyrannicall Dealing of the L. Bishopps
    against Gods Children* 42–45
disenchantment 165, 166
divine right of kings 156
Donne, John 4, 223
    Anatomy of the World 4, 5, 145, 159–77, 179
    Biathanatos 146
    "The Canonization" 167
    "A Funeral Elegy" 163, 169
    Ignatius His Conclave 146, 159
    The Progress of the Soul 163
    Pseudo-Martyr 4, 5, 145, 146, 147–58, 166,
        170, 179
Drayton, Michael 117
Drummond, William, of Hawthornden 171
Drury, Elizabeth 159, 160, 163, 164, 167, 168, 169,
    170, 171
Drury, Sir Robert 161, 162
Dryden, John 223, 224, 227, 230
Dutton, Elizabeth 169, 171, 172
Dutton, John 170
Dyson, Humfrey 211

Edward VI 74, 125
Edwards, Mark 20
Edwards, Philip 122–23
Egerton, Sir Thomas 170
Egerton, Thomas, Lord Ellesmere 170
Eisenstein, Elizabeth 7–8, 9

elect nation 59–60, 183
Elias, Norbert, 223
Elizabeth I 74, 85, 124, 125, 127
enthusiasm 1, 2, 180
episcopacy 83, 89, 103, 156, 157
equivocation 133
Erne, Lukas 120
Eucharist 172
Eusebius 64
The Endightment agaynste Mother Messe 37
"The fatall Vesper" 211

Faulkner, Thomas 201
Faust, Johann 199
Featley, Daniel 13, 206, 210, 212, 213–14, 215,
   216, 217, 218
   Vertumnus Romanus 216
Field, John 97, 101
Fielding, Henry
   The Author's Farce 230
Fincham, Kenneth 205
Firth, Katherine 56
Fish, Stanley 184
Fleming, Samuel 64–66, 69, 71
Foucault, Michel 31, 61, 81, 202
Foxe, John 97, 98, 102–04, 130, 156, 191, 195
   Actes and Monuments 4, 5, 13, 20–21, 56–79,
      124, 125, 149
   *The Whole Workes of W. Tyndale, Iohn Frith,
      and Doct. Barnes* 27, 39
Fuller, Thomas 13, 78, 213–15, 216
   Church History of Britain 209–10
Fulke, William 34

Garrard, George 160
Gascoigne, George 175
Gibson, Abraham
   Christiana-Polemica 13
Gifford, George
   A Dialogue betweene a Papist and Protestant 36
   Country Divinitie 37
Gilby, Anthony 89
Gilmore, Myron 87
Glanville, Joseph 67
Glorious Revolution 225
Goldie, Mark 35, 220
Goodyer, Henry 178
Grafton, Richard 72, 73
   A Manuell of the Chronicles of Englande 71
Greene, Robert 48–49, 50, 117
   A Quip for an Vpstart Courtier 45, 50–54
Greenwood, John 52–53
Grierson, H. J. C. 166
Gunpowder Plot 133, 149, 205
Gutenberg, Johann 199

Habermas, Jürgen 17–18, 34
Haec-Vir: Or, The Womanish-Man 116
Hakewill, George 14
Hales, John 80
Hall, Joseph 13, 160, 161, 215–16
   "To the Praise of the Dead, and the Anatomy"
      160, 163–64, 169, 171, 172
   The Peace-Maker 216
Haller, William
   Foxe's Book of Martyrs and the Elect Nation
      58–60
Hampton Court conference 125, 126
Harding, Thomas 30
Harrington, Sir John 68
Harris, John
   Lexicon Technicum
Hartlib, Samuel 207–08, 209
   The Reformed Spiritual Husbandman 208
Harvey, Gabriel 52, 108, 120, 143
Harvey, Richard 52
   Plaine Percivall the Peace-Maker of England 105
Hayward, John 205
Healy, T. S. 148
Heath, Robert 195–96
Helgerson, Richard 50, 58
Henry VIII 62, 74, 125
Herbert, Mary, Countess of Pembroke
Hic Mulier: Or, The Man-Woman 116
Hill, Christopher 58, 180, 183
Hodgskin, John 80, 82
Holinshed, Raphael 18
   Chronicles 57
Holland, Henry 212
Holme, Randle
   The Academy of Armory 220
Hooker, Richard 105, 130
House of Commons commission 209
Howes, Edmund 211
Hoskyns, John 158
Hunter, Robert G. 140
Hume, David 201–02

Illyricus, Flacius 64
index 62–63, 66–69, 152
Ingram, Martin 97
interest 197
irony 1
Isocrates 194

James VI and I 38, 113, 115, 124, 125–26, 127, 146,
   147, 149, 205–06, 210, 215, 216
Jauss, Hans Robert 45
Jenkins, Harold 113, 114
Jesuits 152
Jewel, John 30

John Bon 37–38
John Fletcher's Head 226
Johns, Adrian 8–10
Johnson, Gerald D. 115–17
Johnson, Samuel 227–28, 229
    Lives of the Poets 228
Jonson, Ben 117, 162, 171

Kahn, Victoria 183
Kastan, David 10
Kennedy, D. E. 205
Kenolde, Dr. 99
Kirkman, Francis 226
Knightly, Sir Richard 80
Knott, Edward 203–04
Knott, John R. 58
Koselleck, Reinhart 19
Kynaston, Francis 206–07, 208

La Primaudaye, Pierre 49
Lake, Peter 205
Lambeth Articles 126
Langland, John 38
Latimer, Hugh 139
Laud, William, Archbishop of Canterbury
    207, 217
L'Estrange, Roger 227
Lewalski, Barbara 163, 169
Lewis, C. S. 46
Lewis, John 13
Ling, Nicholas 113–14, 117, 122, 223
literary 1, 4
literature, category of 140, 144, 223–31
Lodge, Thomas 49
    and Robert Greene, *A Looking Glass for
    London* 50
    Catharos: Diogenes in His Singularitie
        45, 46–48
    Euphues' Golden Legacy 117
Loewenstein, Joseph 192, 223
Long Parliament 181
Love, Harold 114
Luther, Martin 6, 7, 146, 181
Lull, Janice 129

Macaulay, Thomas Babington 6, 18
MacDonald, Michael 130–33
Macham, Samuel 160, 161
McKenzie, D. F. 63, 223
Manley, Frank 178
Marprelate, Martin 15, 40, 44, 52, 80–109
    tracts 4, 5, 35, 38, 42, 124
    The Epistle 57, 83, 87, 90–92
    The Epitome 83, 98, 106

Hay any Worke for Cooper 88, 92,
    104, 106
The Iust Censure and Reproofe of Martin Iunior
    90, 93–94
Theses Martinianae 90, 92–93, 107
Marotti, Arthur 146, 178
Marriot, John 176–77
Marston, John
    Sophonisba 159
martyrdom 44, 47, 149, 151–52
Martz, Louis 163
Marvell, Andrew 203
Mary 125
Mason, Thomas 72, 79
    Christs Victorie over Sathans Tyrannie 76
May, Edward 206
    *A Most Certaine and True Relation of a Strange
    Monster* 206
Mayne, Jasper 176–77
McGinn, Donald 81
McKerrow, Ronald 226
Mede, Joseph
    The Name Altar 12
Melchiori, Giorgio 120–21
Meroz 215
Merritt, J. F. 211, 212
Micaiah 188
Middleton, Hugh 205
Mill, John Stuart 179
Milton, John 4, 74, 133
    An Apology Against a Pamphlet 181
    Areopagitica 4, 180–200
    Colasterion 192
    Paradise Lost 184, 223–25
    *A Treatise of Civil Power in Ecclesiastical
    Causes* 196
Mitchell, C. J. 29
Momus 177
Mouffe, Chantal 18
Mousnier, Roland 202–03
mortalism 137
Morton, Thomas 148, 149, 204
Moseley, Humphrey 223
Munday, Anthony 211
    English Roman Life 117
Murphy, Terence R. 130
Museum Minervae 206, 208

Nashe, Thomas 50
    Pierce Penilesse 49, 117
    The Unfortunate Traveller 57
*A Newe Dialogue wherein is Conteyned the
    Examination of the Messe* 37–54
Nichols, Josias 14, 106

North, Dudley 176
Norton, George 175

oath *ex officio* 103
Oath of Allegiance controversy 149,
    153, 205
Olsen, V. Norskov 68
Ong, Walter J. 18
Orgel, Stephen 121

Parker, Matthew 30
Parkhurst, John 30
Parsons, Robert 130, 153
Patterson, Annabel 18, 147
Peacock, Thomas Love
    Nightmare Abbey 201
Peasants' War 101
Penry, John 81, 82
A Petition Apologeticall 54
Perkins, William 130
Perne, Andrew 57, 99
Pierce, William 104
Pilkington, James 135
Plato 2
Pocock, J. G. A. 180–81, 219
polemic 1, 2, 4, 6, 11–14, 181, 200, 202
    and *ad hominem* argument 96–99
    and citation 29–31
    and logic 95
    and print 14–15, 18
    and the political 16
    and verbal violence 19
    as pejorative 34
politeness 1, 180, 222–23
Pollard, Robert 226
Pope, Alexander 67, 223
Pope Leo X 146
popery 182–83, 189, 215
popularity 118–20, 124
popular pelagianism 52, 132
Potter, Robert 228
Pound, Robert 159, 160
praemunire 88
presbyterianism 68, 70, 80, 84, 89, 100–03,
    109, 156
Prideaux, John 204, 219
Prince Henry 215
print and guns 159, 195–96
print culture 9–10, 179
print, fallibility of 88–89, 193
print logic 179
Protestantism 163, 175, 183, 186, 198, 208
    and print 6–7, 10, 20–27
Proteus 187–88
providence 138–40, 183

publishing event 5
Puckering, Sir John 49
Purchas, Samuel 203
    Purchas his Pilgrimes 206
puritan 107–08
puritanism 150, 224
purgatory 151, 167
Pyrrhonism 129

Rabinow, Paul 31
Rainolds, John 126
Ramus, Petrus 186
Raspa, Anthony 150, 153
Rawls, John 18, 194
Restoration 1, 180, 196, 220, 222, 229
Rieff, Philip 222
Roberts, James 114–15, 122
Rowe, Nicholas 121, 225–26
Royal Society 218, 220
Russell, Lucy, Countess of Bedford 173

Saint-Amand, Pierre 55
St. Paul's Cathedral 207, 212, 216–17
Saunders, J. W. 146
scholasticism 2
Scotus 2
Schmitt, Carl 16, 189
Sensabaugh, George 196
Shakespeare, William 223, 227–28
    Folio 16, 226
    Hamlet 4, 5, 110–44, 168, 179, 225
    Love's Labor's Lost 117
    The Rape of Lucrece 120
    Romeo and Juliet 117
    The Winter's Tale 16
    Venus and Adonis 120
    Tonson / Rowe edition 225–26
The Shakespeare's Head 226
Sharpe, Henry 80
Sidney, Sir Philip 107, 175, 176
    Arcadia 143
Simmes, Valentine 80, 82
Sinfield, Alan 140
Simpson, Evelyn 147
Sirluck, Ernest 185, 188
skepticism 124, 129, 179
Smethwick, John 117
Smith, Henry 185–86
Smith, Nigel 179
Some, Robert 130
Sommerville, J. P. 103
Sowle, Tace 21
Speght, Thomas 120
Spelman, Henry 205
Spenser 175, 223

Spenserians, Jacobean 175
Sprat, Thomas 219
   History of the Royal Society 219
Stanley, Henry, fourth Earl of Derby 80
Stansby, William 159, 161
Star Chamber 181
Stationers' Company 149, 183, 218
Stein, Arnold 175
Stow, John 215
   Survey of London 211–12, 218
Stubbe, Henry
   A Censure upon Certaine Passages Contained
     in the History of the Royal Society 219
Suckling, John 223
suicide 130
superstition 189
Sutcliffe, Matthew 14, 201, 204–05, 206
   The Supplication of Certaine Masse-Priests 31
Swetnam, Joseph
   The Arraignment of Lewd, Idle, Froward and
     Vnconstant Women 116
Swift, Jonathan 1–4, 67
   The Battle of the Books 1–3
   Tale of the Tub 1
syllogism 95–96, 98–100

Tayler, Edward 163
Taylor, Jeremy 197–98
   A Discourse of the Liberty of Prophesying 197
Taylor, John 115
   The Booke of Martyrs 76
technological determinism 8
Theobald, Lewis 121
Thomlin, Arthur 80
Throkmorton, Job 81, 94
Throkmorton, Sir Arthur 159, 160
Thucydides 56
toleration 190, 197, 215, 216
Tonson, Jacob 223–27, 229
Tonson, Jacob, the younger 227
Tonson, Richard 227
Tory 225, 227–29
Tourneur, Cyril
   The Atheist's Tragedy 159
transubstantiation 167
Travers, Walter 85

Tribble, Evelyn 10
Trundle, John 110, 113, 115–17
Tyndall, Dr. Humphrey 127

Udall, John 80
Urkowitz, Steven 124

Vestments controversy 89
von Maltzahn, Nicholas 224

Waldegrave, Robert 38, 42, 46, 51, 52, 81
Walker, Keith 223
Wall, John N. 85
Waller, Edmund 223
Walsham, Alexandra 54
Walsingham, Sir Francis 72, 74
Walton, Izaak 147–48, 150
Whibly, Charles 56
Whig 225, 227
White, John 204
Whitgift, John 15, 36, 42, 53, 58, 68–69, 85, 87, 99, 126
   An Answere to a Certen Libel 29–30
Wigston, Roger 80
Wilcox, Thomas 101
William, Turner 61
Williamson, Thomas 30
   The Sword of the Spirit 21–26
Wilson, Arthur 204, 210
Wilson, Dover 121–22, 136
Wilson, John
   The English Martyrologe 21
Wilson, Thomas
   The Rule of Reason 96, 97
Windet, John 74
Winstanley, Wiliam 16
Wither, George 175
   A Satyre: dedicated to His most excellent
     Maiestie 175
   The Shepheards Hunting 175
Wordsworth, William 179
Wroth, Lady Mary 176
Wyclif, John 74

Zaret, David 17
Zoilus 177